The Study Skills Handbook

Fourth Edition

Stella Cottrell

palgrave
macmillan

First edition 1999
Second edition 2003
Third edition 2008
Fourth edition 2013

First published 1999 by
PALGRAVE MACMILLAN

Palgrave Macmillan in the UK is an imprint of Macmillan Publishers Limited, registered in England, company number 785998, of Houndmills, Basingstoke, Hampshire RG21 6XS.

Palgrave Macmillan in the US is a division of St Martin's Press LLC, 175 Fifth Avenue, New York, NY 10010.

Palgrave Macmillan is the global academic imprint of the above companies and has companies and representatives throughout the world.

Palgrave® and Macmillan® are registered trademarks in the United States, the United Kingdom, Europe and other countries.

ISBN: 978-1-137-28925-4

This book is printed on paper suitable for recycling and made from fully managed and sustained forest sources. Logging, pulping and manufacturing processes are expected to conform to the environmental regulations of the country of origin.

A catalogue record for this book is available from the British Library.

A catalog record for this book is available from the Library of Congress.

10   9   8   7   6   5   4   3   2   1
22   21   20   19   18   17   16   15   14   13

Printed in China

Self-evaluations, checklists, planners and record sheets may be photocopied by individual students for their personal use only.

Contents

Acknowledgements

The author would like to thank the following:

Those who provided encouragement, support and comments for earlier editions of the book, especially Kate Williams at Oxford Brookes, Lynn Chiswick, Robert Simpson, Pam Dixon, David Gosling.

Lecturers across the University of East London (UEL) who used the first iteration – then called Skills for Success – as well as other materials which have been incorporated into this Handbook. I owe especial thanks to the dyslexia support tutors who piloted some of the material with dyslexic students at UEL and elsewhere. I am immensely grateful for the feedback of all these staff on what to include, and on how to adapt some of the early material for later editions.

Lecturers from British and international universities for their constructive feedback on the first three editions; wherever possible their suggestions have been incorporated into later editions. Mary Drury, Karry Omer and Andy Lloyd for specific suggestions for the third edition.

For their insightful conversations that inspired particular directions in the development of the fourth edition, Patricia Owens and Wendy Trevor from the Lifelong Learning Centre at the University of Leeds; Stella Butler and Julia Braham also from the University of Leeds; staff at the British Council in Tashkent; the University of Almaty in Kazakhstan; the University of Liverpool; the Institute of Technology Tallaght; Durham University; and Queens University Belfast. The many other people, teaching staff and students, from around the world who have provided comments and feedback on what they have enjoyed about the book, how they used the material, and what else they would like to see developed. I hope I do justice to their inspiring thoughts.

For the production of this fourth edition: Tina Graham, Jennifer Schmidt, Jim Weaver and Jocelyn Stockley; Suzannah Burywood and other staff at Palgrave for their continued support, enthusiasm and belief in the book over many years.

My partner, who kept everything going whilst I scribbled and typed away, not only feeding me at regular intervals but also contributing so much to thinking through the various updates and proof-reading the drafts.

The hundreds of students who were open to discussing with me what they found difficult about studying and willing to elaborate new and individual ways of approaching their study – to them, and to all future students who may struggle for even a day, this book is dedicated.

Introducing

The Study Skills Handbook

The study skills needed for Higher Education are ultimately gained only through studying at that level. Study skills don't hatch fully formed, any more than a grown hen pops from an egg. They evolve and mature through practice, reflection, trial and error, and feedback from others as you move through the different stages of your course. You may be surprised at how your thinking and language skills develop simply through continued study.

However, there are some basic approaches which can start you off on a good footing, help you cut corners, and accelerate the learning process. This *Handbook* developed out of practical work

undertaken with hundreds of students over twenty years. The core of the book has now been used by hundreds of thousands of students and lecturers worldwide, whose varied comments have contributed to this edition of the *Handbook*.

Quick tips and deeper learning

A reflective, active, self-evaluating approach to learning develops deeper understanding in the long term. However, quick tips are also invaluable to students, especially in emergencies. This *Handbook* offers both approaches. To meet your immediate and long-term study needs, move flexibly between the two approaches.

Aims of *The Study Skills Handbook*

The key aim of *The Study Skills Handbook* is to help you to manage your own success as a student. It does this by:

- encouraging an understanding that success is not simply about being 'bright' or 'clever' – good marks, and other kinds of successful outcome, are possibilities for any student

- supporting you to take individual, or personalised, approaches to study – that work best for you

- preparing you for what to expect from Higher Education at university or college

- offering guidance on how to develop effective study habits and a positive approach to study

- providing strategies and techniques for addressing core academic tasks at this level of study

- offering insights on how to tackle study activities that many students find difficult

- developing understanding of how learning, intelligence and memory work – so you can apply that understanding to your own studies

- developing core methodologies and thinking skills needed in Higher Education

- supporting you in identifying skills you have already, which you need as a student and for working life

- providing the resources to help you evaluate, reflect upon and manage your studies.

How to use *The Study Skills Handbook*

This is a guide that you can dip into as you need – or use by working through the chapters related to a particular aspect of study. You can do as little or as much as you find helpful. Of necessity, the *Handbook* focuses on a different aspect of study in each chapter. However, in practice, these are interconnected: developing one area of your study will also help with other aspects.

Finding what you need

- Each section provides an overview of the cluster of study skills it covers.
- Each chapter begins with an outline of the learning outcomes for that chapter. Browsing through this list may help you decide whether or not you need to read the chapter.
- Each chapter deals with several topics, and each topic is introduced by a heading like the one at the top of this page. These headings make it easier to browse through to find what you need quickly.
- The index (at the back) gives page references for specific topics.

Copiable pages

Pages containing self-evaluations, checklists, planners and record sheets may be copied for individual re-use. (You may like to enlarge some of them onto A3 paper.) If you use such copies, keep them with your reflective journal for future reference.

Using the website

Additional free material can be found on the Palgrave website at www.palgravestudyskills.com. You can download some of the resource materials, rather than copying these from the book.

Cartoons and page layout

The cartoons and the variety of page layouts act primarily as visual memory-joggers. Even if you cannot draw well, you can use visual prompts such as these in your own notes. The visual distinctiveness of the pages along with the page headers will also help you to find things more quickly within the book. This encourages learning through different senses, too – see page 4 below and Chapter 8 for more details.

The self-evaluation questionnaires

The self-evaluation questionnaires will help you in three ways:

- they break down major study skills into their component sub-skills
- they enable you to pinpoint which components make a study skill difficult for you, and to identify steps that you missed out in the past. Often, once you identify that missing step, it is fairly straightforward to address it
- they enable you to monitor your progress and identify your strengths.

Challenging material

If you are returning to study after a few years' absence, or if there are aspects of study that are new to you or that proved difficult in the past, don't let these put you off now.

It is very common for students to find that material which was difficult the first time around becomes comprehensible when they return to it after a gap. Even students who find academic language and methods unexpected or difficult usually adapt to these quite quickly.

Knowledge of specialised terms and of underlying theories empowers you as a student. It sharpens your thinking, allows you to describe things more accurately, and improves your overall performance.

Keeping a journal

This symbol reminds you to note down your reflections in your study journal. For details, see page 99.

Where to begin

- Browse through the *Handbook* so you know roughly what is in it. You may not know what to use until you start assignments.
- Read through the *Seven approaches to learning* used by *The Study Skills Handbook* (page 4). The *Handbook* will then make more sense to you.
- Complete the *What would success look like for me?* questionnaire (page 33). This will help you to orientate yourself as a student.
- Use the *Study skills: priorities* planner (page 48) to focus your thinking.
- If you are unsure where to begin with a study skill, use the *Self-evaluation* questionnaire in the appropriate chapter to clarify your thinking.
- Chapters 1–5 cover groundwork and study management approaches basic to the rest of the *Handbook*. It is generally helpful to gain a grasp of the material in these first.

If you are new to Higher Education …

Start with Chapter 1. This gives you an idea of what to expect as well as guidance on what to find out and do in order to make sense of Higher Education and take control of your experience as a student.

You may also find it helpful, early on, to look at:

- identifying your current skills and qualities (Chapter 2)
- building your confidence in your learning abilities (Chapter 3)
- what will keep you motivated, focused, and help performance (Chapter 4)
- time management (Chapter 5)
- brushing up on reading skills (Chapter 6) and writing skills (Chapter 11).

If you have studied for A-levels, BTEC, Access to HE diplomas or the International Baccalaureate …

You may find that you can browse through the early sections of each chapter quite quickly. Chapters 1, 4, 5, 7, 10, 12 and 13 may be the most useful for you. If you feel uncomfortable about a book that uses images as learning tools, read page 68 and Chapter 8 on *Memory* and the methods may make more sense.

Dyslexic students

There are now thousands of dyslexic students in Higher Education. Many aspects of this book are designed with dyslexic students in mind, including:

- the contents
- the use of visual images
- the book's layout
- the emphasis on structure
- the use of varied and multi-sensory approaches to learning.

Pace yourself

If you have been away from study for a while, or if you are finding study difficult, be kind to yourself. It takes time and practice to orientate yourself to the Higher Education environment and to develop study habits, especially academic writing skills.

Your first-year marks may not count towards the final grade, which means you have time to practise and improve.

Everybody learns in their own way

There are many avenues to successful study. Experiment. Explore. Be creative. Find what suits *you* best.

Chapters 2–4 encourage you to look for your own learning patterns, and make suggestions on how to experiment with your learning.

Seven approaches to learning

The Study Skills Handbook uses seven approaches to learning.

1 Learning can be an adventure

It is difficult to learn if you are stressed or bored. This *Handbook* encourages you to be effective rather than virtuous, and to seek out ways of making your learning more fun. Degree courses take several years, so you need to find ways of making your learning enjoyable.

Small children learn extraordinary amounts without trying particularly hard – simply through being relaxed, observing, playing, role-playing, trying things out, making mistakes, and being interested in what they are doing. They don't regard setbacks as failures; they don't worry about what others think; and they don't tell themselves they might not be able to learn. When a child falls over, she or he just gets up and moves again, and eventually walking becomes easy. Adults can learn in this way too – if they allow themselves.

2 Use many senses

The more we use our senses of sight, hearing and touch, and the more we use fine muscle movements in looking, speaking, writing, typing, drawing, or moving the body, the more opportunities we give the brain to take in information using our preferred sense.

The use of several senses also gives the brain more connections and associations, making it easier to find information later, which assists memory and learning. This book encourages you to use your senses to the full and to incorporate movement into your study. This will make learning easier – and more interesting.

3 Identify what attracts you

It is easier to learn by keeping desirable outcomes in mind than by forcing ourselves to study out of duty. Some aspects of study may be less attractive to you, such as writing essays, meeting deadlines or sitting exams, and yet these also tend to bring the greatest satisfaction and rewards.

It is within your power to find in any aspect of study the gold that attracts you. For example, visualise yourself on a large cinema screen enjoying your study – or your later rewards. Hear your own voice telling you what you are achieving now. Your imagination will catch hold of these incentives and find ways of making them happen.

4 Use active learning

We learn with a deeper understanding when we are both actively and personally engaged:

- juggling information
- struggling to make sense
- playing with different options
- making decisions
- linking information.

For this reason, most pages of this book require you to *do* something, however small, to increase your active engagement with the topic.

5 Take responsibility for your learning

As you will see from Chapter 1, it is generally understood in Higher Education that:

- at this level, it is a good thing for students to take on increased amounts of responsibility for their learning
- *and* you will arrive with sufficient preparation to be able to study in an independent way for much of the week.

It is generally your responsibility to catch up if you are not fully prepared in a certain area, especially for more basic skills such as spelling or grammar.

6 Trust in your own intelligence

Many students worry in case they are not intelligent enough for their course. Some did not do well at school, and worry that being a good student is 'not in their genes'. Panic about this can, in itself, make it hard to learn. That is why this book considers ideas about intelligence (in Chapter 3) and stress (in Chapter 14). Many students who were not ideal pupils at school do extremely well at college, following thorough preparation.

7 Personalise your learning

Recognise your learning preferences

Each of us learns in an individual way – though we also have a lot in common. Some theorists divide people into 'types' such as *visual*, *auditory* and *kinaesthetic*, or *introverted* and *extroverted* – there are lots of ways of dividing people up. The important thing, however, is not to discover which 'type' you are but rather to recognise the many different elements that contribute to how you yourself learn best.

If you regard yourself as a 'type' you may over-identify yourself with that type. You may then get stuck with that image of yourself – and always consider yourself a 'visual introverted' type, or a 'chaotic extrovert'. This may leave you with rigid views about the one way you learn. What you *need* to do is experiment with strategies and skills you currently under-use. The human brain is highly adaptable: able learners move easily between different strategies and learning styles, depending on the task in hand.

The good thing about being aware of how *you* learn best is that you can adapt your learning environment and your approaches to learning to fit where you are now. You may also be able to see more clearly why you did well or badly at school, depending on whether the teaching matched your personal learning preferences.

As you are more in charge of your learning at this level, this gives you opportunities to personalise the learning experience to suit yourself. The various chapters of this book provide ideas about how you can do this.

A new beginning ...

From this introduction, you will probably have gleaned that an important premise of this book is that academic success comes about as the result of many factors. Intellectual ability is one, but not necessarily the most important of these. Whatever your experience of academic study in the past, this may not be the same in Higher Education.

Didn't achieve well in the past?

Many people who didn't do well at school find that they thrive in the very different atmosphere of Higher Education. For some, this is because the approaches taken in Higher Education suit them better; for others, it is because they take a different approach themselves to their work. If you under-achieved in the past, this may come as welcome news. This *Handbook* was designed to help you challenge beliefs that have often led to students under-achieving in the past, and offers practical steps for managing your current studies.

Have always been good at study?

If you did well in the past, you have the benefit of excellent building blocks for study that should boost your confidence. Those who gain the highest marks are generally keen to find ways of studying more effectively. Even excellent students can find ways of saving time, fine-tuning their study techniques, and adapting their approaches to meet the demands of higher level study.

Good strategies count ...

Putting in place the right study skills and strategies can make a significant difference to academic performance. Students are surprised and pleased to find that they can achieve well if they develop study strategies that are relevant to their ways of thinking and working and that draw upon their personal interests and preferences.

Developing study skills in context

Even study skills strategies and techniques are not much use in a vacuum. These are more likely to be effective if they are fine-tuned to the level of study and the study context. For Higher Education, this means considering such factors as:

- understanding what is different about studying in Higher Education
- knowing what is required at your level of study
- understanding the learning process and how you can manage that process to best effect
- being aware of what you want to gain from your time in Higher Education in relation to your longer-term life and career aims.

Before looking at study skills in depth, the following three chapters encourage you to stand back and consider these broader contextual issues. These provide many of the tools you need for applying the specific skills and techniques covered in later chapters.

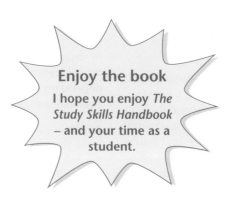

Enjoy the book

I hope you enjoy *The Study Skills Handbook* **– and your time as a student.**

Part A
Managing yourself for study

1 Success as a student
2 Developing your skills
3 Successful study: intelligence, strategy and personalised learning
4 The C·R·E·A·M strategy for learning
5 Time management as a student

In Higher Education, the key responsibility for academic success lies with you. That responsibility increases with each level of study. This change in emphasis can come as a surprise to many students, and can catch many out.

Students who do well tend to be those who appreciate, early on, that higher level study is different from their previous experience, who grasp what this responsibility means, and who have the mind-set and strategies to respond well to the challenge.

Being in control of your own learning isn't easy. It requires a range of personal skills and attributes to manage independent learning successfully, to use time well, to interpret sensibly what is going on when study seems more difficult or your motivation wanes, and to adapt your strategies when your current ones don't seem to deliver what you want. 'Managing yourself' is, then, a key aspect of managing study.

This section, *Managing yourself for study*, provides background and approaches that help you to build a solid foundation in managing your studies. It helps you to understand the context of Higher Education – and why you are expected to take on such responsibility. As you are expected to take charge of your own learning, it is useful to understand what 'learning' is about so that you gain insights into how to do this well. It looks at the range of skills and understandings typically expected of students at this level, so that you can check for yourself whether you are on the right track.

Chapter 1
Success as a student

Learning outcomes

This chapter offers you opportunities to:

- identify what is expected from you as a student
- appreciate how Higher Education differs from previous levels of education
- understand the teaching methods used at this level, and the pivotal role of independent study
- clarify what success at this level would look like for you
- consider how to make best use of the experience
- explore your anxieties and identify resources
- build your resilience as a student so as to maximise your chance of success.

Higher Education involves study at university level, although this may be completed in institutions that are not, themselves, universities. The experience of being a student in Higher Education can be life-changing. Most graduates look back on this time with great fondness. That is because of the unique opportunities to:

- study interesting subjects
- feel stretched intellectually
- explore new ideas
- engage in a wide range of new activities
- find out about yourself, not least how you rise to the challenge of academic study
- consider the kind of person that you want to be in the world
- make friends that will last you for life.

Whilst starting out as a student is exciting, it is also natural to feel some anxieties about what you might be taking on, whether you are up to it, and whether you are doing the right things to achieve well.

Higher level study is different from study at previous levels. This chapter helps you to identify how and why this is the case, and what that means for you as a student. It encourages you to think through what you want from the experience of being a student and to identify things you can do to succeed.

Make the experience work for you

In Higher Education, success lies largely in your own hands. Although help and guidance is provided, it is up to you to take the initiative. This means being active on your own behalf.

Put the hours in

Expertise is largely a factor of how many hours you spend on an activity. This applies to study as for other skills.

Using that time effectively is, of course, also important.

Make wise choices that work for you

Choose ...

- the right degree subject
- the right modules or topics for your level
- the right use of your time in class and outside of class

to achieve what you want to do.

Decide what you want ...

- from your study
- from the broader experience of being in Higher Education.

Think through ...

- how your studies contribute to your broader life plan and career ambitions
- how other opportunities at college or university can forward your ambitions.

Take charge

Plan how you will use your time as a student to gain your broader life and career aims.

Don't wait to be told – find out.

Don't wait to be asked – do it.

Don't wait to be inspired – inspire yourself.

Don't wait for opportunities – create them.

Don't rely only on feedback from others; learn to make sound evaluations of your own work.

Use the opportunities available

Use resources, support and facilities on campus, online, in the local area, through student organisations.

Use feedback from tutors.

Take extra classes, learn new skills, stretch yourself.

Learn something outside of your subject area – take up a new language or complete an enterprise project.

Use chances of a work placement or year abroad.

Network with other students.

Make friends for life.

Be well informed

Investigate. Read. Ask. Double check.

Develop the right mind-set

Intellectually curious and open to new perspectives.

Strongly motivated and determined to succeed.

Resilient, persistent and persevering.

Understand university level study

How and why is it different from previous levels of education?

What is expected of you?

What do you need to know about the conventions and culture?

What is seen as important, and gets good marks, in your subject?

What is expected from you?

It's not like at school where you were stuck in a classroom
from 9 till 4 and teachers told you what you needed to do.

– Ade, first-year student

As a student, you are expected to have
the following characteristics.

Independence

You must be able
to 'stand on your
own two feet'.
However, there is
help available. The
Student Union and
Student Services
will have details.

To cope at this level, you need to be reasonably
good at:

- adapting to new people and environments
- surviving in potentially very large groups
- being flexible in your learning style.

Ability to set goals to improve your work

Self-motivation

You have to be
able to work on
your own a lot.

Ability to organise your time

You need to keep track of time. You must:

- know when and
  where you should
  be for scheduled
  classes, events and
  exams
- know when work
  has to be handed in
- keep to deadlines
  for handing in work.

	MONDAY	TUESDAY	WEDNESDAY
9–10	put notes in order	Ecology lecture Rm G10	prepare for botany seminar
10–11	lecture Dr Shah Rm X22		
11–12	do plan (Science Report)		Botany Seminar Rm R21

(See Chapter 5.)

Openness to working with others

You will need
to organise
study sessions
with friends.

Ability to work out when and how you learn best

Ability to work things out for yourself

Success as a student: where am I now?

Success as a student isn't just about intellectual ability. A wide range of factors contribute, some of which are outlined here. For each statement, circle the emoticon if you feel you are confident in this aspect. Circle the arrows if you want to investigate this aspect further.

Understanding university level study

Clear understanding of expectations

☺ ▸▸ I understand what is expected of me. Page 11.

☺ ▸▸ I know what to expect from Higher Education. See pages 16–17.

Clear understanding of educational context

☺ ▸▸ I understand how higher level study is different from that at previous levels. See page 14.

☺ ▸▸ I have a good grasp of the culture and academic conventions of university level study. See page 15.

☺ ▸▸ I recognise that there will be specialist vocabulary that I need to learn to use myself.

Management of independent study

☺ ▸▸ I understand the role of independent study for university level study. See page 18.

☺ ▸▸ I manage independent study well. See pages 122–33 and 140–9.

Management of assessment

☺ ▸▸ I know how to use course information to help me achieve good marks. See page 323.

☺ ▸▸ I use the marking criteria to help me evaluate and improve my work. See page 323.

☺ ▸▸ I make productive use of feedback from tutors and others. See pages 31 and 324.

☺ ▸▸ I understand how to evaluate my own work. See page 97.

Subject knowledge and understanding

Knowledge

☺ ▸▸ There is a good match between my own knowledge and skills and the starting points on my course. See page 65 (Butterworth, 1992).

☺ ▸▸ I know how to research my subject in order to develop a good knowledge base. See Chapters 6 and 13.

Understanding

☺ ▸▸ I appreciate the difference between information and knowledge. See page 70.

☺ ▸▸ I recognise the importance of developing a deep understanding of the material. See pages 70–1.

☺ ▸▸ I recognise that understanding requires me to spend time reflecting about what I have learnt.

Skills

- ☺ ▸▸ I am aware of the range of academic skills required in Higher Education. See pages 36–7.
- ☺ ▸▸ I am confident that my academic skills are appropriate to this level of study. See page 39.

Learning savvy

- ☺ ▸▸ I understand the difference between intelligence and academic success. See Chapter 3.
- ☺ ▸▸ I know how I learn best. See Chapter 3.
- ☺ ▸▸ I create the optimum learning environment for myself. See Chapter 3.
- ☺ ▸▸ I think creatively about my study. See Chapter 3.
- ☺ ▸▸ I use reflection effectively to improve my academic performance. See Chapter 4.
- ☺ ▸▸ I have effective study strategies. See Chapter 3.
- ☺ ▸▸ I personalise learning so as to build on my strengths and preferences. See Chapter 3.
- ☺ ▸▸ I make the most of my memory. See Chapter 8.

Self-awareness and commitment

Clear vision, direction and motivation

- ☺ ▸▸ I have a clear vision about what success as a student would mean to me. See page 33.
- ☺ ▸▸ I am strongly motivated. See Chapter 4.
- ☺ ▸▸ I use the opportunities open to me so as to support my career aims. See Chapters 2 and 15.
- ☺ ▸▸ I take the right steps to enable me to make wise choices related to my studies. See pages 18 and 387–92.

High levels of personal engagement

- ☺ ▸▸ I understand the high level of commitment required. See pages 18 and 111.
- ☺ ▸▸ I recognise the importance of being intellectually curious and keen to find out more about my subject. See pages 14–15 and 32.
- ☺ ▸▸ I think about the issues for myself. See pages 15 and 32.
- ☺ ▸▸ I understand the importance of reading widely in the subject. See pages 14–15 and 32.
- ☺ ▸▸ I am active in finding out what I need to know for my course and as a student. See pages 30–1.
- ☺ ▸▸ I am able to 'stick with it' in completing tasks and my course. See page 112.
- ☺ ▸▸ I go the extra mile to do well at my studies.

Resilience, self-reliance and self-management

- ☺ ▸▸ I understand what is meant by resilience. See page 22.
- ☺ ▸▸ I am able to identify and manage anxieties. See pages 25–6.
- ☺ ▸▸ I use the support and resources available. See page 26.
- ☺ ▸▸ I keep goals and problems in perspective. See page 22.

Chapter 1

How is higher level study different?

Study is different

As a student in Higher Education, the most noticeably different features are likely to be:

- the teaching methods, especially the emphasis on independent study
- the assumption that you have the maturity and intelligence to 'get on with it', managing your own study, goals and life
- academic work is more difficult and complex
- the strong emphasis on 'understanding' rather than 'information'
- learning how knowledge is created
- that time may seem to operate differently, and good time management skills are essential.

The role of the 'teacher' is different

Teachers at this level are usually known as lecturers or tutors. As well as teaching, they are normally expected to engage in research and scholarship, which may feed into their teaching. When they are not involved in teaching-related tasks, they may be preparing research papers for publication and conferences, or applying research in industry, government and elsewhere.

Creating knowledge

Tutors in Higher Education create knowledge as well as teaching it. Depending on the subject, this is through:

- thinking, discussion and writing to develop theoretical understandings
- experimenting to test out theories
- investigating original sources or past knowledge, finding new ways of looking at these and bringing new interpretations.

Intellectual curiosity; learning community

Studying at this level is about being part of an adult learning community in which everyone, students and lecturers, are active in finding out new things for themselves and sharing them with others. It is assumed that you are intellectually curious, keen to find things out for yourself and to contribute to developing new understandings.

Universities play an important role in:

- encouraging research into new areas
- leading debate on contemporary issues
- critiquing existing understandings
- synthesising knowledge
- generating new understandings of the world
- stimulating economic development
- … as well as teaching students.

Depending on your institution, teaching is likely to be designed in ways that encourage you to do the same. Typically, you are required to:

- engage with debates in your subject
- hunt out answers for yourself
- develop your capacity to think in more creative, systematic and subtle ways
- be open to new perspectives
- undertake projects
- consider the broader significance and relevance of what you find out.

Nobody knows what will happen next …

Studying at the cutting edge of knowledge

Moving beyond generalisations

Study at previous levels often makes learning more manageable by using broader generalisations or 'brush strokes'. These are helpful when you are new to a subject. As you become more expert, you become aware of what lies behind some of the generalisations. As a result, things which had seemed straightforward become more problematic.

Journeying into the unknown

This is especially the case when you come to look at new research. Your tutors' research or scholarship may be at the 'cutting edge' of what is known, as will much of the recommended reading. As a result, course material may take you to that 'edge' too. You may study issues where:

- the answers are not yet known
- there may be no 'easy answers'
- there isn't a clear 'right' or 'wrong'
- research findings are ambiguous or contradictory
- knowledge advances in very small steps – or may seem to be going backwards
- there are conflicting points of view.

You may find this to be frustrating or, alternatively, you may find this to be intellectually exciting and feel driven to think about interesting possibilities.

Culture, conventions and values

Universities have a strong tradition of upholding values such as free speech, independent thinking and criticality. They strive to create objective truths, as far as this is possible, using rigorous and transparent methodologies. In general, each subject discipline has its own:

- ways of looking at the world
- culture, conventions and methodologies
- specialist terminology, so that it can convey precise and specific meanings.

As a student, you are not simply learning about 'facts'. Rather, you are being trained to think in ways that will enable you, in time, to conduct your own research using secure methodologies. This means that you need to learn:

- the specialist language of the subject
- what is valued, and why, within the subject discipline
- how knowledge has developed and is developing in the subject – and how to do this for yourself.

'Learning the rules of the game …'

As with many pursuits, success is easier if you are familiar with the system. In this context, that means understanding such things as:

- how you will be taught: see pages 16–17
- what gets good marks: see page 323
- how language is used and the right style and level of formality: see Chapters 9–11
- academic conventions: see pages 39 and 308–11
- making the best use of opportunities to develop skills and experience: see Chapters 2 and 15.

Chapter 1

Professor Scrubb works at the cutting edge of knowledge

Teaching: what to expect in Higher Education

Teaching methods differ but you can expect at least some of the following.

Lectures

These vary according to course and subject but in general, expect:

- size: 50–300 people
- length: 1–3 hours
- weekly: 5–20 hours
- no individual attention.

See also page 183.

There is usually a set of lectures for each module, unit or option. You are likely to study with different students for each module. Lectures are used to give an overview of the topic. Usually, students listen and make notes whilst lecturers speak or read from notes, write on a board, or project information onto an overhead screen. Some lecturers encourage questions and include activities; others do not. Occasionally, lectures are delivered on video or transmitted from another campus.

Tutorials

These are used to give feedback on your work and discuss your general progress. It may be the only time that a lecturer is able to help you with study problems, so it is important to prepare your questions in advance.

- size: in small groups or on an individual basis
- length: usually an hour at most
- frequency: possibly one or two per term.

Seminars/workshops

These usually involve group discussion of material presented either in a lecture or in set reading. Often, a student (or a group of students) is asked to begin the discussion by making a presentation. It is important to prepare for seminars by reading through lecture notes and background reading, even if you are not asked to make the presentation yourself.

- size: 12–30 people
- length: 1–3 hours
- weekly: varies (perhaps 1–3 each week).

See also Chapter 10, *Working with others*.

Other teaching methods

Groupwork and collaborative learning

This could range from contributing in class and small-group discussion work to undertaking group tasks and projects. You might be asked to complete a class blog or wiki or contribute to a discussion board. Students are often expected to form their own study and support groups. (See Chapter 10.)

Work-based learning and work placements

Foundation Degrees, sandwich courses and other vocational courses require students to be employed or on placement. While there, they may be supervised by a lecturer from the college or by somebody at the workplace – or a mixture of the two.

Laboratory work, studio work and practicals

Science students may spend most of their time doing practical work in laboratories; fine arts students may work predominantly in studio space they are allocated. The amount of practical work of this kind will depend on the course.

Distance learning

Students on some courses study mostly at home. Materials are sent by post or over the internet. Contact with tutors may be by letter, email, video conferencing, Skype, or in local meetings.

Independent study

This is the most common and possibly the most challenging feature of university study. Apart from timetabled elements such as lectures, almost all courses expect students to work independently for the rest of the week. (See pages 18–19.)

Technology-enhanced learning

Most programmes now supplement class-based teaching with a variety of online activities and resources. Depending on the lecturer, a range of technologies may be incorporated into class-based teaching too. (See pages 20–1.)

Seeing your lecturers

For a variety of reasons, lecturers are likely to be less available on demand than at previous levels of education. Typically, a good range of support is provided through a mixture of set appointments, surgery-hours or drop-in times, a help desk, online contact or specialist student support departments.

Lecturers' varied approaches

Different subject areas or departments have their own traditions, and even individual lecturers may have strong personal tastes in how things should be done. You need to be alert to this and notice your lecturers' preferences.

Now let me get this straight. Mr Jiff wants work on both sides of the paper, Dr Lank on one. Ms Snape wants everything word-processed. Mr Kip wants essays sent by email. Ms Snape wants sub-headings …

The study week

Most full-time courses are considered to be the equivalent of an average working week in employment. This means that you are expected to study for 35–40 hours a week, in a mixture of independent study at home or in a library, scheduled classes and activities and, if relevant, in the workplace. The way that time is divided up varies greatly. For more details, see pages 18 and 127.

It is worth booking an appointment in advance …

The role of independent study

What is independent study?

Independent study is a feature of most courses at this level. Typically, this means managing your own study in between taught sessions. For distance learning courses, all study may be by directed independent study.

Guiding yourself

At earlier stages of study, teaching staff often provide much guidance on which pages to read, how to interpret reading material and assignment titles, the information to include in assignments, and how to structure your answers. In Higher Education, you do this yourself. As you become more experienced, you gain increasing amounts of responsibility. This self-direction generally culminates in a dissertation, research project or extended essay.

Varies by programme

There is less independent study on courses that schedule many hours in labs or work-related activity. There is more independent study in arts, humanities, social sciences, business and creative subjects which require reading, writing and practice that do not require a tutor present.

Greater freedom

Independent study can feel lacking in structure, but is also liberating. To take full advantage of this, it helps to understand well how you study most effectively. (See Chapter 3.)

Time management

Managing your own study time can be challenging at first, especially as excuses for missed deadlines are rarely accepted. Good time management skills are essential. (See Chapter 5.)

Keeping going

For independent study, it is important to stay focused and maintain your motivation. Motivation levels can wane over time so it is good to give this some advance thought and to enlist the support of others. See *Motivation* (page 117) and *Study groups* (page 257).

Making wise choices

It is up to you to make smart choices for study options and extra-curricular activities. These have an impact on the coherence of your study and, potentially, on your future career. That can feel rather daunting. However, it can also feel empowering to make such decisions. Guidance will be available, but it is up to you to find out what is on offer.

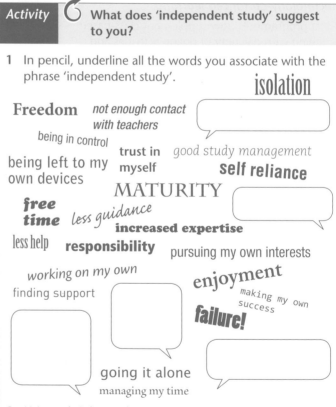

Activity   **What does 'independent study' suggest to you?**

1 In pencil, underline all the words you associate with the phrase 'independent study'.

isolation

Freedom   *not enough contact with teachers*

being in control

being left to my own devices   **trust in myself**   *good study management*

self reliance

MATURITY

free time   *less guidance*   **increased expertise**

less help   **responsibility**   pursuing my own interests

working on my own   *enjoyment*

finding support   *making my own success*

failure!

going it alone   managing my time

2 Using a bright marker pen, circle all the words that describe how you would *like* independent study to be. Use the bubbles to add words of your own.
What do the phrases you select tell you about your attitude to independent study?

Independent study: benefits, challenges, risks

Benefits	Challenges	Risks
More control over your study time	• To manage time effectively. • To meet deadlines.	Losing a sense of time. Wasting time. Underestimating how long study tasks take. Forgetting things that must be done. Missing essential deadlines.
More control over your spare time	• To use spare time effectively in building your personal profile. • To recognise the difference between spare time and independent study time. • To put time aside to relax, rest and enjoy yourself.	Using all your spare time for study. Mistaking time not spent in taught sessions as 'spare time'. Missing opportunities to develop a wider personal profile that will benefit you later when applying for jobs.
More choice about when and where to study	• To create structures for your day. • To organise a place to study. • To work out the best places and times for you for different kinds of study activity.	Not getting down to study. Not creating a place that allows you to study without interruption.
More choice about how you study	• To identify your learning style for different types of tasks. • To take responsibility for your learning and achieving your goals.	Not bothering to explore and develop your learning style. Doing what you enjoy most rather than what works best for you, if these are different.
More responsibility for your own successes	• To identify barriers to your learning and to address these. • To identify ways of improving your own performance. • To make effective use of feedback and to learn from mistakes.	Failure to understand previous barriers to learning. Not addressing weaknesses in your performance. Giving up too easily. Ignoring feedback. Becoming despondent at early failures rather than using these to guide improvement.
More choice about how much energy you devote to topics that interest you	• To find the right balance between a broad set of interests at a superficial level and too much depth in a narrow range of topics. • To broaden your range of interests.	Devoting too much time to topics that interest you at the expense of those needed to complete the programme. Becoming specialised in too narrow a range of topics.
There isn't a teacher looking over your shoulder all the time	• To keep on target with little guidance. • To keep yourself motivated. • To take responsibility for pursuing solutions to problems on your own. • To recognise when you need help and to ask for it.	Letting things slip. Falling behind in your work. Losing motivation. Losing a sense of what you are supposed to do. Not asking for help, not finding out what help is available, or not using it. Running for help too soon instead of trying to solve the problem yourself.
More control over choice of topics	• To create a coherent programme of study that interests you and meets your goals.	Choosing topics that do not fit together well, or that do not contribute towards your goals.

Technology enhanced study

Universities and colleges now routinely incorporate digital technologies into the teaching and learning process. Typical resources are outlined below.

Virtual learning environment (VLE)

VLEs such as *Web-CT*, *Blackboard* or *Moodle* may be used either instead of face-to-face teaching *or to* supplement it, in some of the following ways:

Background information – tutor details, handbooks, support materials, past exam papers, etc.

Up-to-date course materials, such as
- advance preparation for lectures and seminars, electronic version of lecture notes or podcasts of lectures
- digitised reading lists and reading material
- links to electronic journals.

Reminders and guidance – about lectures, events, field trips, and assignment deadlines.

Online learning community – with others on your programme, through chat rooms, discussion groups, webinars or online conferences.

Collaborative learning – messages, conferencing, discussions, notice boards, and opportunities for group activities such as blogs, wikis and projects.

Computer-assisted assessment – exams, tests and quizzes for formal assessment or for practice.

Workplace study – links to resources, tutors and students if your study is based in the workplace.

Webcam and video conferencing

These are especially useful if:
- your class is split between different sites, or if
- some or all of your class is based at home, at work, overseas or on field trips
- your programme has links with students on similar programmes at other institutions.

A student portal

Depending on its design, this might offer:

Programme administration – to check course details such as key dates and exam results.

Programme resources – links to the department website, online notes, VLE or useful websites.

Automatic updates – about the student societies, events and websites you select as of interest.

Messages and bulletins – from tutors, other students, societies and groups.

Easier off-campus access – to the college library and other websites without logging into each individually.

M-learning: using your phone

You may need to use a phone:
- to receive messages about changes to teaching rooms or cancelled classes
- to receive reminders about dates and deadlines
- for notification of events, newsletters, etc.
- for collaborative learning activities and directed chat in lectures and class.

Studying with technology

Your online presence as a student

Bear in mind that tutors and potential employers may access material that you put into the public domain. Take on board the following points.

Consider your future interests: could comments or photos you plan to post come back to haunt you at job interviews or when you go home to your family?

Security: take care not to put yourself, other people or your files at risk in any way.

Netiquette and consideration for others: think whether any of your posts could cause distress to others. Avoid any that might be considered to be offensive, insensitive or bullying.

Tools and apps to support study

There is a growing range of tools and apps that you can use for various aspects of study. You can use these to research topics, record details for references, and for collaborative working with other students. Details of these are provided in the relevant chapters below.

Collaborative learning and group projects

Maintain control of your information: be careful to whom you give access to your details through social networking sites, blogs, etc.

Avoid allegations of cheating: do not share your written work electronically before it is marked as, if other students make use of your academic work in their own assignments, you could be held jointly responsible. Do not cut and paste from electronic material – this too can be detected electronically when you hand in your work.

Find out what is provided for you

Check whether your course provides:

☐ a student portal

☐ a Virtual Learning Environment (VLE)

☐ free use of the internet on campus

☐ free use of the internet from home

☐ easy-to-use links to electronically available academic sources, on campus and at home

☐ shared electronic space for your course such as a student website or intranet

☐ chat rooms or discussion boards for your course

☐ online notice boards

☐ digitised reading lists

☐ digitised reading materials

☐ electronic journals or blogs

☐ podcasts of lectures

☐ writing a class wiki

☐ e-portfolios

☐ video conferencing

☐ collaborative learning projects

☐ assistive technologies for students with disabilities

☐ workshops to help you use any of the above.

☐ Other:

Resilience as a student

What is resilience?

Resilience is the quality of being able to withstand times of difficulty or change in such ways that you can either cope reasonably at the time or bounce back afterwards. It isn't that you never feel stressed, disappointed or out of your depth: it is about developing sufficient inner resources to get through and to keep going. There will be times as a student when resilience will be of real benefit.

How resilience contributes to success

- It helps you manage when things get tough.
- It gives you the experience of recovering from setbacks and of coping.
- It builds your confidence that you can cope, even if everything seems to be going wrong.
- It gives you confidence to take risks, take part, and to take on new challenges.

Resilience helps you as a student when:

- you are experiencing a lot of change: new environments, people, expectations, ways of thinking
- there are challenges and pressures: emotional, financial, academic
- there are many demands to juggle at once: work, study, family, friends
- things don't go as planned: grades lower than you expected; not getting a job you wanted; relationships ending
- you feel down or want to give up on your studies.

Reflection: Resilience as a student

What kinds of situations or issues arise for you as a student where you feel it would help to develop greater resilience?

Rate your resilience

Below is a list of behaviours associated with resilience. Consider your own resilience by rating yourself for each. Use a 5 point scale, where 5 is a high level of resilience.

How resilient am I?

1   **I can bounce back** from knocks.

☹ 1 2 3 4 5 ☺

2   **I look for solutions** that help me to solve problems.

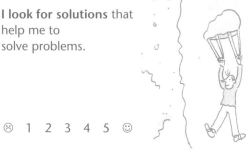

☹ 1 2 3 4 5 ☺

3   **I can keep a sense of perspective** or can bring things back into perspective.

☹ 1 2 3 4 5 ☺

4   **I can manage stress** and keep myself calm.

☹ 1 2 3 4 5 ☺

5 I use support and guidance available.

☹ 1 2 3 4 5 ☺

6 I use my time effectively ... to help me stay on top of all I have to do.

☹ 1 2 3 4 5 ☺

7 I use a routine ... to keep myself on track even when I don't feel like it.

☹ 1 2 3 4 5 ☺

8 I keep myself motivated and am effective in encouraging myself to study.

☹ 1 2 3 4 5 ☺

9 I persevere, even when I don't feel like studying or staying on the course.

☹ 1 2 3 4 5 ☺

10 I build and maintain relationships with others, for mutual support and to enrich my life.

☹ 1 2 3 4 5 ☺

Reflection: Personal resilience

- When am I at my most resilient in life?
- What enables me to be resilient in those contexts?
- How can I draw on those qualities to help me as a student?

Relevant sections of this book

- Identifying resources: page 29.
- Creative problem solving: Chapter 4.
- Managing stress: Chapter 14.
- Staying motivated: Chapter 4.
- Time management: Chapter 5.
- Student support: Chapter 10.

Chapter 1

Managing life as a student

Getting to know people

Student life provides great opportunities for meeting new people, but can also be accompanied at times by feelings of home sickness, loneliness or pressure. This isn't unusual, and many services are there to help. To get through such times:

- study on campus when you can
- get out of your room: use the Student Union and campus facilities
- join in: use clubs, societies, sports
- get to know people one by one rather than only through big groups
- ask people to go for a coffee, a walk, a meal or to see a film
- remember that people who end up as your closest friends may not be those you meet in your first few months.

Using the experience

- Get to know the campus, online resources, library, and facilities. Tour these and consider when and how you will use them.
- Visit Careers services as early as possible, even if only to see what is available.
- Make time to take part in academic and social activities, especially if you are part-time, live away from campus or study by distance learning.

Chapter 1

Taking care of yourself

Although it may seem obvious, it is important to take sensible steps to take care of yourself. With all the things there are to do as a student, this is often put on hold, with unwanted consequences hitting at the wrong time. Give thought to how well you are managing such basics as the following.

Safety   Consider this from many perspectives: accommodation, travel, activities, privacy settings online, who you spend time with.

Sleep   You may well find that your sleep patterns are very different as a student. Getting sufficient sleep is important to such things as keeping healthy, maintaining your immune system so you don't catch infections, taking in information when studying, and being alert generally.

Health   Register with a doctor or health centre once you arrive at university. Take note of any health warnings and of any immunisation programmes that are advised. Take symptoms of ill health or mental ill health seriously and, at the very least, have a check up if you have concerns.

Food   Eat proper food. Use the college refectory or canteen. Find out where you can get different kinds of meal for the lowest prices, or learn to cook if you don't know how already, as this can save you money. Get a good cookbook – there are some designed especially for students, such as *Student Brain Food* by Lauren Lucien.

Money   Keep track of your spending from the first day. Use a financial planning tool such as recommended in Appendix 3. Make sure you are aware of all the sources of support available to you – speak to a financial adviser at the university or college if you are unsure.

See Appendix 3 for useful sources of information.

Reflection: Taking care of yourself

- Which, if any, of the issues identified in the box above are ones that you tend to neglect?
- Make a 'to do' list of things that you could do differently in order to take better take care of yourself.
- Which of the items on your list are priorities – things to do now?

Managing anxieties and resources

It is quite natural to feel some anxiety when you start something new, and many students have concerns about starting at university.

It is easier to work out strategies for handling potential challenges and to manage your anxieties if you have:

- sorted out in your own mind what your worries are
- considered how serious they really are
- realised that many other people feel the same way.

On the right are listed some anxieties which are common amongst new students. Tick the box beside any that apply to you, or add in others in the empty spaces.

Look again at the items you have ticked. Beside each, write the number of the statement below that most closely corresponds with your feeling. Then read the comments on the next page.

1 I expect this to be a minor difficulty: I will get round it easily or in time.
2 I expect this to be quite a serious difficulty: I will work on a solution.
3 I expect this to be a major difficulty: I may need to ask for help.

Reflection: Managing anxieties

- What initial ideas do you have about how you could manage some of these anxieties?
- What strategies have you used in the past to deal with a new or difficult situation? Which of these strategies could be helpful now?

Study and learning

☐ Keeping up with other people
☐ Finding the time to do everything
☐ Understanding academic language
☐ Having the confidence to speak
☐ Developing confidence in myself
☐ Writing essays
☐ Getting used to university life
☐ Meeting deadlines

Personal, family, work commitments

☐ Making friends with other students
☐ Coping with travel
☐ Organising child care
☐ People treating me differently/'fitting in'
☐ Coping with job requirements
☐ Family responsibilities

Others

☐
☐
☐
☐
☐
☐
☐
☐
☐

Study and learning anxieties

It is important to give yourself time to settle in and see what is required. Many institutions pace the first year more slowly to give you time to find your feet.

Focus on planning your own activities rather than worrying about how well other students are doing. Some people play psychological games, claiming that they do no work and can write essays over night. Very few people can really do this; it is certainly not expected of you, and it is not a sensible way to study.

Find support. Many students will be anxious about some aspect of their study and it helps to share concerns. Make time to meet other students in your classes. Once you have formed a bond with other students, you will have more confidence about joining in.

The following chapters make practical suggestions about ways of handling aspects of study such as speaking, essay writing, meeting deadlines, managing stress, and generally setting yourself up to succeed. Focus on your motivation for study, and be determined to enjoy your course. Think of yourself as being on an adventure – not on trial!

Managing other anxieties

There is pressure on students to juggle family and work commitments in ways that were not expected in the past. Students have to be more creative in problem-solving and very organised in their time management.

In many universities and colleges, Student Services and the Student Union offer advice on managing finance, finding work, grants, child care, health care, counselling, disability, and many other issues that arise for students. Use these services to help resolve problems. Advisers can help more successfully if you approach them before problems become emergencies.

Make an action plan

Look back to the items you ticked on page 25.

Set priorities

- What needs to be done immediately?
- Which things can wait?
- In which order do you need to deal with these anxieties?
- Use a copy of the *Priority organiser* (page 135).

Resources

- Find out the sources of help that are available at your college or university.
- Complete: *What are my personal resources?* (page 29).
- Talk to others who may have similar worries. Form a study, discussion or support group with other students with whom you feel comfortable.

Reflection: Thinking things through

It helps if you write down and explore your anxieties and your options.

- Note down your feelings.
- Write down your options and decide between them (see pages 24–5).
- Record how you dealt with each problem so that you can evaluate your progress later.

How do other students manage?

The short passages on the next pages were written by students about their first few months. You may notice that their time seemed very pressurised; being organised is an important theme in these writings. However, these students made time to relax, meet others, use the facilities and opportunities for sports or drama, which are also important to the overall student experience.

Chapter 1

Students' experiences

The first few weeks

I thought I had a pretty good idea of what to expect as I had family at Uni and I had been on a university summer school. These did help but it was very different once I got here ... more people, more reading, more things to do, and everything seemed to sort of 'swim around' – there was so much information and so much to think about. I have become very good at writing lists!

Meenaxi

Making it as a student

I nearly left after the first few weeks. I had already left one uni and I was about to give up on this one as well. I had been studying really hard, so I felt I deserved high marks but that wasn't happening. I was very angry. I felt the tutors didn't like me and were being unfair. At the same time, I realised that I couldn't do more work and I thought I just wasn't up to university.

I told my tutor I was leaving and I am so glad that I did. That was the beginning of really getting to grips with where I had been going wrong. It wasn't that I couldn't do the work, which is what I had thought. I was spending my time doing the wrong things. I wasted a lot of time online and taking copious notes about everything. I didn't have a systematic approach to doing the essays and I didn't believe in my own ideas so these didn't come across in my work. Mainly, I wasn't thinking enough, neither about what I was studying nor about how to go about studying.

I am still building my skills in reading and writing – these underlie everything, really, but my marks are now good and getting better. The main thing is that I can see how having a strategy can make a difference to your study. There is always a way to get things done. Knowing this keeps me looking for ways of doing things, rather than giving up. If I can succeed this far, anybody can.

David

'The mystery of time ...'

Time moves in weird ways – you seem to have loads of time on your hands – empty timetables compared to school, and all those empty evenings in the diary. And then not enough time to fit everything in. It took me a while to realise that I need to be the one who organises things, to see I get everything done if several assignments have to be handed in at around the same time, and just getting out there and mixing so I have a social life.

Olivia

A typical day

On Tuesdays I have a lecture from 10 a.m. to 12 noon. This lecturer does not just talk at us: she breaks the time up into short tasks, discussions, videos, etc. When all 90 of us are discussing something in groups, it can be rather noisy, but you get used to it. The rest of the day is 'free' but as I am already on the site, I go to the library and prepare for the next day's lectures, or do some reading for the seminars I have on every second Wednesday. Some Tuesday afternoons, I go to the gym, and study in the evening instead.

Krishna

Students' experiences

My first term

After the terrible time I had in school, I was very worried about what I might be putting myself through coming back to study as an adult. I was sure I wouldn't be able to keep up. When I got my first few pieces of work back, the marks were not very good, and I felt I ought to leave.

Luckily, I was talked out of leaving. I made an effort to meet other mature students and found many of them were having similar experiences to me. One of them encouraged me to ask my tutors for more detailed feedback on my work. I had not wanted to ask for any help in case the lecturers thought I was not good enough for the course. Bit by bit my marks started to get better, and some were very good. This boosted my confidence.

I had expected study to be difficult. What I had not expected was that other aspects of being a student could be just as hard. It took me ages to build up the confidence to eat in the canteen – it seemed so enormous and bustling. I used to rush away after lectures rather than talking to strangers. My train service is very erratic and I kept arriving late. My sister, who was going to look after my children, moved house. Sorting out all these things has made me very skilled at problem-solving!

I have to say that there are many positive things about being a student. Now that I have got to know other people here, I look forward to coming in to study. I feel like I am escaping into time which is just for me. I like having the library to work in – and not being disturbed while I just get on with it.

I would recommend to new students that they give themselves a chance to settle in, and not panic if anything seems to be going wrong. If they have children, I cannot over-emphasise how important it has been to me to have plans to cover every eventuality. I wish I had had reserve plans for child care right from the beginning because that, more than anything else, had an effect on my studies. I also recommend that new students find other people who have similar experiences to themselves – talking to each other you can come up with good ideas about how to tackle problems, and boost each other's morale.

You are bound to find you think differently about many things by the time you finish your course – for me, discussing things with other people has become a very exciting activity. Above all, I think students have to think, 'I might never get this chance again – how am I going to get the most out of it?' There are many facilities available and it is a very good opportunity to try things you might never have imagined yourself doing – starting your own group, karate, or going on an expedition. It is a wonderful opportunity – but you have to make it work for yourself.

Sasha

My Thursday as a student

Dash the kids to the nursery. Dash into the labs for 10. Suddenly time changes. I am caught up in what I am doing – the project I am working on with two other people. I can spend hours mixing and measuring, comparing my findings with others'. We talk a lot about what we are doing, and why, and make suggestions on why our results are different. I always ask my lecturers if I am unsure – some are very helpful, but some are not. In the afternoon, I have one lecture. Recently, I have arranged it so I can go to drama club on Thursday nights.

Charlie

What are my personal resources?

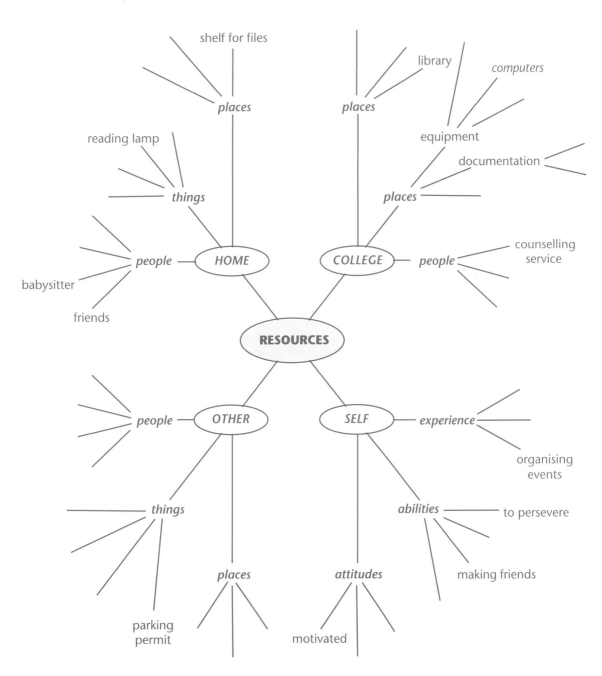

Have you considered all the resources that might be available to you? Try brainsatorming (adding in your own ideas) around key words on the pattern notes below. If you feel you have few resources, it may help if you speak to a student counsellor.

shelf for files

places

library

places

computers

equipment

documentation

reading lamp

things

places

counselling service

people   HOME

COLLEGE   *people*

babysitter

friends

RESOURCES

people   OTHER

SELF   *experience*

organising events

things

abilities   to persevere

places

attitudes

making friends

parking permit

motivated

Chapter 1

Be well informed: find out …

Read what you are given

At this level of study, it is assumed that you will:

- find out what kind of information is available
- read everything that has been provided, thoroughly, and in a timely manner
- work out what it means for you
- ask if you don't understand its significance.

Don't wait to be told

Some students are caught out because they think that, at the right moment, a tutor will remind them of what they should know or do, especially if this is what happened at school or college. Although that may happen occasionally, it is not typical. It is usually up to you to make sure you are up to speed with what you need to know.

Checklist

Find out the following, as relevant to your course. Check ✓ each item once completed.

Find out what you need to know:

- ☐ Make a list of all the information you are supposed to receive and when.
- ☐ Clarify where information is provided.
- ☐ Check that you receive each item.
- ☐ Check where to find the regulations and what is in them in case you ever need them.

Find out programme details:

- ☐ The exact name and code of your course
- ☐ The exact name and code of each module
- ☐ The names and contact details of all the tutors and lecturers teaching you this year
- ☐ Whether there is a programme (and/or module) handbook and where to locate this online
- ☐ The online facilities provided for your course
- ☐ The content of your course (the syllabus).

Find out about levels and credit:

- ☐ Your level of study
- ☐ The number of modules and credits you must take each year and/or for each level (see glossary, page 404)
- ☐ The level and credit rating of each module or unit
- ☐ The right modules/credit to take for what you want to study next year or for career purposes.

Find out about attendance requirements:

- ☐ Start and end dates for terms or semesters
- ☐ The minimum attendance requirements
- ☐ Times you must log on for course-related activity
- ☐ Date and times of any trips or events
- ☐ When your classes start and end
- ☐ Consequences if you don't meet requirements.

Find out about student representation:

- ☐ What kind of student reps system is used?
- ☐ When and how are reps elected?
- ☐ What training is provided for reps?
- ☐ How can you become a rep?
- ☐ How can you get your voice heard as a student?
- ☐ How can you find out what your reps are doing?

Find out about assessment:

☐ The details of how you will be assessed

☐ How marks are allocated

☐ The marking criteria and what these mean

☐ When and how you are expected to hand in your work, such as in person or electronically

☐ The kind of receipt or acknowledgement provided when you hand in your work.

How this level of study is different:

☐ Look out for 'level descriptors' or marking criteria detailed for each level or year of study.

☐ Compare assignment briefs for different levels. Look at such things as word or page requirements, subtle changes to the wording of marking criteria, greater difficulty in assignments, the amount of work you need to do independently.

Find out about feedback:

Feedback on your work may be given in many different ways, from written responses through to informal verbal feedback during a clinical session.

☐ What kinds of feedback are offered on each module or unit of study?

☐ When and by whom is this given?

Find out about resources:

☐ What kinds of learning resources are provided for you online or as hard copy?

☐ When are these updated online?

☐ What kinds of reading lists are set?

☐ Where can you find these lists?

☐ Which items are digitised?

☐ Of the items on your reading list, which can be substituted for others if some are not available?

Get to know your library

☐ Who are your library contacts this year?

☐ If you are not a regular library user, spend time in the library or resource centre. (See page 157.)

Many students are fearful of appearing foolish in libraries, especially when using online catalogues, consulting special collections, or working out the numbering system. It is best to get over these fears before term begins. Librarians are used to people not being able to use libraries: if you need help, ask for it.

Find out about support:

☐ Who is responsible for supporting you this year, such as a personal tutor or year tutor?

☐ What support is available if you struggle with your coursework?

☐ What do you have to do to access this? For example, do you need to email the tutor or book an appointment?

☐ Are support sessions offered, through the library, a resource centre, or the Student Union?

Find out your time requirements:

☐ The number of study hours required. (See page 127.)

☐ The pattern of study on your course – especially the amount of independent study. (See page 18.)

☐ The weekly time commitments expected for different types of study. (See pages 127–8.)

Organise your information

☐ Put together in a separate file or folder all the general information such as college regulations, sources of help, appeals and grievance procedures, and student clubs and facilities.

☐ Put time into your planner to browse it so you know what information is provided.

Chapter 1

Success as a student: what lecturers say

Students who do best at university are those who are very determined to succeed, plan how they will do it, and then keep their plans in perspective.

The students who stand out to me are those who don't just read what is on the reading list, but who genuinely want to know all they can about the subject – who surprise you by having read an article just published or have a good grip on the most recent debates in the subject.

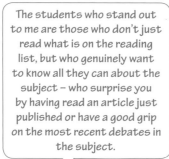

Study is important – of course, I would say that. But college life is about much more than that. It can and should be a life-changing experience – a time to have your ideas challenged, to meet people from an incredibly wide range of backgrounds, to think how your education could change your own life and that of others.

I would say that the key factor is time. If students put in the hours, they tend to do well. Of course, you do need to use the time well too.

Students need to keep their eyes on their long-term goals. If they want a good job, it won't hurt to have a good degree but they also need to show they have experience at other things. They need to get out and do things for the community, get a job, have ideas and opinions, show they are their own person.

What helps students to succeed at Uni? Most students do achieve their degree and then go on to get a job, so that suggests there are many different routes to success. Mainly, it's about the basics. Find out what you have to do, do it, and stay the course. Do more, and your marks will be better.

Universities provide the opportunities. It is then up to the students to make those opportunities work for them.

As a lecturer, I like the students who love their subject and want to know as much as they can about it. As the parent of a student myself, I think it important that students use their time at university wisely. If they want an academic career, then they should put the subject first. If they want a career outside of academia, then they need to think more broadly.

It isn't just about how much work you put in. You can actually get away with doing much less work than others and do better than them – but you can't get away without thinking about what you are doing and what you are learning.

The best students for me are those who really grapple with the issues, who show they have tried to think things through for themselves, even if they haven't got it all right. The worst are those that rely on Wikipedia as their main source of information – and think no-one will notice!

Your vision of success as a student

A return on your investment

Students invest a great deal of time, energy and money in their Higher Education so success at university or at college is usually very important to them. However, there are many different versions of what that success would look like.

The way you spend your time as a student is key to whether you achieve what you really want from the experience. It is largely up to you to decide how you do that. If you can formulate a clearer vision of what success as a student means to you, you are more likely to achieve it.

Reflection: Think forward

Our imaginations are extremely powerful. You can use this to help direct your energies. For example, picture yourself 10 years into the future. Will you be impressed by the choices you are making now, and your use of the time and opportunities available to you? Will you wish that you had done anything differently?

Reflection: Use your vision to direct your energies

What do your choices opposite indicate about:

- what 'success' as a student would look like for you?
- how to direct your energies as a student?

What would success look like for me?

Use the following questions to help you to plan. ✓ Tick all items that apply to you. Then highlight those that are most important to you.

I would feel I had made a success of university/ college if:

Career

☐ I gained a qualification that enabled me to develop my career

☐ I developed skills which helped me find a good job

☐ I made full use of the opportunities available

☐ I took on positions of responsibility that helped my CV

☐ I made good contacts that helped my career.

Transformational experience

☐ I learnt more about who I was as a person

☐ I became a different person as a result of my experience

☐ I developed a range of skills and qualities that improve my life

☐ I developed in personal confidence

☐ I developed a broader understanding of the world

☐ I met and learnt from people I wouldn't have met otherwise.

Subject and qualifications

☐ I learnt a lot about a subject that really interested me

☐ I got a good class of degree

☐ I stretched myself intellectually

☐ I developed academically.

Life and personal

☐ I really enjoyed myself

☐ I made good friends

☐ I developed new interests that enrich my life

☐ I learned to manage myself as an effective adult.

Chapter 1

Review

This chapter was designed to assist new or struggling students to gain a clearer picture of what to expect from Higher Education and to provide a steer on how to place yourself in a strong position to succeed. It provides an overview of the broader academic context in which university level study takes place, in order to help you make sense of its culture, teaching practices and ways of thinking. That context informs the ways that you will be asked to engage in learning and the ways that your work will be assessed.

Depending on your previous education you may be surprised, at first, at the amount of responsibility and independence expected of you at this level: independence of thought, enquiry, decision-making and overall management of your study. It is generally assumed that you will have the appropriate levels of maturity, intelligence and motivation to manage such independence – and to be able and eager to take charge of your own work.

This approach to teaching represents a great deal of respect for your abilities and potential, although it also brings its own challenges. It requires you to be active on your own behalf, working out what you need to do and then getting on with it. This includes grasping that there is information that you need to know and use without always being directed or assisted to do so. It also means that you need not only academic skills, but also a broader range of understandings and qualities that enable you to manage your studies as is expected.

In practice, students vary a great deal in how ready and able they are to take on this level of responsibility at the start of their studies. If it feels daunting to you, then be reassured that there will be others who feel the same way. However, most students find that their skills, including those of resilience and self-management, are stretched and then strengthened as they take on the increased challenges of university level study.

As motivation, self-management and well-founded self-confidence are so essential to success as a student, it is especially helpful if you are clear about what you want to gain from the experience of being a student and use this to good effect in maintaining your morale and sense of purpose.

Finally, the chapter has emphasised the importance of 'taking charge' of your student experience. Plan how you will use your time as a student to gain your broader life and career aims. Don't wait to be told, asked, guided, engaged or inspired. Decide what you want. Search out resources and help. Create your own opportunities. Find ways to energise, motivate and inspire yourself, and look for the enjoyment in your studies that will help to strengthen your enthusiasm.

Chapter 2
Developing your skills

Learning outcomes

This chapter offers you opportunities to:

- reflect on what is meant by terms such as 'skills', study skills and academic skills
- use the APT-S study skills framework
- consider five components that support study skills development
- sharpen your awareness of skills and qualities you bring with you as well as those you gain through your studies
- identify areas of strength in your current study skills and areas to develop further
- set priorities for developing your study skills, monitor your achievements and record these.

This chapter focuses on the skills that you:

- bring with you into academic study
- develop through study
- can transfer to other contexts such as employment.

There isn't a sharp divide between the skills needed for academic study and those used elsewhere. This means that, whatever your previous education, you will have experiences that you can draw upon and adapt to support your studies. Similarly, once you graduate, the academic skills you use as a student will be applicable to other contexts.

Being aware of this can increase your confidence in taking on academic study if you have been out of education for some time or are uncertain about your academic ability. It can also help you to feel more confident about progressing into employment if you haven't had a graduate job in the past.

However, there are subtle differences in the way that similar skills are understood at different levels of education and in the world of work. This chapter provides a means of thinking about the relationship between skills and context. It enables you to audit your current skills and consider how you could make use, in other contexts, of the skills you develop as a student.

What are study skills?

What is a skill?

> **Skill**
>
> To be skilled is to be able to perform a learned activity well and at will.

A skill is a learned ability rather than an outcome achieved through luck or chance and can, therefore, be relied on reasonably securely when you perform an equivalent task again. You can fine-tune skills through practice, feedback and reflection, just as athletes improve their performance by developing underlying skills in movement, breathing and pacing.

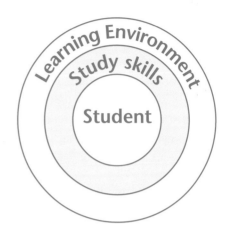

What are study skills?

The term 'study skills' is used here to refer to more than just 'academic' skills. It includes a wider range of abilities that enable achievement in your studies. These can be viewed as four categories of skills:

1 **Self**-management skills for study
2 **Academic** skills
3 **People** skills for studying with others
4 **Task** management skills.

The first of these, self-management, helps you to develop the other three sets of study skills.

The APT-S study skills framework

The skills landscape in Higher Education can sometimes seem complex, as subject disciplines, institutions, employers and professional bodies produce ever longer lists of skills they feel students should develop. The APT-S framework simplifies such complexity by looking at three key things:

1 You, the student, as the starting point
2 The learning environment in its entirety – everything that relates to your study
3 The skills that help you manage that learning environment, its people, tasks, conventions, tools and resources.

You as the starting point

In practice, the skills you will need and acquire as a student will be different from those of other students.

Past experience

Your starting point will be different: your educational history, past opportunities and personal challenges influence the way you are now as a student. They shape your current levels of knowledge, confidence, motivation, study habits, preferences and skills.

Your current experience

- Your choice of subject, course, options and topics will develop specific sets of skills.
- Your own motivation for, and application to, learning new skills will be distinct.
- Many other current factors will also differ, from the people you study with to other aspects of the learning environment described overleaf.

Future aims

Your ambitions for your life and career influence, and will be influenced by, the choices you make for skills development whilst a student.

The APT-S study skills framework

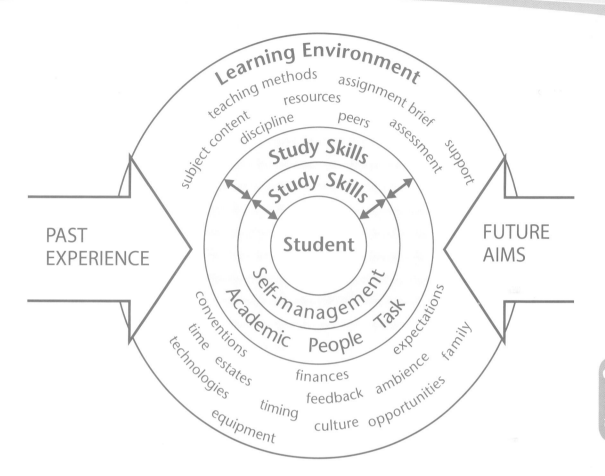

The learning environment

The 'learning environment' refers here to everything that forms part of the wider context in which you are studying. It includes such factors as:

- the academic discipline and its conventions
- the subject content of your course
- the way you are taught and assessed and the tasks and assignments you are set
- the people, tutors, students or others
- the communications required
- technological and other resources available
- the everyday demands on your time that you juggle with those of being a student.

Study skills

Academic, people and task-management skills

As detailed below, your learning environment will frame the particular range of study skills that you will need and develop, and to what extent.

Self-management skills

The sets of interactions between the learning environment and you as an individual are complex. These will change frequently as you progress through your course. Good skills in self-management help you to manage these interactions more effectively and to identify the skills and qualities you need at any given time.

Self: managing yourself for study

Self-management is an essential study skill in Higher Education. It is needed to enable students to cope with the responsibilities of taking charge of their studies and to engage fully in the learning process.

Sort yourself out!

Self management skills in this context involve:

- **Independence**: being a well-informed, resilient, independent student. (See Chapter 1.)
- **Skills management**: understanding and using strengths, and improving your weaker skills.
- **Learning**: understanding and personalising your learning, capitalising on strengths and preferences. (See Chapters 3, 4 and 8.)
- **Strategies**: creative, reflective, effective, active and motivated study strategies. (See Chapter 4.)
- **Time**: managing your study time effectively. (See Chapter 5.)
- **Improving performance**, using feedback from others. See pages 255 and 324.
- **Metacognitive skills**: reflecting meaningfully about how you think, learn and manage yourself for study. See Chapters 3 and 4.

Activity — Managing your learning environment

1 Make a copy of the diagram on page 37.
2 Feel free to add in other aspects of your learning context that are not listed here but which have an impact on your learning.
3 Highlight those aspects of the environment that you find most challenging.
4 List the sort of skills you need to develop in order to manage better the aspects that you highlighted.
5 Which self-management skills will be most important for you in developing those skills?

Personal qualities

Fine-tuning a skill, including a study skill, involves the development of personal qualities too. Of particular importance are:

- self-awareness
- determination
- self-motivation
- commitment
- perseverance
- positive thinking.

Reflection: Personal qualities

- Which qualities do you think are important to the development of good study skills?
- Which of these are strengths for you?
- Which do you need to develop further?

Academic skills

Basic research skills

At each level of study, you will need to use increasingly sophisticated strategies for:

Find out about it!

- **Finding information**: searching for information and knowing what is available
- **Reading** large amounts at speed
- **Using multiple sources** of information
- **Making notes** of what you observe, hear, read and think – and then using them
- **Organisational skills**: sorting, storing and retrieving information for re-use, applying the right tools for the task (see Chapter 6)
- **Using numerical data**: collecting, analysing and presenting these (see Chapter 9)

Thinking skills

At this level of study, this means such skills as:

Think about it!

- **Decision making**: using sound decisions about the material to select and draw upon for your work (see Chapters 6 and 7)
- **Memory skills**, developing strategies for recalling information easily and accurately when needed. (see Chapter 8)
- **Critical thinking skills**: evaluating the quality of sources of information; developing a strong line of reasoning based on sound evidence; interpreting material, data and theories (see Chapter 7)
- **Creative problem-solving and synthesis**: drawing on diverse knowledge and skills to create new ways of looking at an issue or to find new solutions (see Chapters 4 and 7)
- **Understanding**: making sense of increasingly complex and difficult data and concepts, including problems without clear-cut answers.

Understanding academic conventions

For students, that means understanding:

Know your field!

- **Higher Education** as a learning community
- **Your academic discipline**: the specialist branch of learning that underpins your course
- **Foundation concepts** in the discipline – its core theories and ideas
- **Knowledge**: how this is constructed and advanced in your subject
- **Evidence** as the basis of your argument
- **Sound methodologies**, relevant to the subject, used to establish the evidence base
- **Specialist terminology** used in the discipline
- **Academic integrity**, including the use of reputable sources, attributing these correctly, and avoiding plagiarism
- **Ethical awareness**, as relevant to context (see Chapter 13)

Written and other communications skills

In the context of academic study, this includes:

Write it up!

- **Precision**: using words and data accurately and succinctly, and keeping to word limits
- **Structure and clarity**: organising your ideas and using a clear line of reasoning
- **Style and format** for specific kinds of assignment such as essays, reports, case studies, dissertations
- **Audience awareness**: for written, spoken and electronic communication
- **Citing and referencing** sources correctly
- **Subject discipline**: using the style, format and conventions used in your subject.

(See Chapters 11–13.)

People and Task management skills

People: studying with others

Many academic tasks are undertaken in social contexts with other students, the public, clients, face to face or using technology. This calls for such skills as:

- **Taking an active part**, without dominating or letting others take over
- **Contributing constructively** in class, seminars, or in online discussions
- **Peer feedback**: giving and receiving constructive criticism
- **Making presentations**, to a group or as part of a group
- **Collaborative team working and groupwork**, face to face and/or using video links or social networking
- **Supporting others**, encouraging them and sharing ideas without cheating or collusion.

Talk it through!

(See Chapter 10.)

Task management skills

You will need to draw together the above skills in meaningful ways in order to complete required study tasks such as exams or particular assignments. Task management, in itself, requires skills such as:

1) Wake at 7.00
2) Feed fish
3) Observe fish

Take charge!

- **Producing set items** such as essays, reports, portfolios, presentations, case studies applying methodologies, conventions and styles relevant to the discipline
- **Managing the process** of taking a task through from start to finish
- **Meeting given requirements** such as the assignment brief, marking criteria, ethical standards, deadlines and word limits
- **Following the appropriate protocols** and guidance for your subject, such as for lab work, clinical practice, field work, studio, performance, practical or technical skills
- **Using specialist equipment and resources** relevant to your course and circumstances, or using apps designed to support study
- **Project management** of larger, more complex tasks such as research projects, dissertations, exams, field work and end of year shows.

Combining skills

The skills are outlined here, for clarity, as if they were separate categories. In practice, you would combine many skills from each category for most study tasks. For example, you cannot easily separate out basic research tasks, such as searching for information, from the process of thinking through what is relevant for a given assignment in the context of your discipline.

As you develop through your course, you will integrate a wide range of skills fluidly, without noticing that you are doing so.

Which skills?

Which skills will you need?

For your course and circumstances, you may not need to use all of the Academic, People, Task and Self-management skills listed above. Requirements will vary depending on your course. This is exemplified in the 'skills clouds' below. The font size indicates the relative importance of the skill to each course. What kind of course do you think is represented by each cloud?

Skill clouds

Course 1

Analysing data **Maths skills**
Applying formulae   Describing results
Observation   Taking precise notes
Recording details accurately   Writing essays
Working collaboratively on experiments   Presenting results to a group
Reading research papers   Group wiki
Understanding scientific methods   Writing a dissertation
Writing research reports   Group project reports   Understanding and using theory

Course 3

Researching other people's practice   Making presentations
Technical skills   Working with clients   Writing group blogs   **Giving and receiving criticism**
Group discussions   **Reading**   Writing essays
Time management   **Studio work   Portfolio work**
Using numbers
Managing projects

Course 2

Listening in lectures   **Writing essays**
Revision and Exam skills   **Memory skills**   Groupwork   **Writing style**
Using source materials
Thinking critically about texts   Presenting a seminar   **Reading**
Note-making   Using a range of source materials   **Managing independent study**
Contributing to seminars
Technology skills

Course 4

Writing reports
Writing essays   **Project work with clients**   Field work   Communicating with a wide range of people   **Interviewing skills   Making decisions and recommendations**   Thinking critically about texts   Revision and Exam skills
Thinking critically about data   Reading   Listening in lectures
Managing independent study time   **Presenting data**
Note-making   Contributing to groups

Skills clouds for my course

Activity ⟳ **Skills clouds for your course**

Using information available to you about your course, identify the range and relative importance of different skills on your course. Use the boxes below to sketch out the skills clouds for your course.

Skills needed to succeed at this level of my course

Skills that I will develop through my course

Developing skills: five study skills components

1 Self-awareness and self-evaluation

To develop a skill you need first to know where you are starting from. What are your current strengths and weaknesses? What do you want to achieve? Where do you need to improve? How are you going to improve? What are your resources? What could obstruct your goals? Ways of developing such awareness include:

- using self-evaluation questionnaires
- monitoring your progress
- maintaining a reflective journal or blog
- group discussion and chat
- feedback and criticism from other students
- feedback and comments from tutors.

2 Task awareness: knowing what is required

To score a goal you need to know where the goalposts are. In an academic context, this means finding out what is expected of you and what your lecturers are looking for whenever you are set a new assignment.

Essential information is usually provided in course handbooks, webpages, through a virtual learning environment and in assignment briefs. See Chapter 1 for key information to find out and use.

In particular, for each subject, find out about:

- the curriculum – the course content
- the outcomes or objectives – what you must know or be able to do by the end of the course
- how marks are allocated – what gets good marks? What loses marks?
- the special preferences of each lecturer – if in doubt, ask.

3 Strategy, method and organisation

It is easier to study and saves you time if you have a method for working and are well organised. A skilled student uses strategies, and with practice these become automatic.

4 Confidence and sense of 'entitlement'

If you are to succeed as a student, you have to believe that such success is possible for you.

However, many students feel that academic success is for other people rather than for them. This may be because of their experiences at school, or because nobody from their family has a degree. Often, it is because they hold particular ideas about intelligence, especially their own academic abilities, and so do not give themselves 'permission' to do well.

For this reason, Chapter 3 focuses on what we mean by 'intelligence' and 'learning'.

5 Familiarity, practice and habit

All skills improve through practice, feedback and monitoring. The more you study and reflect on your learning, the more you become:

- adept at finding shortcuts
- aware of underlying skills, qualities and habits that you can improve
- able to see patterns in what you do
- able to focus on study for longer
- able to perform skills automatically.

The way to study well and easily becomes a habit. If you have been away from study or are not used to managing so much unscheduled time, you may find you need to build good study habits.

You don't have to be 'clever'!

When you consider these study skills components, it is clear that good study skills have little to do with being 'naturally clever'. They owe much more to awareness, strategies, confidence and practice, leading to an overall development in your learning. Each of these aspects is covered in the various chapters of the *Handbook*.

Recognising your skills and qualities

This section offers you the chance to:

- audit abilities and qualities that you have now
- consider how everyday skills such as observation, selection and support for others can be applied to *academic* study
- identify your current study skills priorities
- consider how academic skills are relevant to future employment.

Skills audits

Skills audits are useful in helping you to:

- become used to forming a judgement of your own performance through self-evaluation, rather than depending on others' estimation
- become aware of your strengths, so that you can present yourself well to others
- develop the confidence and insight to identify areas that need more attention
- set your own priorities for developing skills.

Activity — Skills from experience

Choose one thing you do well, a difficulty you overcame, or a personal achievement, no matter how small. It might be success in arts, performance, sports, with people, coping with illness or life challenges, or being accepted for your course. Use the *beautiful garden* example for ideas.

How did I do it?

1 What did you do to create the conditions that led to success? Did you practise? Did you urge yourself on in a particular way? Did you find people to help? Or did you just believe you could do it?
2 Which skills, attitudes and qualities did you exhibit?

Example: the beautiful garden

Supposing one year your garden or a window box looked absolutely beautiful. How did that happen?

Many small things may have led to a perfect outcome. You may have watered the plants very carefully, depending on the weather. If so, you used powers of *observation* and *deduction*. You may have weeded and pruned in the rain, when you wanted to stay indoors. Here you *kept in mind your long-term goal* for the garden, showing *dedication* and *perseverance*.

You may have *selected* plants from a wide range of options, to match your garden conditions. You probably did *research,* possibly online or by reading gardening books, questioning others who had grown them or watching television programmes. You *followed specific instructions* on how to grow them, and purchased special fertiliser, prepared the ground in a certain way or pruned at particular times: such care requires *method*, *attention to detail*, *time management* and *task management*.

All these skills are relevant to study. Whether your experience is in household management, performing arts, sports or other areas, it is likely that you have developed a range of skills, qualities and behaviours such as those above. The important thing is to recognise these so that you can draw on them when needed.

Your personal skills profile

Reflection: Skills from experience

For the activity above (page 44), were you surprised to find out how many skills you have already? Do you tend to underestimate or overestimate your skills?

By doing the 'Skills from experience' activity, you probably found that you have more skills and qualities than you thought. If not, go through the activity with someone who knows you, or use the list opposite as a prompt. Most people already have qualities and skills which they can adapt to study in Higher Education.

- Those entering from school have the benefit of recent study and established study habits.
- Mature students often bring experience of working with others, responsibility, managing time, and perseverance – all valuable assets when studying.

Evaluating skills and setting priorities

Awareness of your current skills increases your confidence, which in turn increases your chances of success. The following pages offer resource sheets to help you to:

- identify current skills and strengths
- identify study skills strengths
- select priorities for developing study skills
- consider how skills apply in different contexts.

Update your profile

As you progress with the course, your skills profile and self-evaluation will change. Take time to update your skills profile or portfolio, at least once every six months. (See page 56 and Chapter 15.)

Activity **Current skills and qualities**

Use your notes from the 'Skills from experience' activity (page 44) for the following activity.

1 *Make a copy* of page 46, so you can use it again.
2 *Select* ✓ On your copy, check off all the items at which you are reasonably skilled.
3 *Rate* ★★ Use one or more stars to indicate those at which you excel.
4 *Give examples* For each item you selected, starting with those you starred, jot down an occasion when you demonstrated that skill or quality. The 'prompt box' below may help you recall situations in which you might have developed these skills.
5 *Use* Display the list where you can see it and for use later in the chapter.
6 *Congratulate* yourself!

If you did not select many items, search through your past experiences for better examples – or go through the list with a friend. You may be being too modest.

Prompt box: where did I develop/demonstrate my skills and qualities?

- ☐ School or college
- ☐ Employment
- ☐ Applying for jobs
- ☐ Family life
- ☐ Domestic responsibility
- ☐ Caring for others
- ☐ Interests and hobbies
- ☐ Independent study
- ☐ Emergency events
- ☐ Sport
- ☐ Personal development
- ☐ Saturday jobs
- ☐ Unemployment
- ☐ Voluntary work
- ☐ Making a home
- ☐ Friendships
- ☐ Travel/holidays
- ☐ Clubs/societies
- ☐ Personal setbacks
- ☐ Ill health

Current skills and qualities

People

- [ ] Ability to get on with people from different backgrounds
- [ ] Understanding other people's points of view
- [ ] Sensitivity to cultural differences
- [ ] Dealing with the general public
- [ ] Teamwork and collaboration
- [ ] Networking
- [ ] Managing or supervising others' work
- [ ] Teaching, training or mentoring others
- [ ] Negotiating and persuading
- [ ] Helping others to arrive at decisions

- [ ] Consideration of others' feelings
- [ ] Caring for others
- [ ] Supporting and motivating others
- [ ] Understanding others' body language
- [ ] Coping with 'difficult' people
- [ ] Speaking clearly and to the point
- [ ] Audience awareness
- [ ] Taking direction from others
- [ ] Giving constructive feedback
- [ ] Leadership skills
- [ ] Other:

Activities and tasks

- [ ] Creativity, design and layout
- [ ] Innovation and inventiveness
- [ ] Ability to see the 'whole picture'
- [ ] Argument and debate
- [ ] Seeing patterns and connections
- [ ] Attention to detail
- [ ] Searching for information
- [ ] Classifying and organising information
- [ ] Making decisions
- [ ] Managing change and transition
- [ ] Setting priorities
- [ ] Working out agendas
- [ ] Organising work to meet deadlines
- [ ] Facilitating meetings
- [ ] Reading complex texts
- [ ] Computer literacy

- [ ] Technological skills
- [ ] Using social networking tools
- [ ] Working with numbers
- [ ] Selling
- [ ] Problem-solving
- [ ] Quick thinking
- [ ] Practical skills
- [ ] Understanding quickly how things work
- [ ] Seeing practical applications
- [ ] Writing reports or official letters
- [ ] Languages
- [ ] Enterprise and entrepreneurship
- [ ] Business and financial skills
- [ ] Managing difficult situations, emergencies and crises
- [ ] Other:

Personal

- [ ] Setting my own goals
- [ ] Working independently
- [ ] Maintaining a high level of motivation
- [ ] Taking responsibility for my own actions
- [ ] Learning from my mistakes
- [ ] Willingness to take risks and experiment
- [ ] Assertiveness
- [ ] Determination and perseverance

- [ ] Self-reliance
- [ ] Recognising my own needs
- [ ] Taking care of my health and well-being
- [ ] Staying calm in a crisis
- [ ] Coping skills and managing stress
- [ ] Other:

Using personal skills in academic study

The *Current skills and qualities* exercise (page 46) includes specific skills which have more relevance to some courses than others. For example, 'selling' is more relevant to marketing than to history.

The following activity enables you to map out your current skills in terms of the general (or 'generic') skills required for most academic courses, and to rate how well you already perform them. This will give you a better idea of how well you may cope with academic study.

Academic skills (skills used in everyday life which relate to academic skills)	Self-rating 5 = good; 1 = very weak	Examples: where or when you developed this skill
e.g. Managing deadlines	4	Get children to school on time; submitted application form despite illness
1 Managing deadlines		
2 Being self-motivated and able to persevere with difficult tasks		
3 Having the confidence to 'have a go' and to express my own ideas		
4 Finding out information from different sources (research)		
5 Reading complicated texts or forms to find the gist of what they are saying		
6 Being able to select what is relevant from what is irrelevant		
7 Comparing different opinions and deciding what are the best grounds for judging who is right		
8 Being able to weigh up the 'pros' and 'cons', good points versus bad		
9 Writing things in my own words		
10 Being able to argue my point of view, giving good reasons		

Chapter **2**

Study skills: priorities, stage 1

Column A   Tick ✓ if the statement is generally true of you.
Column B   Rate how important it is to acquire this skill: 6 = unimportant; 10 = essential.
Column C   Rate how good you are at this skill now: 1 = very weak; 5 = excellent.
Column D   Subtract the score in column C from that in column B (B – C). Items with the highest scores in column D are likely to be priorities. Then turn to page 49. Repeat later in the year.

Study skills statements I have effective strategies for …	A This is true (✓)	B Skill needed? (scale 6–10)	C Current ability? (scale 1–5)	D Priority (B–C)
1 organising myself for study				
2 using my study time well				
3 thinking creatively				
4 solving problems				
5 reading for academic purposes				
6 searching for information for assignments				
7 making, and using, notes (checklist, page 184)				
8 making good use of lectures/taught sessions				
9 groupwork and seminars (checklist, page 269)				
10 making presentations (checklist, page 267)				
11 managing writing tasks (checklist, page 274)				
12 writing essays using academic conventions				
13 writing reports and dissertations (checklist, page 363)				
14 undertaking a research project (checklist, pages 343–4)				
15 avoiding cheating/plagiarism				
16 citing sources and writing references				
17 using numbers in assignments (checklist, page 220)				
18 thinking critically and analytically				
19 evaluating my own and others' arguments				
20 developing memory skills				
21 taking exams (checklists, pages 372, 375 and 378)				
22 evaluating my work (checklist, page 98)				

Chapter 2

Study skills: priorities, stage 2

Column A Using the scoring from stage 1, decide whether each item really is a priority, whether it could wait, who else could do it, or any other options you have.
Column B Number your priorities in order. Highlight in yellow the one you are going to work on next. Highlight it in red once you have worked on it.
Column C Shows the pages of this *Handbook* related to the given study skill.

Study skills statements I will become more effective at …	A Priority for action? Yes/No/Can wait	B	C Pages
1 organising myself for study			103; 136–8
2 using my study time well			Chapter 5
3 thinking creatively			88–90
4 solving problems			91–6
5 reading for academic purposes			164–70
6 searching for information for assignments			158–61
7 making, and using, notes			184
8 making good use of lectures/taught sessions			184
9 groupwork and seminars			Chapter 10
10 making presentations			265–8
11 managing writing tasks			274
12 writing essays using academic conventions			308–14
13 writing reports and dissertations			358–63
14 undertaking a research project			Chapter 13
15 avoiding cheating/plagiarism			177–8; 258
16 citing sources and writing references			179–81
17 using numbers in assignments			220
18 thinking critically and analytically			Chapter 7
19 evaluating my own and others' arguments			188–96
20 developing memory skills			Chapter 8
21 taking exams			Chapter 14
22 evaluating my work			98

Study skills: action plan

Go back over your answers to the various activities and self-evaluations you completed in Chapters 1 and 2. Bring together your thinking about your current strengths, the areas you wish to develop, and your priorities.

Date:
Summary of my current strengths, skills and qualities: what I have achieved so far
Summary of what I need to work on, develop or improve
My priorities: what I am going to do, when, and how
How will I know that I have improved? (E.g. What changes would I expect in my work, in myself, or in the attitudes of others?)

© Stella Cottrell (2013) *The Study Skills Handbook*, 4th edition, Palgrave Macmillan

Monitoring skills development

Baseline (starting place)

Date: Skill being developed:

My current level of confidence in this skill (circle one):

1 very low   **2** low   **3** OK   **4** high   **5** very high

Aspects of this skill I have already demonstrated:

Goal

What I want to be able to do (aspects, sub-skills, qualities I want to develop):

Record of progress

Note down steps in your development of this skill. Decide what progress would look like in each case. This might be the achievement of a personal goal (such as gaining a particular grade for an assignment), or a step towards achieving a personal goal (such as asking a question in class for the first time, or developing a successful strategy for arriving on time if you find time management is a challenge).

Date	Achievement (what I can do now that I couldn't before)	How you know (evidence or example)

What is a profile?

A profile is simply a snapshot of yourself as you are now – your skills, qualities, attributes and achievements. It is useful for:

- giving you a sense of where you are now, to guide your personal development plan
- developing habits of reflection and self-analysis
- experience in evaluating and describing yourself – this is valuable preparation for job interviews.

In this chapter you have already started to profile your skills, qualities and experience. That will help when writing a curriculum vitae (CV) for job applications. Add in achievements and skills from other areas of your life.

What are recruiters looking for?

The Association of Graduate Employers reports that almost one-third of large employers find it difficult to find students with the right skills to fill graduate vacancies. Although employers still value academic and specialist skills, they also look for a wider range of experience and generic skills, especially 'soft skills'.

Which 'soft' skills?

Employers value soft skills in the following areas:

1 Managing yourself: intra-personal skills

Self-reliance, self-awareness and focus; the capacity to learn, plan action and take the initiative; resourcefulness, motivation and realism.

2 Managing people: people skills

Networking; teamworking; communication skills in negotiating, persuading and influencing; customer focus; leadership and ability to support and motivate others; cultural awareness; languages.

3 Managing projects: task management skills

Ability to get on with tasks without close supervision; devising and implementing an action plan; attention to detail; being logical, methodical and systematic; applying technology; numerical reasoning; problem-solving; versatility, flexibility and multi-skilling; willingness to take risks; being results-orientated and solution-focused; business awareness; work ethic.

Sources

- Graduate Recruitment Survey (AGR: 2012)
- www.prospects.ac.uk (accessed 26 August 2012)
- L. Bachelor, 'Graduate careers: the importance of employability skills', *The Guardian*, www.guardian.co.uk/money/2012/jun/08/graduate-careers-employability-skills (accessed 26 August 2012)

Identify your 'soft' skills

Just as you identified how skills from life can translate into academic skills, so you can also consider how academic study develops 'soft' skills transferable to employment. Some examples are listed on the next page – you will be able to think of others. Use page 54 to map out for yourself the soft skills you develop whilst a student.

Give thought to where you can develop soft skills, either on your course or by taking up opportunities open to you whilst a student. The 'Soft skills' evaluation can be used to develop a skills profile (page 54) for employment.

For more about developing soft skills, see:

- Stella Cottrell (2010), *Skills for Success: Personal Development and Employability*, 2nd edition (Basingstoke: Palgrave Macmillan)
- Free resources on www.palgravestudyskills.com

Activity	Which skills do employers value?

- Browse advertisements for graduate jobs, and websites such as www.prospects.ac.uk, noting the skills employers ask for.
- Which of these skills could you develop whilst a student?

Transferable and soft employment skills

Area of academic activity	Examples of potential transferable and soft skills which could be developed
Personal development / personal planning	Self-management; forward planning; taking responsibility for improving performance; increasing personal effectiveness; reflective skills.
Independent study	Working without supervision; organising your own time and work; taking personal responsibility; self-reliance; knowing when to ask for help.
Lectures	Listening skills; identifying and selecting relevant points; recording salient information; preparing for meetings; using the information heard.
Seminars, groupwork, team projects, collaborative learning	Listening; teamwork; negotiating; oral communication; giving and taking directions; taking responsibility; working with people from diverse backgrounds; cultural sensitivity; dealing with differences in opinion; sharing knowledge; contributing to meetings and discussions.
Lab work	Following protocol and instructions; taking responsibility; designing tasks for particular purposes; precision and attention to detail; attention to health and safety requirements; ethical understanding; measuring change; recording results; being systematic; drawing conclusions.
Oral presentation	Speaking in public; persuading and influencing others; making a case; time management; presentation skills; using audiovisual aids; planning; sharing knowledge; adapting communication style.
Writing essays and other forms of academic writing	Task analysis; structuring writing for specific audiences using relevant style and conventions; developing an argument; making a strong case; working to word limits and deadlines; sharing knowledge; breaking tasks into component parts; attention to detail.
Maths and statistics	Problem-solving; presenting information; interpreting data; sharing knowledge.
Observations	Listening skills; working with people from a variety of backgrounds; information management; attention to detail; drawing conclusions; making precise and accurate notes and reports.
Research projects	Time management; using search tools; managing large amounts of information; working to deadlines; decision-making; project management; using technology; developing ethical understanding; taking responsibility for larger pieces of work.
Exams and revision	Planning; working towards deadlines; using time effectively; decision-making; managing stress; coping with challenges; resilience.

Chapter 2

Turning academic skills into transferable and soft employment skills

Drawing on activities you undertook for this chapter, use the chart below to profile the soft and transferable skills you are developing as a student. Look especially at page 46, *Current skills and qualities*. The four items already written in often appear at the top of employers' lists. Add others relevant to you.

Skills, qualities, attributes and achievements	Specific examples
☐ Self-awareness and self-reliance	
☐ Verbal skills	
☐ Team working	
☐ Practical skills in managing projects	
Other transferable skills I can offer	
☐ Driving licence ☐ Technology skills ☐ Languages:	

Recording achievement

Celebrate success

When you have achieved a goal, or taken a significant step towards a goal:

- *Acknowledge your achievement* Give yourself credit for what you have done.
- *Celebrate* Give yourself a reward, appropriate to the significance of your achievement.
- *Record it* Note down what happened.
- *Use it* Use your success as an example of what you can achieve when you focus your energies. When applying for jobs, or to build personal motivation, use your records to find examples of different kinds of achievement.

Records of success and personal records

Records of achievement can vary from a list of qualifications to a portfolio of work. Your university or college will issue a formal transcript listing subjects studied, your marks or grades and, in some cases, additional information about skills and experience (see page 57). However, only *you* will know:

- how your confidence has grown
- how you have developed as a person
- personal goals you have achieved
- how you did it – the steps you took and the personal qualities you called upon
- how you kept yourself motivated
- what you learnt about yourself in the process.

It is useful to maintain records of *how* you achieved your goals, as well as *what* you achieved. These enable you to make use of your experience and to chart change over time. Records of this kind are sometimes referred to as 'portfolios', 'progress files', 'records of achievement' or 'personal records'.

Maintaining a personal portfolio

A portfolio is a file or folder where you bring together materials on a theme, such as art work or evidence of occupational competencies. A personal portfolio is your collation of key materials about you. To keep this meaningful and easy to use:

- divide it into sections
- label everything, and use a contents page
- update it regularly, removing old materials
- include an updated personal statement.

Personal statements

A personal statement draws together details of where you are now, where you want to be, and how you will get there. It can be brief. Include such things as:

- career and life goals
- what you have done so far towards achieving these (at school, college, university, or work)
- the personal significance of goals/achievements
- what you learned about yourself along the way (e.g. how to stay motivated or to perform best)
- skills and qualities you have achieved, with examples that demonstrate these
- what your next steps will be.

Academic portfolios

Some programmes of study require you to hand in portfolios with evidence of your work for tutors to grade or provide feedback. For such portfolios:

- Follow instructions: include only what is required.
- Be selective: choose good examples, rather than 'dumping' everything in the file for the tutor to see.
- Number all pages and compile a contents page.
- Provide a brief, clear opening summary to draw together your learning/main points.
- Indicate exactly where tutors can find each piece of evidence to support each point you make in your summary and/or to meet assignment criteria.
- Annotate or highlight the evidence in the file.
- Observe confidentiality: edit names, materials and details that could identify people or organisations, unless you have their signed consent.

Developing a portfolio

What is the purpose of a portfolio?

A portfolio has several uses:

- it keeps related documents together
- it helps you stay organised
- it helps the process of reflection
- it gives the process of self-evaluation and personal development a higher focus in your life
- in some vocations, you can take it to job interviews
- it can hold relevant examples and information for when you need them, such as when applying for work placements, work or other courses.

Do you have to keep a portfolio?

A portfolio may be compulsory for your course. However, even if you don't *have* to keep a portfolio, you will probably find it *helpful* to do so – to organise your thinking about what you need to do, and to monitor your progress.

Checking and updating your portfolio

Update your portfolio regularly – at least once or twice a year, and whenever you achieve something new. Re-reading or rewording what you have written may refocus your energies.

What to put in your portfolio

1   Full contents list for each section.

2   Self-evaluation and profile sheets, planners and action plans.

3   A profile of vocational and technical skills you have developed.

4   An up-to-date list of courses and training.

5   Certificates (exams, courses, achievements, etc.).

6   An up-to-date list of your work experience, with the dates, addresses of employers, brief job descriptions, your main responsibilities, skills or qualities you demonstrated, and what you learned from doing that work.

7   Your curriculum vitae (CV). (A careers adviser can help you to compile this.)

8   Your ideas about where you would like to be in seven years' time, and what you need to do to achieve this goal.

9   Examples of your work and interests, if relevant – but without breaching anyone else's confidentiality. Examples include a copy of a report undertaken during a work placement, slides of your artwork, or a copy of an article you wrote for a student magazine.

10   Personal statement – see page 55.

11   Degree or course certificates; transcript.

Choices, skills and career development

Use your choices wisely so that they support your longer-term academic and career ambitions.

Skills development

Most universities and colleges provide opportunities to develop a range of skills and experiences that help you as a student and for your future career. Each takes a different approach. For example, yours may:

- encourage a specific set of skills which defines its graduates
- develop and assess skills through coursework
- offer modules to develop specific skills
- offer specialist skills sessions through the Careers Service, library, or a resource centre.

Making use of skills opportunities

Universities and colleges offer many opportunities to develop responsibilities, abilities and knowledge across a wide range of areas. When you apply for jobs, your employers will know that you have had such opportunities, and will be interested to see how well you used them.

I've written my action plan. Would you check it out?

327 STEPS TO FAME

Careers Service

Reflection: Using the opportunities

How well do you make use of the opportunities at your university, college, and in the local area to try out new things, take on responsibility, meet different kinds of people, and develop a wider range of skills and qualities?

Personal development planning

It is likely that your university or college will provide opportunities for personal development planning at all levels of study. Most offer such activities as:

- work experience, placements or internships
- work-related study or enterprise projects
- volunteer work such as mentoring or coaching in local schools or the community

- careers advice
- guest speakers from relevant professions
- being a 'student representative'.

Some will also structure the curriculum to increase opportunities for personal development. For example, they may offer academic credit for career planning, skills development, or work-based learning. There will also be many opportunities through student clubs, the Student Union, and the local community.

Transcripts and records of achievement

When you graduate, you will receive a transcript with details of your studies. At many institutions, this itemises skills developed, prizes gained and evidence of activity such as community volunteering and positions of responsibility such as student rep.

Activity   Your transcript

- What information is recorded on the transcript or record of achievement provided by your institution?
- How will your study choices and the way you spend your time as a student affect what is recorded for you?

Personal records

Maintain your own records to track your progress and achievements in ways that are meaningful to you and for future employers. Your records could contain:

- a personal plan of which skills and experience you want to gain and how you will achieve this
- a journal, log or blog to reflect on what you are learning about yourself, your ambitions and the ways you are going about achieving these
- a portfolio or similar record (see page 56).

(See also Chapter 15.)

Review

Every university and college identifies skills and qualities that it wants its graduates to achieve. The list of desired skills keeps growing, and students can find the length and complexity of the skills requirements bewildering. The APT-S framework outlined in this chapter is just one way of simplifying the skills needed as a student. It makes it easier to:

- see how the range of skills fits together, and
- navigate your way through an otherwise complex skills landscape.

The APT-S framework and skills cloud activity draw attention to the differences in skills and attributes developed by each student. Students arrive with different starting points and focus on particular areas during their course: all graduates are not the same. It is for you to consider, early in your course, what you can do to ensure that your profile of skills and qualities will make you stand out from others in ways that you will want.

This chapter has encouraged you to look at your current qualities and skills. The process of self-evaluation can begin in quite mechanistic ways, such as filling in questionnaires, rating yourself, setting priorities, and assembling information about yourself. In time, however, this can develop into a deeper process of self-reflection and self-development that benefits any aspect of your life, including your study.

This chapter and Chapters 3 and 4 emphasise that real progress in study skills occurs when skills development is treated as part of a wider, general process of learning. At its best, this is a process in which you learn about yourself and how you perform to your potential under *any* circumstances, not just academically. It involves developing an understanding about how personal opinions, attitudes and states of mind influence your success. Fundamental to that process is self-awareness, based on reflection and self-evaluation, so that you know what you do well and why, and what needs to be improved and how.

Some students feel as if they have no academic skills. Others, especially those who entered Higher Education courses straight from school, can be anxious about having the right skills to find employment when they leave. It is useful to look for parallels between skills used in academic study and those used elsewhere. Everybody brings experiences and skills that are transferable to academic study.

In turn, academic study develops skills and ways of thinking that are of benefit in employment. Skills are generally most transferable from one situation to another when you can *see* similarities in the two situations. This takes creative reflection, but it is worth the effort. Graduates who do well in the job market are not necessarily more skilled than others, but they have learnt to *identify* their skills and can therefore talk about them confidently and with examples of their application.

Students may also feel that they do not know where to begin to develop their study skills. The ideas of mapping or profiling skills, identifying weak points for improvement, setting priorities, and drawing up action plans, are themes that run throughout this book. However, it also encourages you to look at opinions, states of mind or belief systems that can affect learning. Chapters 3–4 focus on attitudes, beliefs and approaches that can help or hinder study.

Chapter 3
Successful study
Intelligence, strategy and personalised learning

Learning outcomes

This chapter offers you opportunities to:

- reflect on your own views about intelligence and learning, considering how these affect your confidence in your academic abilities
- identify your learning styles and preferences, and ways of drawing on these to personalise your learning
- consider ways that you can optimise your own academic performance through taking strategic, personalised approaches to study.

Three essential steps in developing good skills are:

1 **self-awareness**, including insight into how your own and other people's opinions about your intelligence and academic abilities impact on your capacity to achieve at your best

2 **strategy**: understanding that successful study is largely about understanding the field, developing good study habits and applying good approaches and techniques – rather than how 'bright' you are

3 **personalised approaches**: being able to adapt your study strategies to suit your strengths, interests, and circumstances.

Students do not, typically, give much time to thinking about these three aspects of study: it can feel easier to launch into the more tangible study skills of making good notes or writing an essay. However, it is worth putting time aside to think more strategically about what learning is, what impacts on successful outcomes and how, through reflection and planning, you can exert greater control over your own academic performance.

This chapter focuses on the learning process itself, looking at how intelligence develops through learning, the conditions that are necessary for learning to occur, and how you can take an active role in creating the optimum conditions for your study.

It is often taken for granted that academic success is the result of 'being clever' or 'bright' and that this is something you are blessed with – or not – at birth. Such thinking creates barriers to success. It leads students to assume, falsely, that they will either:

● continue to do well academically, on the strength of being 'clever' alone, or

● fail to achieve the highest marks because they are inherently less intelligent than others.

'Am I intelligent enough for university?'

This question haunts many students even if their marks are excellent. They worry that 'secretly' or 'deep down' they aren't clever enough to succeed.

Your marks were OK last time – but that was a fluke. This time you might fail, and you'll be so embarrassed because now everyone expects you to do well.

So far I've been lucky ...

It is very common for students to underestimate their potential or to lose confidence, especially if, as happens to most students at some point, they receive a lower mark than they had hoped for. Many students can remember an occasion in the past when someone such as a teacher or relative undermined their confidence in their abilities. Such memories can resurface, exercising a disproportionate power to undermine self-belief.

Reflection: The impact of views of intelligence upon academic confidence

Jot down your initial thoughts about how your own views of intelligence, and those of other people, may have affected your previous academic performance – in both helpful and unhelpful ways.

One reason students can become anxious about their capabilities is that they haven't been taught to evaluate their own work or to develop criteria for doing so. As a result, they feel prey to the whims of chance: good or bad marks 'just happen', or depend on the luck of the draw of how 'naturally clever' they are or which tutor they get.

Such thinking leaves people feeling disempowered or adrift, even if their marks are good. They worry about suddenly being exposed as stupid. Anxiety can create a vicious cycle in which students:

● can't settle down to study

● can't concentrate or focus their attention

● can't take in what they read

● can't remember what they learnt

● are reinforced in their suspicions that they 'really' lack intelligence.

This is very common, so it is important to look at what we mean by intelligence.

Intelligent study

Intelligent study means applying good strategies to study, appropriate to the academic level and to your own ways of learning. University level study makes greater demands, so requires new approaches. The right strategies and mentality can bring success to any student, whereas failure to apply these can result in any student under-achieving.

Chapter 3

What is intelligence?

What is intelligence?

Tick ✓ any response that you feel is true.

- ☐ 1 Intelligence is an underlying, general cleverness which, because it depends on genetics, is fixed for life.
- ☐ 2 There are many kinds of intelligence.
- ☐ 3 Intelligence can be developed.
- ☐ 4 Intelligence depends on your life opportunities.
- ☐ 5 What is regarded as intelligence depends on the environment and the culture.
- ☐ 6 Intelligence is about applying what you know easily to new contexts.
- ☐ 7 Intelligence is a question of how much you know.
- ☐ 8 Intelligence is easy to measure.
- ☐ 9 Intelligence is about applying effective strategies that can be learnt.
- ☐ 10 Intelligence is a question of habit and practice.

Reflection: Thinking about intelligence

Jot down your initial responses to these views of intelligence.

Read the pages that follow.

Then return to the notes that you jotted down above and add to them. Note in what ways, if any, your opinions about your own intelligence change as a result of reading and reflection.

Ten different views of intelligence

1 Intelligence is a general, underlying 'cleverness' which is fixed for life

Early psychologists such as Spearman (1927) and Terman (1916) believed that each individual has a general level of intelligence, known as the *intelligence quotient* or IQ. They regarded intelligence as a single, fixed, underlying capacity: a person who did well on one test would do well on all or most intelligence tests; and no matter what happened in life, those born 'very intelligent' would remain generally more intelligent than those born 'less intelligent'. More recently, psychologists have used studies of identical twins to support this idea, arguing that some traits, including intelligence, are up to 80 per cent dependent on genetic inheritance.

However, other psychologists, using the same data, argue that genetic influence is as little as 20 per cent or even zero (Gardner 1993). Pairs of twins used in twin studies are often brought up in similar environments and, as they look the same, they may evoke similar responses in other people so that their experiences may be unusually alike.

There is also strong evidence to suggest that environment plays a great part in intellectual performance. For example, the *Raven's Progressive Matrices* – an intelligence test used to measure abstract reasoning ability – were designed for use with people of any language, age or culture. The person being tested has to choose a visual pattern from a selection of options, in order to complete a larger visual sequence. Scores are graded, according to age, to give an IQ score. Scores for Raven's correlated very well with those of other IQ tests, including language-based tests. So far, this supports the notion that intelligence is 'general'.

A Raven's-style question

 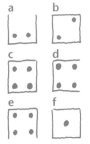

Identify which option from a–f fits the space at '?'

However, although Raven's is supposed to be culture-free and language-free, it was found that Asian children's scores, scaled according to age, went up by 15–20 points after they had lived in Britain for five years – a very significant change (Mackintosh and Mascie-Taylor 1985). This suggests that what is measured by an intelligence test is at best only a snapshot of a person's experiences and learning up to that moment. It is not necessarily a true indication of the person's underlying intelligence or potential.

We feel she has infinite potential for future improvement.

A snapshot of current performance

2 There are multiple intelligences, not one general intelligence

Thurstone (1960), after experiments involving hundreds of college students, concluded that there was no evidence of any *general* form of intelligence. Similarly, Gardner (1993) argues that intelligence consists of many separate, independent systems, which interact with each other. For Gardner, there are at least seven main 'intelligences'; each consists of abilities to solve the problems or produce the objects that are relevant within the person's culture and environment.

Research in neuropsychology suggests that different cognitive abilities, such as speech, may be semi-separate 'domains' of ability, controlled by different circuits within the brain (Karmiloff-Smith 1992). Some people show a weakness in one area, such as a complete inability to recognise faces. Other people show poor development for most skills, but have an outstanding ability in one area, such as drawing or mathematical calculation.

This supports Gardner's view that intelligence is 'multiple' rather than 'general'.

It is obvious that most of the intelligences on Gardner's list can be developed. For example, people can attend workshops to develop interpersonal skills, and counselling or meditation to develop intrapersonal awareness. A scientific way of thinking is formed through practice, training and exposure to the language and conventions of scientific research (see pages 311–12). Skill in writing poetry or essays can also be developed through practice.

Gardner's multiple intelligences

1 Linguistic
– such as reading, writing, talking, listening, or poetry

2 Logical, mathematical
– such as ability with numbers, or legal or scientific thinking

3 Spatial
– such as navigating a boat or plane, driving, or architecture

4 Musical
– such as singing, composing, playing an instrument, or appreciating music

5 Bodily-kinaesthetic
– such as sports, drama, dance, or making things

6 Interpersonal
– such as counselling and teaching skills, or understanding others

7 Intrapersonal
– such as self-understanding, self-management, or reflection

Reflection: Multiple intelligences

For which of Gardner's multiple intelligences do you show most aptitude? What reasons might there be for your having developed those intelligences rather than others?

Chapter 3

3 Intelligence can be developed

In Japan, the Suzuki Violin Talent Education Programme has trained many children to play the violin to virtuoso level. The programme begins with exposure to music from soon after birth, and involves daily practice from an early age. Even the less remarkable students perform to a level that in other cultures would be considered that of a child prodigy (Gardner 1993).

Similarly, children exposed to several languages from an early age tend to become multilingual quite naturally. People who start later in life can also develop into good violinists or linguists. The Suzuki Programme suggests the importance of the belief that *anyone* can learn to a high standard, as well as showing the role of environment and practice in developing skills. Excellence need not be the preserve of the few.

Just as we would not, in general, expect excellent violin playing from somebody who rarely played the instrument, we would not expect outstanding intellectual performances from people whose minds are not regularly challenged by ideas and problems. University provides part of that necessary stimulation. As you go through your course, the language and thinking styles of your subject will become part of your own thinking processes and linguistic expression.

4 Intelligence depends on life opportunities

As the Suzuki example illustrates, life opportunities can make a significant difference. Academic intelligence may be fostered by opportunities such as these:

- easy access to books, equipment, and appropriate teaching
- sufficient time to study, think or practise
- stimulating conversations that require active engagement and reflection
- validation by people who are important to you, of your specific learning interests, whether for geometry, philosophy or *cordon bleu* cookery
- being part of a culture that values academic intelligence.

There are ways in which you can increase these opportunities, such as making use of local libraries, doing courses at a local college or university, and even through your choice of newspaper and radio or TV programmes. If you did not have ideal opportunities for learning when you were younger, or if you were not then ready for them, it may take some time to catch up. But it can be done – and it *is* done, every year, by thousands of adult students.

Reflection: Using opportunity

In what ways could you make more of the opportunities currently available to you?

5 Intelligence depends on what is needed and relevant within a culture

According to this view, intelligence is not just something that individuals carry around in their heads, but includes the equipment and tools available to them – their filing systems, the amount of memory on their computers, the sophistication of the tools they can use, the lines of communication within their society, the people they meet. Intelligence is not cut off and measured in relation to individuals, but regarded as a *social* phenomenon (Vygotsky 1978; Resnick, Levine and Teasley 1991).

For example, the intelligence needed in industrial settings may be very different from that required for a rural economy or for life in the mountains. Similarly, the education valued for girls, or for the youngest child within a family, may be different from that sought for boys or for older children. Children are skilled at adapting to what is expected of them.

Sternberg (1985) described intelligence as being, in part, a sensitivity to the environmental context. This can apply to learning contexts also. One learning environment may match what a person is used to, making learning easy. For another person, the same teaching methods may not work. Some people learn best in quiet stillness; others find that sitting quietly is a torture. Some find it difficult to learn from books and learn better by ear. Some learn best when the curriculum is very structured; others when it is flexible and open.

If you did not do as well at school as you might have done, it may be worth reflecting on how *you* learn best – then compare this to the way you were taught. You might also consider what you were good at when you were a child, and what you valued as important. Were your interests shared and valued by the people around you – your teachers, parents and friends? If not, this may have made learning more difficult for you.

Are the things you value *today* shared by the people around you? Do they understand and support your desire to study? If not, as an adult, you can now take responsibility for setting up the right environment for yourself as a student. You may need to find a table you like in the library, or set up a space to study that nobody else can use.

Similarly, you can organise information in a way that suits your learning preferences. For example, you could record your materials or convert information to images – whatever works for you. On the whole, your lecturers will not be able to create the ideal environment *for* you, as each person's needs will be different. So it's up to you to look after your own needs.

Reflection: Managing your learning environment

How could you change your total learning environment so that you don't repeat earlier learning experiences? Do you need to surround yourself with more people who support your study ambitions? (Chapters 1, 4, 8 and 14 may give you some further ideas.)

6 Intelligence is about applying what you know to new contexts

Sternberg (1984) emphasised that any skill is made up of underlying processes and sub-skills; he saw intelligence as the ability to transfer those skills easily when confronted with a new task. What is important is not just that you are able to perform a given task, such as making a pancake or writing an essay, but that you are able to apply what you know to new situations, such as making a cake or writing a report.

However, it is not necessarily an easy matter to transfer a skill from one learning situation to another. Research into mathematical problem-solving suggests that for skills to be transferred from one problem to another, the student has first to be helped to identify their common features and the underlying principles in solving that kind of problem. If students can recognise that two problems have similar underlying structures, they can apply the principles for solving one problem in solving the other.

Also, unless the teacher makes the link between the old and the new learning explicit, the student may not realise that two problems are connected. Further, the new learning needs to be at around the same level of complexity as that already covered (Reed, Dempster and Ettinger 1985).

If teaching has not followed these lines, the student may feel lost and give up. In addition, the student may think that the fault lies with her or his intelligence, rather than in the way the problem was presented. A good teacher will help students to see what they already know, and to use this as the basis for the next step in their learning.

Applying multiple intelligences to study contexts

Gardner suggests that different intelligences interact. Students who work in a multi-sensory or a multi-disciplinary way often find that learning in one area enhances learning in other areas. If you develop a sense of rhythm, this can improve not only music and dance, but maths and spelling. Similarly, students who are sensitive to shades of colour can use these to structure and organise information visually and spatially, which in turn can help memory and understanding.

It is important to look for connections between the intelligences you have already developed and those in which you feel you are weak. You don't need to be a genius in music or art to harness music, colour, shape, and movement as learning tools. Croaky singing of chemical formulae, imagining your relatives as courtroom personalities for law revision, or using the rainbow to sequence paragraphs from pattern notes, are ways of using multiple intelligences to make studying easier – and more interesting.

Reflection: Working from your strengths

Look back to your reflection on multiple intelligences (page 62). How could you transfer abilities from your area of strength to help your learning?

7 Intelligence is a question of how much you know

The popular view of intelligence is that it is an ability to answer the type of closed questions set on *Mastermind*. This does not take into consideration aspects of intelligence such as creativity or coping in real-life situations. Another view is that intelligence is a capacity for abstract reasoning, such as formulating general hypotheses, and that you don't need to *know* much at all to reason well.

Donaldson (1978) argued that the way we reason depends upon the particular context we are in and on what we already know. For example, she demonstrated that both children and adults interpret what they hear by attending not just to the meaning of words, but also to their understanding of those words based on their own thoughts and previous knowledge. It follows that the amount and kinds of background knowledge you bring to academic study will affect the ease with which you can process new information and reason with it.

Our ability to think in abstract ways about something may depend on having already had real-life experience of similar problems. Butterworth (1992) describes how abstract notions such as 'generosity' are actually concrete social realities. The real-life, concrete experience allows us to develop a mental model, and this model later provides the basis for abstract thinking. If we have gaps in concrete experience – for example, with manipulating numbers – we are likely to find it harder to move on to more abstract examples until we have filled the gaps.

Butterworth suggests that when presented with a familiar problem in an unfamiliar context, we may be unable to recognise that the two are the same. This can make us look like complete beginners when we are not. We may need somebody to point out the similarity between what we already know and the new learning. When we see the link, we can do the problem.

Plastic brains

The brain has 'plasticity': it is capable of change and development. When a person takes up a new skill, millions of fresh connections are set up between different neurons in the brain to deal with the new information – rather like a set of telephone wires relaying information. The more you develop an ability, the more elaborate the neural networks or wiring system, and the faster your brain can process information related to that skill.

When you begin to study a new subject, the speed at which you will be able to take things in and make sense of them will depend on how far your brain can use past learning experiences. If you have studied something very similar in the past, you may experience the new learning as quite easy.

If a subject is very new, however, there is little foundation for you to build upon. Your brain has fewer connections it can use to make sense of the new information. If the language used is also unfamiliar to you, the brain will need to build connections for this too. You may *experience* this as finding it harder to listen or harder to read: you may get tired more quickly, or you may feel that your brain is 'dead', or that nothing makes sense. As you go over the same material from different angles, though, the new connections will get stronger and learning will become easier.

8 Intelligence can be measured

IQ tests only measure things that can be measured! Many areas of human excellence, however, cannot easily be measured – such as artistic and musical creativity, emotional maturity, intuition, sensitivity to the needs of others, keeping a cool head in emergencies, being able to impersonate other people, and inventiveness. Some people may excel in these areas and yet perform poorly in tests that are language-based. Students who have failed in language- or number-based GCSEs often do very well on university courses in the arts. Similarly, some people who are poor at languages are excellent at computer sciences.

Einstein's schoolwork was not very good – yet IQ tests are supposed to correlate well with school performance. Einstein claimed that his initial ideas on the relativity of time and space struck him in a moment of inspiration while he was daydreaming that he was riding on a sunbeam. This kind of imaginative thinking is difficult to measure using IQ tests.

9 Intelligence is about applying effective strategies that can be learnt

This book is based on the premise that what we regard as intelligence is often a question of good study strategies and skills that you can develop. For example, research shows that students who do best at problem-solving spend longer than other students in working out exactly what the problem is before trying to solve it. Other students look at the surface of the problem and do not see the underlying structure which connects it to problems they already know how to solve. Some students fail because they don't spend enough time considering the examples and information they are given; others copy out examples without reflecting on the underlying purpose of the activity (Keane, Kahney and Brayshaw 1989). Successful students use strategies that can be learnt.

Although the research mentioned above referred to a particular *kind* of problem-solving, its findings apply to university study in general. Some students skim across the surface of their learning, copying a bit from one book and a line from another, without really looking at why the work was set, what the information means, or its relevance to themselves. With most university assignments you will benefit from taking time to reflect, clarifying what is really being asked, the issues within the title, the reasons for that piece of work being set, and the best strategy to use. Over time, this way of working becomes a habit.

10 Intelligence is a question of habit and practice

As with any skill, study skills develop through frequent use until your application of them is like a reflex and feels instinctive. Rapid and skilful reading comprehension develops through constant reading, and familiarity with specialist texts typical of your subject. The more you write, the better your writing skills are likely to be. The more you apply your mind to thinking in critical analytical ways, the more fine-tuned such thinking skills become. If you want to achieve well, constant practice, coupled with critical reflection on your work, is essential.

Reflection: Views of intelligence

- With which of these ten views of intelligence are you most familiar?
- Which make most sense to you?
- Which best encourage learning?

What is 'learning'?

We have looked at how intelligence can be fostered though a learning process, but what is 'learning'?

Learning as process

Learning is clearly more than just intelligence or study skills. It is, rather, a multi-faceted process, involving such factors as:

- each individual learner
- and his or her learning history, knowledge, skills, ambitions, interests, attitude, motivation and current circumstances
- the current learning environment, including teaching methods, resources, materials, other students as well as the physical environment
- the content and expected outcomes of the learning being undertaken
- and the interactions between these.

We can say that learning has taken place when we both understand something and can explain, teach or demonstrate it to others.

Five learning dimensions

Many different routes can be followed to arrive at the point where learning has taken place. These vary in level of enjoyment and active engagement, and we may not even be aware that learning has taken place. Below are five dimensions along which learning activity can vary.

> ### Five dimensions of learning
> 1 Conscious or unconscious
> 2 With different levels of attention
> 3 Via different sense sequences
> 4 By detail or by the whole picture
> 5 By fast track or by the scenic route

1 Conscious or unconscious

Conscious learning

Learning is conscious when we are *aware* that we are learning, as when we set out to memorise a poem or an equation, or when we recognise that we have understood new material. Typical methods of learning consciously are:

- repeating something
- writing it out
- checking that we have remembered it
- telling someone else what we know.

Unconscious learning

We are aware of a small part only of information taken in by the senses, which the brain processes. Learning is unconscious when we are unaware of it happening. Occasionally, unconscious learning may emerge into consciousness later, as when we feel we 'just know' something we didn't realise we had learnt. You may have experienced suddenly recognising which way to go on an unfamiliar car journey, or surprising yourself by answering a question without thinking, and then wondering, 'How did I know that?'

Conscious learning   Unconscious learning

 Reflection: Unconscious learning

How could you create conditions which assist easy, unconscious learning of course material?

2 With different levels of attention

Our level of attention may vary, depending on:

- our mental or physical state for learning
- the way information is presented to us
- whether the material is completely new.

As we saw from the example of Einstein and the sunbeam (page 66), learning can take place in a relaxed, aware state – it does not always require effort and concentration. You will be able to recall many occasions when you tried hard to remember something but forgot it quickly, while remembering easily something to which you had paid little attention, such as an advertisement or song.

3 Via different sense sequences

Each of us has our own preferred sequences for seeing, hearing, speaking, writing, and manipulating information in order to learn it.

Activity ⟳ Find your preferred sense sequences

Identify some material that you need to learn – it could be a list of words you have difficulty spelling or course work that you are revising for an exam. Experiment with different sense sequences and motor movements to see which work best for you when learning that material.

Three examples:

1 Look at it (sight); say it aloud (sound); write it (sight/motor); check what you've written (sight and/or sound).

2 Draw it; look at it; say it aloud; write it; check what you've written.

3 Say it; record it; listen to it; repeat it; write it; check what you've written.

For similar visual, auditory and kinaesthetic activities, see pages 204–5.

4 By detail or by the whole picture

Some people learn best when they see the overall picture first; they are confused or overwhelmed by too much detail early on. Others learn best through building up details, allowing the whole picture to emerge. This whole picture may be meaningless to them until they have a flavour of the specific details.

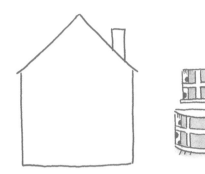

5 By fast track or by the scenic route

Some people find efficient 'motorway routes', learning exactly what they need and only that. Others take scenic routes, gathering material which may not be essential but which makes the learning more interesting. The scenic route can lead to deeper processing, and can be a richer experience. However, it can also generate a lot of information that is not essential to the task in hand. Which way is appropriate depends on what you have to learn, why you are learning it, and how long you have in which to learn it.

Learning across the dimensions

At any one time, we occupy different positions along each of these five dimensions, depending on information from the environment and according to our needs and focus. It is easier to design effective study strategies when you are conscious of these dimensions and can use them to advantage.

Chapter 3

Six conditions for learning

For learning to occur at all, and for us then to know that the learning is complete, we need:

1 New experiences
2 Foundations
3 Rehearsal
4 Processing
5 Understanding
6 Demonstration

1 New experiences

In order to learn, we need to be exposed to novelty: to new ideas, new information, new situations, new challenges, new emotions.

Imagine, for example, discovering that when Hannah put her hand in a flame, she did not feel pain. This discovery might challenge your previous learning: that fire burns and is likely to cause pain. It might stimulate a series of questions about why and how this might *not* happen.

A new experience is an opportunity to learn – based on curiosity, a desire to know, a wish to see how everything fits together. Our brains try to fit new information into what we already know: to assimilate it. If that is not possible, the brain adapts previous knowledge to accommodate the new data.

2 Learning foundations

Learning is easier if it builds on earlier learning – if it can use similar or related experiences as a foundation to 'make sense' of new information. Thus, if we look at the object in the diagram and are asked what we know about it, we can only describe what we see.

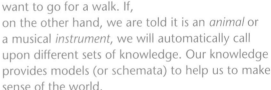

However, if we are told it is a *fruit*, we know how to react to it, what to expect from it: it can be eaten, it will probably be sweet; it is unlikely to move, make a noise, attack us, or want to go for a walk. If, on the other hand, we are told it is an *animal* or a musical *instrument*, we will automatically call upon different sets of knowledge. Our knowledge provides models (or schemata) to help us to make sense of the world.

The same is true of academic learning. For example, it is easier to read when we have a good vocabulary. If we need to keep looking up words in the dictionary, our attention to what we are reading is continually interrupted – we lose the flow, which affects our comprehension. We also have to try to make sense of what we are reading, whilst simultaneously remembering the meaning of the new words and fitting it all together. This leads to overload, and is often the point where people feel they 'can't learn'. In reality, they are learning a great deal – but too much at once.

Your brain will take time to assimilate new information, and may need to see how it all fits together, as well as what all the parts are individually, before it feels it 'knows' what it is taking in. People who seem to learn things very quickly may simply have good foundations of information, and practice in similar problems.

3 Rehearsal

Academic learning is similar to learning physical activities, such as dance or football. We generally need to repeat the action or the new information several times to take it in, and we need to come back to it or practise. Otherwise, we become 'rusty' and forget. This is just as true of writing essays or reading academic books as it is of football, drawing, playing a violin or making a soufflé.

If you think back to what you learnt at school, you will probably be aware of a vague overall knowledge of some subjects even though the details may seem hazy. You would learn these subjects more quickly a second time around. Just glancing again at some old schoolbooks may bring whole areas of knowledge flooding back.

4 Processing new information

Superficial or 'surface' processing

We may process new information at a superficial level. For example, we may just note and remember that Hannah (page 69) does not feel pain, and then think no further about this. We may learn it by heart as a fact, like learning maths tables, or record it as an entry in our notebooks.

Memory and recording are only part of learning, however. If we use only surface methods, we don't develop a sense of the underlying structure or the significance of what we learn. This makes it more difficult to apply the new knowledge in other situations.

Deep processing – making sense of what you learn

Alternatively, we may try to make sense of Hannah's experience, looking for explanations. We may ask ourselves questions to stimulate our thinking, exploring the problem from many angles. Perhaps Hannah is very good at exercising mind over matter? Maybe she has a neurological condition that prevents her from feeling pain? Maybe she *does* feel pain, but hides this?

We may also start to wonder what pain really is. How does it work – is it regulated by the brain? Or chemicals in the body? Or our attitude? Or maybe the flame was different from the flames we are used to? Maybe the answer is not in Hannah but in chemistry?

As you analyse the experience from different angles, raising new questions and experimenting with possible answers, you process at a deeper level.

'No, I don't need to practise – I have a natural gift!'

5 Moving to another level of understanding

In order to understand a new phenomenon, such as what happens when Hannah's hand is in the fire, we may have to change our previous views of the world. We may have thought that everybody would feel pain from fire.

- When we realise that there are situations in which people don't feel pain in quite the same way as others, we move to a different level of knowledge.
- When we know why this occurs, we move to a deeper level of understanding.
- When we appreciate how we came to hold our previous set of beliefs, and why we now hold a different set, we are learning at an even deeper level – understanding how knowledge is constructed, and how we come to know and understand at all.

Understanding derives from seeing things in a different way

When we learn in this way we have to be prepared to open our minds to new ways of seeing and doing things, even to new ways of thinking about ourselves, looking at how we came to believe what we believe. This makes study exciting, and is one reason why so many students return to postgraduate study.

6 Demonstrating learning

We are not really sure of our knowledge until we have put it to the test – demonstrating to ourselves and others that we really do *know* it.

One way of testing our understanding of new material is to put it to use. In some cases there may be a practical use, such as fixing a piece of machinery or producing a new design. In other cases, such as understanding how pain works, we can demonstrate learning by explaining it to other people. If we can do this

- in writing, speech, diagram, or by practical demonstration
- without checking the details as we do so
- and in a way that is clear and makes sense to our audience,

then our thinking is also likely to be clear, and a stage in our learning is complete.

If we *cannot* demonstrate what we think we know, then our knowledge and understanding are likely to be incomplete. We may need to check back over what we have learnt. It may help:

- to take a different angle on the issue
- to use a different book
- to see whether we missed a step earlier.

See also page 210 and *The C·R·E·A·M strategy for learning* (Chapter 4).

Learning at university level

Some people think that memorising 'facts' is all there is to learning. Certainly it *is* useful to have information readily available when you need it. For most courses, however, what counts is not how many facts you can fit into your answers, but how you *use* information.

You will be expected to demonstrate:

- that you can evaluate and select what is relevant and important, and what can be omitted
- that you know how ideas are linked and interconnected
- that you have made sense of your course
- that you can structure your ideas and knowledge to make a convincing argument.

What is my learning style?

Below are a range of approaches to learning. Identify which, if any, most aptly describes you. Note your learning strengths, and things you could develop to broaden your study strengths.

The diver

Characteristics

- [ ] You tend to jump in and have a go.
- [ ] You like to get things over with.
- [ ] You like to see if things work.
- [ ] You like to get on to the next thing quickly.
- [ ] You work well with short bursts of activity.

Learning strengths

- [ ] You don't waste time worrying.
- [ ] You start tasks early.
- [ ] You can motivate others.
- [ ] You are good in role-play activities, problem-solving, and crises.

Areas to develop

- [ ] Reflection and planning.
- [ ] Creative thinking.
- [ ] Considering alternatives.
- [ ] Listening to and working with others.
- [ ] Increasing your personal interest, so that you can work for longer periods.

Reflection: 'Diver' characteristics

Do you have any strong 'diver' characteristics? When are these most apparent in your study?

The dreamer

Characteristics

- [ ] You think a lot about the subject.
- [ ] You like to research things thoroughly.
- [ ] You put off practical aspects such as writing.
- [ ] You have no idea where time goes.
- [ ] You continually rewrite your time-planner.

Learning strengths

- [ ] You reflect and evaluate well.
- [ ] You are creative, with lots of ideas.
- [ ] You get to the root of things.
- [ ] You listen well and sensitively to others.

Areas to develop

- [ ] Effective learning strategies.
- [ ] Timekeeping and organisational skills.
- [ ] Taking responsibility for self and others.
- [ ] Participating.
- [ ] Setting priorities and taking decisions.
- [ ] Assertiveness and risk-taking.

Reflection: 'Dreamer' characteristics

Do you have any strong 'dreamer' characteristics? When are these most apparent in your study?

Chapter 3

The logician

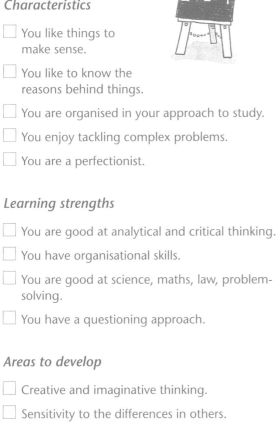

Characteristics

- ☐ You like things to make sense.
- ☐ You like to know the reasons behind things.
- ☐ You are organised in your approach to study.
- ☐ You enjoy tackling complex problems.
- ☐ You are a perfectionist.

Learning strengths

- ☐ You are good at analytical and critical thinking.
- ☐ You have organisational skills.
- ☐ You are good at science, maths, law, problem-solving.
- ☐ You have a questioning approach.

Areas to develop

- ☐ Creative and imaginative thinking.
- ☐ Sensitivity to the differences in others.
- ☐ Personal reflection.
- ☐ Working with others.
- ☐ Stress management.

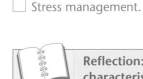

Reflection: 'Logician' characteristics

Do you have any strong 'logician' characteristics? When are these most apparent in your study?

The searcher

Characteristics

- ☐ You find everything interesting.
- ☐ You like to see the big picture.
- ☐ You have bits of information on lots of things.
- ☐ You are fascinated by details but don't remember them.
- ☐ You find it hard to select what is relevant.

Learning strengths

- ☐ You have high motivation and interest.
- ☐ You have broad general knowledge.
- ☐ You can see connections between things.
- ☐ You are creative and inventive.

Areas to develop

- ☐ Setting goals and priorities.
- ☐ Analytical and critical thinking.
- ☐ Categorising and selecting.
- ☐ Editing skills.
- ☐ Developing memory for detail.

Reflection: 'Searcher' characteristics

Do you have any strong 'searcher' characteristics? When are these most apparent in your study?

Learning types or personal learning style?

Treating learning styles as 'types'

The activity on pages 72–73 divides learning styles into four types. You may have found that:

- one type summed you up accurately
- no type summed you up accurately and fully
- some aspects of each type were true of you
- you could think of occasions when you might adopt each of the styles detailed.

There are many psychological theories that divide people into a small number of basic types as in the activity above. Some students find it helpful to identify with a type and consider this offers insights into, or explanations for, how they learn. However, we bring to each learning situation different levels of knowledge, confidence and skills that impact on how we learn. It isn't necessarily helpful to reduce such individual complexity to a small range of types based on a few shared characteristics. It can limit our understanding if we look only to a given learning 'type' for explanations.

Style, habit, attitude, preference and experience (SHAPE)

In practice, we each draw on a complex and individual combination of styles, habits, attitudes, preferences and experiences.

- Learning **S**tyle: how we learn best
- Learning **H**abits: how we have become used to studying
- **A**ttitude: the mind-set we bring to study
- Learning **P**references: how we like to study and approaches we enjoy even if not always the most effective for us
- **E**xperiences: the educational and life history that impacts on how we study.

Awareness of these factors can help us to make conscious choices about how we study so as to use time more effectively, with more enjoyment and better results.

Rather than focus on our 'type', it can help to consider the particular factors that seem to work for us – and how these might change depending on when, and what, we are learning.

Learning experiences

Activity **How do you learn best?**

Enjoyable learning experiences

Think back to a time when you found something very easy or enjoyable to learn. It might have been at school, home or work.

Jot down your thoughts about *why* this was the case. What made it into a good learning experience for you?

For example:

- Was it the teaching?
- Your interest in the subject?
- The teacher's faith in you?
- Because it was visual?
- Because each step was clear?

Your notes for the activities on pages 44–5 can help with this activity.

Difficult learning experiences

Now think of a time when you found something difficult or unpleasant to learn. Jot down your thoughts about:

- What happened in this second example that was different from your first example?
- What could have made the second experience more manageable?

Learning from your experiences

- What do these two experiences tell you about how you learn best?
- What light do they throw on your learning habits and attitudes to learning?

Personal learning style

Your personal learning style will be much more individual than the broad 'type' of learning style that you considered on pages 72–3.

The following pages provide material to help you investigate further your own unique learning style – or styles.

Chapter 3

Identify your personal learning style

Draw a ring round those factors below that you consider contribute to your performing *at your best*. There may be many or just a few. Add in any others that you consider relevant to you.

1	**Social** On my own. With friends. With other students. A mixture. It depends on the day or task.
2	**Input from others** Motivating myself. Working to my own agenda. Working things out for myself. Studying collaboratively. Sharing ideas. Encouragement. Support. It depends on the day or task
3	**External direction** Detailed instructions. Lots of guidance. Some guidance. Some instructions. Freedom to study my way. Some choice. Few choices. Lots of choice. It depends on the day or task.
4	**Timing** Start early. Well-paced. Last minute. No fixed pattern. Studying for hours uninterrupted. Studying for a set amount of time. Lots of short breaks. Studying with no fixed pattern. Breaking up time with different tasks. It depends on the day or task
5	**Sensory** *Visual*: Colour; Shape; Film; Layout; Seeing material on the page or screen; observing. *Auditory*: Listening to lectures/podcasts/recordings of own voice; Singing/rapping information. *Kinaesthetic*: Moving around; making things; making a diagram or model of the problem; writing. It depends on the day or task.
6	**Planning** Systematic. Well-planned. Clear priorities. Using lists. Studying what I feel like at the time. Going with the flow. Creative chaos. Organic development. Browsing. It depends on the day or task.
7	**Global: detail** Seeing the big picture first. Sorting out the details first. Moving back and forth between the big picture and the details. It depends on the day or task.
8	**Location** On campus. At home. In a library. In a set place. Anywhere. It depends on the day or task. It makes no difference.
9	**Noise** In silence. With music. With the TV on. It depends on the day or task. It makes no difference.
10	**Light** Bright light. Dim light. Average light. It depends on the day or task. It makes no difference.
11	**Medium** Paper-based. Electronic. It depends on the day or task. It makes no difference.
12	**Other things that characterise the way I learn best:**

Chapter 3

What kind of learner are you?

Student comments

Jumoke – I selected 'It depends ...' for nearly every answer. For example, for new topics and problems we have to solve, I develop my ideas best when we chat about these in the library or on a discussion board. But I get to a point when I want to clear my head about what I really think. Then, it is better if I withdraw to a quiet place where I can work through my thoughts without interruption.

Milan – I want to say 'creative chaos' is my style as that suits my nature. But actually, what works best for me is to plan everything phenomenally well so nothing can deflect me from what I have to do. This counteracts my natural disorganisation and tendency to drift into what entertains me.

Louis – Although I think of myself as an introverted person, I am quite a social learner. If I talk about lectures or what I read, it becomes clearer to me and I remember it better. I learn a lot from sharing ideas in groups – they just need to be small, quiet groups that are focused on the task.

Adele – I work best in a heightened environment – bright light, lots of space, big tables so I can spread out my books and papers and have everything opened at once, lots of stimulus to keep my ideas flowing. If I am at home, I put the TV on in the background – I don't really watch it, but it blocks out other distractions.

She says she's experimenting with her learning style.

Reflection: Characteristics of my personal learning style

Using the evaluation from page 75, consider the following:

- What characterises the approaches that help you to study at your best?
- Can you detect any patterns in the factors that help you to study best?

Activity ⟳ **Name that style**

It is useful to name your own personal learning style.

- It helps you to formulate in your own mind what is distinctive about how you learn best.
- It helps you to sum up the factors that contribute to your learning best.
- When you sit down to study, this helps you to remember to apply the specific approaches that help you achieve best.

Choose a word or phrase that accurately sums up how *you* learn. Make this as individual and specific as you can so that you are more likely to remember it – as in the example below.

Student examples: Name that style

Saskia: 'Ninja Learning Style': I think of learning as a secret mission where I have to sneak up on myself and get engaged before the boredom baddies get me.

Mark: I call my style 'Extreme Learning' as I work best in extremes of quiet, applying all my attention.

Abi: Squirrel Learning Style, that's me. I squirrel away lots of details that I think nobody else will find out, little nuggets of information, and then feast on them when I have to write my assignment.

Learning preferences and habits

The way we enjoy learning, our preference, is not necessarily the same as our learning style, or what produces our best work.

Etienne I *prefer* to spend my time browsing interesting facts on the Internet, especially late at night, and then assembling these into some sort of order for my assignments. My *learning style* is 'Global chatter', as I work best when I get a sense of the overall subject from discussing it with others. It took me a long time to realise this as I don't really enjoy working that way.

Claire I get my best grades when I start early, am methodical, make a lot of notes, and work on a draft over several sessions. I call that my *All Method No Madness* learning style. In stark contrast, my learning preference could be characterised as *High Pressure High Intensity*. When I studied to my preferences, I used the approach of 'get in, do it, and get out quickly'. This meant reading whatever I could get my hands on fast, ignoring any material unavailable on that day, and rushing out a rapid piece of work with no drafting or proof-reading.

Nita By preference, I am very competitive and enjoy studying on my own, using every minute effectively. I don't like groupwork as I don't really want to share my ideas and it can feel like a waste of time, a bit slow. Overall, my learning preferences and style match each other, as I do get good grades. However, even though I find collaborative work annoying, I have found that I get my very best grades from this: the range of ideas and perspectives stimulates me to come up with richer answers.

'Actually, I think I prefer to learn at this angle.'

Harnessing your learning preferences

It makes sense to find ways of using approaches we enjoy – if we can make them work for us.

Reflection: Style versus preference?

- How different are your learning preferences (above) from your learning style (page 75)?
- How can you adapt your study methods so as to gain a good balance between those you enjoy (which are likely to motivate you and keep you on task), and those that help you gain the best results?

Activity Study habits

What study habits have you developed over the years? How far do these equate with each of the following:

1 your learning style (what helps you learn best)?

2 your learning preferences (what you like doing)?

3 your early learning experiences rather than what you need now?

4 the attitude, or mind-set, that you bring to your study?

Which study habits might it be useful to change?

Activity Identify your learning preference

Return to page 75, *Identify your personal learning style.* This time, highlight in a bright colour those factors that you *prefer* when studying – that is, those factors which you think help you to engage with study and enjoy it.

Personalise your learning

Once you have analysed your style, habits and preferences, use your insights to create the optimal set of conditions for your study. Personalise your learning through creating study environments and selecting strategies that suit you best overall. Look for the ideal combination that helps you to:

- engage effectively
- enjoy your time studying
- achieve your best possible grades.

Adapting your course to suit you

If your course is not structured in a way that matches your learning preferences, 'adapt' it through the way you choose to study.

> ### Example 1
>
> #### Prefer studying with others
>
> Organise a study group, or arrange to work with a friend. Work in libraries and get involved in student activities. Use your social networking tools to connect with students outside of class. Ask questions about material you are studying. Comment on ideas that others raise. Make opportunities for collaborative study, such as creating a class wiki or setting up a discussion board.

> ### Example 2
>
> #### Prefer working to own agenda
>
> Focus on time management so that you have maximum control over where time goes. Look for articles that nobody else is likely to use; find examples and details that others may not think of. For each study brief you are set, look for your own angle. If you are required to work with others as part of your course, take charge of your own contribution: consider what kind of constructive role you could take within that group and play an active part.

> ### Example 3
>
> #### Prefer learning through listening
>
> Use any podcasts that are provided. Record lectures, extracts from books, your notes, ideas, lists of key points, formulae or quotations – or make a podcast of these. Listen to them whilst travelling. Look for computer-voiced text you can download as a podcast and other information that can be downloaded to a portable device such as your MP3 player. Investigate assistive technologies such as screen readers, and software such as *Texthelp!* that enables you to listen to words, sentences or paragraphs of text as you type or highlights them as you listen. Form a study group – to learn via discussion.
>
> See also *Individual memory styles,* page 204.

Gain a rounded skills portfolio

Whilst personalising your learning, take care also to vary your study choices and strategies so that you gain the widest set of perspectives and skills. For example, if you prefer to work on your own, create some opportunities to develop teamworking and people skills, so that you are able to draw on these when needed for assessed group projects or for future employment. Conversely, if you always work with others, make time for independent study and thinking things through on your own.

> ### Reflection: Varying study approaches
>
> It is important to consider approaches that we find more difficult and what we lose if we avoid these completely.
> - Which methods of study do you try to avoid?
> - Which skills and insights might you miss out on as a result?

Using technology to personalise learning

Some students prefer to work completely online; others prefer face-to-face learning; others a combination of methods. Experiment to find the best combination for your study. You may prefer, for example, to search for materials online, but read books in hard copy. You may find chat rooms useful for general discussion but prefer to meet face-to-face for particular aspects of study such as preparing for a group presentation.

Taking part

Make use of the opportunities that are available so that you have the widest range of methods from which to choose. For example:

- If there is a chat room or discussion board set up for your programme, contribute to it. Once they are used to them, students often prefer to exchange ideas in this way.
- Use the links that are built into electronic learning materials. You lose these links when you print out the materials.
- Turn up to face-to-face study activities more than once so as to give them a chance. Get to know some of the other people. Make an active contribution before deciding whether this is the right method for you.
- Once you have met group members and have a sense of what they are like, you may prefer to use social networking tools to maintain contact with them.

Reflection: Taking part

In general, do you have a preference for taking part in activities and discussions face-to-face, online, or a combination of these?

Keeping organised

- Maintain an electronic diary. Set this to give you advance reminders of appointments.
- Maintain a paper-based planner, so that you can keep track of appointments when you lack an internet connection.
- Investigate bespoke student planners in online and paper-based form.

Reflection: Keeping organised

What kinds of planning and information do you prefer to work with in paper form, such as a student planner or address book? Which do you prefer to use through your computer, tablet and/or phone?

Using library resources

Work out the best pattern for you when working with materials in libraries and resource centres. It is useful to visit the library in person to:

- get to know the librarians and gain a sense of who to ask about different enquiries
- make use of the different kinds of learning spaces provided: many libraries provide spaces where you can study quietly without disturbance and places for group study
- gain from the ambience, which can help you to remain focused on your work
- use time well if you have occasional hours between classes
- access services and resources not available online. See Chapter 6.

On the other hand, many traditional library services are now also available online, such as:

- ordering books and articles
- digital copies of texts and learning materials, including audiovisual
- open source materials.

Reflection: Using library resources

What kinds of library-related activities do you find work best for you when present in the library itself, and which online?

Managing information

Consider the optimum combination for you in recording, maintaining and accessing your notes from lectures, reading and thinking about course material.

If the choice is available to you, you may prefer to take all your notes onto a tablet device. However, you may find it more convenient, and easier to remember material, if you take notes by hand, especially in class. You may choose to type up highlights of handwritten notes later so they are easier to read. Alternatively, you may find it easier to use and recall material that you work with more actively, such as by making visual posters, charts or flash cards.

However you prefer to work, it is usually worth maintaining an electronic bibliography of all the texts you read. This will save you rewriting details if you use the same resource for another piece of writing. There are apps designed to help you record material for use in references. See Chapter 6.

Reflection: Managing information

What kinds of material do you prefer to work with in hard copy? And which electronically?

Capturing and developing your ideas

Experiment with using:

- a notebook and pen or pencil
- a dictaphone to record your voice
- a flip camera, phone or tablet to video yourself or your practical work 'in progress'.

Designing materials for assignments and revision

Consider working on paper, in notebooks, on large card, and using software such as Impress (which is Open Source), Publisher, Powerpoint or Adobe Illustrator for:

- designing posters for assignments
- making charts and posters to organise information for revision.

Use video, photography and drawing software to find alternative methods of laying out information in ways that help you to make sense of it and to recall it. For example, if you make large charts or pattern notes (page 173) to organise material visually, you could use your phone, tablet or flip camera to record this and play it back at intervals whilst you are on the go, to help you remember it.

Using apps for study

Experiment with different apps to see which you prefer for study. Visit apps stores at:

- https://play.google.com
- www.itunes.apple.com
- www.uk.blackberry.com /services/appworld
- www.android.com/apps

Activity **Personalised use of technology for study**

You can enhance your study by using varied combinations of technologies, drawing on those provided for your course and those that you enjoy using in everyday life.

Use the chart on page 81 to stimulate your thinking about which of the following uses of technology would work best for you for each aspect of study. Use a ✓ to indicate the technologies you would choose to use for each aspect of study.

Consider the different ways that you could combine these technologies and approaches to make some aspects of your study more interesting and effective.

Personalised use of technology for study

Aspect of study / Technology	To keep myself organised	To research and understand the subject	To get the most out of taught sessions	To work on group projects /activities	To learn from practice and feedback	To produce essays, talks, reports, etc.
Videos, photos, animations						
Course-based discussion board						
Online practice tests						
Social networking e.g. Facebook						
Micro-blogging tools e.g. Twitter						
Podcasts						
Blogs						
Wikis						
Lecture chat						
Apps (e.g. referencing tools)						
How I would use the technologies in combination:						

Chapter 3

Study strategy – individual or social?

For each aspect of study, a different combination of approaches a, b, or c below is best for you. Jot down which combination of these you would use, and how, for the following 9 aspects of study.

Aspect of study	(a) Studying on my own (b) Studying with others face-to-face (c) Studying with others online
1 Preparing in advance for taught sessions	
2 Engaging and maintaining my interest in the subject	
3 Reading around the subject and researching new topics	
4 Understanding difficult concepts and making sense of material covered in taught sessions	

Aspect of study	(a) Studying on my own (b) Studying with others face-to-face (c) Studying with others online
5 Making sense of assignment briefs	
6 Keeping motivated and staying on task	
7 Developing my ideas and gaining different perspectives	
8 Managing time and being organised for study	
9 Reviewing and revising material	

Chapter 3

Optimal learning

When you are in a physical state to learn

- You can't learn easily if you are tired, stressed, hungry, dehydrated or on a high-sugar diet.
- A glass of plain water several times a day helps neural activity in the brain, and releases energy. Other drinks do not have the same effect. If you tire easily when studying, or if your thinking is muddled, drink some water.
- Foods such as cereal-based products (rice, oats and wheat), which release natural sugars slowly, help balance your energies.

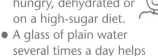

- Stress may put you into 'survival mode', diverting your energies away from your brain to your muscles (see page 209). We learn best when relaxed, interested and motivated.
- Sleep helps the brain to absorb and recall information, as well as helping you cope with stress.

When you *believe* you can learn

- Believe in your intelligence (Chapter 3).
- Allow yourself to do well.
- Create a positive state of mind for learning.

I can do this!

Learning is easier and more effective when ...

When the material suits you

Take action, where possible, to ensure that:

- you are on a course you find interesting and relevant
- the material you use is at the right level. If you don't have background knowledge in the topic, start with basic texts and build to specialist ones.

ROCKET SCIENCE MADE SIMPLE

When the time is right

- at the right time in your life
- at the best time of day or night to suit your learning of that material for that kind of activity
- when you have cleared away distractions
- when your time is planned out well to make the study session interesting
- when you can learn at your own pace and without undue haste.

See Chapter 5.

PLANNER 365

Chapter **3**

When you use the 5 learning dimensions to best effect

Create opportunities for:
- conscious and unconscious learning
- varying your level of attention
- using your senses in preferred sequences
- learning from detail or globally
- at different speeds and intensity.

See pages 67–8.

When you combine technologies to suit you

- Experiment with paper-based and technology enhanced learning to find the combination that is most effective for you in practice.
- Combine technologies with each other to find the optimum selection for the activity.

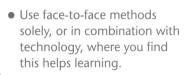

- Use face-to-face methods solely, or in combination with technology, where you find this helps learning.

When the medium suits you

- Rewrite, draw, act, record, photograph, video, or sculpt new information so that it is easier to absorb – whatever suits you best.
- Experiment with different layouts, colours, fonts, etc.

When information is organised

Organise information so that it is easier for your brain to structure it (see page 215).

When you use C·R·E·A·M strategies

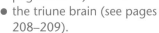

Be creative, reflective, effective, active and highly motivated (see Chapter 4).

When you use your whole brain

Take full advantage of your brain. Use:

- all your senses to encode information (see page 212)
- both the 'left' and 'right' sides of your brain (see pages 207–8)
- the triune brain (see pages 208–209).

When five key study-skills components are in place

You need:
- self-awareness
- awareness of what is required of you
- methods and strategies
- confidence and permission
- familiarity, practice and habit. See page 43.

When you enjoy what you learn

Make the learning fun. Make sure:
- that it has meaning for you
- that you really care about the outcome, attracted to success like a bee to honey
- that you are fully engaged in what you are learning
- that you create points of interest, challenge and enjoyment where these do not occur naturally for you in a given text, topic or learning context.

When you put into place the 6 conditions for learning

See pages 69–71.

When you work with others

- for interest and enjoyment
- for support and solidarity
- for different viewpoints
- to use time effectively.

See Chapter 10.

When you personalise study to suit you

- Keep experimenting.
- Be honest about what really works best for you.

Reflection: Optimising my learning

List five things that would optimise your learning that you are willing and able to undertake now.

Chapter 3

Review

Learning is a complex process and many factors impact on our capacity to learn new material easily, effectively and with enjoyment. Amongst these are, first and foremost, our attitudes towards, and understanding of, the learning process itself.

This chapter has provided an opportunity to reflect upon what is meant by intelligence and learning and the different conditions that give rise to intelligent learning. Understanding more about these can help to make sense of what affects your ability to achieve well on your current course, and to design personal study strategies that are likely to be more effective for you.

There are many different views about intelligence. Some traditional attitudes have been limiting. They reduced people's self-esteem, making it more difficult for them to learn and undermining their potential to achieve. Different cultures and environments require, appreciate and develop different aspects of intelligence. These differences, and their impact on individual students, haven't always been fully appreciated in academic contexts.

Your early learning environments and previous study attitudes, habits and experiences may have been of help in preparing you for your current academic study. Alternatively, you may have experienced these as disadvantageous. They do not, however, prevent you from developing new habits and strategies relevant to your current course.

One of the reasons why students have under-achieved in the past is because much of their formal learning took place in class in conditions that didn't necessarily suit the way they worked. In Higher Education, however, much of your study is by independent learning where you have far more choices and control. You can decide when and how you want to learn.

The chapter has encouraged you to consider influences on your own learning, and provided you with some ideas about how you might personalise your study to enhance your academic performance. Chapter 8 provides further ideas about personalising your approach to study with a focus on memory. Once you give these some thought, it is likely that you will find many other ways that you could adapt the content, pacing and timing of your study and develop new strategies.

Chapter 4
The C·R·E·A·M strategy for learning

Learning outcomes

This chapter offers you opportunities to:

- become aware of the contribution of each aspect of the C·R·E·A·M strategy to the learning process
- develop ideas on how to take more creative and active approaches to your study
- understand the difference between being a *virtuous* student and being an *effective* student
- consider effective approaches for different kinds of study
- clarify your motives for study and develop strategies for maintaining high levels of motivation
- build upon the reflective work of previous chapters.

C·R·E·A·M

C·R·E·A·M stands for:

C – Creative
Have the confidence to apply imagination to your learning and problem-solving.

R – Reflective
Be able to sit with your experience, analyse and evaluate your own performance, and draw lessons from it.

E – Effective
Organise your time, space, priorities, state of mind, resources, and use of technology to maximum benefit.

A – Active
Be personally engaged physically and mentally, in making sense of what you learn.

M – Motivated
Be clear about the outcomes you want to achieve, the steps you need to take to achieve these, and what you will do to build and maintain your engagement and enthusiasm.

Developing each of these aspects strengthens all the others. For example, being motivated involves reflection about what you really want. Active learning and creativity require motivation and help you to stay motivated. Effective organisational strategies benefit from imagination and reflection – and so on.

Creativity is especially important for generating ideas in the early stages of new assignments. You can use more logical approaches later, to evaluate which creative ideas to use.

Attitudes that prevent creativity

- 'It's a waste of time.'
- 'It's childish.'
- 'There's a time for work and a time for play.'
- 'There's a right way of doing things.'
- 'It's not logical.'
- 'I'm not creative.'
- 'I can't.'

Reflection: Creative blocks

Do you express any of the above attitudes? Were you given any messages when you were younger which stifle your creativity now?

Approaches that foster creativity

'Play' and lateral thinking

Select any two random objects, such as a cup and a plant. Find as many connections between them as you can (e.g. by size, colour, owner, the way they break, how they spin, when they were bought). How could you apply this type of 'play' to your coursework?

You find what you are looking for

- Find ten round things in the room.
- Find ten things that 'open'.

Once you start to look, you may find your attention drawn to many such items. If you look for new strategies or answers, it is more likely that you will find them too.

There's more than one right answer

Once you have come up with an answer, look for more. These may be better – or give you a way of fine-tuning the first idea.

Combine things

Take the front half of one animal and the rear of another. What new animal have you invented? The essence of invention is mixing two different ideas or contexts to create a new variety. This helps in academic thinking too – such as comparing viewpoints.

Metaphor

Let one thing stand for, or represent, another: that is, use metaphor or analogy. Look at objects, or study problems from different perspectives, making these visual or concrete in playful ways. Take an issue out of the academic context and see what it looks like in the world of oranges and apples, or knives, forks, salt and pepper.
If an issue doesn't make sense to you, map it out with objects on a table – just as generals mapped out military strategies using 'toy' soldiers.

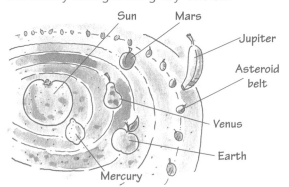

'**Suppose this apple is the earth, this orange is the sun, and these other fruit are the rest of the solar system …**'

Activity ↺ Search for connections

See how many ideas you can generate by completing the sentences below.
- Writing an essay is like making cakes because …
- Study is like a game of football because …
- Being a student is like being a sandwich because …
- What other metaphors can you think of to describe what study or learning is like?

Be a professor – and other ideas

Give yourself a new sub-personality

In our minds, we carry various sub-personalities, such as an internal *critic* who tells us off, a *playful child* who sees the funny side of things, a *hero* who wades in to save the situation, and many others.

If you pay attention to your thought process, you can become aware of those different characters within.

Add to your dramatic cast and find a professor within you

Keep an ideas notebook

Value each passing idea, as writers and artists do. Jot ideas down at once in a notebook or on sticky labels. Keep paper and pen by your bed.

Go through the ideas later to see which you can use. Many will lead nowhere – that's part of the creative process – but sometimes one will be just what you need.

Be curious about what you don't know

Creative people are curious. They want to know everything – just in case it fits together with something else one day.

It is difficult to be creative if you fear or resist what you don't know. Be open to the curious child in you who wants to have a go at everything.

Create opportunities to break a routine

When you take a different route, even if it is not the quickest way, you discover new things of interest.

Examine your routines. Ask:

- Why am I doing it this way?
- Have the original reasons now changed?
- How else could I do things?

Imagine alternatives

Ask 'what if …?' questions

What if the weekend were three days long? What if this essay had to be in tomorrow? What if I were only allowed 100 words to write up my research – what would I include?

How would others do it?

Consider: how might Pablo Picasso approach this study problem? Or Nelson Mandela? Aung San Suu Kyi? J. K. Rowling? Mozart? Beyonce? A politician? A choreographer? Your mother? Your internal professor? Whose approach would most help and inspire you?

Activity **You are the world's leading expert**

Experts don't find problems easy, but they are more open to dealing with the seemingly impossible. Those working at the forefront of research cannot look up the answer in a book – it isn't there yet! Like Einstein daydreaming on a sunbeam (page 66) they may play with ideas, juggle with options that seem crazy, and go on flights of fancy, imagining 'what if …?', generating lots of possible answers, and then examining them more closely to see whether any could actually work.

You can do that too. When you cannot think of a way of doing a piece of work, imagine that you are a professor or inventor dealing with a world-important problem. What does your internal professor look like? Sound like? How do you move your hands and head when you are in 'professor' mode? Let your professor come alive, and talk to you about possible approaches to study problems.

Creative learning

People devise many different strategies to help them to learn. Here are a few.
Tick the box beside any *you* could use. What other methods can you think of?

© Stella Cottrell (2013) *The Study Skills Handbook*, 4th edition, Palgrave Macmillan

Creative problem-solving

What?

Problem-solving takes different forms such as:

Real-life, everyday situations in study, personal life or work.

A 'teaser' question or activity in class or on a discussion board for a group to solve. This could be a game or puzzle.

A case study that provides a problem-based or enquiry-based, approach to a complex issue such as in healthcare, politics or business, and often requiring you to make recommendations.

A mathematical problem requiring an answer using specific measures (of time, distance, length, energy, etc.)

Why ...

Exercises in problem-solving train you in a range of thinking skills. They enable you:

- to develop creativity and reasoning abilities in generating potential solutions and deciding between them
- to research issues from different perspectives
- to develop your understanding of theory and principles and put these to practical use
- to practise specific procedures.

You can apply a problem-solving approach to any research or study activity.

Easy problem-solving

Problem solving is easier if you use the following approaches.

Mind-set Approach it as a puzzle rather than a 'test'. As this is more enjoyable, it is more likely that you will stay on task in a relaxed, engaged mental state until you arrive at a solution.

Time Spend as much time as you need to really tease out precisely what is needed before you start to search for and apply solutions.

System Use an organised, step by step approach, so that you take account of all important information and clues with which you are provided, and so that you cover all essential stages in the right order.

Knowledge Call upon what you know. As a student, it is likely that any problems that you are set will relate in some way to material covered previously in class or about which you can find essential information in the reading materials and resources provided.

Preparation Research the problem carefully before deciding on a solution. Assemble all the information and material that you need. Go through your formulae, or undertake the background reading or investigations.

Typical mistakes

Do any apply to you?

☐ **Rushing at the problem**
... rather than taking the time needed for the early stages in defining the task. This can create difficulties later, and leads to students thinking that they can't solve problems they could manage.

☐ **Being imprecise**
... about the specific nature of the problem; not examining the details in a systematic way.

☐ **Jumping to conclusions**
... about the strategy or formula to use before thinking through all the options.

☐ **Missing out on clues**
... rather than using the initial information provided in order to work out further information, which they need in order to solve the problem.

☐ **Giving up too early**
... rather than keeping going, looking for new angles, or researching examples that throw new light on the set problem.

☐ **Under-use of material**
... such as course work and texts that could have thrown light on how to understand the problem and solve it.

☐ **Disorganised working**
... jumping steps in the process; misreading their own working out.

Creative problem-solving: stages in problem-solving

Stages in problem-solving

1   Define the task.

2   Identify a strategy.

 • *Draw upon familiar problems.*

 • *Weigh up alternative approaches.*

 • *Make a decision.*

3   Work it through systematically.

4   Check your answer.

5   Write it up.

6   Evaluate.

1   Define the task

The most important part of problem-solving is 'elaborating' what is being asked of you (see page 66). This usually provides a pointer to the kind of answer required, which in turn can prompt a means of finding the answer. Unless you recognise the nature of the task instantly, you may need to move back and forth between the following strategies until you are clear what is being asked.

(a) Put it into your own words

Reword the problem to check you understand it.

(b) What *sort* of answer will it be?

A formula? Actions? A decision? A set of conclusions? A particular unit of measurement? Recommendations?

(c) Verbal sketch

Jot down a quick outline of the problem.

What do you know? What are the key facts in the information supplied?

What do you need to find out?

What kind of a problem is this? How does it compare with problems already covered in class?

Simplify: If relevant, identify a formula or equation that represents the problem in a generalised way.

(d) Sketch it as a diagram

For mathematical problems, and for other problems if it helps, make a rough sketch to outline the problem. Use stick people, symbols or basic shapes that help you to see at a glance how one part of the problem relates to another.

On your diagram, mark in:
• what you already know
• anything you can work out
• what you need to find out.

(e) What information do you need?

• Which of your notes, texts or other resources are relevant?
• Which theories, case studies or formulae apply?

(f) Define it

Write it out clearly
Once you are clear in your thinking about what kind of problem it is, write this out as the first part of writing up the problem.
Keep referring back to this ... so that you remain focused on the precise task in question.

Chapter 4

Defining the task: clarify the problem precisely

Before spending months resolving the problem of *how* to build a bridge, be sure the problem is not actually about *whether* to build one or not

---

Defining the issue: the tortoise and hare

One hot day, a tortoise and a hare decided to race each other. The hare shot away quickly whilst the tortoise followed at a very slow pace. The hare was nearly at the finishing line when he decided he could afford to stop for a drink. In the heat of the day, he soon fell soundly asleep. Many hours later, the tortoise crept past the sleeping hare and crossed the finishing line first.

A question of speed?

If you were set the problem of whether the hare or tortoise was faster, you would need to attend to the exact wording of the problem. A hare can run faster in general terms, and did so for the greater distance. The tortoise took less time to complete the race overall. To calculate speed, you divide the distance by the time taken:

$$\text{Speed} = \frac{\text{Distance}}{\text{Time}}$$

As the tortoise completed the whole distance in the least time, it was faster. The correct answer would depend on the exact wording of the problem set.

---

2 Identify a strategy

For your subject, there will be formulae, precedents or protocols that would be applied to the kind of problem you have been set. If you identify the nature of the problem correctly, this generally gives you a clear steer about the steps needed to arrive at a solution.

Draw upon familiar problems

Of problems covered previously on your course or in the recommended course materials:

- Which are the most similar to those you have been set? How might their solutions help here?
- In what ways does the problem you are working on differ from previous problems you have worked on? As a result, how might the solutions to this problem also be different?

Weigh up alternative approaches

Jot down a list of strategies that might, potentially, lead to a solution to the problem. Give initial thought to where each might lead.

- What are the advantages of each solution or combination of solutions?
- What might be the disadvantages?

Make a decision

Make a reasoned decision about which is the best approach for arriving at the solution. Apply this to the problem to test it out.

Difficulties finding a solution?

If the answer isn't immediately apparent, work creatively to find a different approach.

(a) Simplify

Remove unnecessary detail: sift the essentials from the broader background information. Hone this down to get to the core of the problem.

Generalise: Find points of commonality with other material you have covered.

- In maths and sciences, this usually means identifying the appropriate formula, as in the Tortoise and Hare example above.
- For other subjects, look for features or characteristics such as structure, sequence, protocols, genre or theories that enable you to make cross-comparisons with other events or situations in your discipline.

Make broad assumptions that help you generalise the problem. In the Tortoise and the Hare, if we didn't know the hare fell asleep, we would solve the problem of relative speed by making reasonable assumptions based on the known typical average speed of hares and tortoises.

(b) Consider alternative ways of looking at it

Take a different angle

If you find it difficult to understand a problem:

- Rephrase it.
- Look up similar examples of the problem.
- Use analogies to gain insights into this problem.
- Consider who might benefit from the solution.

Make it real

It can be helpful to relate problems to parallel, concrete problems from real life: when might you or others apply this kind of problem to a real situation? What would you need to know or do? Which parts of that real-life issue match which parts of the problem you have been set?

Combine the possibilities

Consider combining solutions from diverse problems you have solved in the past. Could the problem have several parts to it that each need to call upon a different aspect of previous course work?

3 Work it through systematically

- Think through, step by step, the implications and potential outcomes of your preferred method or strategy.
- For problems which require you to apply formulae, write out each step you take, so that you can see how you arrived at each stage of your working out.
- Consider which aspects of the solution might not work – and what might work instead.

4 Check back over your work methodically

- Check that you interpreted the problem correctly.
- Check each step of your working out for errors.

5 Write up the problem

- Write out precisely and succinctly the nature of the problem and its solution.
- Set out the steps you would take to solve the problem – your method or 'working out'.
- Make sure that the solution, whether a number, recommendation or conclusion, is set out clearly.

6 Evaluate your work

- Did you spend long enough considering the nature of the problem and what was required?
- Were you able to find similar problems that might help?
- Did you 'play' sufficiently with possible alternative solutions and combinations?
- Did you leave enough time to work it out?
- Do you need help understanding the coursework?

Creative problem-solving: identify the task

It may help to draw up a chart. An example is provided below, that you can copy or adapt for your use.

1 Definition of the problem	
Put in your own words What exactly are you being asked to do?	
Sketch it ● How do the different parts of the problem relate to each other? ● What information can you write in? ● What else can you work out and add in that would help? ● What do you need to find out?	
Similarity to other problems? Which kinds of problems have you solved before that were similar in some way to this?	
Other information? Which of your notes, texts, learning resources, websites etc. would be of most use?	

Creative problem-solving: organise your approach

2 Identify a strategy: weigh up alternative problem-solving strategies	
Strategy A (advantages)	*Strategy A* (disadvantages)
Strategy B (advantages)	*Strategy B* (disadvantages)
Strategy C (advantages)	*Strategy C* (disadvantages)

Decision made about which problem-solving strategy to take

Working through, checking and writing up *(Fill each box with a ✓ once the stage is completed.)*

3 ☐ I have worked through the problem systematically.

4 ☐ I have checked back through my solution, step by step, to check for errors and omissions and to see that it works overall.

5 ☐ I have written out the problem succinctly and accurately, demonstrating clearly how I arrived at the solution.

6 Evaluate your work *(See step 6, page 94 above.)*	

Chapter 4

☀ Reflective learning

As a student in Higher Education, you are responsible for your own progress – for your development as an autonomous learner. Although you will receive formal assessment (marks, grades and comments) from lecturers, it is important not to be dependent upon the assessment and views of other people. You benefit from being able to work out for yourself, through a process of analysis and reflection, what you do well, what you need to improve, and your priorities. You started work on this process in Chapter 2.

Developing the habit of reflection

Your performance as a student is likely to improve if you develop the habit of putting time aside to reflect on *how* you learn. You will find that you study more effectively if you consider, for example:

- changes in your motivation levels
- changes in your attitudes and ideas
- the appropriateness of your current study strategies to the tasks you are undertaking
- which skills you need for different kinds of assignment
- what is blocking your learning
- gaps in your knowledge or your skills.

Five methods of developing reflection

1 Keep a learning journal or blog (page 99). Use prompts such as the questions in this book to help structure your reflective thinking.
2 Use the self-evaluation questionnaires.
3 Keep an updated profile or portfolio (page 56).
4 Make constructive use of feedback from tutors (page 324).
5 Fill in progress sheets regularly (page 98).

Evaluating your own progress

Questionnaires and checklists

- Use these as starting points to focus your thinking about your learning.
- Select a few points from each questionnaire to consider in your journal.

Be fair to yourself

When you decide that you are 'good' or 'bad' at something, consider your *reasons* for thinking that. What criteria are you using to assess yourself? Work out what is involved in the task, breaking it into smaller tasks or sub-skills. Are you better at some parts than others? What makes some parts more difficult than others?

People may easily underestimate themselves when:

- they have been out of formal education for a few years
- they learn more about a subject (the more we know, the more we are aware of what we don't know, and that can be unsettling).

Monitor your performance

- Photocopy the questionnaires and fill them in again later in the term. Compare answers, looking for progress.
- Read through your journal regularly. Comment on your progress.

How well am I doing?

Course, unit or module:	Date:
Level:	Year of study:
1a Generally, how well am I doing in this unit?	**1b** On what am I basing this self-evaluation? (My marks? Feedback from tutors? Self-monitoring? Other ways?)
2a In this unit, I am best at: What makes me better at these aspects?	**2b** On what am I basing this self-evaluation?
3a To do better in this unit, I need to improve: What prevents me from doing as well at present?	**3b** How will I bring about this improvement? My timescale for this improvement is:
4a What have I already learnt, or improved, since starting this unit?	**4b** How do I know this? How do I measure or monitor what I have learnt? (How long it takes? My level of confidence? My understanding? My level of enjoyment?)

Chapter 4

☼Reflective learning journals

In a strong notebook, or using your computer or mobile device, start a reflective learning journal.

Start a reflective learning journal now!

Why?

- The act of writing things down helps you to clarify your thoughts and emotions, work out strategies, and focus on your development.
- A written record will help you see your progress and improvements: it can be easy to lose sight of this otherwise.

Who is it for?

For yourself – to help you focus on your own performance.

What do you write?

Anything which helps *you* to reflect on:

- your feelings about the course, the lecturers, other students, your progress
- things you find difficult: challenges
- changes in your attitude or motivation
- how you tackle tasks – your strategies
- things you find out about yourself
- thoughts about how you learn best
- ideas that arise from your studies
- how different areas of study link up
- how your studies relate to real life.

Use the *How well am I doing?* sheet (page 98) to prompt ideas. Identify the criteria you are using to evaluate yourself.

'… I can't believe the difference between my first essay (very bad!!!) and this one. Keeping an ideas book has helped.'

'I used to read the hardest books first – to be a 'real' student. Now I look for a simple overview first.'

'Why am I always late? I think it's because I always try to get somewhere on time, whereas I should think about getting there 5 minutes early – then I might be on time!'

Other uses of reflective learning journals

As a basis for discussion

It can be helpful to discuss your journal or blog entries with other students on your course. How do their experiences of the course compare with your own? Do they use strategies which you could adopt too?

Preparing for tutorials

Go through the journal and make a list of issues that you want to discuss in your next tutorial. Put these in order of priority. If you have any problems, think through some possible options, so that the discussion with your tutor will be more focused.

Risky writing

Keeping a private journal helps to develop your writing. You can experiment with different styles if you want to. You can take risks. The journal is for *your* benefit – and for your eyes only. This may make a welcome change from writing to the demands of your course or tutors!

Reflection

This sign is used in the guide at points where it may be useful to stop, think, and write in your journal.

Reflection: Start now

How do you feel about starting your course? What challenges do you anticipate? How can you use your experiences to help you to meet these challenges? See Chapter 2.

Chapter 4

Virtue versus effectiveness

Studying hard is not the same as working efficiently or effectively. Consider the table below, which shows the study strategies of one student, Leila. Leila feels she should get good marks because she works very hard. She studies 50 hours a week, and gets all her work done by the deadlines.

 Reflection: Ineffective strategies

Can you see why Leila's marks are getting worse, even though she is working harder? Note your thoughts in your journal.

Leila's study strategies	
Leila feels virtuous because …	**… Yet her study strategy is weak because …**
1 Leila reads every book on the reading list, and searches the internet constantly.	• The same information is repeated in several books. She does not select from one book to another.
2 She reads every book from cover to cover.	• Not all of the book is equally relevant. She does not use smart reading techniques (see pages 165–7).
3 She writes very detailed notes.	• She has more information than she needs. • Her notes are repetitive and take a long time to read. • She doesn't think much about what she is noting down. • It takes her a long time to find things in her notes. • She has to rewrite her notes to revise from them. • She copies out large sections – and then copies these into her own work – which loses her marks.
4 She writes her notes neatly, and in full sentences.	• Using abbreviations would save time. • As long as she can read her notes and find information easily, they do not need to be neat.
5 She works long hours with few breaks.	• She gets tired and cannot think as clearly. • She gets bored and loses interest easily. • Her mind wanders and she forgets what she has read. • Sometimes she takes notes without realising she has done so – with no idea what they say.
6 She locks herself away to work solidly.	• She misses out on other people's opinions, suggestions and perspectives.
7 She never asks for help or attends support workshops.	• She would benefit from guidance on how to use her study time, and the experience of being a student, more effectively.

Activity — Virtuous or effective

Do you think the following examples are 'virtuous' or 'effective' ways of studying – or neither?

In the boxes below, write:
V for Virtuous   **E** for Effective   **N** for Neither

1 ☐ Linking new information to what you already know or have studied.

2 ☐ Learning difficult information 'off by heart'.

3 ☐ Copying chunks from textbooks – because the writer says it better than you could.

4 ☐ Questioning whether what you have heard is really true or representative.

5 ☐ Writing fast so that you can take down almost everything the lecturer says.

6 ☐ Reading your essays and other writing slowly and out loud before you hand it in.

7 ☐ Studying when you are too tired to concentrate.

8 ☐ Changing to a new topic or type of study activity if you find that your mind is wandering to other matters.

9 ☐ Asking for help as soon as you find something difficult.

10 ☐ Relating your studies to real life.

Answers are given on page 407.

Reflection: Effective strategies

- Jot down any other examples of ineffective study that you have noticed either in yourself or others.
- What strategies would be more effective in these examples?

Unhelpful thinking

Do you:

- feel guilty if you are not working?
- feel you are cheating if you don't read a book from cover to cover?
- worry if you cannot remember every detail of what you have learnt?
- worry that other people have taken far more notes than you?

Instead, work out a strategy for learning in the most effective way. See below and page 102.

Start tasks early …

- You only need an available computer or a piece of paper and a pencil to get started. Don't wait until you have all your books, or tidied your desk (excuses to put off getting started).
- If you don't feel like studying, give yourself permission to study for only ten minutes. Quickly jot down questions to focus your ideas; write a list of things you need to do, etc. Attend to the 'excuses' afterwards – if you still want to. You will probably find you are 'hooked' into the study and want to keep going.
- Get your mind working on a problem as soon as you can. It will continue working on it even when you move on to something else. This is why it pays to start looking at new assignments as soon as you receive them.

Chapter 4

☀️Effective study checklist

Check your own effectiveness as a student. For the following items, indicate (✓) all that apply to you already. Follow up on areas for improvement using the relevant chapter or pages.

1 ☐ I take the initiative

As we saw in Chapter 1, in Higher Education, success lies mainly in your own hands. It is up to you to be proactive on your own behalf.

2 ☐ I find out the 'rules of the game'

As with many pursuits, success is easier if you understand the 'rules'. Find out such things as:

- How Higher Education works. (See Chapter 1.)
- Academic conventions. (See Chapters 1 and 12.)
- Expectations in your subject. (See page 314.)

3 ☐ I make excellent use of my time

This is an essential component of effective study. (See chapter 5.)

4 ☐ I am highly organised

Good organisation of your life, study space, materials, notes, online time and searches saves time and effort. (See pages 103–4, 134–5 and 182–4.)

5 ☐ I use sensible short-cuts

It makes sense to use efficient study methods, freeing up time and mental effort for where you need it most. (See page 100, *Virtue versus effectiveness*, and Chapter 5.)

6 ☐ I personalise study

At this level, you have far more opportunity to adapt your study methods to suit your preferences. (See pages 76–83.)

7 ☐ I maintain high motivation

Find ways of keeping in touch with your reasons for study. Look for ways of staying engaged and interested.

(See pages 111–18.)

8 ☐ I use active strategies

These can help maintain your attention and focus. (See pages 108–10.)

9 ☐ I reflect on my own performance

Effective study means being able to recognise when your work is good and how to make it better – rather than relying on grades or feedback from others. (See pages 97–8.)

10 ☐ I look for ways to 'up my game'

Each year of full-time study is referred to as a 'level'. At each level, there isn't simply a change in the material covered, there is also an increase in difficulty and complexity. Consequently, your study skills, strategies and coping mechanisms need to improve year on year. To some extent, this happens naturally, but you can benefit from putting time aside each year to reflect on what is needed.

Reflection: Higher expectations

- In what ways will the demands of your programme require you to refine your skills or change your approach in order to 'up your game' in the year ahead?
- What will you do differently in order to gain the marks that you want?

Chapter 4

Effective organisation: space and resources

Dedicated study space

Create a separate space for study where you can leave things and come back to them. If you don't have access to a desk or table, use a shelf or cupboard to keep all your study things together.

Light and comfort

It is good to work near a window so that you have adequate light. Sitting with the window behind or to one side will cut down on distractions. A reading lamp and natural daylight bulbs are a good investment if you study in the evening.

Make the study area a pleasant one to come back to, preferably with a comfortable chair, so that it encourages you to return to study. As far as possible, keep surfaces clear and papers organised. This not only makes it easier to find things, but is relaxing for study.

Good broadband or wireless connection

If you need to go online to access material or link in with tutors, make sure that you have a strong and reliable connection before you start to study.

Study resources

- A table clear of clutter
- An adjustable, stable chair for working
- A computer, laptop or tablet
- Memory sticks
- Flexible lighting
- A diary or planner – ideally with 'a week to view'
- Essential books (make sure you know which of the books on your reading list you are expected to buy)
- A4 lined, punched paper
- An A4 ringbinder for each subject – use different colours
- Lots of coloured file dividers
- A smaller folder to carry your day's work. Use file dividers to separate the contents by subject
- An attractive notebook for your reflective journal
- A dictionary and a thesaurus
- A calculator
- Large sheets of paper or wallpaper (or backs of posters) for wallcharts
- Lots of coloured pencils, felt-tips, pens and highlighters, plus a ruler, correction fluid, glue, etc.

Optional items

- MP3 or MP4 player
- Digital recorder
- Flip camera

Chapter 4

Organisational skills on your computer or mobile device

The most challenging aspects of working electronically are:

- keeping track of where information is filed
- losing information, if something goes wrong.

The following suggestions can help to organise your work and save time in the long term.

1 Name new files when you create them

Make sure you do name each file and folder.

Choose filenames carefully

Use names that will help you recall the contents.

Name and date it in the footer

As soon as you name a file, type this in the running text at the foot of each page, so that it will appear on the document when you print it. This helps you to find it again when needed.

2 Keep file sizes manageable

Avoid creating large files, as these slow you down.

3 Use a different file for each draft

Add a number or letter to indicate each new draft: e.g. 'piaget1a' and 'piaget1b.doc'.

4 Save your work

If there is a computer glitch or loss of power, you could lose all work completed since the last time you saved it. This can be very frustrating. To protect your work, save it frequently or set the computer to save files automatically every few minutes. Copy files to a memory stick, save to cloud storage or email to yourself.

5 Organise your electronic storage

Copy important files twice. Keep your memory sticks where you can find them easily. Accessorise or paint them so you can identify them easily.

6 Group your files

Most computers have some way of grouping files or folders. Use this to keep files relating to a particular subject together so you can find them again at speed.

7 Keep a list of filenames

Opening files repeatedly to check what they contain wastes time. Print out a list of the files contained on your memory sticks and store this with them. Add brief details of file contents, especially if you are limited to a short filename which cannot tell you very much about the file.

8 Save files online

You can store files online such as through Google Docs and Dropbox. Files saved online can be accessed from any computer or mobile device, provided you have a wifi connection. This has many advantages such as saving time retrieving material, not having to copy material across from one device to another or save everything to sticks.

9 Be aware of compatibility issues

Make sure your own software is compatible with that of your institution. Install antivirus software and update regularly. Many antivirus programs update automatically whenever you are online.

10 Leave time for hitches

Leave time for hitches such as not being able to open large files or documents in certain formats. Tutors expect you to plan for such hitches and do not usually accept them as reasons for late work.

11 Use opportunities selectively

The opportunities offered through electronic media are vast. On the internet, for example, there are fascinating forums, chat groups, and distribution lists. Choose carefully what is really valuable for you, so that such facilities don't eat into your time. Select just a few such groups at any one time.

12 Use the online tools available

There are many study apps and tools available that help with study tasks such as searching for, and referencing, information. See page 400.

Combining work and study effectively

Students may combine work and study in various ways and circumstances, such as:

- part-time students in employment
- students whose work is home-based, including family and care commitments
- full-time students who need to work for money or help out with a family business
- students whose programmes or options include work placements
- students on programmes that are primarily work-based, such as for medicine-related professions and Foundation Degrees.

Benefits

Which of the following potential benefits of combining work and study are relevant to you?

- ☐ A broader range of experience and skills.
- ☐ Greater confidence in adult work settings.
- ☐ Increased maturity and self-reliance.
- ☐ Professional and/or business awareness.
- ☐ Understanding how academic theory relates to professional practice.
- ☐ Income from work.
- ☐ Networks and work contacts.

Reflection: Working whilst studying

- What other benefits would work/study combinations bring for you?
- What arrangements would you need to make?

Before you start

If you want to combine study and employment, it is worth investigating, early on, potential obstacles and ways of managing these. For example:

- ☐ Check that you can attend as required.
- ☐ Find out if there are tutorials, trips and other non-timetabled events you need to attend.
- ☐ Plan out typical weeks to see whether your proposals are manageable.
- ☐ Check how your timetable might change from one term or year to the next.
- ☐ Sort out your finances – study costs, loans and financial support can vary depending on what you earn and your mode of study.

Look for creative and efficient work/study synergies

If you are already in employment and have sympathetic employers, talk to them about how best to manage your work alongside study:

- Are there ways your study could be counted as professional development as part of a work-related appraisal scheme?
- Can you undertake relevant work-based projects that could count towards your qualification?
- Would your employer be willing to provide study leave, quiet space and time to study at work, or support towards costs?
- Some jobs lend themselves less easily to work–study combinations than others, but appropriate projects may still be possible.

Some jobs lend themselves more easily to work/study combinations ...

Chapter 4

Effective management of work-based projects

Most academic aspects of work-based projects use skills that are outlined elsewhere in this book. Such projects have specific logistical issues you must also learn to manage. Some key issues are identified on this page and the next.

Do you need your employer's agreement?

Before undertaking a work-related project, check whether you need your employer's agreement. For assignments that are more theoretical in content, or that call upon informal observations and your own experiences, you will often not need permission. On the other hand, you *will* need your employer's permission, for example:

- if you would be using work time or your employer's resources in carrying out an assignment
- if you would be making use of certain types of information acquired in the workplace (such as confidential or commercially sensitive information)
- if the nature of your assignment is such that you might lose the trust of your employer or your colleagues if they were unaware of it in advance
- if you are likely to produce work that could be published or stored, and in which your employer or clients might be identifiable.

Before giving you permission to carry out a work-based project, your employer may wish to impose conditions: if so, put these in writing so that you are both clear about what has been agreed.

Organise yourself for the project

- Check legal 'data protection' requirements and consider how you will meet these.
- Gain permission for use of workplace data and information.
- If you are using observations, photographs, client material, or the like, obtain written agreements from those concerned.
- Schedule interviews and observations early on to be sure that colleagues will be available when needed.
- Find out whether you yourself need to undergo any formal checks, such as clearance from the Disclosure and Barring Service (formerly the CRB) if children are involved (or the equivalent, depending on which country you are studying or working in). Arrange such checks well in advance.

Workplace mentors

Students generally find it very helpful if they have a mentor to provide support. Ideally, this will be someone in the workplace who:

- knows the pressures the student might be under
- can help to negotiate access to data, relevant work tasks, study time or other resources
- can be a sounding board for ideas about what is feasible in the workplace
- can provide current professional and practical perspectives on issues.

Effective use of workplace mentors

- Build your relationship with your mentor. Show your appreciation for her or his time.
- Clarify what you need from your mentor, and when. Check before you start that he or she is able to provide these.
- To help your mentor support you as effectively as possible, identify what she or he will need from you for meetings, observations and at other times, and when this is needed.
- Arrange dates and outline agendas in advance for a series of meetings.
- Arrive prepared for each session. Ensure that you have completed whatever is asked of you.

Project-based skills: related sections

- *Working with others: collaborative study.* Chapter 10.
- *Core research skills.* Chapter 6.
- *Research projects, case studies and dissertations.* Chapter 13.

Chapter 4

Effective management of study leave

Employers may offer study-leave time at work or off-site. If managed well, this is a valuable resource.

Student comments

> Half a day a week study leave made all the difference to me. It meant I could get onto campus to sort out administrative bits and pieces, meet tutors and so on, that would have been hard to do outside college hours.

> For me, an afternoon a week was OK. I went to the library to read things that weren't online.

> I didn't get much out of study leave. By the time I did the shopping and got home, the day was almost over and I had to start the family's dinner.

> I tended to use the time to catch up on other things – not much on study.

> I meant to take the half day but something always came up at work so it didn't happen.

> I preferred taking a whole study day once a fortnight rather than a half day each week.

Reflection: Study leave

- What do the experiences of these students suggest to you about how best to approach and plan any time you have as study leave?
- What kinds of circumstances might prevent you from making best use of study leave time and what would you do to manage these?

Half-day or full-day study release?

Half-day study leave can be the more difficult to manage effectively. It can mean time is wasted in travel, and it provides less opportunity for consolidated study. It tends to suit people who:

- prefer short bouts of academic study
- like to study 'little and often'
- have little travel to undertake
- manage study time well.

Reflection: Making best use of time

If you prefer more concentrated bursts of study time, see whether you can consolidate weekly study leave into longer, less frequent periods of study leave.

Making effective use of study leave

- Plan ahead so that you make the most of the time available. For example, identify tasks that could be completed in the study-leave time for that week, so that you gain a sense of achievement at the end of the study period.
- Check whether there is a quiet room at work that could be used for study, to save travel time.
- If you have negotiated study time in the workplace, see whether you can connect to appropriate online study resources from there. If not, would you study more effectively on campus?
- Plan use of your half-day study within the context of your overall working week. It may be more useful to rationalise certain activities at particular times. The specific time given for study leave might be best used for other activity if, for example, that cuts down on your overall travel time.
- If you find it better to use study leave for non-study purposes, ensure that you do put aside equivalent study time elsewhere in your schedule.

Chapter 4

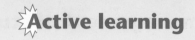# Active learning

Why is it important to develop the habit of active learning techniques?

1   Look at the illustrations on page 109.
2   Consider the characteristics of both passive and active learning, summarised in the chart below.

From these, you should be able to see for yourself why active learning methods make success more likely.

Reflection: Active or passive?

What initial reflections and ideas do you have about whether your study habits are passive or active?

Characteristics of passive learning	Characteristics of active learning
1 You wait for directions and information to be fed to you.	1 You look for ways of being more involved in what you are learning.
2 Information is delivered to you – you just follow what is said or written, and do as you are told.	2 You are engaged in the whole learning process (and in a position to see why information has been selected).
3 Different pieces of information are treated as separate units.	3 You look for links between different things that you discover.
4 You repeat information without understanding it.	4 You make a conscious effort to make sense of, and find meaning in, what you learn. Understanding is usually deeper.
5 You don't reflect upon what you have learnt.	5 You are involved in reflection and self-evaluation.
6 You may become bored and tired easily.	6 Your attention span is longer because your mind is more fully engaged.
7 You use surface processing (see page 70), in which case you are less likely to understand or remember.	7 Long-term memory is assisted. If you understand what you learn, and keep relating what you learn to what you already know, you are more likely to remember what you have learnt.
8 You are less likely to be able to use what you learn.	8 Linking information helps you to see how you can apply it to different situations.
9 What you study may seem irrelevant.	9 Learning is personalised and interesting.
10 You expect others to prompt you or to remind you of steps, stages and deadlines, so you often feel uncertain about what to do next.	10 You take charge of your learning and manage it like a project, so you feel confident that you know what to do, when, and why.

Chapter 4

Emphasis on action!

Reflection: Active learning strategies

Consider the illustration below and the ideas on page 110. Jot down any ideas you have about making yourself a more active learner.

(A) Inactive learning strategies

A1

A2

A3

A4

A5

(B) Active learning strategies

B1 Prepare for lectures

B2 Set yourself questions

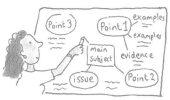

B3 Rework your notes

B4 Link ideas and information

B6 Mull things over

B7 Organise information

B8 Draft and redraft work

B9 Evaluate your own work

B5 Discuss with others

B10 Use feedback constructively

Chapter 4

Active learning strategies

1 Put a tick by any of these active learning strategies you could try.
2 Select *two* to try this week.
3 Select *two more* to try later this month.

☐ Summarise a passage in 8–12 words. This makes you think about what you have read.

☐ Make spider diagrams – or other patterned notes. (See page 173.)

☐ Think of 3–5 real-life examples of what you have learned. This helps you to apply what you learn.

☐ Work out which is the best example, and why. This will help you to prioritise and evaluate.

☐ List 50 mini-questions about one aspect of the subject ('what, why, who, where, when, how did *x* happen?) This helps you to explore the subject.

☐ Answer your own mini-questions. This helps you to research in an organised and focused way.

☐ Draw a diagram or a cartoon to illustrate a theory or concept.

☐ Write action plans – of things to do today, or this week, or this term.

☐ 'Teach' what you have learned to a real or an imaginary person. Imagine you are giving a lecture or instructions.

☐ Keep a reflective study journal.

☐ Sum up the three most important points of a lecture. Which is the *one* most important point? This helps you to evaluate and select salient points.

☐ With other students, start a wiki.

☐ Make a wallchart or a large plan, linking all you have learned about an aspect of your studies.

☐ On your wallchart, in a different coloured ink, link information from another area of your studies.

☐ Which is the one best book for the subject you are studying now?

☐ Which section of the book you are reading is the most interesting or useful?

☐ Pretend you disagree with everything you are reading – how would you argue your case? What examples and evidence would you use?

☐ How does what you have learned link with your work or your everyday life?

☐ Invent titles for essays or reports. Give yourself 5 minutes to write a quick outline plan for one of these.

☐ List all the key points for one aspect of study.

☐ Draw a simple picture or symbol to remind you of each aspect.

☐ Discuss your ideas – or your difficulties – with other people.

☐ Contribute to your course chat room, or start one.

☐ Write key points on index cards or sticky labels. Juggle these around to see how many ways you could organise the same information.

Motivation

Your level of motivation will affect your success. No matter how much you love your subject or want to gain a good degree, there may be times when you don't feel like studying or wonder whether you would be better off doing something else. You need strong motivation to keep yourself going at such times.

What affects motivation?

Motivation can be affected by all kinds of things, from changing your mind about the career you want and the qualifications you need, through to your friends leaving the course. Most students experience periods of lower motivation at times, though they usually work through these.

Key influences on motivation

Motivation to study is affected by such things as:

- clarity of purpose
- being on the right course
- managing the 'boring bits'
- confidence of the outcome
- using time well.

Reasons for weak motivation

- loss of direction
- boredom, resulting from poor study strategies
- too much or too little challenge
- crises of confidence.

Signs of weak motivation

- finding excuses not to study
- not being able to settle down to study
- losing interest in the subject
- becoming easily distracted
- giving up quickly.

How strong is your motivation? Make a frank evaluation of your own motivation. Rating: 1 = low; 5 = high.	Rating
1 I have a strong sense of purpose	1 2 3 4 5
2 I know my reasons for study	1 2 3 4 5
3 I am clear how my study will benefit my life	1 2 3 4 5
4 I set myself clear targets for completing tasks	1 2 3 4 5
5 I am driven to achieve well	1 2 3 4 5
6 I can get going quickly when I sit down to study	1 2 3 4 5
7 I have strategies for getting myself down to work	1 2 3 4 5
8 I stay focused once I sit down to study	1 2 3 4 5
9 I always complete work by the deadline	1 2 3 4 5
10 I create the time I need to complete tasks well	1 2 3 4 5
11 I set personal challenges that inspire me	1 2 3 4 5
12 I take pleasure in achieving milestones/goals	1 2 3 4 5
13 I study well even when I don't feel like it	1 2 3 4 5
14 I keep going even when things get tough	1 2 3 4 5
15 I give thought to how to keep myself inspired	1 2 3 4 5
16 I find ways of making study sessions enjoyable	1 2 3 4 5
17 I make the subjects I study interesting to me	1 2 3 4 5
18 I avoid actions that might sabotage my study	1 2 3 4 5
19 I use criticism as a spur to doing better	1 2 3 4 5
20 I manage anxieties and crises of confidence	1 2 3 4 5
Total score out of 100	

What do you think that your overall score and your rating of individual items tell you about your motivation?

Keeping motivated

Below are some strategies that can help to raise and then maintain your motivation. Identify ✓ which ones would work best for you.

☐ **Clarity of purpose**
Be clear about your reasons for studying this course, and how you will benefit. If you are excited about your course now, you may not feel this is necessary. However, it is well worth spending time doing this.

☐ **What I want from my study**
Use the reflective self-evaluation *What I want from my study* on page 114 to focus your thinking.

☐ **'I am doing this because ...'**
Jot down your response to this prompt, drawing on your ratings for the self-evaluation above. List as many reasons as you can. Underline those that are most important to you.

☐ **Link to longer-term goals**
Make a list of all the ways, directly and indirectly, that your studies will be of benefit to your life, personal and professional, over the longer term. Use your reflective journal to think this through.

☐ **Motivational chart: sticking with it**
Using your responses to the activities above and to that on page 33 in Chapter 1, write out your reasons for sticking with your studies. Do this in a way that will keep you inspired. Add photos, newspaper clippings or other material that reinforces your sense of purpose. Update this as relevant.

☐ **Make a screensaver of your motivational chart**, so that you are continually inspired.

☐ **Make good choices**
- Find out as much as you can about your course and options, so that these support your overall objectives.
- Be active in finding points of interest and relevance.
- If necessary, speak to financial and careers advisers about either (a) changing course, or (b) how your current course can help meet your objectives.

☐ **Seeing results: short-term goals**
The end of your course may seem a long way off. It is natural to want to see results. You can gain a better sense of this by setting short-term goals, milestones, targets or challenges that are:

- meaningful to you, and
- can be achieved in small steps in the near future.

See *Managing the challenge*, page 117.

☐ **Give yourself a precise focus**
If you are easily distracted from study, start each session by jotting down a quick list of the things to complete in that session. Check these off as you complete them.

Make Mum & Dad proud

I want a degree

Work overseas

RJP Ltd Grad Jobs

REWARD SYSTEM
study
1hr= 15mins surfing
4hrs = go for swim
8hrs = watch DVD

EMERGENCY MEASURES
RING JOHN TO TELL ME TO KEEP GOING

Develop a routine

If you find it difficult to put time aside for study, take a more structured approach. Write specific times for study into your diary, and keep these as appointments. Where possible, study at the same time and place each day. See Chapter 5 on time management.

Manage the boredom

- Clarify exactly why the task is relevant and what you will gain by completing it.
- Be active in searching for points of interest, either in the material or the way you design the study session for yourself.
- Use active learning strategies to break up time and focus the attention. See page 110.
- Set yourself short-term goals and mini-challenges. See *Managing the Challenge*, page 117.
- Manage your time effectively. See Chapter 5.

Awareness of positive triggers

Take note of the conditions that encourage you to get down to study, and then create these around you. So, if you work best with others, set up a study group. If you work best under pressure, set yourself demanding challenges to complete during a study session rather than leaving work to the last minute.

Awareness of negative triggers

- Become aware of the circumstances that demotivate you; plan how you will avoid these.
- Take note of the people around you who have a demotivating impact on you.
- Notice those aspects of your own thinking or behaviour that demotivate you. Devise a strategy for using your positive triggers instead.

Manage anxieties and confidence

Academic study is demanding, so you may feel anxious at times about what you can achieve.

- Take note of your feelings but don't dwell on them. Speak to a counsellor to gain a clearer picture of what you need to do to succeed.
- Set yourself short-term goals to provide focus and a sense of achievement.

Use a 'supporter'

Ask a friend for motivational support, such as:

- checking in with you occasionally to see that you are on task
- reminding you of your goals and ambitions
- reminding you of your strategies.

Meaningful reward

Give yourself treats for undertaking the aspects of study you find least motivating. Identify different kinds of reward, proportionate to how much time or emotional effort it takes to undertake the activity.

Have a 'Motivation plan'

Feelings of low motivation may just pass, but it is wise to plan for such occasions.

- Decide which strategies you are going to use for various kinds of circumstance.
- Write these out and put them where you can see them.
- Put the necessary resources into place (such as putting money aside for rewards, or time to spend with a mentor).
- In your diary or planner, write in times when you will check whether your plan is working. If it isn't, revise it so that it does.

Clarity of purpose: what I want from my study

What are the outcomes you wish to achieve from your studies. Draw a ring round the number that indicates how important each potential outcome is to you.

Outcome	Less important								Very important
Personal development									
To prove to myself I can do it	1	2	3	4	5	6	7	8	9
To feel better educated generally	1	2	3	4	5	6	7	8	9
To develop higher level skills	1	2	3	4	5	6	7	8	9
Course-related									
To find out more about a subject that interests me	1	2	3	4	5	6	7	8	9
To develop an area of personal expertise	1	2	3	4	5	6	7	8	9
To have the opportunity to study	1	2	3	4	5	6	7	8	9
To get a good grade	1	2	3	4	5	6	7	8	9
To gain the qualification	1	2	3	4	5	6	7	8	9
I just want to get through	1	2	3	4	5	6	7	8	9
Life and work-related									
To get my life out of a rut	1	2	3	4	5	6	7	8	9
To improve my career opportunities	1	2	3	4	5	6	7	8	9
To be better at my current job/employment	1	2	3	4	5	6	7	8	9
To improve my chance of promotion / higher salary	1	2	3	4	5	6	7	8	9
Other outcomes									
To show my family/friends that I can do it	1	2	3	4	5	6	7	8	9
To make up for missing out on education earlier	1	2	3	4	5	6	7	8	9
To be a role model for my children	1	2	3	4	5	6	7	8	9
Other reasons									

Reflection: Motivation for study

Select two outcomes you have decided are important to you. Write in more detail about what you aim to achieve.

Look back at this from time to time to see if your aims, and motivation for studying, are changing. Use pages 115–18 to explore your goals further.

Using your goals to guide your study strategy

Your reasons for studying and your goals can guide the way you proceed with your study, as in the following examples.

Goal A: to learn about the subject

If learning about the subject is the most important outcome for you, then reading around the subject and doing what interests you may be more important than following the curriculum.

Goal B: to have a good grade

If your chief priority is getting a good grade, then it is likely to be important that you 'play the game' and find out exactly what is required.

Goal C: just to get through

If you have many other demands on your time, or gaps in your education, you may have to limit yourself to covering essentials. What is important is that you know how to find and use information to get you through – you can fill gaps in your knowledge later in life.

Stating your goals

Goals are most motivating when stated in the present:

> I am able to achieve a 2.1!

It is also best to state them as positive objectives:

> I am able to gain a good job.

Negatively worded goals, such as 'A degree will help me to escape from my current employment', are less effective in providing motivation.

> **The effect of thinking negatively**
>
> Having a negative outcome is like going shopping with a list of what you are not going to buy.
>
> O'Connor and McDermott (1996)

Analyse goals in detail

The following questions are based on an approach known as Neuro-Linguistic Programming (NLP). For each goal, go through the following questions and the resource sheet on page 118.

Are your goals 'well-formed'?

- Are the goals clear and specific?
- Are they at all limiting?
- Do they help you?
- Are they realistic?
- Are they sufficiently motivating?
- Are the outcomes worth it?
- Are they really desirable?
- How will you know you have achieved the outcomes – what will be different?

What are the implications of having these goals?

- Will you need to put everything else on hold?
- Will you have to change your study options?
- Who else will be affected?
- Are there other implications?

What are the potential gains?

- Will you feel more in control of your life?
- Will you have more respect for yourself?
- Are there other potential gains?

What are the potential losses?

- Will you see less of family and friends?
- What sacrifices are involved?
- Are there other potential losses?

Visualise yourself in the future, having achieved your goals

- Where are you as a result of your achievement?
- Are there any good or bad consequences?
- What has changed for you?
- Are you as happy as you thought you would be?

Using your goals to guide your study strategy

What will you do to achieve your goals?

Visualise or consider exactly what you will do and when. For example, for an assignment, see the time laid out in your planner; watch yourself doing the required study. Ask yourself:

- Where am I?
- What am I writing on?
- What do I have available to drink or eat?

What obstacles might prevent you achieving your goals?

Look at problems in advance.

- What could stop you achieving your goals?
- Have you set yourself too much to do?
- Are there people who would suffer?
- Who might try to stop you?
- What other obstacles might there be?
- How will you overcome each of these obstacles?
- Visualise yourself overcoming obstacles in the same way you did above, in relation to achieving the outcomes.

Fine-tune your goals and objectives

Keep modifying your goals and objectives until these feel, sound and look right for you.

- Use the chart on page 118 to clarify and focus your thinking about each of your goals.
- Do you need to revise or reword your original goals so that they are more realistic and motivating?

Make a clear mental plan

Create in advance the mental plan for as much of an activity as you can. Your mind will now orientate you to achieve it.

Self-sabotage

It can sometimes be hard to accept that we may *achieve* our goals. Many people have set patterns that they use in their daily life to sabotage their own best-laid plans.

It is not clear exactly why this happens. Sometimes it is simply hard to accept that we might now be successful where once we struggled. If we do succeed, we may start to feel that we should have tried harder in the past. If we fail now, however, this will 'prove' that we were 'right all along' in believing that we could not do something. At other times, we may fear failure so much that we just want it to happen quickly so that it is over with: waiting to see whether we can succeed may be too difficult.

Kinds of self-sabotage

Students sabotage their studies in all kinds of ways. Examples include:

- not turning up to lectures
- leaving work until the last minute and then missing deadlines
- not turning up for exams because they feel they will fail them
- filling their time with any activity *except* study
- refusing to enter a library
- spending all their time in the bar.

There are many more to choose from!

- What kinds of self-sabotage are you most likely to engage in?
- What kinds of events are most likely to trigger you into self-sabotage?
- How could you recognise that you had started to sabotage your studies?
- Is there anybody whom you would trust to point this out to you?
- What would you do to turn this around?

Motivation: managing the challenge

Setting goals

These can give you a sense of momentum and early success.

Give yourself manageable short-term goals

Set yourself mini-goals as milestones, so that you have a sense of achievement. In time these add up to greater achievements.

- Break larger assignments, such as writing a report, into smaller tasks: 'Read course notes', 'Find resource materials', etc.
- Break each of *these tasks* into smaller ones: 'Make notes of pp. 20–40 *Media Now*.'
- Set a realistic time allowance for each mini-goal: 'Make notes on pages 31–70: 20 mins.'
- Give yourself a start time – and stick to it!
- Set a target end-time and work to that. The key aim isn't to keep to time but to *complete* the goal, so keep going until you do.

Effective mini-goals or milestones are:

- *integrated*: clearly linked to a larger plan, such as your essay, project, or your overall motivation for the course
- *manageable and realistic*: set yourself achievable goals
- *specific*: decide precisely what you are going to tackle
- *measurable*: such as a set number of pages to read, or a report section to write
- *flexible*: plan time in for emergencies; be ready to change things round if necessary.

Celebrate successes

Increase your chances of early success by setting targets and deadlines you know you can meet. When you achieve a target (such as two hours' reading), reward yourself (such as taking a half-hour's break). Give yourself bigger rewards for completing whole tasks, to encourage yourself next time.

> ### Mark success
>
> Note down your achievements and successes in your reflective journal. It is important to note what you do well, so that you can do it again! After a few months, look back on your early work. Give yourself credit for any progress you have made.

Aim for higher peaks

When you achieve one set of goals, set new ones, making these a little more challenging.

The peaks are calling me.

Victory!

Keep setting yourself new goals and challenges

Achieving goals

Goal *State this here with positive wording, in the present tense*	
Potential gains	
Potential losses	
How I'll recognise when the goal has been achieved	
Targets (short-term goals and milestones)	
Possible obstacles	
Steps to overcoming obstacles	
How I'll celebrate success	

The C·R·E·A·M strategy for learning © Stella Cottrell (2013) *The Study Skills Handbook*, 4th edition, Palgrave Macmillan

The C·R·E·A·M strategy

C·R·E·A·M strategy	How I will incorporate this strategy into my study
Giving more freedom to my imagination	
Finding ways to increase my enjoyment in study	
Personalising what I learn, and the way I study it	
Being flexible in study strategies and having plenty of variety	
Reflecting on my learning and evaluating my progress	
Organising time and space, and being in the right state of mind for study	
Seeing where I waste effort by being over-virtuous	
Linking learning in one subject to other subjects and to real-life issues	
Increasing my motivation	
Formulating clear outcomes and milestones	

Review

The C·R·E·A·M strategy is a general principle or 'meta-strategy' which you can apply to any area of life. It is applicable, for example, to graduate jobs: creativity, professional reflection, independence, self-reliance, self-motivation and evidence of personal effectiveness are valued and rewarded by employers.

This chapter encourages you to develop attitudes and approaches that make learning, simultaneously, more interesting as well as more efficient and effective. You are more likely to maintain the high level of application needed for success as a student if you are:

- *creative*, finding ways to make study enjoyable, varied, imaginative and dynamic

- *reflective*, pausing at frequent intervals to reflect on your performance, checking whether your studies are working out as you would wish, and adapting your study strategies accordingly

- *effective*, making good use of the time and effort you put into study, so that you see positive outcomes from these as well as being able to fit other things into your life

- *active*, designing personalised strategies in self-reliant, imaginative and energetic ways, rather than awaiting direction from others or attempting to absorb information in passive ways

- *motivated*, being clear about your purpose and goals, and organising your study in such a way that you gain a sense of progress and achievement.

This means planning not just *what* you study and when, but also *how* you will study.

Plan study sessions as you might other kinds of project or event. Start with the learning preferences that you identified in Chapter 3. Create the physical and mental space that enables you to learn at your best. Use initiative in thinking through how you will keep yourself on track, such as by building variety and points of interest into each study session. Use your time to best effect. Chapter 5 enables you to look at time management in more depth.

Chapter 5
Time management as a student

Learning outcomes

This chapter gives you opportunities to:

- understand the key importance of effective time management to successful study
- consider the time requirements of your own programme of study
- gain a clear sense of where you spend your time now and where you want to spend it in future
- apply time management strategies to help you make good use of time put aside for study and identify where you can save time
- organise your independent study in ways that make the best use of your time.

Introduction

As a student, only part of your week and year will be formally timetabled. You are responsible for organising most of your study time for yourself. This can be challenging. It is likely that you will:

- experience many demands on your time: from study, jobs, family, social life, sports, music, personal interests, shopping, eating, travel, moving across campus, and managing other basics of day-to-day living
- have to manage competing deadlines, with several assignments to turn around in quick succession or for the same hand-in date
- spend much of your time in independent study and online, both of which provide interesting but time-consuming diversions.

If you feel that your time is pressurised, or you suspect that you waste time that could be better spent on other things, then it is worth developing your time-awareness and time management skills.

This chapter provides strategies, approaches and tools to help you to:

- evaluate how you use your time currently
- decide how you want to use it
- organise your time so that you feel that you are in control
- save time for the things you really want to do.

Oh my days! I thought the ark was leaving next week.

How well do I manage my time now?

For each of the items below, circle the response which best fits you. Then follow up the 'Next step' to check for strategies that could help you fine-tune any areas in which you want to improve.

Item	Do I ...	Response			Next step See page(s)
1	have a good sense of why time management is important for students?	Yes	No	Don't know	123–4; 127
2	usually *know* where I should be and at what time?	Yes	No	Don't know	136–7
3	usually *turn up on time* to where I need to be?	Yes	No	Don't know	136–7
4	keep good track of all the things I need to do?	Yes	No	Don't know	128; 136; 138
5	have an accurate sense of where my time goes?	Yes	No	Don't know	129; 131–2; 149
6	use breaks and blocks of study creatively, to support effective study?	Yes	No	Don't know	140; 141; 147
7	know how many study hours are expected for my course?	Yes	No	Don't know	128
8	know how many hours I am expected to spend across the year in different kinds of study?	Yes	No	Don't know	127
9	prioritise effectively the things I most need to do?	Yes	No	Don't know	134–7
10	use a planner or diary effectively?	Yes	No	Don't know	134; 136–7; 139
11	know when all assignment deadlines and/or exams fall?	Yes	No	Don't know	139
12	map out in my planner how I will organise my work so as to meet all deadlines?	Yes	No	Don't know	136–7
13	use my time online effectively?	Yes	No	Don't know	104; 142; 146
14	know how to manage distractions?	Yes	No	Don't know	140; 142; 146–7
15	use time management strategies effectively?	Yes	No	Don't know	125–6; 141; 143; 145; 148–9
16	have time for myself and to relax?	Yes	No	Don't know	133

Reflection: Evaluating my own time management skills

- What do your answers to these questions suggest about how well you manage your time now?
- Do you need to change any of your attitudes to time in order to manage your studies well?

Why time management matters to students

Time management = study success

Your success as a student will be strongly affected by the combination of two time-related factors:

- **How much** time you spend in study
- **How well** you use that time.

The more time you put into the various tasks of reading and thinking about your subject, preparing for exams or fine-tuning your assignments, the more likely it is that you will do well.

If you both spend more time in study AND manage that time effectively, you are much more likely to achieve well and have a great time as a student.

You feel more confident that you are in charge and can cope – and that you don't forget or miss out on things that are important.

You make sure you have time to do the basics, such as eating and sleeping properly and making friends.

You learn to juggle the various demands of study, social life, employment, family, and personal interests and commitments.

You learn where you can take short cuts that save you time.

Time = choice

If you use time effectively, this gives you choice in how you spend the time saved, such as in ...

- pursuing some topics in more depth, so that you are more expert in these and so that your work stands out
- reinforcing what you have learnt, so that it makes more sense to you
- preparing for exams and assignments so as to achieve better grades
- being with your family
- enjoying your social life.

What students say

Emails are the worst. You can kid yourself that they are really urgent. You need to make yourself ignore the flashing signal that says there is a new email in the box.

I am very selective about which search engines I use – there isn't much point using lots of search tools when a really good one gives you as much as you are likely to need.

I just don't waste time reading material on sites where I can't validate the source or the reliability of the information.

My advice to other students would be 'Don't have your treats before you get down to work. Do the study first or else it's much harder to make yourself do it! '

Know your weak points and don't pretend they don't matter! Mine is Twitter. I want to tweet all the time and I'm useless at doing bits of study between tweets so basically it is no tweeting for me when I am studying. It's just easier. I know I can send some smug tweets at the end of the day about how much work I have done!

Sorting out how you use time – that is the one big thing to get right about study – especially if you go online a lot. In my first year, it just disappeared before I knew it and everything was rushed and my marks were OK but not great. This year, I am the other extreme. I am constantly thinking about how I am using the time I have.

I thought time management was just a catchphrase, not something I should actually think about. I had no idea how much time I wasted until I actually started to take note of it. It made me realise all the things I could do if I was more disciplined in how I use time – so now I am!

The thing about studying so much on your own is that you realise how you rely on other people, teachers or just others working around you, to help stay concentrated yourself. When it is just you and the computer, you drift off more easily, so you need to give yourself ways of staying focused. I always start out by making a list of things I have to do – there's always more to add than I imagine, and that usually shocks me into getting down to it.

When you are researching online there is always the temptation to look up just one more thing or to see what one more search engine turns up. You have to know when enough is enough.

Reflection: Learning from others

Are any of these students' experiences similar to your own? What could you learn from their experiences and strategies?

I make myself study for 45 minutes and then I let myself 'play' – play is looking at football scores, music videos, emails, games, anything I want. I need constant reward, so that is how I do it.

10 steps to effective time management

10 steps to good time management

1. **Be systematic** in your time management
2. **Find out** your time requirements
3. **Clarify** how you use your time currently
4. **Decide** how you want to spend your time
5. **Prioritise** what is most important
6. **Plan** what you will do when
7. **Do it**, keeping to your plan
8. **Apply time management techniques**
9. **Manage distractions** and procrastination
10. **Monitor** Keep checking it is all working

1 Be systematic …

- in thinking about time management
- in developing an understanding of how you use your time
- in working out how best to manage your time to achieve your priorities
- in planning your time.

How and when am I going to handle time management?

2 Find out your time requirements

- Find out the pattern of study required for your programme – and how much time you will need to spend in independent study. See page 127.

How much time am I expected to spend on study as a minimum? How long does it take me to travel from A to B? How many hours do I need to work a week?

3 Clarify how you use your time now

Be aware of how much time it takes you, personally, to do things. Use or adapt the resources on page 149 to check:
- where you *think* your time goes
- where it *actually* goes.

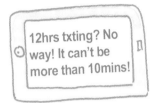

12hrs txting? No way! It can't be more than 10mins!

4 Decide how you want to use your time

- Use the charts on pages 128–30 to work out how you will spend your study time.
- Use the time circles on pages 131–3 to decide how much time you want to give to different activities. Compare this with the way you actually spend your time.

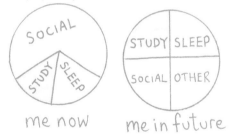

me now   me in future

5 Prioritise

You may find it hard to fit in everything you would like to do and some things will be more urgent than others. Identify your priorities and set a time by when these must be completed (pages 134–5).

Which is more important for me to do first? Buy socks or hand in these equations?

6 Plan

Be very specific and comprehensive in your time-planning.

- Keep a detailed diary/planner (see pages 136–7).
- Work backwards from deadlines such as assignment hand-in dates (see page 139).

7 Do it

- Put your plan where you will be reminded of it easily.
- Implement your plan to schedule.
- Work out what might sabotage your plans.

8 Apply time management techniques

Experiment with ways of saving and managing time, so that you find out what works for you and have more time for things you really want to do.

Essay done! Time for a nice lie in!

9 Manage distractions and procrastination

Build your understanding of when and how you become distracted from using time effectively, despite your best intentions.
Plan strategies to manage this. (see pages 146–7).

Yes – I will manage procrastination and distraction but ... um ... later.

10 Monitor

Check that you are sticking to your plan. If not,

- either update your planning to make it more realistic, OR
- work out what you need to do to stay on target.

It's taking all my time to manage my time management.

Working through the 10 steps to effective time management

The following pages provide strategies and resources for each of these ten steps.

- Browse through these resources.
- Work through the 10 steps, focusing especially on those which will most improve your own time management.

How much time should I study?

How many hours must I study?

Hours per year

Each year of successful full-time study on a degree programme is assumed to be the equivalent of 1200 hours. For work-based courses, those hours may include clinical practice or workplace activity.

Hours per week

The number of hours of study per week will vary depending on how many weeks off you take.

- 1200 hours = 23 hours a week for 52 weeks.
- 1200 hours = 27 hours a weeks for 45 weeks, if you take 7 weeks of breaks.
- You could distribute your time in different patterns for term-time and holidays.

Nominal hours versus actual hours

The figures above are a nominal requirement – that is, a general assumption of how long it takes to cover the work for that level of study. In practice, the time required varies from student to student, depending on such factors as:

- how much additional work they undertake out of interest or to gain higher marks
- how quickly they get through the work
- the amount of care they take in fine-tuning their work
- whether they find study hard or easy
- the demands of work-based practice.

Part time study

The number of hours depends on the proportion of the qualification you study each year.
If you study the equivalent of 50% of a full-time degree, that would amount to around 600 hours a year or an average of 12 hours a week.
If you study 80%, that would mean around 960 hours a year or an average of 18 hours a week.

How many hours for your programme?

Total study hours expected per year   [   ]
Average hours per week   [   ]
Average hours per week during breaks   [   ]

How much compulsory attendance?

Approx hours required on campus   [   ] hrs
Hours of compulsory attendance   [   ] hrs
Approx number of hours expected
for independent study (including
online study)   [   ] hrs

Where study time is spent

In practice, 1200 hours can mean very different things depending on your programme.

I spend 20 hours a week in laboratories and the rest studying online.

I spend 4 days a week at work – and it counts towards my degree. I have classes two evenings a week.

I spend 6 hours a week in lectures, seminars and tutorials, and the rest of the time in the library or online.

All of my programme is provided online.

How are you expected to spend those hours?

Within the overall number of study hours, there will be broad expectations of how those hours will break down into different kinds of study. These may be detailed in your course handbook.

A blank chart is provided below so that you can map out roughly how much time you are expected to spend on different kinds of activity.

Expected weekly study requirements

Using your course materials to guide your estimates, shade in the time you are expected to spend in each kind of activity each week. The pattern may differ across the year, so copy this sheet for re-use. Then go to page 129 to compare these expectations with how you actually spend your study time.

Activity/Time in hours	1	2	3	4	5	6	7	8	9	10	11	12	13	14	15	16+
Lectures																
Seminars																
Tutorials																
Practical studio/field/clinical/lab/work-based																
Face-to-face study groups																
Other classes or workshops																
Independent reading/thinking																
Organising and planning																
Using online course materials																
Online reading/research																
Online directed study activities																
Online tutor contact																
Online study group(s)																
Writing a blog and/or reflective journal																
Writing up and fine-tuning assignments																
Other activity:																
Other activity:																

Current use of study time

PLANNING TOOL

Copy this sheet for re-use. Over a period of 1–3 weeks, use these copies to shade in how much time you actually spend on each type of activity. Compare this with the programme requirements (see page 128).

Activity/Time in hours	1	2	3	4	5	6	7	8	9	10	11	12	13	14	15	16+
Lectures																
Seminars																
Tutorials																
Practical studio/ field/clinical/lab/ work-based																
Face-to-face study groups																
Other classes or workshops																
Independent reading/thinking																
Organising and planning																
Using online course materials																
Online reading/ research																
Online directed study activities																
Online tutor contact																
Online study group(s)																
Writing a blog and/or reflective journal																
Writing up and fine-tuning assignments																
Other activity:																
Other activity:																

Chapter 5

Preferred use of study time

You may wish to spend more, or less, time on some activities than is outlined in the course requirements. Plan out how much time you will spend on each type of activity. This may differ each term or semester, and during breaks. Compare this with the programme requirements and consider the reasons for differences in your own planning. Copy this sheet for re-use.

Activity/Time in hours	1	2	3	4	5	6	7	8	9	10	11	12	13	14	15	16+
Lectures																
Seminars																
Tutorials																
Practical studio/ field/clinical/lab/ work-based																
Face-to-face study groups																
Other classes or workshops																
Independent reading/thinking																
Organising and planning																
Using online course materials																
Online reading/ research																
Online directed study activities																
Online tutor contact																
Online study group(s)																
Writing a blog and/or reflective journal																
Writing up and fine-tuning assignments																
Other activity:																
Other activity:																

Where does the time go?

As a student, there will be many other demands which eat up your time apart from study. Clarify where your time goes by pencilling into your diary everything you do for a few days – sleep, exercise, lectures, etc. – noting this roughly every hour. Chart this using the *Time circle*. Then use the second time circle to chart how you would *want* to use your time each day. Compare the two.

Circle 1: How I use time now

Using different colours or graphics for each type of activity, mark in where your time usually goes in a day. Treat each segment as roughly one hour. Which activities are left out or don't receive enough time? Which activities take up too much time?

Example

- sleep – 10 hr
- eating – 2 hr
- socialising – 3 hr
- personal/home – 3 hr
- travel – 1 hr
- lectures, seminars, tutorials – 2 hr
- reading – 2 hr
- writing – 1 hr
- thinking – 0 hr
- exercise/relaxation – 0 hr

Circle 2: How I want to use my time

On the second circle divide the day into how you would *prefer* to use your time so that your day is balanced between different activities. This is your goal for you to distribute your time.

Example

- sleep – 8 hr
- eating and socialising – 3 hr
- personal/home – 2 hr
- travel – 1 hr
- lectures, seminars, tutorials – 2 hr
- reading – 3 ½ hr
- writing – 2 hr
- thinking – 1 hr
- exercise/relaxation – 1 ½ hr

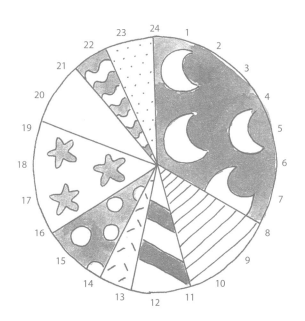

Time circle

Date:

How I use time now

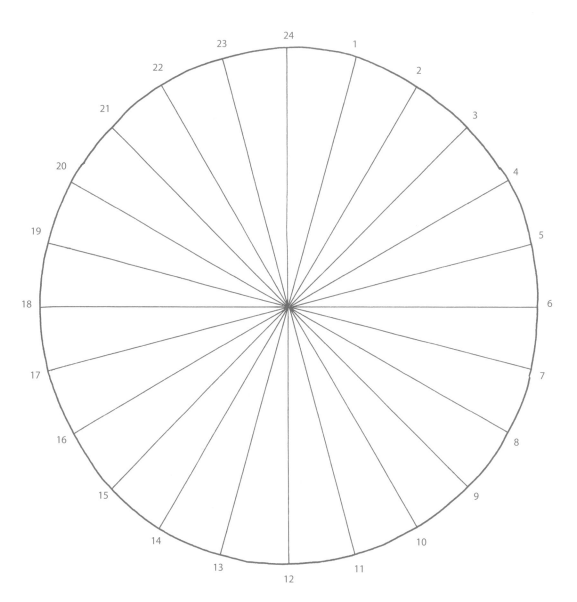

Key to shading

☐ _____   ☐ _____   ☐ _____

☐ _____   ☐ _____   ☐ _____

☐ _____   ☐ _____   ☐ _____

Time circle

Date:

How I want to use my time

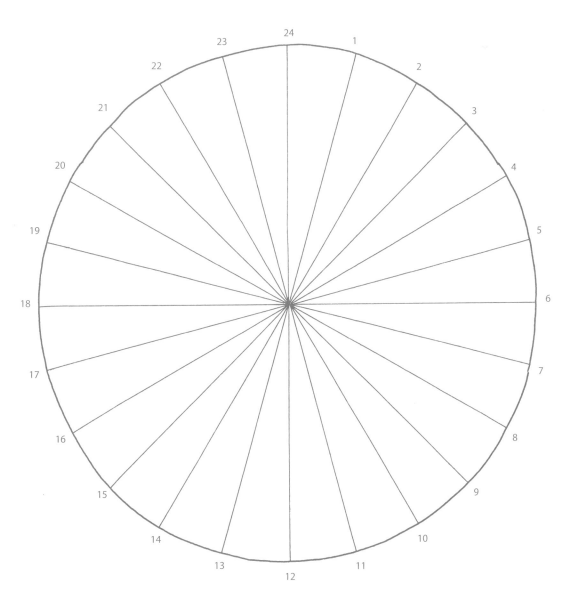

Key to shading

☐ _____   ☐ _____   ☐ _____

☐ _____   ☐ _____   ☐ _____

☐ _____   ☐ _____   ☐ _____

Chapter **5**

Set your priorities

You may find that you have more things to do than there is time to complete. If so, you will need to set your priorities for the day, week or year. The following checklist helps clarify what to do and when.

Priority-setting checklist

Done ✓

☐ 1 Write a 'To do' list of everything I have to do.

☐ 2 Highlight or underline in bold the essential tasks.

☐ 3 Identify the most urgent items on the list (those with the tightest deadline).

☐ 4 Identify the most important items on the list (those with the most serious consequences if not completed).

☐ 5 Number the items in the best order to do them.

☐ 6 Work out how long I can spend on each.

☐ 7 Decide what might have to be missed out.

☐ 8 Enter into my timetable or planner the times put aside for each stage of all essential tasks.

Working out the best order

Decide the best order for completing tasks depending on such considerations as:

● the most urgent

● the most logical order, such as tasks that should precede others, or which can be grouped according to location, travel routes or the people involved

● whether you find it more motivating to get started on the easiest things first, or prefer to get the most difficult tasks out of the way first.

Rating your priorities

If you have difficulties with prioritising, it can help to use a rating system.

● Use one rating to identify the level of importance.

● Use a second rating to decide on urgency.

● Weigh up the scores for one against the scores for another, as in the *Priority Organiser* on page 135. The rating system for that is described below.

Using the Priority Organiser (page 135)

Use rating system

Column A: Importance. Rate how important it is for you to do this task at all. (6 = unimportant; 10 = essential.)

Column B: Urgency. If this is to be done at all, how essential is it that you do it soon? (1 = must be done at once; 5 = it can wait.)

Column C: Balance the scores. Subtract the score in column B from column A. The highest scores in column C are the most likely to be priorities. However, double check to see if that is really the case.

Decide on the order

● *Column D* Be guided by your ratings to work out the best order to complete tasks.

● Then number tasks in the order that you will complete them.

● Write down the time or date to do each.

● Write these into your planner.

Monitor completion

● Highlight in yellow the task that you will complete next, so that it stands out for your attention.

● When it is complete, highlight it in green to indicate that it no longer needs your attention.

Priority organiser

Complete the organiser below, following the directions on page 134 above.

List of things to do	A need to do (scale 6–10)	B do now (scale 1–5)	C (A–B)	D order of priority/when

Effective planning and diary-keeping

A good student planner or diary can be invaluable in managing your time. A 'week to view' diary for the academic year is ideal.

What to put in about your study

A comprehensive record

To be effective, your diary or planner needs to be a *complete* record of what you have to do. Write in:

- all non-study activities, such as family holidays, medical appointments, work hours, birthdays, volunteering, travel, etc.
- exam dates, field trips, work placements, deadlines for handing in assignments, etc.
- exactly where, and with whom, each appointment or lecture is
- specific study tasks, such as 'Read Chapters 2–4 of *Urban Ecology*'
- dates and times when you need to log-on for specific activities or when course resources are made available online
- free time, to be used to catch up on things you missed, emergencies, unforeseen events, rest, and enjoyment.

A plan for completing assignments

Map into the diary the times when you will:

- think about the subject
- prepare for lectures and seminars
- prepare for other formal sessions
- plan your work
- research each subject, including conducting searches, reading and making notes
- organise and condense your notes
- reflect on your learning
- discuss work with others
- write early drafts, and edit and redraft these
- check your work.

A strategy for managing deadlines

Use the 'Working backwards from deadlines' sheet (page 139) to work out the time you will need for each stage of your assignments, before entering these into your planner. Organise everything else around your deadlines.

Colour codes and symbols

Use colours and symbols to indicate different activities and subjects in your diary. If you use these consistently, you will find that after a while you don't need to 'read' the entries: you will be able to note at a glance what is there. Use a positive or energising symbol for activities you dislike.

Examples of symbols you could devise

Diary entries

Make your planning work for you

Using your planner

Your diary or planner will be effective only if you keep it up to date and *use* it.

- Carry it with you at all times.
- Add all commitments straight into this so that you cannot forget them.
- Write inessential appointments in pencil, so you can make changes easily.
- Organise entries so you can see at a glance which time is filled; make sure you cannot double-book your time.
- Be rigorous in reorganising appointments straightaway if more than one falls at the same time. Avoid leaving this until later.
- Check it several times a day, especially at night and first thing in the morning. See whether there is anything you need to organise for the next 24–48 hours.

Write 'To do' lists in your planner and update these every day. Look ahead to the end of the week in case future activities require you to add anything to today's 'To do' list. See page 138.

High visibility

- Highlight all key dates such as deadlines so that they stand out from other activities in your planner.
- Enter items legibly and in full so that, later in the year, you know what each refers to.

Be specific

Enter brief but clear details that will help you to be in the right place at the right time. These include start times, people's names, locations and room numbers. The example below is taken from *The Palgrave Student Planner*.

Reflection: Using your planner

- What are your current strengths in maintaining a diary or planner?
- What improvements could you make to make your life more organised?

14 MONDAY			
Time	Activity	Where	To do today
9–12	Modern aesthetics (lect.) (leave before 8!)	H - A401	
12:15	Lunch w/Sean and Yoshio	Green Caff	- Coffee/rice
1 pm	Go over seminar with JK for this pm		- Reserve Gombrich books
3–5	C19 tech. Seminar: JK & me presentat.	Carpt. 22b	
5:30–7	Gym. Meet Susie inside.		- Ring home
			- card for Claire
8:20?	Film at Phoenix. Ring for seat.		- pick up slides

Using 'To do' lists

Why use 'To do' lists?

Checklists are a simple but effective way of drawing together everything you need to do and keeping track of what has been completed.

Even the simple act of writing a good 'To do' list can be helpful. It can reduce stress by enabling you to feel you are getting started on a task. The more precise the actions, times and details on your list, the less you need to remember, so reducing mental 'clutter'. The more your brain feels you are in charge of completing a task, the less it gives you a nagging sense of things yet to do.

Diary 'To do' lists

- Write a fresh list of things to do on a piece of paper or sticky note.
- Divide the list into 'Today' and 'Soon' (so you are aware of what you need to do long-term).
- Write items under headings so that they are easy to see: 'Study', 'Home', 'Other' (or whatever headings suit you).
- Be as precise as possible about what exactly you are going to do.
- Star or highlight the essential items.
- Attach or paperclip the list to the page opposite the current page of the diary.
- Cross out all completed items so that you are clear what is left to do.

Map out the time for 'To do' lists'

- Organise your list into a sensible running order
  – which are most important?
  – which are best clustered together?
- Jot down the maximum time to spend on each item or cluster of items.
- Jot into your planner the start and end times for the most important items on the list.
- Take note of things that take longer than planned. Take account of this in future planning.

'Next step'

For larger items on the 'To do' list, jot down what you will do next. This will help you to:

- get started on doing it
- reduce distracting thoughts about unfinished tasks.

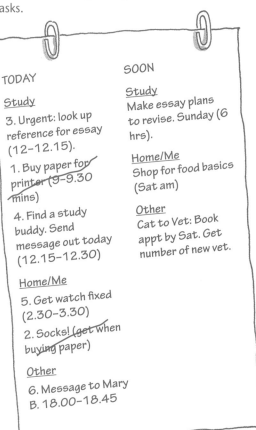

TODAY

Study
3. Urgent: look up reference for essay (12–12.15).
1. Buy paper for printer (9–9.30 mins)
4. Find a study buddy. Send message out today (12.15–12.30)

Home/Me
5. Get watch fixed (2.30–3.30)
2. Socks! (get when buying paper)

Other
6. Message to Mary
B. 18.00–18.45

SOON

Study
Make essay plans to revise. Sunday (6 hrs).

Home/Me
Shop for food basics (Sat am)

Other
Cat to Vet: Book appt by Sat. Get number of new vet.

Making new 'To do' lists

At a certain point, you are likely to have a list with many items crossed off, and others still remaining to do. Once your list starts to feel old, cluttered or confusing, start a new list, transferring over any unfinished items.

Note whether there are items that you put off continually. Decide whether you really are going to get round to them. If so, put a precise time into your diary and stick to it, so you can clear it off your list.

Chapter 5

Working backwards from deadlines

	How long will it take?	When will I do it?	How long it actually took
Preliminaries			
● Early brainstorming, reflection and discussion with others	_____	_____	_____
● Working out what is required	_____	_____	_____
Research			
● Working out which research methods to use	_____	_____	_____
● Working out what information/data I need	_____	_____	_____
● Assembling information (to search, read, gather data, experiment, etc.)	_____	_____	_____
● Digesting and reflecting on the information collected	_____	_____	_____
Organising the content			
● Grouping and organising information	_____	_____	_____
● Selecting what to include	_____	_____	_____
Writing draft versions			
● Thinking about and improving each draft	_____	_____	_____
● Writing each draft	_____	_____	_____
● Likely number of drafts	_____ _expected_		_____ _actual_
Completing the task			
● Writing up the references	_____	_____	_____
● Writing the final draft	_____	_____	_____
● Checking through the work	_____	_____	_____
● Final deadline	_____	_____	_____

Use this information in planning your next assignment. Write the time for each stage into your planner.

Chapter 5

Apply time management techniques: time blocks

Select ✓ those techniques that you think would be most effective for you to use.

☐ Choose the right time

Some people study best at night when all is quiet; others think more clearly first thing in the morning; others study 9–5, following a working day.

- Choose the time when you are most alert mentally and best able to remain focused.
- Avoid times when you may be interrupted.
- Match the study task to the time available.

Reflection: Which times work best for you?

At what times of day (or night) are you at your best for different kinds of study activity?

☐ Use workable blocks of time

Some students study best for bursts of 30 minutes, separated by 5-minute breaks. Others find it hard to settle after breaks and work better in longer study sessions. Organise blocks of study time that:

- help you stay focused and interested
- enable you to do a significant piece of work
- avoid time-wasting.

Reflection: Which blocks work for you?

- What kinds of study block suit you best?
- Does this vary depending on the study task?

☐ Mix it up

If you get bored with routine, then divide your time into blocks of different lengths, allocating these to activities that either lend themselves well to shorter bursts or need sustained application.

- Follow longer blocks of study with short ones.
- Build-in breaks of different lengths too, so that your use of time feels less regimented.
- Move frequently between tasks such as reading, noting, writing, thinking, calculations and so on, to keep your mind alert.
- Intersperse online study with other activities.

Reflection: Maintaining concentration

How could you plan out a session of independent study time to best maintain your concentration and interest whilst using all the time effectively?

☐ Plan efficient breaks in study

Longer breaks are important for rest and for enabling the brain to absorb information. Too many breaks can disrupt concentration, making it harder to refocus on the material. Taking no breaks at all suits some people, but tends to lead to tiredness, boredom or taking ill-advised short-cuts.

☐ Build in some longer breaks

Time these so that you can:

- clear your head and keep your thinking fresh
- rest your eyes and check your position if you have been on-screen for some time
- check that you are spending time as planned.

☐ Take micro-breaks

- Take micro-breaks of 2–10 minutes.
- Whatever the length of the break, give yourself a set time by which you must return to study.
- Move right away from your books or screen so that you don't get drawn back into study or online activity. Go to a different room or outside so that you have a complete change of scene.
- Get a drink or snack if needed. Move around so that you stretch your limbs and unwind.

Reflection: Which breaks work for you?

Is your study more effective with frequent breaks? Or does that disrupt your concentration?

- How long does it take you to settle down to study when you take a 3-minute break? A 20-minute break? A break of an hour or more?

Chapter 5

Apply time management techniques: multiple methods

Work to your rhythm

Take note of how you respond to different kinds of study task. For example, if you are slow to warm up to study, schedule short activities such as brainstorming ideas early in the day. You may find you are increasingly engrossed by study as the day progresses, and can settle down to complex reading or to writing tasks once you have 'warmed up' with shorter or simpler tasks. Look for ways of scheduling activities to suit your study rhythms.

Set early deadlines

Set yourself deadlines for completing assignments earlier than the official hand-in time. This gives you time to fine-tune your final drafts and manage unforeseen emergencies.

Keep track of time

- Jot down as a list your start times for each new activity.
- Put this where you can see it easily, such as on a sticky note on your diary or computer.
- Check it frequently as you study. Adapt your times sensibly if you start to fall behind.

Use a timer

- Use a timer on your computer or phone, or an old-fashioned alarm clock. Set it to go off a few minutes before the time you wish to start on your next activity.

Stop the Tweets! Time for Keats!

- When the timer goes off, be strict in bringing your current activity to a close so that you can start the next.
- It may take some experimentation to work out realistic amounts of time to set for each type of activity.

Use support networks

If you have demanding commitments outside of study, it helps to build the kind of support networks that fit your life style. For example, if you volunteer or work part-time, there may be ways of sharing shifts with others so that there is cover available for when you need to be in class. If you have children, you may be able to organise childcare with other students who are parents.

Organisation = time-saving

Good organisation is a key way of saving time.

- **Manage your files**, so that you don't keep more material than you need.
- **Organise space**, including your online space, so that you can find everything quickly.
- **Name it and label it**, so you can find things easily.
- **Plan your day** so that you use pockets of time well.

Apply time management techniques: online study

☐ Beware the addiction...

Surfing, browsing and communicating online make study more interesting but can be addictive – and more time-consuming than we realise. Listen to those who say they never see you! Be rigorous in monitoring how long you spend in online activities.

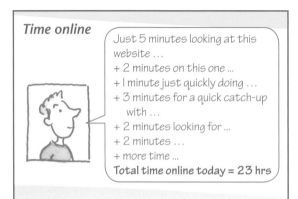

Time online

Just 5 minutes looking at this website ...
+ 2 minutes on this one ...
+ I minute just quickly doing ...
+ 3 minutes for a quick catch-up with ...
+ 2 minutes looking for ...
+ 2 minutes ...
+ more time ...

Total time online today = 23 hrs

☐ Monitor time used for online study

You are likely to engage in online activities to support your study, such as:

- browsing for material for an assignment
- watching online videos
- listening to podcasts of lectures
- sending messages to students on matters related to your study.

As these activities are study-related, it is easy to persuade yourself that it is all beneficial for your study, even if you spend more time on them than is helpful. This can mean that you run out of time for other aspects of your study, such as reading, analysing material or proof-reading assignments.

- Find out exactly how much time you spend on each type of online study activity.
- Consider whether that time allocation is working well for your study.
- If not, decide on the times you want to spend on those activities – and stick to these.

☐ Monitor online distractions

When timing your online activities, be scrupulous in timing how much time you spend on things that distract you from your main study plan.

- Include distractions that take 'just a minute'.
- Note how much time it takes you to settle down to study after each break or distraction.
- Note whether the occasional minutes are really just that or whether they add up to significant distractions.
- Add up the total study time lost to these distractions over an hour, day, week and year.
- Consider whether that is how you still want to spend your time online.

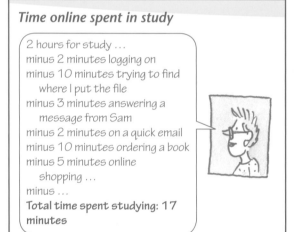

Time online spent in study

2 hours for study ...
minus 2 minutes logging on
minus 10 minutes trying to find where I put the file
minus 3 minutes answering a message from Sam
minus 2 minutes on a quick email
minus 10 minutes ordering a book
minus 5 minutes online shopping ...
minus ...

Total time spent studying: 17 minutes

☐ Plan-in response times

If you will need to await responses from others, including tutors, in order to complete aspects of your study, work on the assumption that they may take 24 hours or even several days to get back to you. It isn't realistic to expect everyone to get back to you immediately.

Ten time-saving strategies

1 Save time writing notes

- Write your notes directly onto a laptop, computer or mobile device.
- Avoid writing notes in full sentences – use headings and keywords.

2 Save time copying between files

- Use Dropbox, Google Docs, or similar software to access the same documents from any computer or device that you use, rather than copying across from one to the other.
- If you use Pages on an ipad, email documents to yourself in WORD format so that you can save them into Dropbox.

3 Make the most of spare moments

Make a list of tasks that you could complete in spare moments such as when queuing, or that you can combine with other activities that require little mental input. Ideal study tasks include listening to podcasts of lectures or revision points, memorising flash cards, or reading short sections from books.

4 Save time looking for notes

- When making notes, write each major point under a different heading. Use a large bold font for headers so you can find points quickly when browsing your notes for specific items.
- Name and date your folders and files clearly.
- Maintain an updated contents guide to your folders and files, so that you know exactly where to search for what you need.
- Keep detailed records of source materials and page numbers in your notes, so you can find them again easily if needed to check details.

5 Save time reading

- Use 'smart reading' strategies (*Am I a smart reader?*, pages 165–7).
- Read only what is relevant to this essay or assignment. If something looks interesting for the future but is not relevant now, make a note of it rather than becoming distracted by it now.

6 Save time in writing references

For every book, article, etc. that you read, keep a full record of the details required for your references (see pages 179–181). Do this electronically for ease in pasting into your assignment, or use electronic referencing tools. See page 182.

7 Use word limits to focus your energies

Usually, you won't need to read, note and include as much for a 1000-word essay as for a 2000-word one. Map out how much you really need to read, note and write to match the word limit (pages 290–1).

8 Save time thinking

- Carry a small book to capture ideas as they occur.
- Use 'brainstorming' and pattern notes to generate ideas quickly (pages 279 and 173).

9 Save time organising information

- Don't note down the same information twice. If two writers make the same point, note a reference to the second source in the margin next to the first time you noted that point.
- Use shading on the computer, or highlighter pens on paper, to group information relevant to the same section of your assignment.
- Cut and paste together items shaded the same colour. Read these again once regrouped.
- If you have the option, read your shaded notes on a page or in a window alongside the one in which you are writing your assignment.
- Use a folder or a resource such as *The Palgrave Student Planner* to draw together study-related information in one place (see Appendix 3, page 402).

10 Avoid duplicating effort

Find a study partner to bounce ideas, exchange study strategies and share permitted study tasks.

Manage procrastination and distraction

Effective study depends on having your state of mind, space, time and materials organised in the ways that best suit your learning.

Creating a state of mind for study

Many students find it difficult to get into the right mood for study. They put it off to another day. Everyone has their own particular distractions: endless cups of coffee, texting and tweeting, phone calls, TV, browsing online, housework, anything rather than settling down to study.

Give yourself study triggers

Many people need a 'trigger' to start a study session. One student clears his desk each time he finishes studying: his study trigger is a clear, inviting surface. Another has a 'ritual' of switching on the computer, bringing in a glass of water and then opening her books at the appropriate pages before she feels she is ready to begin. Another begins by making a coffee while standing in the kitchen, brainstorming ideas onto paper. He feels he has already started to study before he sits down.

Reflection: Study triggers

What actions or thoughts can trigger you into 'study mode'? If you don't know, experiment until you find triggers that work for you.

Create the right environment

Make a conscious note of the kind of environment that suits you best for different study tasks. Do you need quiet, music, background noise? Is study better at home or in a library? Alone or with friends? In clear space or chaos? What else do you need?

Reflection: Study environment

What kind of study environment works best for you? Does this change for different aspects of study?

Use your distractions to help you study

Study on the move

If your distractions involve movement (such as sport, shopping or housework), spend ten minutes first browsing a chapter or going over notes. Then give in to your distraction if you still want to – but go over what you have just read as you do it. If you are an active person, combine sport or movement with study tasks such as thinking through how you will approach an assignment, or rehearsing material covered in class to see how much you remember. Some people learn better 'on the move'.

'Stealth study'

If you find it off-putting to be 'obliged' to study, begin by allowing yourself a limited time to study initially – maybe just 5–10 minutes. Ease yourself gradually into increasingly longer spells. Alternatively, after ten minutes, move away from your study, changing activity, but doing something that enables you to continue thinking about what you have just studied. Set yourself questions to answer if that helps you to remain focused. For example, consider whether you agree with what you have read, or decide how you would use it in under 30 words in an assignment. Jot down any ideas or phrasing that occurs to you.

If you feel compelled to sit down to check a point or write something up, then do so. You may find you become engaged in your study at that point.

Use distractions as resources

If you tend to phone or text friends as a distraction, ask them to help you focus on your work. Tell them to ask you about the assignment or use them as a sounding board, but be considerate – your friends will probably be delighted to hear from you, but may also be trying to concentrate on their own study. Set time limits for calls

Connect to your motivation

See pages 111–18.

Getting down to study

Settling down to study is a common difficulty for students, even those who enjoy study once they get going. If this is true of you, it may be because you have not established the right conditions for you for that aspect of study. For example, do you know what kind of task you do best early in the day or late at night? Do you know the best time and place for you to redraft a piece of writing or to read difficult texts?

Experiment until you find the times and places that suit you best for different study tasks. Whenever you struggle to get down to study, check your responses to the following questions.

Organise your time, space and mind for study

Reflection: Getting down to study

For each of the five areas below, write at least one suggestion of a change you could make now to improve your studying.

---

1 Am I doing this for myself?

☐ Am I clear about my motivation for doing this?

☐ Could I make this task more interesting?

☐ Could I make this task more enjoyable?

2 Are my expectations realistic?

☐ Am I taking things step by step?

☐ Do I need to set smaller milestones?

☐ Do I need a better reward system?

☐ Am I taking the right kinds of breaks?

☐ Have I worked for too long without rest/sleep?

☐ Am I getting enough to eat and drink?

☐ Have I set myself enough challenge?

3 Am I in the right place?

☐ … for this aspect of study?

☐ Do I have a good surface to write on?

☐ Do I feel comfortable?

☐ Do I have good light and ventilation?

☐ Do I have the equipment I need?

☐ Am I likely to be uninterrupted?

4 Am I working at the right time?

☐ Do I work productively at this time of day?

☐ Is this the best time for this activity?

☐ Am I completing tasks in order of priority?

5 What are my excuses for procrastination?

What kinds of excuses do I use for putting off getting started ('First, I just need to …')?

1 . . . .

2 . . . .

3 . . . .

I will manage these excuses by:

Chapter 5

Identifying and managing distractions

Time-eating 'danger zones' online

As time spent online often creates the greatest challenges to students' time management, it can help to identify your personal 'danger zones'. These are the websites and e-resources that take up a disproportionate amount of your time. They could be useful sites that you over-use, distract you too easily from your main purpose or serve too easily as launch pads to other sites.

- Note which sites, apps and tools you use most.
- Decide how much time you really want to spend on these.
- Decide how you will build a reasonable use of your favourite sites or resources into your day.
- Consider how you will keep yourself to that amount: how will you monitor how long you are using each? How will you motivate yourself to close the site or app?

My 'danger' apps

The apps that take up a disproportionate amount of my time or distract me from study are:

(1)

(2)

(3)

(4)

(5)

I'll manage my time using these by:

My 'danger zone' websites and tools

The main websites and resources that take up too much of my time or distract me from study are:

(1)

(2)

(3)

(4)

(5)

(6)

(7)

(8)

I'll manage my time using these by:

Other distractions

You may find that you are also easily distracted by friends, family, personal interests, games, day dreaming, or a host of other things.

Other key personal distractions

The other main distractions that prevent me from settling down to study or draw me away from study once started are:

(1)

(2)

(3)

(4)

(5)

I'll manage these distractions by:

Chapter 5

Staying on task

Once you have started on a task, the next time management challenge is staying on task. This is sometimes referred to as 'stick-with-it-ness'.

Using the first few minutes effectively

It can help to stick with a task if you feel you have made a good start. To achieve this, set yourself a time challenge to complete in the first 10–15 minutes of each period of independent study.

Reflection: The first 10–15 minutes

- How effectively do you use the first 10–15 minutes of study?
- What kinds of challenges could you set for yourself to use those initial few minutes in effective and motivating ways?

Remaining focused

Some of the reasons that students give for not staying on task are listed below. Which, if any, apply to you?

1. ☐ continuing the same activity for too long
2. ☐ getting bored
3. ☐ finding the material too difficult
4. ☐ not seeing the relevance
5. ☐ getting tired.

Strategies for remaining focused

- Break up your study time into blocks of different lengths: see page 140.
- Set yourself specific challenges for each block – with just enough time to complete them. Don't give yourself the luxury of thinking there is time to waste.

- Set a schedule of tasks for the time allocated. Alternate tasks of reading, noting, writing, listening to podcasts, thinking, searching, etc. to maintain your interest through variety.
- Set short questions relevant to your assignment to focus your attention for that study session.
- Look for the debates and controversy in the topic: these add interest. Consider how these will impact on your own perspectives on the issues, and on your assignment and revision.
- Consider spending some time working with others – agree a time schedule together for staying on task.

Reflection: Remaining focused

What could you change about the way you study to help you to remain focused on the task?

Life balance

Organise your time so that you take care of yourself generally and can replenish your energies. It is better to plan these into your week along with time to deal with unforeseen circumstances. Make sure you get enough time for:

- sleeping and relaxing
- eating
- exercise
- family, friendships and social activities
- having fun.

Reflection: Life balance

- To which aspects of life, work and study do you pay most attention?
- How effective are you at replenishing your energies? What could you plan differently?

Activate your time management strategies

Reflection: Which strategies?

Which of the strategies from pages 125–47 above could you adopt or adapt to manage your time?

(1)

(2)

(3)

(4)

(5)

(6)

(7)

What other strategies, if any, could you devise for yourself to improve your time management?

(1)

(2)

(3)

(4)

(5)

Activity — Next steps for putting time management strategies into action

For the strategies that you identified as right for you, decide how you will plan these into your daily routine. Start the ball rolling by identifying the next set of steps you need to take in order to effect a change in your time management.

For example, if you need to use a planner, your first step might be to find a website or shop to purchase one. If you need to manage your online time better, then identifying your personal online 'danger zones' (see page 146) may be your next step. Jot down your 'next steps' as a 'To do' list.

To do: (what and when)

(1)

(2)

(3)

(4)

(5)

(6)

(7)

Monitor your use of time

Use a photocopy of this sheet for each study period until you are happy with how you use your time.

Column 1 (fill out during study)	Column 2 (fill out after study)
Date: Where: Time I am starting: Study conditions:	Were the conditions, time and place the best possible? Could I improve anything?
How long am I going to study for altogether?	How long did I study for?
How many breaks do I intend to take? Times of breaks (approx.)? Length of breaks?	When did I take breaks? Did I stick to the break time? If not, what do I need to do to get back to study?

Interruptions that occurred

Type of interruption	Length	Time finished	Total time worked
1			
2			
3			
4			
5			

How could I prevent these interruptions?

Actual time spent really studying:

Thoughts and observations about my study habits and time management

Chapter 5

Review

Time management is an essential skill for students. Student life can be very demanding and that is especially the case if you combine study with other commitments such as work, volunteering, family and caring responsibilities, sports or creative and performing arts. It is easy to assume that there is more time available than is the case, and to believe that study tasks can be completed more quickly than proves possible in practice.

It is not unusual for people to forget to put any time aside even for such essential tasks as preparing food, eating, travelling between home and college, celebrating a friend's birthday, finding course materials they have been told to use, or planning out their assignments. It pays to develop a sharper sense of what exactly needs to be done, and by when, and how long it takes to complete each aspect of the task.

Investigate as early as possible the amount and nature of expected study commitments for your programme, so that you can plan for these well in advance. Develop a keen sense of the total range of tasks that you will need to complete for study and for everyday life, and plan into your diary or planner exactly when you will do these.

It is unlikely that you will need the same level of monitoring of your use of time throughout your time as a student. However, most students experience periods when it is hard to get down to study, or to stay on task, or to fit in everything they need to do. At such times, it can help to focus in on your time management strategies, using those techniques and resources outlined in the chapter that you find of most use.

This chapter has outlined a 10-step strategy for effective time management. All 10 steps are important – you can't really pick and choose, or opt to miss any out, and still be managing your time to best effect.

However, it is likely that you will be more effective in some areas than others. Good self-knowledge, planning and organisation help with most aspects of time management. You can draw upon the chapter for ideas for more elaborate strategies to address those areas you find most problematic.

Part B
Academic skills

6 Core research skills: reading, note-making and
   managing information
7 Critical analytical thinking
8 Memory
9 Confidence with numbers

Study skills consist of more than simply academic skills, but academic skills are a key aspect of what we understand by the term 'study skills'. Chapter 2 outlined a wide range of skills that could be considered to be academic skills. This section focuses on just four sets of academic skills that are essential to most courses of Higher Education.

As research of one kind or another is central to academic work in Higher Education, you are expected to have the strong core skills relevant to researching your own assignments. These include finding good quality information at speed, reading selectively and at speed, and using taught sessions to help you build your information base in support of independent study. They also include knowing how to use the information you find in appropriate ways.

As well as finding information, you need to be able to select and interpret it with a critical eye. Critical analysis is an essential skill for

reading and listening in Higher Education. You will be expected to demonstrate this in your written assignments. Depending on your course, you will need to be able to recall, at speed, your course material in a range of settings: in discussion, for exams or for practical application. Many courses expect at least a basic understanding of, and confidence in, manipulating numbers.

Although the subject specialist aspects of research, statistics, maths and critical analysis of sources are generally included within courses, it is generally expected that you have a good grasp of the basic underlying concepts. These are addressed by this section.

It would also be expected that you have good basic skills in writing. Those academic skills are covered within the context of writing specific assignments, in Part D on task management skills.

Chapter 6
Core research skills
Reading, note-making and managing information

Learning outcomes

This chapter offers you opportunities to:

- fine-tune your skills in information-finding, reading and note-making for higher level study
- understand the processes involved in managing information for academic tasks
- appreciate what is meant by 'good quality' sources
- consider how to adapt your reading and note-making for different types of study task
- know what is meant by 'plagiarism' and how to avoid it
- learn how to cite sources and reference your work
- make effective use of lectures and taught sessions.

The nature of research

Research, or 'finding out', is something we do all the time, whether we want to know more about music, people, sport, shopping or following up an item on the news. Our methods vary depending on the topic, how much we want to know, and the availability of the material. Likewise, for academic study, there are different methods of researching a topic, depending on the subject discipline, level of study, source materials and the assignment.

Using 'informed opinion'

At this level of study, you are expected to use more than just opinion, common sense and spur-of-the-moment responses and to develop informed positions on issues. You do this through activities such as reading, debate, experimentation and critical reflection. You are expected to demonstrate a deeper understanding, and to use more precise information, than the average person in the street.

In practice, this means searching out information to use to produce assignments and contribute to projects, taught sessions and discussions at an appropriate level. As you progress through your degree, you build your research skills, making more advanced searches, reading greater amounts, using specialist material, collecting your own raw data or using original documentary sources, and working with information to make it meaningful in the context of your course and assignments.

You start the process of developing your research skills by honing pre-existing skills in finding information, reading and note-making. This chapter looks at ways that you can develop these core skills, along with skills in extracting useful information in taught sessions, and appropriate ways of acknowledging your sources. Such skills provide a solid foundation for the specialised research skills that you will learn within your academic discipline.

Just a 2,000-word report ...

Managing information for academic study

(1) Defining the task, identifying precisely what you need

Work out what you really need...

Use assignment titles and the background information provided about the assignment in order to identify key words, dates and places that will help you to focus your search more precisely.

Be as clear and precise as possible in your own mind about the kind of information that you are looking for so that you can define your searches closely, saving time and effort.

(2) Using material of suitable quality and content

Recognising what you need when you see it ...

(a) being able to identify material of good quality for academic purposes
(b) identifying material that is directly relevant to the purpose, such as your assignment or research project
(c) being able to tell quickly what to reject, so that you don't waste time on material you are not going to use.

Managing information for study

Managing information for study means:

1 defining the task, identifying precisely what you need
2 using material of suitable quality and content
3 knowing where to look for it
4 using the right tools
5 using search methodologies that offer the most direct route
6 applying effective reading and note-making strategies to extract and record the information you need
7 storing information so that you can find it again easily for use in your studies or work
8 sharing information appropriately for group assignments
9 applying information in a way that is fit for purpose, using appropriate conventions, citations and attributions
10 moving back and forth flexibly and easily between the above stages – with the least time and effort.

(3) Knowing where to look

Knowing where to start a search for which kinds of information ...

- library catalogues
- Google Scholar
- Athens
- bibliographic databases
- gateway services
- digital repositories.

(4) Using the right tools

Knowing which tools are available to help you to conduct, online ...

- searches
- storage
- referencing
- sharing.

(9) Applying information and attributing sources

Knowing how to use the information in your assignments ...

(a) selecting the most appropriate material
(b) using information to stimulate your own ideas
(c) combining and synthesising material from many sources
(d) drawing on sources for evidence to support your reasoning
(e) giving due recognition to those whose work or information you use.

It also means:

● knowing what is meant by plagiarism and cheating
● understanding how to cite your sources and provide appropriate references. (See pages 179–81.)

(8) Sharing information for group assignments

Knowing about tools and methods that can help you to study collaboratively with others online or in study groups ...

● taking care to avoid accidental copying or plagiarism
● sharing bookmarks
● using Google Tools.

(7) Storing for academic use

Knowing how to store or tag information so that you can ...

(a) find it again quickly if needed for assignments
(b) cite and reference it appropriately

● Downloads
● Memory sticks
● Bookmarks
● Delicious
● Reference management tools.

(5) Using the most appropriate search methods

Knowing the search methods to use to:

(a) limit your search to find just what you need
(b) extend your search if you haven't found what you want
(c) make advanced searches, including use of Boolean operators.

(6) Applying effective reading and note-making strategies

(a) read at the right speed for the purpose
(b) adapt your reading strategy to suit your learning style and the task
(c) make useful notes when reading, listening and using audiovisual material.

Defining your research task

The nature of the task

We saw above (page 66) that successful students tend to spend more time at the start of an assignment, working out exactly what is required. Before launching into any piece of work, take time to clarify exactly what is required and plan your approach. Being clearly focused from the outset will save you time later.

1   *Organise and plan your work,* allocating your time according to what you are expected to produce.

2   *Read carefully through the guidelines for the assignment.* How many parts are there to the question? What is really being asked? (See pages 284–5.)

3   *Consider the purpose of the assignment.* Why this particular topic, and why this particular wording? Is the assignment one that is always set on your course because it covers essential background? If so, what is there that you need to know? Or is it topical, related to recent research or an issue in the news? If so, what is that issue?

4   *Consider your end-point.* What should your work look or sound like when it is finished? (See Chapters 12 and 13.)

5   *Use the marking criteria.* Display them where you can see them, and use them to guide your work.

6   *Scale your research to the time and the word limits.* Consider what is expected, given the length of the assignment. Be realistic in how much you plan to read and note.

Start by surveying the field

What do I need to find out?

You undertake research of some kind for every piece of academic work. This might include:

● background reading to explore the subject

● identifying the leading experts in this topic – those whose primary research, theories or writings are regarded by academics as essential background knowledge – even if you do not read their work in detail

● some investigation into the variety of views held on the subject: what has been written on the core issues? Do the experts agree or disagree, and in what ways and why?

● some specialist reading, such as a recent or important journal article, or an essential text or set of texts on a given topic.

In other words, start by surveying the area. As an undergraduate you may not need to read a great deal on any one topic, but you do need to be aware of your field of study – what is important, what stands out, and why. Develop a feel for which topics are worth focusing on, and which are peripheral.

Managing the peripherals

As you carry out your research, you will come across all kinds of information that will intrigue or fascinate you and that you may want to pursue. You will not have enough time to follow up everything that catches your attention, so you will need to:

● decide what is essential

● decide what you have time to pursue now

● make a list of topics to follow up later and put these aside for now.

Making the most of the library

Library services

The starting place for most research is the library. Join your college library as soon as possible, and find out about the range of services available. Typically, these include:

- support and resources for using the library and for finding material online
- silent areas, study rooms and reference sections, and discussion areas
- books, papers and academic journals, in print and electronically
- specialist collections
- photocopiers, laminators, binding facilities
- computers and wireless areas for laptops
- DVDs, film, tape, slide, microfilm and digitised materials from your reading list
- specialist resources for disabled students
- facilities for making audiovisual aids for your presentations.

If your institution is based on more than one campus, find out what is available on each. Find out how you can access books and resources at each site.

The library catalogues

Most catalogues are now electronic. Your library may have specialist collections in your subject, or the index for a national collection. It is quite usual to need help using these. If you are uncertain, don't be afraid to ask.

Make the library your own

To join the library you will usually need your student number and/or identity card, so make sure you take these with you. Walk around the library and become familiar with the atmosphere. Sit at different tables – try out different spaces. Where would you work best?

Look up books from your reading list, using the technology, checking what is available on the open

You did say to make myself at home in the library.

shelves and what you can call up from stores or on loan from elsewhere.

Find out basic information

- Where are books in your subject located in the library? How are they classified?
- How many items can you take out at once?
- How many items can you take home on loan – and for how long?
- How long does it take for books to arrive once ordered?
- Can you reserve books?
- How do you reserve or renew by phone or online?
- Are there fines?
- How do you request inter-library loans? How much do these cost?
- Are there subject-specialist librarians?

Activity **Classification system**

Check the classification system (or systems) used to group books in your library – Dewey Decimal Classification (DCC), Library of Congress (LC), etc. Which number range applies to your subject for each system?

Finding information: getting started

The reading list

The most important tools for getting started are usually those provided through your course. Typically, these are:

- reading lists
- course handbooks
- resources mentioned by teaching staff, provided as handouts or in the course's virtual learning environment
- references made within set texts or course materials, to other materials.

Use these to build up a sense of the academic community in the discipline, to identify the people respected and to recognise the kind of sources regarded as useful and reliable.

Build your own trail

- Note who you are asked to read.
- Find out more about the other works they have written.
- Check the references at the end of the item. Call up some of these for yourself and then check their references in turn, to call up further items.
- Look for patterns in who is writing about which topic and whose work is most respected and used in references.
- Decide which sources you find most useful and interesting.

Indices and abstracts

Indices and abstracts are separate publications which give brief details of journal articles, including who wrote what and where to find it. In an index, you can search by subject heading and by keywords for all the articles on a given subject. They are updated regularly and are well worth using.

Finding academic sources online

Google Scholar search engine

Google Scholar is the main search engine to use for your work as a student. It is:

- extensive: it draws on a very wide range of subject databases relevant to students
- based on a keyword search
- predictive: it brings up results based on the individual user's pattern of searching
- personalised: it draws on your previous searches, so you gain unique search results.

Research tools

You can find additional research facilities online, such as those available at www.iTools.com/research. With these, you can access definitions, maps, quotations, language translations, synonyms, and much more.

Athens

Athens AMS manages access to sites of interest to researchers. As a student, this usually gives you free access to many electronic journals and databases.

Bibliographic databases / gateway services

These are maintained by professional academics, which helps to quality assure the materials. You can search by keyword, author or journal to help you find books, articles, reports, papers and documents in your subject. Your library website will have details for each subject.

Digital repositories

Banks of digital materials with millions of resources suitable for academic study are being grown by HEIs and other bodies. These are usually free to search but you may need to enter a repository to search it.

Useful resources

See pages 400–1 (Appendix 2) for useful databases, services, repositories and tools.

Conducting an online search

Starting an online search

- Go online and search for Google Scholar.
- Type your chosen keywords into the search field and click on the icon to the right
- A list of possible leads will appear below, typically summary descriptions or partial quotations from websites, with web addresses.
- Click on entries that look promising: the links will take you automatically to those web pages.

'What exactly am I looking for?'

If you enter a general keyword, such as 'mouse', you will be offered *millions* of options – on rodents, electronic mice, cartoon mice, pest control, science experiments, mice in children's story books and so on. A search on Google Scholar (15 July 2012) gave the following results:

Search string	Number of entries
mouse	289,000,000
fieldmouse UK	219,0000
fieldmouse habitat UK	1,170
fieldmouse urban habitat and owls UK	154

Narrow your search

To narrow your search to more relevant items, include more keywords in your 'search string' and choose your search string with care.

- Which keywords best describe what you are looking for? Which are most likely to be used as keywords for making electronic links?
- Consider synonyms (words with the same meaning such as 'city', 'town', 'urban' and 'metropolitan').
- Might unrelated subjects share keywords with your topic? If so, use at least one keyword that applies *only* to your topic.
- Which *specific areas* of your topic do you need to focus on? Which keywords identify these?
- To find additional material, use new keywords.
- If a search string proves particularly useful, note it down for future use.

Searching for journal articles online

Electronic versions of journals may be free to students and available through a 'host' such as:

- ABI Inform
- EBSCO EJS
- IngentaConnect
- Athens AMS

When looking for journal entries, search first for the name of the *journal*, not the name of the article.

You can search journal databases for authors, journal titles, article titles or keywords, and call up short abstracts to see what an article is about.

For speed, type in words such as 'research', 'journal', the names of leading theorists or schools of thought as well as the topic.

Conference papers

If you have an Athens authentication number, conference proceedings and papers in your subject are available through the 'Web of Knowledge' at: http://wok.mimas.ac.uk (select *ISI Proceedings*).

Saving web addresses

For useful sources, save their web addresses as a 'favourite', 'bookmark' or 'mark' it. Set up folders to group your most used addresses. Name these clearly, just as you would with your files. If you use a free social bookmarking tool such as Delicious, you can save your bookmarks online and access them from anywhere with online access.

Automated searches using eTOC

Some bibliographic databases let you save searches and return to them later. For many, you can request to be emailed details of all publications that meet your search criteria. For journals that you find especially useful, request an eTOC – the electronic copy of its contents. You can receive these by email, with direct links to the articles.

Narrowing or extending your online search

You can vary your search by using OR, AND and NOT (known in this context as 'Boolean operators'), and truncation symbols or wildcards. These allow you to broaden or narrow your search in order to find the most relevant pages.

Too many items? Limit your search

AND

If you type **AND** between two keywords, the seach will produce only those pages that include *both* of the keywords. For example, **field AND mice** would find only pages that contain both **field** and **mice**, not those containing only one of these keywords.

Inverted commas (" ")

In many situations you can use double inverted commas to specify a phrase rather than a single word. This will narrow down the search and reduce the number of items you find, but must be used with care. For example, **"electronic mouse"** would yield references to computer mice, excluding those that mention rodents, but equally it would only list pages where those two words appeared together in exactly that form.

NOT

Use **NOT** to *exclude* items from your search. For example, to find references to mice but not to pest control, you could enter: **mice NOT extermination**

More keywords

The more keywords you use, the fewer pages are listed. For example, a library database search may allow you to specify the author's name, words in the title, the publication date, and so on. The more of these you provide, the more precise your search will be.

Too few items? Extend your search

OR

Use **OR** to search for pages that contain *one* or *more* of two or more words. For example, a search for **car OR bicycle** would list pages that include **car** but not **bicycle**, pages that include **bicycle** but not **car**, and pages that include both **car** and **bicycle**. This kind of search is useful when authors may use different terms for the same topic (often synonyms or abbreviations): **"vitamin C" OR "ascorbic acid"**

Truncation symbol (*)

The truncation symbol can be used to find variations of a keyword that begin with the same set of letters (the 'stem'). For example, **crit*** would find **critic, critical, critique** and **criticism**.

Wildcards (?)

Wildcards find variations of a keyword, such as alternative words in a phrase or alternative letters in a word. The exact operation of **?** varies between search engines: check the help system.

- Alternative words: **car ?** would search for **car** plus any other word, and might find **used cars, sports cars, car insurance, car hire**, and so on. Beware: this may yield a long list. In a publications database, for example, **Smith ?** would list publications by *any* author named **Smith**; it would be better to include a specific initial to limit the list (**Smith W**).
- Alternative characters: **wom?n** might find **woman** and **women**; **organi?e** might find **organise** and **organize**.

Advanced online searches

Advanced searches

With some databases you can use a more sophisticated search string that uses parentheses ( ) to link operations and to specify their order of precedence. You can continue to use operators, truncations and wildcards (page 160), within and between the groups of keywords.

You need to put some thought into what you are including and excluding. However, experiment and you will soon get a feel for whether your search strategy is finding the kinds of items you need.

Example 1

Suppose you wished to find articles about mice in cities. You might try this search string:

(mice NOT rat) AND (urban OR city OR metropolitan NOT field)

The search engine would list items in the database that:

- include the keyword **mice** but do not include the keyword **rat**

and also

- include any combination (one or more) of the keywords **urban**, **city** or **metropolitan**, but *not* the keyword **field**.

However, this search might exclude some useful articles that mentioned 'rat' or 'field' even once.

Example 2

"global warming" AND (glaciers NOT North)

The search would look for items that:

- include **global warming** as a phrase (excluding items that contain the words **global** and **warming**, but not together)

and also

- include the word **glaciers**, but do *not* include the word **North**.

Again, this would exclude any articles that mentioned the word **North** even once.

Efficient search strategies

An efficient search strategy is one that:

- finds the most relevant items
- does not exclude relevant items
- does exclude irrelevant items
- is successful in the fewest attempts.

Activity **Advanced searches**

1. If you use AND in a search, you are likely to find additional references. True or false?

2. If you use OR in a search, you are likely to find additional references. True or false?

3. Which search string would find most items?
   - A global OR world
   - B global AND world
   - C global NOT world

4. Which search strategy would find the fewest items?
   - A graphic OR design
   - B (graphic OR design)
   - C "graphic design"

5. How could you enter the keyword 'design' to find references to 'designs' and 'designers' also?

6. For the following topics, how could you search for references to items using alternative versions of the keywords?
   - A A compendium of nursing methods
   - B Monopoly as a trend in world trade

7. Which search string is likely to be most efficient in finding references to the impact of global design trends on designers?
   - A global AND design AND trend
   - B global? AND (design* AND trend?)
   - C global* OR (design AND trend)

Answers are given on page 408.

Using material of suitable quality and content

Using 'authoritative sources'

Only a small portion of the vast amount of information available in print and online will be suitable for academic assignments. Being able to identify good quality material is an essential requirement of study at this level.

You can find excellent materials online as well as in print. Little of what is printed or put on the internet is subjected to academic scrutiny so it is useful to know:

● where to find good materials, especially those that have been peer-reviewed

● how to differentiate between good and poor quality material for yourself.

New research and theory is developed as part of an international academic community. As you read and develop expertise in your subject, you will come to know the experts in your field and to recognise reliable information quickly. You also become familiar with institutions, organisations and centres associated with excellent work in specific areas

Who is who?

● Look out for the names that appear in research papers, book reviews and on the editorial boards of journals. Do other academics make positive references to their work?

● Google the authors – find out what they have written more recently.

● Check whether there are reviews of their work in journals and read these.

● Check the qualifications, experience and occupation of the authors: are they academics such as doctors or professors at an HEI, or otherwise leading experts in the field?

Characteristics of good quality sources

Even if you do not recognise the authors or editors, you will become familiar with the characteristics of good quality sources for your subject. Typically, you would look for:

● where items appear: are they in a reputable series, in a peer-reviewed journal or by an academic publisher?

● the number and quality of the references they make to other experts in the field

● use of original source material and data

● clear references and details of source materials, such as would enable readers to check these sources for themselves.

Using peer-reviewed items

'Peer-review' means that a recognised group of experts in the field have scrutinised published work to quality assure it from an academic perspective, prior to publication. Reviewers consider such matters as:

● the appropriateness of the methods used to gather, analyse and present information

● ethical considerations

● whether sufficient use had been made of previously published research findings

● whether data were interpreted correctly

● whether the evidence supports the conclusions

● whether anything is misleading in the way the material is presented.

Just because a book has been reviewed it does not mean that errors and inconsistencies are eliminated or that you need to take on board its findings in an uncritical way. The issues listed above are ones that you are also expected to consider for yourself. These are covered in more detail in Chapter 7.

Journals or periodicals

These tend to be good quality sources and many are now available online. The articles and book reviews they contain are written by experts for experts and so assume a certain level of background knowledge in the subject.

Journals are published at regular intervals during the year. They are collected into numbered volumes, usually one for each year. To find a journal article, you can browse using keywords, but you may need to use a specialised database to find the item. It helps if you know:

- the title of the journal, the year it was published and its volume number
- the name and initials of the author
- the title of the article.

Use abstracts and book reviews in journals

Most articles open with a short 'abstract' or summary. Browsing through abstracts and reviews helps you to keep up to date with research and publications in your subject, and to identify items to call up to read in full for your assignments. Often, the abstract provides sufficient information for undergraduate assignments, especially in the first years of study.

Podcasts

A podcast is an audio file or audiovisual file that can be downloaded from a web-based source onto your computer or a portable media player such as an MP3 or MP4 player or mobile phone.

- Lecturers may make some or all of a lecture available as a podcast.
- Study resources may be available as podcasts: e.g. www.palgravestudyskills.com
- Good sources for students are: iTunes, Juice, Podnova, podcast.com and ted.com
- Check details of the speaker in order to find out whether the material in the podcast is likely to be reliable.
- Check the date to see if it is recent.

Advantages of podcasts

You can listen to the material when you like and where you like, and as many times as you wish in order to fully understand and remember it.

Wikis and Wikipedia

A wiki is a website to which many people can contribute by editing or adding to existing items or creating new pages. There are many kinds of wiki, from corporate and student-created wikis through to large free online resources. The best known are:

- Wikimedia Commons: a large free respository of materials
- Wiktionary: a large, free, online dictionary and thesaurus
- Wikipedia: a free encyclopaedia that aims to provide a neutral viewpoint.

Using Wikipedia selectively in your work

Wikipedia can be a useful starting place when researching a topic. However, it is advisable to use it with caution for assignments.

- Look up and read its references, and then refer to these rather than to Wikipedia in your work.
- For academic work, use specialist texts rather than Wikipedia or other encyclopaediae.
- Use your course reading list and the references in academic texts to develop your information trail, rather than relying on any one source.

How I love to see so many references to Wikipedia in a student's work.

Identifying and selecting relevant information

Reading selectively

Use the reading list

Some courses give long reading lists, and expect you to select items from these. Others provide a short list, expecting you to read everything on it. If in doubt, ask what is expected.

Select the latest information

- To keep up to date, look under 'new titles' in bookshops and look for the latest issues of journals on the library shelves or in the computerised catalogue.
- Check whether statistics and similar data are up to date. Are more recent figures available? If so, should you use these?

Select the most relevant information

- Look for the information that relates most exactly to your assignment.
- Draw up a trial essay plan and see what information you will need. Which themes came up in lectures and seminars?
- Check the back of the book, the contents list and the index to see what the book covers.
- Quickly scan the introduction or conclusion: these may indicate whether the book is worth reading. They may even provide all the information you need.
- Browse through the headings to gain a feel for the book.

Select by reliability

- Is the source a well-known one in the field, such as a recommended academic journal?
- Is the source likely to be biased? If so, does the bias matter in this case?
- Does the text have a good bibliography? Is it clear where any evidence comes from?
- Is the source from a publisher respected in your subject area? (Information in newspapers or from friends is not usually considered reliable.)
- See also *Critical analytical thinking*, page 187.

Select by amount

- Use your essay plan to work out a word limit for each major theme, and then for each topic or example. You will find that you will have very few words to write about any one item.
- Use your word limits to guide you on how much to read and note. If you can only write a line or paragraph about something, you probably don't need to read and note very much.
- Consider whether an article goes into too much depth for your purposes: you may only need to read the abstract or one section.
- Keep asking whether material is relevant to the title of the project, essay, etc.

What do I actually need to read?

If you usually read books from cover to cover, try the following exercise to see how little you could read and still get what you need.

Activity **How much do I need to read?**

- Read any information on the back cover. Browse the contents page, section headings, and the last chapter. Make a few quick notes on what seem to be the main points of the book. Record only the gist of what you read.
- Read the introductory and concluding paragraphs of each chapter. When you finish reading, note any extra important information.
- Read the first line of each paragraph. Note any additional important information.
- Now, read the whole book. How much really important *additional* information did you gain by reading the whole book? Which parts of the book were essential? How little could you have read to grasp the essentials?

Am I a smart reader?

Do you have strategies for approaching your reading? Which of the following do you do?

Know exactly what you are looking for

☐ Do I consider the questions I'm trying to answer?

☐ Do I consider what information I need?

Use reading lists selectively

☐ Do I use the recommended reading list?

☐ Do I know what I *need* to read?

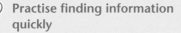

RECOMMENDED READING   *need to read*

1 Jones, E. (1952).   *pp.66-80*

2 Smith, B. (1998).   *Chs 4-6*

3 Atkins, J. (1952).   *intro*

Examine sources for suitability

For each source, do I consider:

☐ whether it's on the reading list?

☐ whether it's up to date or fairly recent?

☐ whether it looks readable and manageable?

☐ whether it has the information I want?

Activity   Practise finding information quickly

Using an index (at the back of the book):

- Select an item to look up.
- Note the page numbers given.
- Using these, find the item in the book as quickly as you can.

How long did this take you? Could you get faster? Did you notice that when you know what you're looking for, your eyes can pick out information on the page more quickly?

Select relevant parts of the book

☐ Do I browse the book quickly?

☐ Do I use the contents page, the headings and the sub-headings for guidance?

☐ Do I identify which parts of which chapters I need, and put markers in these?

Find information quickly

☐ Do I make good use of the index?

☐ Have I got faster with practice?

Select relevant parts of the page

☐ Do I read the chapter heading?

☐ Do I read any sub-headings?

☐ Do I read the first sentence of each paragraph (which should introduce the topic or idea)?

☐ Do I look at any diagrams, graphs or charts?

☐ Do I read any summaries or conclusions?

Chapter 6

Core research skills

Use photocopies

- ☐ Do I make copies of important pages?
- ☐ Do I use marker pens to highlight important words and phrases (only)?
- ☐ Do I jot ideas and thoughts in the margins?
- ☐ Do I make notes about the points I highlighted, to help myself remember them?

Chart the main ideas

- ☐ Do I map out ideas so that I can see how everything fits together?

Practise prediction

- ☐ Am I active in anticipating what is coming next, or what the conclusions will be?

Read interactively

- ☐ Do I think about what I'm reading?
- ☐ Do I question what I'm reading?
- ☐ Do I look for answers to my questions?
- ☐ Do I make notes of the important points, and ideas triggered by what I read?
- ☐ Do I challenge the assumptions of the writer, the logic of the arguments, and the validity of the conclusions?

Vary reading speed and method

- ☐ Do I keep changing my pace, according to the needs of the text? (See page 169.)
- ☐ Do I scan rapidly for specific information?
- ☐ Do I read quickly to get the general sense of a passage, and then read difficult or dense parts slowly?

What is the main point or basic idea I have just read?

Can I sum it up in 10 words?

Do I agree?

Engage with your reading

Be active in your reading. As you read, always have paper and pen to hand.

Use markers

☐ Do I label a corner of my own texts with a keyword summary?

☐ Do I insert labelled bookmarks so that I can find details easily, and need fewer notes?

☐ Do I use tabs and give star ratings to useful pages, making them easier to find later?

Maintain your attention

> I read that three times and I don't remember a word...

There are three major conclusions ...

Listen to yourself read

☐ Do I record myself reading important passages?

☐ Do I listen to these as I travel, or work around the house?

Using two recorders

If you have two recorders, speak your ideas into one as you listen to material on the other.

Create ideal conditions

☐ Do I read with the light from behind, sufficient to light the page but without glare?

☐ Do I sit with a relaxed, upright posture?

☐ Do I take in what I read?

☐ Do I make sure I'm doing so, by:
  - summing up each section?
  - taking regular breaks?
  - reading interactively?
  - moving on when material isn't relevant?

Reading off the computer screen

☐ Do I read best from screen or from paper?

☐ Do I adapt text on my computer to make it easier to read?

Consider time and place

☐ Do I read when I am sufficiently awake and alert?

☐ Is my study environment conducive to reading in a focused way?

> I prefer Arial font 16 blue

Chapter 6

Improving reading comprehension

Do I understand what I read?

Do you:

- understand most of what you read?
- know how much you understand?
- understand material you don't find interesting?
- actively monitor your understanding?
- know how to improve comprehension?

If you answered 'no' to one or more of these questions, experiment with these reading strategies to improve your comprehension.

Active reading strategies

Start with something general

Reading is easier if you have a sense of the context and a general overview of the material. Read a very basic text first, to familiarise yourself with the main issues and the vocabulary.

Monitor your comprehension

Read a few sentences, then stop. Without looking back at the text, sum up what you have read in just a few words. Say these aloud or jot them down. If you cannot do this, read back over what you have read, using an additional strategy from below.

Guide your reading

Set yourself specific questions to start off your reading. Write them down. Adapt the questions as your reading progresses. The clearer you are about what you are trying to discover, the easier it is to find it in the text.

Re-read difficult passages

Academic texts often contain difficult passages. Don't panic! You are bound to need to re-read some passages slowly, several times.

Highlight key words and phrases

On your text, photocopy or screen, underline the information you think may be relevant. Look especially at headings and first and last sentences of paragraphs. Select a few of the key words you underlined and highlight them in colour. Use bold or add a symbol such as a star to indicate the most important points. Be selective: if you underline or highlight everything, *nothing* will stand out as important.

Colour-code information

Use different colours for different kinds of information – for example, one colour for reference names and dates, and one for each of the main schools of thought or major theories for the subject. Later, just seeing that colour combination on the page may bring back to you what the page was about.

Ask 'depth questions'

Look for the underlying issues:

- What point is the writer making?
- Why is this detail relevant?
- Is the writer trying to answer a particular question?
- What lessons can be learnt from this text?

Apply the C·R·E·A·M learning strategy

Consider how you can apply the C·R·E·A·M strategy (Chapter 4) to your reading.

Relaxed reading

Reading comprehension is improved when the body is relaxed. Use appropriate lighting; have music or silence, as you prefer, and drink plain water. See page 381 on relaxation.

Reflection: Smart reading strategies

- How do I approach reading tasks now?
- How could I spend my reading time more effectively?

Improving reading speed

Understanding is the most important aspect of reading, but you will find it helpful if you can also improve your reading *speed*.

How to check your speed

- Find something familiar to read.
- Set the alarm for ten minutes.
- Read for ten minutes at a speed that allows you to understand what you read.
- Count how many words you read.
- Divide this number by ten, to find out how many words you read in one minute.
- Do this using different texts. If you read fewer than 200–250 words per minute, even with material that is clear and interesting, it is worth trying to increase your speed.

Vary your reading strategies

Inspect

Check the title, the contents page, the index, the writing style, and the details on the back cover. Flick through to get the feel of the book. Do you *want* to read it? Do you *need* to read it?

Scan rapidly

Scan the page. Which key words leap out at you? You may sense the 'pattern' of the argument or the general subject matter. Is information organised in a way that helps you? What can you pick up from section headings, diagrams, the first lines of paragraphs, and conclusions to chapters and the text?

Question

Keep asking questions: What am I trying to find out? What do I need to know? Exactly which parts do I need to read?

Locate specifics quickly

To find a specific piece of information quickly, use the index. Go straight to the right page. Move your eye quickly down the page to find what you are looking for.

What is slowing down your reading?

Below is a list of some factors which can slow down reading. Do any apply to you? If so, try the relevant strategies for speeding up your reading (page 170).

- [ ] 1   Do you read advanced texts very infrequently?
- [ ] 2   Do you track with your finger along the line?
- [ ] 3   Do you read out loud under your breath, or mouth the words?
- [ ] 4   Do you read books from cover to cover?
- [ ] 5   Do you start reading before you have worked out what you need to know, or what you are looking for?
- [ ] 6   Do you read word by word?
- [ ] 7   Do you keep checking back along the line, re-reading what you have just read?
- [ ] 8   Do you read difficult sections before you have worked out the general gist?
- [ ] 9   Do you find that the words seem to jump up off the page or that text moves or glares?

Read at the right speed

Read at the appropriate speed for the task. This may be fast for case studies, novels and well-developed arguments, and slowly for texts which condense detailed information into short passages or use unfamiliar specialist vocabulary. As you become more familiar with the ideas and vocabulary used, your speed will increase.

Recall and review

Check that you understand what you have read. What is the basic argument or idea? Does the text answer your questions? Are you convinced by the evidence and the arguments offered? How does what you have read relate to what you already knew? Does it confirm or challenge your views? What else do you need to find out?

Strategies for increasing your reading speed

For each of the problems noted on page 169, there is something you can do to improve matters.

1 Read more advanced texts

Reading improves with practice. Your brain becomes more used to seeing unusual words, and your mind to dealing with complex sentences and ideas. Also, look for subjects that interest you and read more for pleasure.

2 Finger-tracking

Move your finger down the page, directly from top to bottom, to train your eye to move more quickly down the text.

3 Know when to read aloud

Some people read out loud from habit. Reading silently can speed up reading in such cases. However, other people can only understand what they read if they *hear* the words. If you read aloud for this reason, have a go at recording yourself so you can re-read 'by ear' rather than by eye.

4 & 5 Read selectively and actively

Be choosy in what you read. Use the active reading strategies suggested on pages 165–8, such as working out what you are looking for. You will finish reading more quickly, even though your reading speed may be the same.

6 Read larger chunks

Allow your eyes to take in larger chunks, either by resting them less frequently along a line, or by taking in larger sections of text as you browse. Experiment with holding the book further away, so that your eyes can take in more at once. This is also less tiring for the eyes, which allows you to read for longer periods.

7 Build up to difficult texts

Background knowledge of a subject helps to increase reading speed and understanding. If a text looks hard, start with something simpler on the same subject, or read the easiest sections first. You can return to complex sections or more difficult books later.

8 Keep your eyes moving forward

Which of these sentences is easier to read?

A Checking back over back over what what you have read makes understanding checking back makes understanding checking back over makes understanding difficult.

B Checking back over what you have read makes understanding more difficult.

Most people find **B** easier to read because they can take in a larger chunk of memorable 'sense'. Encourage your eyes to keep reading forward to the end of a sentence (to the next full stop). You will then be reading larger units of sense rather than just words and phrases. You can read the whole sentence again if necessary.

9 Jumping and glaring text

- Coloured filters (such as see-through plastic folders) placed over the page can reduce 'jumping' and 'glaring'. Experiment with different colours and see if one suits you best. Using tinted paper may help.
- Consult an optometrist for advice – you may need spectacles with coloured lenses or a particular filter.
- Enlarged photocopies of text can help.
- If the problem is serious and you prefer to 'read by ear', speak to the disability adviser at your institution. There may be specialist equipment to enable you to scan texts and have them read aloud to you, or reading services which record books for you.

Put comprehension first

In some cases slow reading is preferable:

- for texts with condensed information, such as many science and medical texts
- for detailed instructions
- for formulae and equations
- for close analysis of texts, such as for law, literature and history.

Making notes

Why make notes?

How many reasons can you find for making notes? After you have noted some, look at the diagram on page 172. Are your reasons the same? Which of these matter most to you?

Activity **Note-making**

Select a passage from a book and make notes on the main points of what you read – or find some notes you have already made.

Compare your notes with the suggestions made below. Consider whether you could improve your note- making strategies.

A method for making notes

- Put your pen down – so you won't be tempted to copy out of the book.
- If you are typing your notes, don't type as you read.
- Read – to answer your own questions.
- Identify and sum up the main ideas. (Hear them in your own words.)
- Jot down a few words to summarise these.
- Summarise points. This also helps ensure that the notes are in your own words and not accidentally copied from texts into assignments.
- Note *exactly* where information comes from.
- Note real names and quotations *exactly* as they are written.
- Leave space to add details later.

How to make notes

There is no one 'best method', but it is worth considering the following points.

What do you need to note?

Be selective: write just what you need. Consider:

- 'Do I really need this information? If so, which bits exactly?'
- Will I really use it? When, and how?
- Have I noted similar information already?
- What questions do I want to answer with this information?

Organise your notes

- See *Recording and using information* (page 176).
- See *Organising information: planning your writing* (page 289).
- Use a separate file/folder for each subject area.
- For paper notes, use file dividers to separate topics.
- For electronic notes, use separate files for each topic.
- Arrange points under headings or questions. (Notice how information is organised in this *Handbook*.)
- Label everything clearly.
- Number and label pages so you can find them easily.
- Keep an updated contents page at the front of each file.

Note-making styles

Nuclear note-taking style: why take notes?

Is making notes a useful activity? Why make notes at all?

A. Useful record
1. of important points for future use
2. of where the information comes from.

C. Helps understanding if you:
1. focus on selecting info. to note
2. think through where everything fits
3. build levels of detail outwards from core concepts and information.

WHY TAKE NOTES?

B. Helps completing assignments
1. Helps ideas flow.
2. Helps planning – you can see what info. you have.
3. Assists organisation – you can rearrange and renumber notes in a different order.
4. Helps you get started.

D. Helps memory
1. Summing things up briefly helps long-term memory.
2. The physical act of writing helps memory.
3. Pattern notes can be more memorable visually.

E. Helps exam revision
1. Material is well organised.
2. More info. is already in memory.
See example on page 173.

Linear notes: strategies for making notes

① Good note-making: general
1.1 Think before you write
1.2 Keep notes brief
1.3 Keep notes organised
1.4 Use your own words
1.5 Leave spaces – to add notes later

② Useful strategies
2.1 Note keywords and main ideas
2.2 Write phrases – not sentences
2.3 Use abbreviations
2.4 Use headings
2.5 Number points
2.6 Make the page memorable – with colour, illustrations, and so on
2.7 Link up points – using arrows, dotted lines, colour, numbers, boxes
2.8 Note sources of info. exactly
2.9 Write quotations in a different colour

③ Unhelpful strategies
3.1 Copying chunks and phrases
3.2 Writing more notes than you can use again
3.3 Writing out notes several times to make them neater

④ Tidying messy notes
4.1 Shade, or draw a 'square' around, sections of notes in different colours to make them stand out.
4.2 Use shading, changes of colour and headings to divide pages up into clearer sections and to make each page more memorable for revision.
4.3 Link stray pieces of information by arrows or colour. Number the sequence in which to read them.

Pattern notes: an example

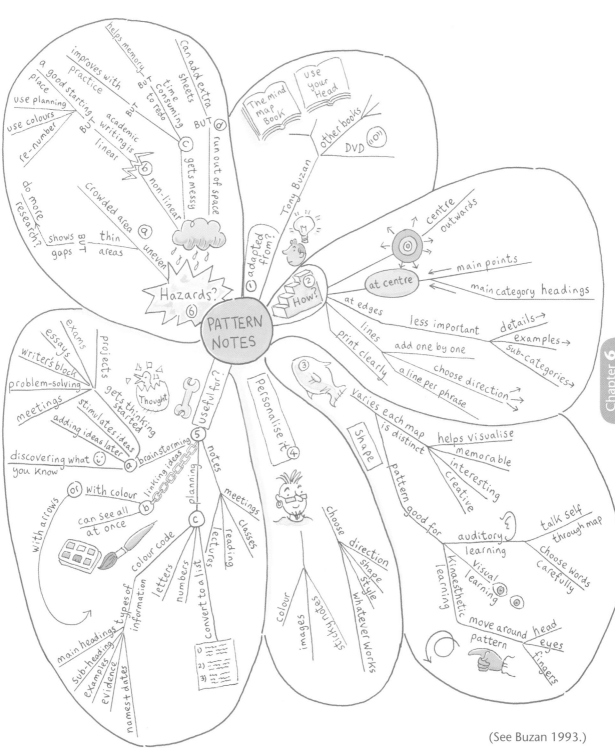

(See Buzan 1993.)

Shortcuts in note-making

Plan for amendments

Leave space in your notes, and a wide margin, so that you can add new information and ideas later. (This is quicker than *rewriting* your notes to incorporate the new information.) Alternatively, word process your notes so that you can summarise, edit, highlight and rearrange them easily.

Make just one set of notes

Aim to have just one set of notes. Visual familiarity will make it easier to find information later, and to recall information during exams.

Use sticky notes

Carry these with you and use to jot down ideas as they occur. Stick them into a plastic folder. You can add these to charts or posters, moving them around to organise ideas for assignments.

Number the pages

Label and number pages. Cross-refer to information already noted elsewhere – for instance, 'see red file, page 24, Amphibians'.

Use abbreviations

Abbreviations save time. Use them in your notes, but not in assignments.

● Work out a system you'll remember.
● Stick to your system.
● Introduce a few at a time, so that your notes make sense.
● Keep a 'key' to your abbreviations to hand.

Useful common symbols

& (+)	and
+	plus, in addition to
>	greater/more than/ better than
<	smaller/less than
=	is the same as/equal to
≠	is not the same as
\	therefore
[\]	because
w/	with
♀	woman/female
♂	man/male
→	this leads to/ produces/causes

Useful common abbreviations

e.g.	for example
i.e.	that is, that means
etc.	and the rest
NB	important, notice this
p.	page (pp. = pages)
para.	paragraph
Ch.	chapter (Chs. = chapters)
edn	edition
info.	information
cd	could
wd	would
Govt	Government
Educ.	Education
impt	important
devt	development
C19	nineteenth century

Which abbreviations are used in *your* subject areas?

Making notes with confidence

Students' solutions

Sonja and Charlie are two students who used to have great difficulties making notes. Here are their accounts of how they tackled their difficulties, with help from a study-skills tutor.

Sonja

There are two things which I find difficult about making notes.

Firstly, I am not very confident about using my own words – the book always seems to say things better. It is very tempting to use nearly the same words as the book. I imagine that I will rewrite them in my own words later – but then I don't have the time, or I forget which bits are taken from the book, and end up with the words of the book in my essay without even realising.

The second thing I find difficult is working out what to take notes about, especially keeping to essentials. I worry in case I miss out information I will need in the future. I can end up with 10 sides of notes from reading only a few pages. It takes ages and there is too much to even look at a second time. When I came to revise for my first exams, I had too many notes to revise – there were simply too many to read, never mind learn.

Now I spend more time thinking and planning before I even touch a book. I try to work out what information I want. I draw a mind-map with everything I already know, and what I need to find out. If I have an essay title I do a rough plan really early, even before I start reading – just to get the shape in my head.

I always start with the easiest book – just to get a picture of what it is all about. With other books, I use the contents page and headings to work out where information is. At this stage I don't write much except something like 'gold – producer countries: p. 248 and pp. 265–9'.

When I have more idea of what I am looking for, and where that information is, I take more detailed notes. Sometimes, I do this by writing a question and putting the information as an answer. When I am not sure if I want some information, I just write a few lines onto an index card, saying where I can find that information later if I really need it.

Charlie

It's taking notes in lectures that I find hardest as I either day drift off and forget to note anything, or I type notes up as I go and make far more notes than I need. It's hard to keep track of what is being said and to select out important points at the same time.

I find it helps if I prepare before the lecture. I browse the topic online and look over the chapters quickly. If something looks complicated, I work out, if I can, what it is about before the lecture. I make notes in advance, or just make a list of the things I have information on already. I make a list of the questions I still need answers to. I don't need to make loads of notes in class then.

We sometimes get podcasts of lectures and I listen to the bits of these that I think will be most useful.

Reflection: Note-making strategy

These are just two approaches to dealing with note-making. Do any of their ideas appeal to you? Or do you have a better system?

Reading, recording and using information

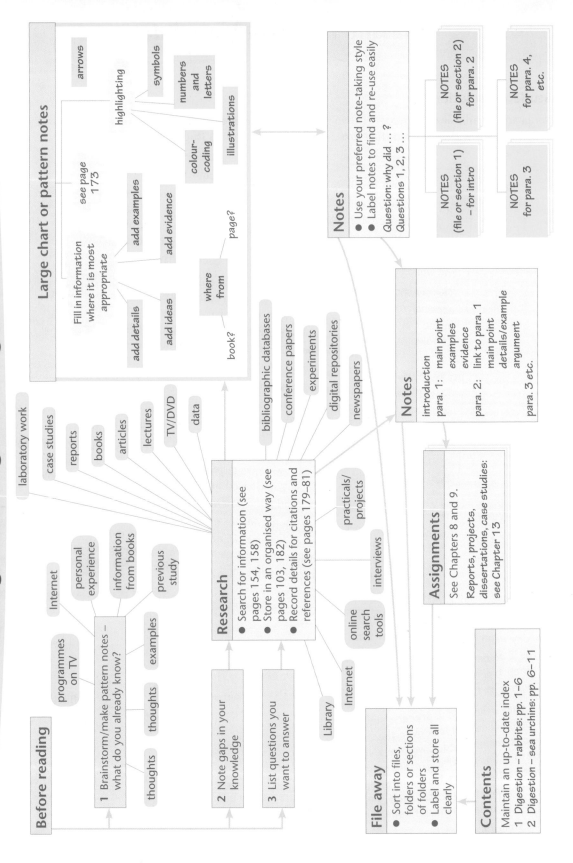

Before reading

1 Brainstorm/make pattern notes – what do you already know?

- programmes on TV
- Internet
- personal experience
- information from books
- previous study
- thoughts
- thoughts
- examples
- thoughts

2 Note gaps in your knowledge

3 List questions you want to answer

Research

- Search for information (see pages 154, 158)
- Store in an organised way (see pages 103, 182)
- Record details for citations and references (see pages 179–81)

- laboratory work
- case studies
- reports
- books
- articles
- lectures
- TV/DVD
- data
- bibliographic databases
- conference papers
- experiments
- digital repositories
- newspapers
- practicals/projects
- interviews
- online search tools
- Internet
- Library

Large chart or pattern notes

Fill in information where it is most appropriate

- add details
- add ideas
- add examples
- add evidence

where from
book?
page?

- highlighting
- colour-coding
- illustrations
- arrows
- symbols
- numbers and letters

see page 173

Notes

- Use your preferred note-taking style
- Label notes to find and re-use easily

Question: why did ….?
Questions 1, 2, 3 …

NOTES (file or section 1) – for intro

NOTES (file or section 2) for para. 2

NOTES for para. 3

NOTES for para. 4, etc.

Notes

introduction
para. 1: main point
examples
evidence
link to para. 1
para. 2: main point
details/example
argument
para. 3 etc.

Assignments

See Chapters 8 and 9.

Reports, projects, dissertations, case studies: see Chapter 13

File away

- Sort into files, folders or sections of folders
- Label and store all clearly

Contents

Maintain an up-to-date index
1 Digestion – rabbits: pp. 1–6
2 Digestion – sea urchins: pp. 6–11

Plagiarism

What is plagiarism?

Plagiarism is the use of the work of others without acknowledgement of your source of information or inspiration. This includes:

- using words more or less exactly as they have been used in articles, lectures, television programmes, books, or anywhere else
- using other people's ideas or theories without saying whose ideas they are
- paraphrasing what you read or hear without stating where it comes from.

Even if you change a few words or sentences you have 'borrowed', or if you reordered them, the result is still plagiarism.

Plagiarism is treated very seriously, and plagiarised work is usually disqualified. This can have a major impact on your marks or grades.

Using quotations

Quotations should be:

- used sparingly – and only if the words really are worth quoting
- brief – a few words or, at most, a few lines.

In writing a quotation you should:

- copy words and punctuation *exactly*
- use three dots (…) to indicate omitted words
- put 'quotation marks' around the words you quote: *'Stunning,' wrote the artist*
- state exactly the source of the quotation (see page 180).

Develop confidence in your own words

Use your own words, even if you don't think you write well – they count for more than copied text.

Other people's words make for a poor survival strategy

How to avoid plagiarism

- Write all your notes in your own words.
- Note down *exactly* where you read the information you put in your notes.
- In your assignment, cite the sources of ideas and information. Do this even when not giving a quotation. Make it clear when you are using a direct quotation.
- At the end of your work, write a full list of references.
- For details of how to cite your sources and give quotations, see pages 179–82.

Avoid accidental plagiarism

If you have a habit of copying:

- Put your pen or keyboard out of reach.
- Read a passage without taking any notes.
- Stop reading and cover up the page.
- Sum up what you have read. If possible, say this aloud, or record yourself, so you hear your own words and in your own voice. If this remains difficult, look back to *Improving reading comprehension* (page 168).
- Once you can say what the passage is about, note it down in your own words.
- If you want to copy material to use as a quotation, write it in a different colour so that you can find it easily. The colour will also show you how much you copy.

Detecting plagiarism and copying

eggs
cheese
potatoes

Read each of the pieces of text below and decide whether the text is an example of plagiarism, and why. The original text, on which the examples are based, can be found on pages 60–6.

Text 1

Research shows that students who do best at problem-solving spend longer than other students at working out exactly what a problem is before they try to solve it. Weaker students look at the surface of the problem and do not see the underlying structure that makes it similar to problems they already know.

Text 2

Many people undervalue their own intelligence because they hold mistaken views about what constitutes 'intelligence'. This is partly because too much emphasis has been placed upon the idea of 'IQ'. In addition, early educational experiences can damage self-esteem or be demotivating, undermining a natural interest in learning. There is a body of research that argues that outstanding performance in almost any field of human activity can be fostered if the right conditions are in place. Those conditions include finding the right learning strategy for each person.

Text 3

There is strong evidence to suggest that environment plays a great part in intellectual performance. In Japan, the Suzuki Violin Education Programme has trained many children to play the violin to virtuoso level. Being part of a culture that values academic intelligence also helps. Donaldson (1978) argued that the way we reason depends upon the particular context we are in.

Text 4

'There is strong evidence to suggest that environment plays a great part in intellectual performance' (Cottrell, 2013). Cottrell writes: 'In Japan, the Suzuki Violin Education Programme has trained many children to play the violin to virtuoso level.' She also points out: 'Being part of a culture that values academic intelligence also helps.' Cottrell cites Donaldson (1978), who argued that the way we reason depends upon the particular context we are in.

Text 5

The reasons for appearing 'intelligent' or not may depend upon a complex set of factors, all of which interact (Cottrell, 2013). Butterworth (1992) suggests that we can even believe ourselves to be incapable of a task that is well within our capacities. This can occur simply because we do not recognise the similarity of two tasks when the circumstances appear different. This view is supported by research. It has been demonstrated that students who spend more time early on actively looking for similarities between writing tasks and areas of existing expertise are then more successful at the writing task (Bloggs, 2014). This suggests that academic success may be more a question of good strategy and of building upon experience rather than underlying 'intelligence'.

Text 6

Various psychologists have used experiments on identical twins to suggest that anything up to 80% of our intelligence could be genetically based. Others argue that twins' similar physical appearance and cultural upbringing could account for similarities in their performance. Whilst people who do well on one intelligence test do well on other such tests, there is evidence that such performance is also affected by familiarity with the culture and thinking of those who designed the test.

See Answers, page 407.

Citations and references

Why are references needed?

In academic writing, it is essential to acknowledge, or 'cite' the sources of ideas and information. Such citations allow readers to refer back to the sources for themselves.

There are five main reasons for acknowledging your sources through citations and references.

1 It is a courtesy to the person whose idea or words you have used or referred to.
2 By giving the source you make it clear to the reader that you are not trying to pretend somebody else's work is your own. (You are not 'plagiarising' their work.)
3 It helps your readers to find the original texts or webpages to read themselves, should they wish.
4 If you need to check something later, the reference will help you find it again more easily.
5 People will have more confidence in your assertions if they know where your information comes from. Thoroughness in referencing suggests that you will also have been thorough in checking your facts.

When must you cite your source?

You do this whenever you draw on a source of information:

● as your inspiration (in general)
● for a particular theory, argument or viewpoint
● for specific information, such as statistics, examples, or case studies
● for direct quotations, reproducing the writer's exact words
● for texts and information that you paraphrase or allude to rather than quote.

What information do you give?

Imagine that you wished to read for yourself a source text used by another author. What information would *you* need to locate that source easily? The information usually provided includes:

● the name and initials of the author(s)
● the title, in full
● the year of publication
● for journal articles, the name of the journal and the number of the volume
● the edition, if relevant
● the name and location of the publisher
● relevant page numbers
● for electronic materials, the URL for the webpage and the date it was downloaded.

Provide extra information if needed. For example, to find a photograph, print or manuscript you may need the name of the library, the collection, and the catalogue number of the item within the collection. The important question to ask is, 'Could somebody else *find* this source from the information I have given?'

Where do you put this information?

Citations in the body of the text

Whenever you refer to someone else's work, either directly or indirectly, indicate whose work this is.

Use the format recommended by your tutors. Usually this will be simply the surname of the author(s), the year of publication and possibly the page number(s), using brackets in one of these ways:

> … and as noted by Cohen and Smith (2013), there are many …
>
> … and as noted by Cohen and Smith (2013, p. 56), there are many …
>
> Evidence for this is well established (Cohen and Smith 2013).

References at the end of the assignment

Write out full details in a list of 'References' – see page 181 for guidance, and pages 415–17 for an example of such a list.

Citing your sources

There are various ways of acknowledging your source materials. Check whether you are expected to use a particular system for your course. If not, use the Harvard (author–date) system.

The Harvard system

When you have used, quoted or paraphrased a source, acknowledge it. Either within the sentence or at the end of the sentence, write in brackets the author's name, the date of publication and, if required, page numbers. Full details of the source should be written out in the reference section.

Text citations

Here are three different ways of using sources.

Short direct quotation – within the text

> Nonetheless, the film was deliberately inaccurate about the life of José Martí. Jesus Colon (1982, p. 82) pointed this out when he wrote, 'José Marti never had a mansion or a hut of his own. Needless to say, he never had slaves.'

Paraphrasing

> Nonetheless, the film was deliberately inaccurate about José Martí, who, contrary to the image depicted in American films, spent much of his life in poverty (Colon 1982, pp. 81–2).

Longer direct quotation

A few words, carefully chosen, make the most powerful quotations, and demonstrate that you can select appropriately. Avoid long quotations; they are rarely needed. If the exact wording of a long quotation is essential, however, indent it and leave space above and below (as shown on the right). Incorporate the quotation clearly into your writing with linking sentences and by discussing its relevance.

References list

In the 'References' at the end of the essay, the reference to Colon would appear in this form (and in alphabetical order):

> Colon, J. (1982). *A Puerto Rican in New York and Other Sketches*, 2nd edn. New York: International Publishers.

Note that for books you don't give page numbers in the 'References'. For a journal article you give the page numbers for the whole article.

Useful phrases to introduce references

- As *X* points out, …
- According to *X*, …
- To quote from *X*, '…'
- *X* states/suggests that …
- *X* tells/shows us that …
- In an article entitled *Name of Text*, *X* makes the point that …
- Referring to …, *X* says that …
- As *X* stated/wrote/said, …
- In *Name of Text*, *X* wrote that …
- Writing in *Name of Text*, *X* explained that …
- Writing in 1926, *X* argued that …

Angry at Hollywood versions of Latin American history, Jesus Colon wrote:

> After pictures like *Zapata* and *Santiago* we can only hope that these Hollywood vulgarisers and distorters, without the least bit of respect for the history and culture of our Latin American nations, won't lay their bovine eyes upon epic themes like the Aztec struggle against Cortes' conquest of Mexico, or Sandino's fight against American imperialism … (1982, p. 84)

Here we can see that Colon is very critical of versions of Latin American history produced in the USA.

Writing out your references

At the end of your assignment, provide a full list of your references – all the sources to which you referred within the assignment. Each time you draw on a source of information in any way to inform your own work, record the details that you will need for your list of references. See page 179 for a list of the details to include.

Reference Management Tools

A number of tools are available free online and make it easier to record details for references.

Mendeley, Zotero, Endnote, Reference Manager: all allow you to import references from digital sources, databases and pdfs, and use these to produce your list of references in word-processing tools.

CiteULike: useful for storing articles, adding notes and tagging sources you might wish to cite and reference.

Conventions in writing references

- Don't number the items.
- Begin each source on a new line.
- List alphabetically, by author's surname.
- If you use more than one work by a given author and published in the same year, label these a, b, c … (2013a, 2013b, 2013c, …) in the text and in your References.
- Order information as in the examples here (author, date, title, location of publisher, publisher) or as recommended by your tutor.
- Italicise titles of books or journals.
- Use 'single' quotation marks for the title of an article within a journal.
- Include every source referred to in your assignment, including DVDs, TV and online sources, but not dictionaries or reference books.
- Don't include in your 'References' materials that you have not used for your assignment.
- List additional sources, which you read but did not use, in a 'Bibliography'.

Sample references (see also pages 415–17)

A book:

> Bailey, P. (1978). *Leisure and Class in Victorian England*. London: Methuen.

A chapter in a book:

> Humm, M. (1991). 'Landscape for a literary feminism: British women writers 1900 to the present'. In Forsas-Scott, H. (ed.). *Textual Liberation: European feminist writing in the twentieth century*. London: Routledge.

A journal article:

> Jones, C. (1980). 'The welfare of the French footsoldier.' *History* **65** (no. 214), 193–213.

Material cited within another text, where you have not quoted the original source:

> O'Connor, J. and McDermott, I. (1996). *Principles of NLP*. London: Thorsons. Cited in Cottrell, S. M. (2013). *The Study Skills Handbook*. Basingstoke: Palgrave.

An electronic reference (include the URL and the date on which you downloaded it):

> http://www.foe.co.uk. 6 July 2013.

Bibliographies

A bibliography is a list of everything you read for the assignment, whether or not you referred to it in your writing. Your tutor may require both. Write out using the same conventions as for references.

Tools for storing, retrieving and sharing information

Saving work

- Always make more than one copy, especially of assignments. Loss of material is not usually accepted as an excuse for handing work in late and penalties can be harsh.
- Save to one or more locations: memory sticks, online storage such as Dropbox, Google Docs or cloud, as an email attachment, and to your hard drive.

Storing useful websites

Store the addresses of useful websites marking them as favourites or bookmarks, so your browser can then find them easily for you in future. You can build up named collections of your own bookmarks.

You can tag pages that you want to use again, using keywords relevant to your assignment. This enables you to retrieve relevant pieces of information easily from within sources that you have bookmarked.

Storing with Delicious

If you do this using a social networking tool such as Delicious, then you can also:
- access these from anywhere with access to the Internet
- share bookmarks with other students, such as those in your project group.

Sharing information for group assignments

Most universities and colleges now set assignments that require you to work collaboratively with other students, and some of the skills you will need for such joint working and group projects are looked at in Chapter 10. Such groupwork is made easier by tools that enable you to share information and work collaboratively online.

Google Docs

- Use to create, store, update and share documents, data, project work and group presentations, free and online anywhere.
- Share documents with other students in your group – and edit them together online from anywhere with an Internet connection.
- Google Docs lets you see revisions to the documents made by all users, and to revert to an earlier version of the document.

Dropbox

Dropbox is a free online storage facility that lets you work on documents online anywhere, and synchronises them across multiple devices. You can invite other people to access your folders and files and work in Dropbox collaboratively.

Sharing References

Reference management tools

You can use Mendeley, Zotero, CiteULike, and Reference Manager to share references.

> ### Check whether sharing is permitted
>
> Always check whether such sharing is permitted within the brief set for your assignment. Sometimes, sharing will be encouraged, but for other assignments, you are expected to undertake all tasks independently without sharing.
>
> It would usually be reasonable to share bookmarks with other students, to let them know about material you have found interesting on the Internet. You may need to use shared references and Google Docs more selectively.

Using information from lectures and taught sessions

Lectures and other taught sessions are designed as useful starting points for your study. They give a general overview of the main ideas, theories, debates and recent research in the subject, as a guide to your own reading and reflection.

Before the lecture or class

The better you prepare in advance, the easier it is to make sense of information in class, what you need to check and what is worth noting.

- Gain a feel for the subject of the next lecture or session. Read (or browse) a book about it. Look for themes, issues, and headings. Look up any technical words you don't understand.
- Write down questions you want answered. Leave space to write the answers under each question either during or after the lecture.
- Jot down your own opinion. Notice if it changes during the lecture.
- Glance through your notes from the previous class, and look for links with the next one.

During the lecture or class

Teaching staff vary in whether they prefer questions during or after the lecture or class. They usually go through the subject quite quickly, and expect you to jot down main themes and references.

- To focus attention, listen for clues from the lecturer about the direction of travel. For example: 'There are five major categories of …', 'Now, I want to look at …' or 'So, why does this happen?'
- Good teachers tell you at the beginning which main topics will be covered and in which order, or write up headings. Use such information to help you structure your notes.
- Note down headings, questions, points and references provided during the session.
- Avoid writing details you can easily get later from a textbook. Keep your attention for your listening. If you are not clear on the source of information, ask.
- Mentally challenge what is said: this helps focus your attention. Ask yourself, 'Is this always the case?', 'How representative is this?', 'Why is this?' and 'Do I agree?'
- Note down interesting questions and points made by other students.

After the lecture or class

- Label and file notes and handouts.
- Read through your notes. Fill in details from your reading or research.
- Discuss the lecture or class with others. Compare your notes and fill in any gaps.
- Use any podcasts and follow-up materials provided online.

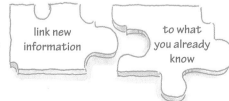

How helpful are your notes?

Using notes provided for you

In advance of a lecture or class, during it or after it, your tutors may give you printed notes. These may be transcripts of their presentation, *PowerPoint*® handouts, outline notes, or background text. They may be printed out for you or posted on a website, or available through the Virtual Learning environment (VLE).

Knowing that you have these materials, you may be tempted not to make your own notes – or you may be overwhelmed by having so much to read all at once.

- If you are given a large set of notes at the beginning of term, check how much you need to read each week.
- Whenever possible, read handouts before the lecture or class – to help you to follow what is said in class.
- When you are given printed notes, make them your own by highlighting, condensing or annotating them.

Notes for Week 1.

MORE ON-LINE COURSE NOTES

Many of the reasons for making notes outlined on page 172 apply even when you are provided with excellent printed notes. By working on these notes to produce your own set, you will:

- ensure that they make sense to you
- make the content your own
- absorb and remember the information.

outlined on page 172

How helpful are your notes?

For each of these sets of opposite statements, tick along the line depending on how far it is true of your own notes.

Reflection: Improving your notes

Record your ideas about how to improve your notes. What is the priority?

Easy to read	Hard to read
Brief, to the point	Too detailed
Easy to understand	Hard to understand
Well organised	Poorly organised
Pages numbered/labelled	No system
Easy to learn from	Difficult to learn from
Well abbreviated	No abbreviations
Important ideas stand out clearly	Not easy to see important points
In my own words	Chunks copied from books or lectures
My words clearly separated from quotations	Easy to confuse my words with quoted material
Source material clearly referenced	Hard to see where material comes from

---

Information gained from practical and laboratory work

What are practicals and laboratory work for?

These vary a great deal from one subject to another, but some general principles are outlined below.

Practicals

Practicals are designed to help you:

- practise using equipment, procedures and techniques
- test theory and previous research findings through your own empirical enquiry
- learn how to design experiments so as to gain the data needed for specific purposes.

Health and safety

Make sure you know and understand any Health and Safety Regulations – and follow them carefully.

Laboratory work

Laboratory work is designed to help you develop skills in

- working in a systematic way, usually to an agreed, planned methodology
- accurate observation
- recording data precisely
- interpreting data
- evaluating your own, and other people's, findings in a constructively critical way
- reporting clearly on your methods, findings and conclusions
- clarifying your thinking about the aims and purpose of specific experiments.

It helps you to develop an understanding of such things as:

- how and why knowledge usually moves forward in small, incremental steps, building on what is already known
- why results are often unpredictable
- why it can be difficult to devise perfectly controlled conditions that give you results that are straightforward to interpret.

Basic principles

Be assertive

Make sure you get your fair share of time using equipment. Don't be content watching others – have a go yourself.

Ask

If you are concerned about using equipment with which you are not familiar, ask for help.

Find out

Clarify which theory or experimental findings the practical is supposed to be testing or demonstrating.

Discuss

Discuss your findings with your lecturer and with other students.

Read

Read around the subject. How is the theory or the experiment applicable to real life? What kinds of results have others gained? What impacts on results?

Record

Record *exactly* your methods and what happens. Don't change your results to what you think the 'right answer' is. Many experiments work only in ideal conditions. Your lecturers will know this and will be looking to see how you record your method and data, and your discussion of why you think you got the results you did.

Write it up

Write up your method, results and conclusions neatly and clearly. Find out the required format for writing up practicals and experiments in your subject area. Are you expected to include diagrams, tables and graphs?

Review

As a student, you will be required to undertake background work, or research, into the topics you are set for assignments. This chapter has looked at generic skills useful for most academic disciplines. These cover the core processes needed to find and make use of information for academic purposes.

The underlying research processes are not necessarily very different from those you would use for everyday purposes. The key differences lie in such considerations as:

- **Being able to recognise material** that is of suitable quality for academic purposes
- **Knowing where to look** for good quality sources relevant to your subject
- **Managing very large amounts** of material
- **Using effective search strategies** so you can find the right material quickly within the vast range of sources available
- **Generating your own data**, such as through experiments
- **Creating useful notes** when reading, from experiments and in taught sessions, that help you to make use of information
- **Storing and retrieving information** effectively, so you can find it and make sense of it again quickly when needed
- **Drawing upon material appropriately** within your assignments
- **Citing and referencing** sources correctly, following recognised conventions.

As you move through your course, it is likely that you will develop further your underlying skills in reading at speed and with improved comprehension, being able to focus your listening, taking more selective notes, identifying key points more quickly, generating your own data and working with more specialist texts and sources. Reading widely will build your expertise in the knowledge base, concepts and specialist vocabulary of the subject.

Later chapters look at other skills that support the kind of research that you will undertake for student assignments. These include:

- using numbers
- analysing sources and data using critical analysis
- generating your own data and presenting these
- selecting and applying data to meet given assignment briefs
- writing up your findings within typical academic structures such as essays, project reports, case-studies and dissertations.

As you develop such skills and apply them, you will find that they are mutually reinforcing. The more critical an eye you bring to your resources, the faster and more adept you will be at recognising good quality material and selecting exactly what you need. The better you are able to manage information, the better use you will make of your time and the more you will improve the standard of your academic work.

Chapter 7
Critical analytical thinking

Learning outcomes

This chapter offers you opportunities to:

- understand what is meant by taking a critical or analytical approach
- become more aware of how to use critical and analytical thinking when reading and writing
- develop criteria for evaluating an argument or a line of reasoning in a piece of writing
- develop criteria for evaluating the evidence given in a piece of writing
- learn how to identify and draw valid conclusions.

Critical thinking

Critical thinking means weighing up the arguments and evidence *for* and *against*. Edward Glaser, who developed a test of critical thinking, defined it in this way (1941):

> Critical thinking calls for a persistent effort to examine any belief or supposed form of knowledge in the light of the evidence that supports it and the further conclusions to which it tends.

In other words, Glaser emphasises the importance of the following:

- *persistence*: considering an issue carefully, and more than once
- *evidence*: evaluating the evidence put forward in support of the belief or viewpoint
- *implications*: considering where the belief or viewpoint leads – what conclusions would follow; are these suitable and rational; and if not, should the belief or viewpoint be reconsidered?

Critical analytical thinking

Critical analytical thinking involves additional processes:

- standing back from the information given
- examining it in detail from many angles
- examining material in terms of its component parts; identifying how these relate to each other
- checking closely whether it is completely accurate
- checking whether each statement follows logically from what went before
- looking for possible flaws in the reasoning, the evidence, or the way that conclusions are drawn
- comparing the same issue from the point of view of other theorists or writers
- being able to see and explain why different people arrived at different conclusions
- being able to argue why one set of opinions, results or conclusions is preferable to another
- being on guard for literary or statistical devices that encourage the reader to take questionable statements at face value
- checking for hidden assumptions
- checking for attempts to lure the reader into agreement.

Develop a detective-like mind

To develop critical and analytical thinking ability, you might imagine that you are developing a detective-like mind.

Reading

Critical thinking when *reading* involves the following:

1 identifying the line of reasoning in the text
2 critically evaluating the line of reasoning
3 questioning surface appearances and checking for hidden assumptions or agendas
4 identifying evidence in the text
5 evaluating the evidence according to valid criteria
6 identifying the writer's conclusions
7 deciding whether the evidence given supports these conclusions.

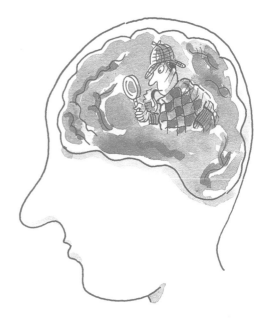

Writing

Critical thinking when *writing* involves comparable processes:

1 being clear on your position on the issue, including hypotheses and/or conclusions
2 constructing a clear line of reasoning – an 'argument' leading to your conclusion
3 presenting evidence to support your reasoning
4 analysing issues from multiple perspectives, weighing up the evidence for each
5 drawing together information and analyses, synthesising these to construct your position in the issues
6 writing in a critical, analytical style, rather than in a descriptive, personal or journalistic style
7 reading your own writing critically, as above, as well as your sources.

Listening

Critical thinking when *listening* involves the same awareness as when reading, plus:

1 checking for consistency in what the speaker is saying – does the speaker appear to contradict herself or himself; and if so, what is going on beneath that contradiction?

2 checking that body language, eye contact, and speed and tone of voice are consistent, or 'congruent', with what is being said: does the speaker look and sound as though he or she believes what he or she is saying?

These issues have been touched on in earlier chapters: the following pages explore them in more detail, and include some basic exercises so that you can try out your critical thinking skills.

Critical questions

In general, when working in a critical way you will be asking questions such as those below.

● Why?
● How far?
● How much?
● How often?
● To what extent?
● How do we know this is true?
● How reliable is this source?
● What could be going on below the surface?
● What do we *not* know about this?
● Which is preferable?
● For what reasons?

Critical thinking when reading

Critical thinking when reading is essential to academic success, as much of the writing you do for assignments will include critical analysis of the work of other people.

1 Identify the line of reasoning

Most of the texts you are required to read as a student will include an argument. In academic writing, an 'argument' is:

● a line of reasoning *or*
● an angle or a point of view *or*
● a position that is being defended *or*
● a case that is being made
  – backed up by evidence and examples and
  – leading to conclusions.

When reading, you need to keep asking yourself, 'What are the main things this writer wants me to accept? What reasons does she or he present to encourage me to accept this?'

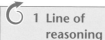

Activity 1 Line of reasoning

Identify the main line of reasoning – the main argument – in Passage 1, 'Rochborough Health'. (See page 408 for feedback.)

Passage 1: Rochborough Health

Outdoor play has beneficial effects for children in terms of both their health and their levels of social interaction. According to clinical trials carried out by Rochborough's Health Council Advisory Body in September this year, children who played outside for over fifty days in the year had a 20% higher lung capacity, and 30% lower incidence of asthma and bronchial conditions than children who played indoors. Children who played outdoors also reported having more friends than those who played indoors. A survey of 30 families by Rochborough Social Amenities Committee found that parents were more likely to let their children play outdoors if they had their own gardens or if there were supervised play areas nearby. Mr Arkash of Milton Road said his children did not feel safe playing on the Children's Meadow on the outskirts of Rochborough, as his son had been frightened by a fox there in the past. His little son looked quite tearful as his father spoke. 'He often cries because he has nowhere to play,' said his father. Supervised play areas can be expensive to provide. However, only 18% of homes in Rochborough have gardens. Therefore, to improve the health of all its children, Rochborough needs to provide more supervised outdoor play areas.

Rochborough Playcouncil Newsletter

---

2 Critically evaluate the line of reasoning

An argument can be critically evaluated in terms of whether it contains:

● relevant, contributing and sufficient propositions (reasons)
● logical progression
● false premises
● flawed reasoning.

Each of these is explored below.

Relevant, contributing and sufficient propositions

The Rochborough Health passage makes a number of statements or *propositions*. For example:

● Outdoor play improves levels of social interaction.
● Only 18% of Rochborough homes have gardens.

These are some of the reasons it gives to support its argument.

When examining the line of reasoning, you need to consider whether the reasons given are relevant and whether they support (that is, contribute to) the overall argument. For example:

- The reference to the isolated incident of a fox is not very relevant to the argument about health.
- The reference to the expense of supervised play areas *is* relevant to the argument – however, it weakens or undermines the argument rather than contributing to it, because the piece does not make clear how the expense could be met.

It is important to check that reasons and evidence are both relevant and supportive of the main argument, as this helps you to identify whether the writer's conclusion is valid. Even if the writer has given relevant reasons that contribute to the argument, however, she or he may not have given sufficient reasons to prove that this is the *only* conclusion that could be drawn.

Passage 2: Injuries

There has been a tremendous rise in the rate of industrial injury. This year there were over thirty reports of repetitive strain injury in the factory (Smilex Injury Report 2013). All those injured worked in the fibre department. Ten years ago there were no reported injuries. This shows that our work conditions are taking a more serious toll upon our health than in the past.

Smilex News

The writer of Passage 2 begins from the premise (starting point) that there has been a great rise in industrial injury. The conclusion is that work conditions are having a more serious effect on health than in the past. The writer gives a relevant and contributory reason: the rise in the number of reported injuries. However, the writer does not consider other reasons why the number of reported injuries might have increased – such as whether repetitive strain injury was known about thirty years ago, or whether people were less likely to report accidents in the past.

In addition, the writer has not looked at figures for any other types of injury, or at the health of

workers in other departments. He or she makes generalisations based on only one kind of injury and one part of the factory. The writer may still be *right* about the rise in industrial injury, but has not proved this. He or she has not given sufficient reasons (or evidence) to justify the conclusion.

Logical progression

In everyday conversation, it is common practice when someone is speaking to assume that there is a logical connection between one thing that is said and the next. For written arguments and in academic contexts in general, you need to question whether one point does indeed follow logically from another. A line of reasoning will:

- begin from a premise
- follow in logical stages (*A* leads to *B*; *B* leads to *C*; *C* leads to *D* …)
- lead to a conclusion that follows directly from what has gone before (there are relevant reasons, in a logical order, which build towards the stated conclusion).

The premise in Passage 1 is that outdoor play is good for children's health. The logical progression would be:

- local evidence supports the health argument (that outdoor play is desirable)
- parents' attitudes support this argument
- a lack of facilities prevents outdoor play
- more outdoor play facilities are needed.

False premises

If there were a reason why outdoor play was *not* good for Rochborough children, the writer of Passage 1 would have started from a 'false premise'. The writer of Passage 2 may indeed have begun from a 'false premise' – believing that industrial injury is on the rise in the Smilex factory. No conclusive evidence of this is given, so it may not be true.

It is useful to be on the lookout for false premises: many arguments are based on weak foundations of this kind.

Flawed reasoning

Here are some examples of 'flawed reasoning'.

Assuming a causal connection

If two things occur at the same time or place, it is

easy to assume either that they must be connected or that one must have caused the other. For example:

> I revised really well for that exam and got a low mark, so next time I won't revise and I should get a better mark.

This assumes a connection between revision and failure, without considering other possible reasons for failure. Similarly:

> The number of cows in Britain has gone down, and the amount of cheese consumed is on the increase. Psychologically, people seem to eat more cheese when they feel that it will run out.

This assumes that the increase in cheese consumption is related to the number of British cows, whereas it may have been for other reasons such as increased vegetarianism, or a rise in cheese imports. The decrease in the cow population might relate only to herds reared for meat – perhaps the number of milking cows is unaltered.

These examples are chosen to highlight the faulty logic, but flawed reasoning of this sort is not always easy to spot.

Drawing general conclusions based on one or few examples

> The woollen jacket caused a serious skin reaction in the three-year-old, so sale of woollen clothing should be banned.

Here a generalised conclusion is made on the basis of a very small sample of experience – just one example. (The importance of using an adequate sample is explored further below.) There may have been reasons for the reaction unique to that child.

Inappropriate comparisons

In Passage 1 a comparison is drawn between children who play indoors and those who play outdoors. However, it may have been that the children who played outdoors were already healthier, and those who played indoors did so because of poor health which might get worse if they played outdoors. For example, asthma sufferers are often allergic to pollen and might have been discouraged from playing outdoors.

3 Question surface appearances

Critical thinking requires that you examine these factors:

- Is the evidence what it appears to be?
- Might there be other explanations apart from the obvious one?
- Has all necessary information been given, or might other details lead to a different conclusion?
- Are there interested parties who would gain if the conclusions were accepted?
- Are there hidden assumptions or agendas?
- Does the evidence come from a reliable, disinterested source?

Activity **2 Vested interests**

Look again at the 'Rochborough Health' passage.
- What hidden agendas might there be in this piece?
- What information may be missing that might lead to a different conclusion?

(See page 408 for feedback.)

4 Identify evidence in the text

Identifying evidence in the text is usually fairly straightforward. Look for statistics, examples, case histories, findings from experiments, surveys, questionnaires or case studies. The evidence may be anecdotal – that is, stories told by one or a few people about their experiences.

Activity **3 Types of evidence**

What evidence is given in the 'Rochborough Health' passage? (See page 408 for feedback.)

5 Evaluate the evidence

It is not enough for a student to write in an essay or report: 'There is evidence on both sides.' Evidence is not all of equal weight. How can we decide which evidence is better? Some basic guidelines are outlined below.

Use valid criteria to evaluate evidence

Critical thinking involves identifying valid criteria against which something can be evaluated.

For example, in declaring that somebody is healthy, a doctor takes into account certain criteria, such as body temperature, blood measurements, and the absence of known (or common) symptoms of illness. He or she evaluates whether signs of potential ill health are matters for concern and, on the basis of experience and established medical knowledge, comes to a conclusion about whether the evidence points more towards good health than to sickness.

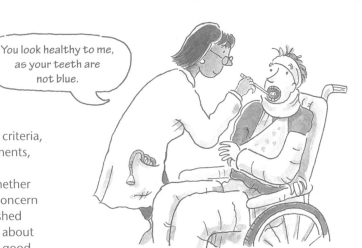

> You look healthy to me, as your teeth are not blue.

The following sections give some criteria against which you can evaluate evidence in academic texts and for your own research.

Check the date of the research

Data may be out of date or conclusions based upon it may have been revised. How would your attitude to the 'Rochborough Health' article change if you found out that it was written in 1300, or 1927, or 2013?

Check the source of your information

Articles in academic or professional journals and in recommended textbooks are usually based on in depth research, and are regarded as more reliable than findings recorded in magazines and newspapers. Newspapers and magazines may be useful primary sources for some subjects such as cultural studies, but are not generally regarded as 'authorities' to quote in essays.

Check for bias in your sources

Bias may not be obvious, and it does not necessarily mean that your source was being 'dishonest' or 'prejudiced'. If somebody has a strong interest in the survival of a particular hospital, for example, the evidence they present may be accurate, yet not the whole story. When thinking critically, we need to be continually questioning in our minds whether there may be hidden agendas, or reasons why the evidence appears to point one way rather than another.

It is always worth considering what political or economic interests might prevent the whole truth from emerging. Consider also how easy it would be, or would have been, for alternative views to be printed and circulated. For example, in some societies, such as sixteenth-century Britain, people who spoke, printed or sold certain viewpoints could be punished by death or loss of limb.

Today, it can be difficult for small organisations or individuals to get the funding they need to research and validate an alternative viewpoint. The overall picture may be distorted if not all the evidence has come to light.

Whilst it is not necessary for you to write about issues of economics, politics and media access in every essay, it is important to be aware of who has access to power, resources and information, who does not, and the possible implications.

Beware the allure of numbers and statistics

It is important to check numerical data, and words that *imply* numerical data, as these are often misused and amounts misrepresented in order to sway the reader – see Chapter 9, page 219.

Most/many

Notice words such as 'most' and 'many':

> Most people said that they preferred oranges to apples.

'Most' is a very vague amount. If it *mattered* whether this statement were true or false, we would need more details. How many people were asked? How many preferred oranges? Under what circumstances?

Percentages   Notice when percentages are given. Supposing, instead, the statement above read:

> 60% of people preferred oranges; 40% said they preferred apples.

This looks convincing: numerical quantities are given. But is the difference between 60% and 40% *significant*? Here we would need to know how many people were asked. If 1000 people were asked, of whom 600 preferred oranges, the number would be persuasive. However, if only 10 people were asked, 60% simply means that 6 people preferred oranges: '60%' sounds convincing in a way that '6 out of 10' does not. As a critical reader you need to be on the lookout for percentages being used to make insufficient data look impressive.

Sample size   Notice also that if just 2 more people arrived who preferred apples, there would be 6 of each. A very small increase in the *sample* (the database of people asked) could easily overturn the original percentage, changing it to 50% for apples and 50% for oranges – no difference at all.

The sample size is the number of people, animals or objects used in the research, whether it's an experiment, a survey or whatever. Small samples give very unreliable information. All other things being equal, the bigger the sample, the more reliable the data. A thousand participants is often taken as a reasonable number for considering statistics to be 'significant'.

Representativeness   The sample should be representative of the overall group being studied. If all those asked about fruit preference came from Seville and made their living from oranges, we might not consider them to be either typical or reliable as a sample. Similarly, if all those asked about their preferences were women, or aged ten, or from the south of England, it would not be safe to generalise from them to the rest of the population. To make the sample representative, researchers aim for a good mix of men and women, of different ages, backgrounds and interests.

Conditions of data collection   If you found out that those who said they preferred oranges had each been given one free by the person conducting the survey, you might wonder whether the participants had had an ulterior motive in giving their answers, and whether the data were reliable.

Similarly, if the data were collected in face-to-face interviews by personnel wearing the logo of a company known for its orange juice, it is possible that some participants wished to please the interviewers. It is important to find out, where possible, about the conditions in which data were collected, to determine how trustworthy they are. Articles in academic journals usually give full details about the research conditions.

Emotive language and persuader words

Certain words can be very persuasive, and can trigger a position of trust in the reader. Which words they are will vary from subject to subject. For example, for some people the word 'experiment' summons up notions of scientific accuracy and reliability. However, the fact that an experimental approach was used does not in itself mean that the evidence is sound.

Emotive words   The use of words and phrases such as 'cruel', 'unfair', 'abuse', 'natural', 'normal', 'commonsense', 'innocent child', 'old', 'little', 'massive', 'unique', 'extremist', 'radical', 'youth', 'new' and even 'final offer' can prompt emotional responses that may lead the reader away from an accurate appraisal of the evidence presented. Emotive images, such as people crying, can be used in a similar way.

Persuader words   These words and phrases draw you in by appealing to what they claim is evident. It may be true that what follows is evident, but you still need to be on the alert when you see such words. They include 'surely', 'clearly', 'obviously', 'it is evident that', 'it is plain to see that', 'naturally' and 'of course'.

 Activity   4 Evaluating the evidence

Evaluate the evidence given in the 'Rochborough Health' passage, using the criteria outlined above. (See page 408 for feedback.)

6   Identify the writer's conclusions

Conclusions generally come at the end of the piece of writing. However, they may also be found at the beginning of the text or even in the middle. They are then harder to find and tend to be less effective.

Often conclusions are indicated by 'trigger words', such as 'therefore', 'so', 'hence' or 'thus'; or by the use of imperatives – words indicating that something *has* to be done, such as 'must', 'should' or 'need to'.

 Activity   5 Conclusions

Identify the conclusion in the 'Rochborough Health' passage. (See page 408 for feedback.)

Sometimes, the conclusion may not be stated at all – it may only be implied by the arguments and evidence. There may also be more than one conclusion to draw from a text, with some conclusions stated explicitly and others implicit. For implicit conclusions, you need to consider whether further conclusions are implied by the reasoning and the context. For example:

> In Jonah Smith's new book, the characters are compelling, the story is interesting, it is very atmospheric, and there is a surprising twist to the plot. The book is excellent.

Here, the *explicit* conclusion is that 'The book is excellent', and the reasons for this judgement

have been given – the characters, the story, the atmosphere and the twist to the plot. The *implicit* conclusion is that you too would enjoy this book.

 Activity   6 Implicit conclusions

For each of the following short texts:
- Decide whether there is an explicit conclusion and, if so, say what this is.
- Say what you think the implicit conclusions would be.
1   You want a plant. You like this one and you can afford it.
2   The election closed very early, but only Happy Party voters had been told this would happen. Happy Party supporters prevented some opposition party voters from voting. Therefore, the election was unfair.
3   The tree is dangerous. It is leaning over the children's playground. It is heavy, rotten and could break at any time.

(See page 409 for feedback.)

7   Evaluate whether the evidence supports the conclusions

A writer may present evidence which could be considered reliable, being based on good research, but then draw conclusions which are not warranted by the evidence. An exaggerated example illustrates this:

- Proposition 1   *The karate champion is a woman.* (Verifiable fact.)
- Proposition 2   *My mother is a woman.* (Verifiable fact.)
- Conclusion   *My mother is a woman, therefore she is a karate champion.* (False conclusion.)

Check for hidden false assumptions

In the above example, the faulty reasoning was based on the false assumption that if *one* woman is a karate champion, then *all* women are karate champions. This false assumption is easy to spot, but it is not always so simple. Researchers may try to be objective, but it is very difficult to stand completely outside of the commonsense views and ideological context of the society in which one is writing.

Example

Consider the ideas discussed in the student essays about Bowlby's influential studies of the 1950s (pages 325–7). Bowlby's findings (1951, 1969) suggested that infants who were separated from their mothers at an early age had behavioural and emotional difficulties later. This was used to argue the case against mothers working outside the home. The argument for mothers to stay home was no doubt based on genuine concerns for children's well-being, but the conclusion also suited the economic conditions of the time, as there was a shortage of jobs for men who had returned from the Second World War (1939–45).

Later, the conclusion that children were damaged by absent mothers and child care was heavily criticised (Clarke and Clarke 1976; Clarke-Stewart 1988; Tizard 1991). For example, it was argued that Bowlby's data was based on children in very extreme conditions, such as frightened war orphans and sick children in bleak hospitals and institutions of the 1950s. These children were not typical, and needed to be compared with average, healthy children attending friendly, well run nurseries, who saw their mothers every day. However accurate Bowlby's research may have been, his findings may not have justified the conclusions drawn from them. It is quite likely that Bowlby was affected by the dominant belief system of his day, that a woman's place was at home with the children, and that this influenced his interpretation of the data. It is also likely that his opponents were influenced in their research by changing ideas such as feminism, or by the rising number of women in part-time work.

It is quite typical for research to progress in this way, with advances being made as later researchers question aspects of earlier research, such as whether the sample was representative or whether the research contained assumptions which were invisible to the researchers at the time.

Activity **7 Use of evidence**

Do you consider that the evidence in the 'Rochborough Health' passage supports the conclusion drawn? What assumptions are made in the passage? (See page 409 for feedback.)

Critical analytical thinking

Now that you have worked through one passage step by step, try analysing Passage 3, 'Children at Play'. This writer covers issues similar to those in Passage 2, so you can compare the passages.

Activity **8 Critical analytical thinking**

For Passage 3:
- Is the line of reasoning good?
- What is the conclusion?
- How strong is the evidence?
- What are the underlying assumptions?
- How well do the reasoning and the evidence support the conclusion?

(See page 409 for feedback.)

Passage 3: Children at Play

Children need to play outdoors and yet it is amazing how few children get that opportunity today. Although Smith (2004) argues that 48% of children prefer to play inside, Jones (1964) found that 98% of children in Britain prefer to play outdoors. I spoke to some parents in Rochborough who said their children missed out by not being able to play down by the river or roam the countryside in safety. Most children are now television addicts or, worse, are addicted to computer games. Everybody knows that this is damaging children educationally, and yet nothing is done about it. This is certainly true of Rochborough's children, and the main reason is that they do not have anywhere to play. Hardly anybody in Rochborough has a garden. It would be better for their health if they played outdoors, but parents say they won't let them unless supervised play areas are provided. The parents are worried that they cannot see their children when they are playing. What chance is there for the health of citizens in Rochborough if its children do not get to play outdoors, and end up as TV addicts?

Critical analytical thinking

Use the following checklist to analyse a piece of writing that you need to read for an assignment. You could also use this list to analyse your own writing.

Critical questions	Analysis of the writing
What is the main line of reasoning (the main thesis or argument)?	
Is the line of reasoning clear both in the introduction and in the conclusion?	
What is the key evidence used to support the line of argument? Is the evidence presented in a way that develops the argument and leads clearly to the conclusion?	
When was the evidence produced? Is it up to date? Is it still relevant?	
Is there sufficient evidence to prove the case? Is the evidence relevant? What might be missing?	
What (if any) would have been a better order in which to present the evidence so as to strengthen the line of reasoning?	
Are there any examples of flawed reasoning? Attempts to persuade the reader through an appeal to the emotions? Is evidence interpreted and used correctly?	
Has the writer given sufficient consideration to alternative points of view? Give examples.	

Critical thinking when writing

Critical thinking when *writing* includes most of the elements of critical thinking you would use when *reading*. It can be more difficult to analyse your own work critically, however, and to recognise and admit to your own opinions and bias.

Be clear about your position on the issue, including hypotheses and conclusions

Students' writing is often weakened because their thinking is not clear before they start to write their final draft. Time spent in such critical analysis is equivalent to 'elaborating the problem' – a process which, as we saw in Chapter 4, was one way in which those who achieved good marks differed from those with poor marks.

Be clear about your conclusions

It is not unusual for students to hand in work which shows that although they have done the necessary reading and even given their work considerable thought, they are not sure of their conclusions. The whole of the piece of writing should lead to its conclusions: if these are vague, understated or poorly formulated, *all* of the writing loses its force.

As soon as you are given an assignment, write out your initial position on the issue and what you think your conclusion will be: what is it that you are trying to prove? Put this where you can see it.

Whenever you find out something that requires you to revise or fine-tune your conclusion, write out a new one. It may seem paradoxical (or back to front), but your writing will be clearer if you write your conclusions first. If you are testing a hypothesis, keep clear records of evidence that either supports or does not support that hypothesis.

Construct a clear line of reasoning

If your conclusions are clear, your argument or line of reasoning is likely to be clear also. The conclusion gives you a goal at which to shoot.

Keep your writing focused, rather than rambling. Bear in mind four guidelines:

1 Early drafts help to elaborate and refine thinking. Your final version should state your position clearly.
2 Create a writing plan that sets out reasons, examples and evidence in the most logical order.
3 Consider how best to link up your material, so that your writing is not just a list of facts but an organised, well-developed argument.
4 Keep your argument clear: including too much detail can obscure it. Draw together your best material and ideas, selecting carefully. Shape these to support your argument. Use paragraphing, link words and phrasing to signpost points clearly.

Use evidence to support your reasoning

A large part of your assignment will consist of evaluating and presenting the best evidence to support your case.

Take multiple perspectives

The best answers identify how and why various experts agree or disagree on an issue, and demonstrate how the evidence supports, or does not support, their positions. This means considering strengths, weaknesses, and grey areas. The answer is seldom a straightforward one of right or wrong. Usually there are many contradictory pieces of evidence to weigh up and evaluate against each other. Your final position or conclusions may be a synthesis of these.

Analyse your own work critically

Your tutors or examiners will take a critical reading approach when marking your work. Before handing in an assignment, analyse it critically as you would other material you read. Be a fierce critic of your own work so that you can spot weaknesses and address them, and ensure that you are clear about the strengths of your own argument.

Critical analytical writing vs. descriptive writing

Critical writing

In general, students lose more marks for lack of critical analysis than for any other single weakness in their work.

Good critical writing generally makes the difference between getting the highest grades for a degree and getting a lower grade. Typical tutor comments on student writing include:

- 'More analysis needed.'
- 'Less description, more critique.'
- 'Too descriptive.'
- 'Descriptive rather than analytical.'
- 'You have told me what the theory is rather than how you evaluate it.'

Finding the balance

Both descriptive and analytical writing have their place. *Descriptive* writing is needed to give essential background information so that the writing makes sense to the reader. However, this should usually be kept to the bare minimum – if you use up most of your word limit on description, you will have fewer words to use for the *analytical* writing that could bring you high marks.

Skilled writers use descriptive writing in the appropriate sections of their writing (see **Writing the report**, page 360), or weave small amounts of descriptive writing *into* their critical writing. Some of the main differences between these two types of writing are outlined in the table below.

Descriptive writing	Critical analytical writing
states what happened	identifies the significance
states what something is like	evaluates strengths and weaknesses
gives the story so far	weighs one piece of information against another
outlines the order in which things happened	makes reasoned judgements
instructs how to do something	argues a case according to the evidence
lists the main elements of a theory	shows why something is relevant or suitable
outlines how something works	indicates why something will work (best)
notes the method used	identifies whether something is appropriate or suitable
states when something occurred	identifies why the timing is of importance
states the different components	weighs up the importance of component parts
states options	gives reasons for selecting each option
lists details	evaluates the relative significance of details
lists in any order	structures information in order of importance
states links between items	shows the relevance of links between pieces of information
gives information or reports findings	evaluates information and draws conclusions

Identifying critical and descriptive writing

Descriptive writing: an example

My name is John. I live at 33 Acacia Drive. I have five sisters and brothers. I am good at team games, and enjoy football, cricket, and baseball. Team games were encouraged by both my parents. All of my family took part in sport. Our teachers at Beckfield School were very interested in sports sciences. We were encouraged to drink lots of water to improve our performance. Our team always did well, so it seems to have worked. I also like to go running. I live in the beautiful Welsh borders, so it is a pleasure to take a healthy run each day.

Almost all of this passage consists of statements and descriptions. There is an evaluative comment ('our team always did well') and this is linked to possible reasons (drinking lots of water). However, this link is not *analysed* in depth. The passage overall is descriptive. Compare this with the passage below.

Critical analytical writing: an example

At Beckfield School, teachers took a scientific approach to school sports over a ten-year period. In particular, pupils were encouraged to monitor their intake of liquids. All pupils were required to drink a minimum of eight glasses of tap water a day. The school did consistently well in sports competitions over this period, and the teachers claimed that this was proof of the importance of liquid intake to good performance. However, it is not clear that the school's sports performance can be attributed to water intake. Beckfield School's claims were investigated by an independent researcher, Martinez (2013). Martinez argued that although Beckfield's performance was good, its performance in competitions was consistent with what would be expected of a school of its size. In addition, interviews with pupils showed that most had not followed the school regulations on drinking water. Most pupils stated that they drank less than one glass of tap water a day. Although other research does suggest that water intake benefits performance (Fredo 2010; Mitsuki 2010), Beckfield School's claims about the benefits of tap water in its sports success have not been proved.

This is critical analytical writing. There is a clear line of reasoning which takes the reader through what the school claimed and the basis of the school's arguments. The writing then weighs the school's claims against other evidence. It draws upon published evidence rather than personal opinion. The writer considers both sides of the argument, taking account of published evidence that does support the importance of drinking water. This research has been weighed against the facts of the case. The writer draws conclusions: the 'school's claims about the benefits of tap water … have not been proved.' The conclusion is based upon the evidence.

The passage does contain descriptive writing which gives background detail, such as the first four sentences. Although the passage contains many statements of fact, such as 'most pupils stated that they drank less than one glass of tap water a day', these statements are ordered in such a way that they build up the argument. They are also supported by sentences that introduce the argument, such as 'However, it is not clear that the school's sports performance can be attributed to water intake.'

Activity 9 Descriptive or critical?

Identify whether the following passages are examples of descriptive or of critical writing. (Feedback is given on page 410.)

Passage 1

In the West, all life forms are divided into one of two categories: plant or animal. Animals move and take in food. Plants are rooted into the earth in some way and lack locomotion. They photosynthesise their food. Zoologists study animals, and botanists study plants. Bacteria were classified as plants because many kinds of bacteria photosynthesise their food. However, they also have locomotion. Recent research has shown that there is an enormous variety of bacteria. Some are able to survive at extreme temperatures and in the absence of oxygen. Most plants cannot usually survive in those conditions. Therefore, even though bacteria photosynthesise, they are not now regarded as plants.

Passage 2

The difficulty in categorising bacteria was partly based on the assumption that all life forms were divided into two main categories, plants and animals. Organisms that photosynthesised and lacked mobility were classified as plants; those that had locomotion and ingested food were classified as animals. Bacteria were traditionally categorised as plants because many forms of bacteria photosynthesised their food like plants. However, bacteria also have locomotion, associated with animal life. Genetic research has now shown that there are at least eleven major divisions of bacteria, all of which are more genetically distinct than plants are from animals (Fuhrman *et al.* 1992). In addition, the minute organisms formerly described as 'bacteria' are now found to consist of several major kingdoms and domains of unicellular and multicellular life (bacteria, archaea, eucarya) (Woese 1994). This research is significant as it has shown that the fundamental division of all life forms into 'plant' or 'animal' was an error, and that plants and animals form only a very small part of a much more diverse range of living organisms.

Passage 3

Scientists do not agree about the extent to which creativity can be linked to activity in the right hemisphere of the brain. It is known that the biochemistry of the two hemispheres of the brain is different. For example there is more of the neurotransmitter, norepinephrine, in the right hemisphere than the left (Oke *et al.* 1978). Norepinephrine is associated with increased alertness to visual stimuli. It has been suggested by Springer and Deutsch (1981) that this may lead to increased right-hemisphere specialisation for visual and spatial perception. However, this link is not yet proven. It is not yet clear whether one hemisphere of the brain can be responsible for any creative task. Moreover, although it might seem reasonable to assume that responsiveness to visual stimulus may be an important factor of creativity, this has also not yet been proved.

Passage 4

The brain contains millions of neurons. These communicate with each other through electrochemical activity at the synapses found at the end of each neuron. The chemicals that enable this communication to take place are known as neurotransmitters. Each neurotransmitter is associated with different kinds of message. The different messages to the brain influence the way we respond to events that take place in our internal or external world. Some neurotransmitters are associated with mood swings, with depression, with rapid responses, and so forth.

Passage 5

Bowlby's Attachment Theory argues that child development is affected by the closeness of the bond between mother and child. Bowlby claimed that even short spells away from the mother during infancy could have a profound effect upon a person later in life. This became known as 'maternal deprivation theory'. According to this theory, the relationship with the mother during an early 'critical period' gives the developing child an 'internal working model'. This model then forms the foundation of all future relationships.

Critical thinking when listening

When would I do this as a student?

- In lectures and classes.
- When using podcasts of lectures.
- When using audio-material online.

Listening to audio material

It isn't always possible to go back over what was said, so it can be more difficult to catch flawed reasoning. It is also easier to be carried along by the skills and qualities of the speaker.

Prepare in advance Read or browse a reputable text before listening. If you are already informed about the subject, it is easier to identify flaws in the arguments or evidence.

Identify the thread Focus on the line of reasoning, or argument, just as you would when reading. This will help you avoid being distracted by interesting or emotive details and anecdotes.

Question closely what you hear, even if it sounds plausible or it is your lecturers speaking. Take nothing at face value.

Evaluate the evidence Identify the evidence used to support the argument. Apply the same critical approaches as when reading.

Check when listening …

Check whether you are being swayed unduly by such factors as:

- the fame of the speaker
- impressive verbal fluency or vocabulary
- clever phrasing
- use of humour
- the passion of the speaker
- appeals to your emotions
- use of possibly irrelevant facts, used to make speakers sound more authoritative
- repetition used to emphasise some points at the expense of others
- speakers hopping between topics, preventing you from analysing their logic
- interviewers' use of unfair questioning techniques.

Chapter 7

Critical selection of podcasts

The value of podcasts

- There are podcasts of excellent academic quality, available as open source, giving you access to cutting edge research from around the world.
- You can listen back over the material, to help you analyse it critically and check the details.

Select good podcasts such as:

- Podcasts provided by your lecturers –– as most likely to be relevant for your course.
- iTunesU: offers podcasts from all kinds of universities and colleges worldwide.
- Podcasts by known subject experts or produced by academic publishers.
- TED www.ted.com: offers free audiovisual sources in a wide range of disciplines.

Content over style

When listening to podcasts created by lecturers, such as on iTunesU, listen for the quality of the content – even if the sound quality and production values are not excellent.

How could you not trust someone with an accent like this?

Moon = cheese

'… so that proves the moon is made of cheese …'

Review

Critical analytical thinking is an essential skill for most undergraduate and postgraduate study, and for many courses it is the most important single aspect of study.

As a student, you need to read, listen, write, speak, think, create and work with increasing critical awareness. You will be expected to bring a critical approach to every aspect of your study. You will be expected to examine arguments, evidence and conclusions closely, as well as the links between these. You will be asked to evaluate other people's reasoning and evidence, using criteria to guide you.

Tutors often use the terms 'critical analysis' and 'analytical writing' interchangeably. Both terms refer to the 'detective-like' approach outlined on page 188, and to your ability to explain how people arrived at different conclusions or results.

The more advanced your level of study, the more sophisticated you will need to become in the way you engage critically with the debates in your subject. As you progress through your programme, you will be introduced to further teaching methods and specialist texts that will refine your critical thinking skills.

In the debates that you encounter as a student, in the media or at work, be *active*. Look for strengths and weaknesses. Take note of how your tutors and peers evaluate evidence and theories, and learn from the way in which they draw on evidence and argue their own case.

This chapter has presented approaches for developing your critical skills that build on what you have learnt from earlier chapters. You should now feel confident that you have a mental toolkit that will allow you to approach new material in a critical manner and to incorporate critical analysis into your writing.

If you are interested in developing your critical and analytical thinking skills in greater depth, you may find it helpful to look at: Stella Cottrell, *Critical Thinking Skills: Developing Effective Analysis and Argument*, 2nd edn (Palgrave Macmillan, 2011).

Chapter 8
Memory

Learning outcomes

This chapter offers you opportunities to:

- understand more about your own memory style and about strategies that suit you
- learn general strategies that assist memory
- optimise the way you use your brain in order to assist learning and memory
- understand how 'stages' of the memory process can be used to assist memory
- develop ideas on how to 'encode' information so as to make it memorable
- learn the importance of organising and 'chunking' information
- understand more about memory in general, and how to use it to your advantage.

Remember, remember ...

There are times when we want conscious recall of specific information. This may be for everyday purposes – to have information at our fingertips when we need it, to save time by not needing to check information, or for social occasions such as taking part in a quiz. If as a student you are required to sit exams you may be expected to memorise some details, but it also builds confidence when you know that you can remember your material.

People generally underestimate their memory. They focus on what they forget rather than what they remember, and rarely appreciate how sophisticated the memory is.

For example, to read this paragraph requires extraordinarily complex feats of memory. You have to remember the complex workings of a language which took you years to learn; you call upon a memory of thousands of known words; you match the look, sound and meaning of particular written symbols to a memory store of thousands of symbols. You integrate all of this in memory and make sense of what you read. You do all of this within fractions of seconds.

People worry about memory deteriorating with age. Research by Harris and Sunderland (1981) suggests that older people remember some things better than the young. Older people often expect that their memory will be worse, so notice more when they do forget – yet greater age means that they also have more to remember. Buzan and Keene (1996) argue that learning *improves* with age – and learning involves memory.

Our brains take in much more information than we need: if we don't make active use of the information, it is as if the path to it becomes lost or overgrown, making it hard to access. The *way* we take in information also affects what we remember.

The more you know about how the brain and memory work, the more you can develop techniques to remember *what* you want to remember, *when* you need it.

Individual memory styles

We each have a combination of memory strategies that work best for us. We each use varied strategies to remember different kinds of information.

You probably used different strategies to remember the phone number than to recall your first day at school. You may have used some of the following strategies – if not, experiment with them now.

Fact strategies

Many techniques may help in learning a fact such as a telephone number. You might try:

- chanting the rhythm of the number
- using your fingers to map out the pattern of movements needed to dial the number
- seeing the number in your mind
- hearing your voice saying the number
- drawing out the digits with your finger
- writing the number down quickly
- noting any memorable peculiarity of the number, such as a repeated pattern (2727) or a reversible number (1331)
- noting any smaller numbers of personal significance to you, such as the year you were born or a relative's house number, contained within the number.

Event strategies

Trying to recall your first day at school may have called up different types of memory.

- The emotional memory of the event may have come to mind – your excitement at starting school, or your distress at being left by your mother, or your fear of the teacher. You might experience this physically in your body, as a tightening of the stomach muscles, for example, or a change in your breathing.
- You may have a strong visual memory of the journey to the school, or of moments during the first day. These may run through your head like a film or a series of snapshots.
- You may be able to hear the noises of the school – the shouts in the playground, or the school bell. You may remember certain smells, or even the taste of chalk on your fingers.

Other strategies

In remembering the six items above you may have used quite different strategies.

- To remember how to use a pencil sharpener you may have moved your hands to guide you through the sequence of movements.
- To remember what you wore, you may have recalled the place where you were.
- To remember where your clothes are now, you probably used a mixture: visual recall of where they usually are, and a check through your memory of recent events to see if there was any reason why they might be somewhere else.
- For the postbox, you may have visualised the local geography, or remembered a time you posted a letter, or imagined the walk to the box, or repeated instructions under your breath.

Check your memory style

What helps *you* remember things? Here's a simple way to find out.

- Highlight, in colour, 10 words on the word chart on the right.
- Read through the chart for 2 minutes, then cover it completely.
- Write down all the words you can remember.
- Read the following section as you check your results.

sea	Lenin	dog	merry	PINK	chair
saucer	cog	kitchen	LOG	hobby	butter
cheese	circus	green	Spain	essay	harp
windy	glink	student	jog	pills	sandwich
	walnut				
sick	Fred	pong	doctor	Gandhi	plate
JAM	happy	sneeze	sad	maybe	holiday
fog	lost	tutor	INDIA	hand	bandage
blue	bread	table	book	kneel	gloom

What helps you remember?

Look at the words you recalled. Does the selection of words you remembered suggest that you used any of the strategies below? If so, you have valuable clues about how you can arrange information you *want* to recall.

Your memory may be assisted by any or all of the following.

Recency effect ☐

You may have remembered best the words you learnt last.

Primacy effect ☐

You may have remembered best the words you learnt first.

Sound ☐

You may have remembered rhyming words, odd-sounding words, or words that you heard together in your head.

Locus (place) ☐

You may have associated a word with a place you know.

Real names ☐

You may have a particularly good memory for names.

Visual features ☐

You may have noticed the look of a word (such as the words in capitals or those with shapes around them).

Visual association ☐

You may have linked words with pictures or mental images.

Visual arrangement ☐

You may have remembered where items were on the page. (If so, you may find it easy to recall flowcharts or pattern notes, or be helped by visual spacing or making links with a picture.)

Semantic association ☐

You may have remembered words with meaningful associations, such as bread, butter, sandwich.

Being bizarre and unusual ☐

You may have noticed odd things, such as the words 'pong' and 'glink' which stand out. (If you did, you may find it helpful to link ordinary things with bizarre images or sounds.)

Stories ☐

You may have linked unrelated items so that they made a story. (This can help with the letters of a difficult spelling. For example, 'liaise': Liam Is Always In Such Ecstasy.)

Colour and activity ☐

If you remembered several of the words you highlighted, you may be sensitive to colour; or perhaps you benefit from *doing* things with information you are learning.

Musical association ☐

Did you try singing, chanting, or rapping words? These can be useful aids to memory.

Improve your memory

Memory aids

Particular practices can help you remember things. Below are some that are well known, and you may have others of your own.

Self-awareness

Know what tricks and methods you *already* use to remember things.

Repetition or over-learning

This is essential. Go over information at least three times. Check back often, for short lengths of time (rather than once for a long time).

Association

Link what you need to remember with something you already know. See also *Active learning* (pages 108–10).

Mnemonics

Any trick to help you remember is a mnemonic (pronounced *nem-on-ic*). One common mnemonic is to use the first letter of each keyword to make a new 'word' that sums up the whole subject – just as 'CREAM' sums up Chapter 4. It doesn't matter if the letters don't make a real word.

Active listening

Discuss what you're trying to learn with friends. Listen to your voice saying or reading it. Tape yourself. Exaggerate. Use accents. Be dramatic.

Writing things down

In your own words, write things out over and over again.

Personalising it

Relate what you learn to yourself. (For example in what way does it *affect* you? Does it remind you of someone you know, or somewhere you have been?)

Play

Play with information. Look for the fun in it. Relax and enjoy the process.

Think about advertisements

Advertising agencies deliberately set out to make us remember their advertisements. The 'tricks' and 'devices' they employ to prompt our memory can also be used to help us to remember what we study.

> **Reflection: What makes it memorable?**
>
> Think of three adverts (from TV, magazines, hoardings, etc.). What makes these three memorable for you?

Devices used by advertisers

Which of these devices are most effective in helping *you* remember?

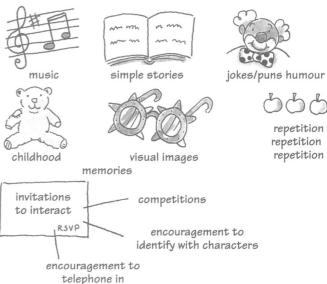

music simple stories jokes/puns humour

childhood memories visual images repetition repetition repetition

invitations to interact competitions

RSVP

encouragement to telephone in encouragement to identify with characters

Using the brain

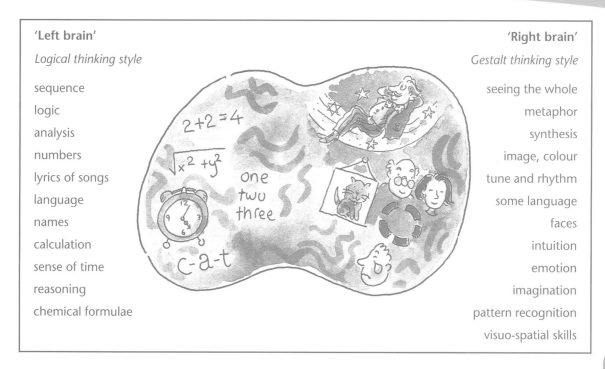

'Left brain'

Logical thinking style

sequence

logic

analysis

numbers

lyrics of songs

language

names

calculation

sense of time

reasoning

chemical formulae

'Right brain'

Gestalt thinking style

seeing the whole

metaphor

synthesis

image, colour

tune and rhythm

some language

faces

intuition

emotion

imagination

pattern recognition

visuo-spatial skills

Left brain–right brain

The brain is divided into two *hemispheres*, left and right. Research into brain damage shows that different mental functions are affected depending on which hemisphere is damaged. This understanding led to the idea that each hemisphere is generally associated with particular thinking and memory styles.

- The two hemispheres are linked by over 200 million nerve fibres (known as the *corpus callosum*).
- There is a crossover effect: each hemisphere controls the opposite side of the body.
- The body is designed to help the two hemispheres to work together.
- Each hemisphere is also skilled in the mental capacities of the other hemisphere.

The hemispheres work together

Most activities involve using both hemispheres. For example, to remember a song, you need to bring together both the lyrics (left hemisphere) and the tune (right hemisphere). To remember a person, you need to link the face (right hemisphere) and the name (left hemisphere).

If something in one part of the brain makes learning difficult, the brain has a tremendous capacity for finding a different route to learning. This suggests that if something proves difficult to learn or memorise in one way, there is likely to be a different way your brain could learn it.

Many people identify more with either the logical or the Gestalt thinking style. Do you think you are more 'left brain' or 'right brain' dominant? You can use your preferred style to link information across the hemispheres. This encourages the parts of the brain to work better together and makes learning easier.

Using left and right brain to improve memory

Although the brain uses both hemispheres for almost any activity, you can encourage this process, giving greater brain integration, and making use of more of your brain.

If you have a 'right brain' preference

- Draw a diagram or picture to show how varied information links up.
- Personalise information – find a way to make it relevant to your own life or experience.
- Use shape and colour to highlight and organise information.
- Use different colours for different topics.
- Sing the information you have to learn.
- Move around as you learn – as you do the housework or walk to the bus stop, see if you can recall what you have just learnt.

If you have a 'left brain' preference

- Write out the information by hand.
- Turn the information into lists.
- Number items of information so that the sequence is clear.
- Use headings to break up the information into different categories.
- Turn information into flow diagrams so you can see progression.
- Build up from details until you get the whole picture.

Locate the information in the brain

Make an experiment. While trying to visualise or recall information, first look up and to the left; then do the same but looking up and to the right. Also try looking left, then right, and then down to each side.

Which direction worked best? Does this hold true for different kinds of information? When you need to recall something, look first in the direction that is appropriate for you for that specific kind of information.

For optimum memory, combine different methods

Whatever your left- or right-brain preference, find a way of linking those skills to the skills associated with the other side. For example, if you are a picture thinker, number and sequence your pictures. If you use lists, then sing or colour them. 'Left brain' thinkers need to ensure they have the whole picture and can see how everything fits together. 'Right brain' thinkers need to ensure they appreciate the sequence, order, and hierarchy of importance.

When learning something, combine a mixture of memory strategies –

- look at it
- repeat it with rhythm
- write it
- number it
- give it a shape
- turn it into a diagram
- say it aloud
- sing it
- draw it
- colour it
- act it out
- make it bizarre

– and use any other device you find useful from this chapter.

The triune brain

The brain is also divided 'top-down' into three main areas of activity: *reptile brain*, *limbic system* and *neo-cortex*. McLean (1973, cited in Rose 1985) referred to this as the 'triune brain'.

The neo-cortex

The neo-cortex is what people generally think of when they speak of 'grey matter' or imagine a brain. It controls intellectual processes such as language, thinking, and handling numbers.

However, the neo-cortex is only part of the story: other parts of the triune brain also affect what can be learnt and remembered.

The mammalian brain (or limbic system)

The mammalian brain is located above the brain stem, roughly in the middle of the brain, and consists of a number of organs which control functions such as emotions, pleasure, moods, romance, and immunity to disease.

The reptile brain also affects study

In evolutionary terms the reptile brain is the oldest part of the brain. It is situated in the brain stem at the base of the head, and manages our basic instinctual and survival responses.

The reptile brain interprets stress or anxiety as a danger to our survival. It tries to help us 'escape' by drawing the main resources of the body to the large muscles and producing extra adrenalin so that we are in a heightened, alert state, ready to run away. Resources are taken away from the areas of the brain that we use for academic study: logical argument is not needed for basic survival. Being in 'survival mode' is not very helpful to study – if we don't use up the adrenalin by moving the big muscles, we may feel tense, over-alert, easily distracted and unable to concentrate.

Learning

Learning involves interaction between these three aspects of the brain, which are linked through the limbic system.

Some psychologists believe that emotions are the main link between the three areas. Emotions are a great stimulus to memory. The Accelerated Learning Movement uses music, images, colour and associations to create unconscious emotional arousal, facilitating faster learning.

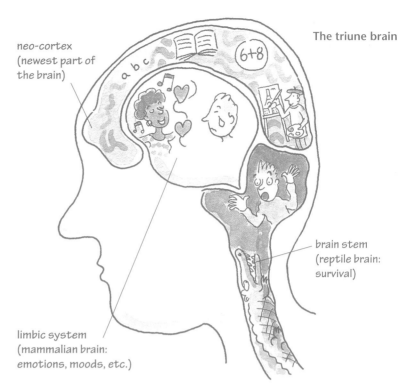

neo-cortex (newest part of the brain)

The triune brain

brain stem (reptile brain: survival)

limbic system (mammalian brain: emotions, moods, etc.)

A state of 'relaxed alertness' helps the imagination, and increases suggestibility and openness to new information. It can also stimulate left–right brain interaction (Rose 1985).

Optimising study with the triune brain

The following guidelines will help you study as effectively as possible.

- Stay relaxed, so that you avoid 'survival mode'. If you feel tense, go for a walk, stamp your feet, exercise or move around as you learn: this will use up excess adrenalin.
- Once you are relaxed, give yourself a positive emotional outlook on the task in hand: that it is easy, enjoyable, exciting, fun, interesting, full of surprises.
- Use your imagination to 'reframe' difficult or boring subjects as challenges. Set yourself targets, such as 'I'll learn three pages in the next half-hour' or 'This will be the most creative set of pattern notes I have made so far', so that your interest and emotions are involved.
- When studying, listen to music which has an expressive and recognisable melody played on string instruments, and has a steady bass rhythm of about 60 beats per minute. Possibilities include classical Baroque music (such as Bach or Vivaldi), classical Indian music, and New Age healing tapes.
- Use your imagination to make strong visual links between ideas.
- Make your notes visually striking, pleasant and appealing to the eye.

Stages of the memory process

Another way of using the brain to improve memory is to work with the different stages in the memory process (see page 211).

Four stages in the memory process

1 *Taking in information* – noticing or attending to information, and absorbing it.

2 *Retaining it* – in short-term memory.

3 *Encoding it* – interacting with the information in working memory so that the brain can store it in long-term memory.

4 *Recalling it* – retrieving or remembering information, whether on purpose, by accident, or in dreams. Recall can seem accurate even when it is not.

Stage 1: Taking information in

What we already know and have a name for affects how we direct our attention, what we notice, and therefore what goes into memory. We need to maintain our attention in order to remember.

If you study on 'automatic pilot', little attention is involved so you will remember less. You will remember more if you:

- direct your attention consciously and purposefully
- focus in a relaxed way – not with hard concentration
- take breaks and make changes in what you are doing, so as to maintain relaxed attention – a few minutes moving around or doing something different is sufficient
- link information to what you know
- give names and labels to information
- deliberately arrange or adapt information so that it is structured and yet stands out as odd, distinct, different or more interesting – so that it grabs your attention.

Stage 2: Retaining information long enough to remember it

Rehearsing new information in short-term memory helps the working memory hold onto it. Repeating it gives the brain time to call up stored memories to help you make sense of the information and encode it for storage.

Rehearsal must start within a few seconds, as information fades quickly. Rehearsal is a useful strategy for holding onto names, dates, numbers, formulae and instructions for long enough to write them down. You can then employ other memory strategies to remember the information long-term.

Stage 3: Encoding information – the key to memory?

The brain encodes new information so that it can be represented in the memory. Codes may be oral, auditory, kinaesthetic (using touch and feelings), verbal, semantic (related to meaning), visual, emotional, or motor (using a muscle sequence).

For example, when you tell a story, the brain encodes the pattern of fine-muscle movements you used to speak and stores them. It can also encode and store the sound of your speech on your own ear; the images and emotions that the story brought to mind; the look of the text; and details such as who was in the room, or the buzzing of a neon light. The brain links information it has encoded – so any one aspect could trigger the whole memory later. The more facets of an experience the brain has encoded, the more triggers there are to memory.

It follows that you can assist your memory by *choosing* to encode information in several ways. Some are suggested below, but create your own too.

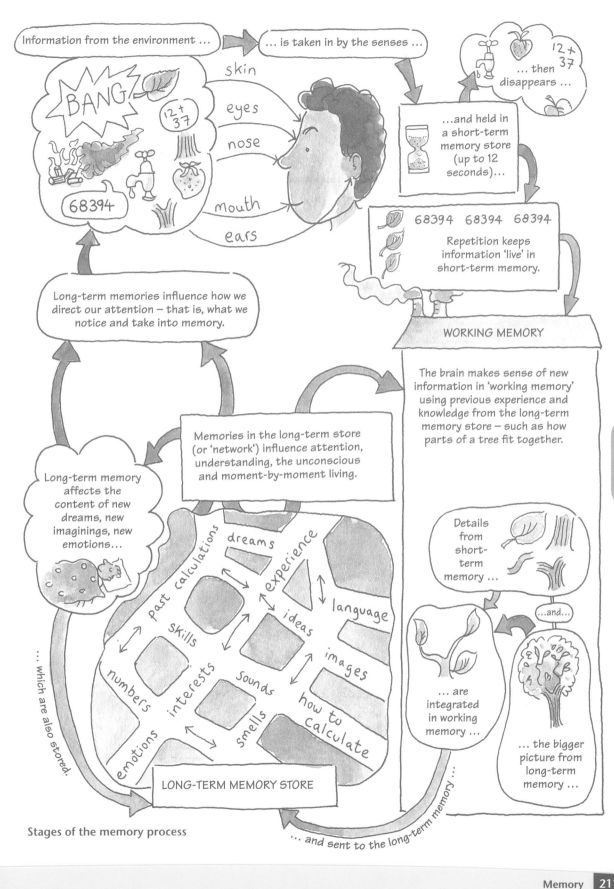

Information from the environment ...

... is taken in by the senses ...

skin

eyes

nose

mouth

ears

BANG

12 + 37

68394

... then disappears ...

12 + 37

...and held in a short-term memory store (up to 12 seconds)...

68394   68394   68394

Repetition keeps information 'live' in short-term memory.

WORKING MEMORY

Long-term memories influence how we direct our attention – that is, what we notice and take into memory.

The brain makes sense of new information in 'working memory' using previous experience and knowledge from the long-term memory store – such as how parts of a tree fit together.

Memories in the long-term store (or 'network') influence attention, understanding, the unconscious and moment-by-moment living.

Long-term memory affects the content of new dreams, new imaginings, new emotions...

Details from short-term memory ...

...and...

past calculations   dreams   experience

skills   ideas   language

numbers   interests   images

emotions   sounds   smells   how to calculate

LONG-TERM MEMORY STORE

... which are also stored.

... are integrated in working memory ...

... the bigger picture from long-term memory ...

... and sent to the long-term memory ...

Stages of the memory process

Suggestions for multiple encoding

Use your environment

- Use a different room for each subject.
- Notice aspects of the environment such as the light or feel of the room – how do you feel in that place?
- Attach your notes to the furniture. Notice their location.
- Associate a different location with each subject. Associate furniture, windows, plants and ornaments with particular topics.

Use your clothes

- Associate items of clothing with topics in your learning – a shoe could represent one aspect of foreign policy; each button on a shirt could represent a quotation. Clothes with patterns, pockets and buttons are especially useful.
- Wear these clothes into the exam room as a memory trigger.

Use the parts of your body

Parts of your body are especially helpful as triggers to memory, as your body will be there in the exam room!

For example, each hand could represent an essay plan – each finger one major topic; each segment of each finger a principal reference you would use. The fingernails could represent counterarguments; the knuckles could be associated with relevant quotations.

Use motor memory

- Study on the move. If you exercise, associate each movement with something you wish to remember. To refresh the memory, go through the exercise in your mind.
- Writing, drawing and speaking also use motor memory: the fine-muscle sequence is recorded by the brain.

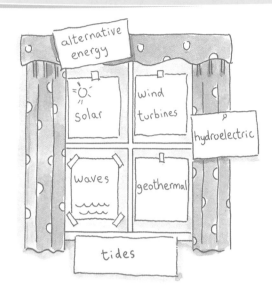

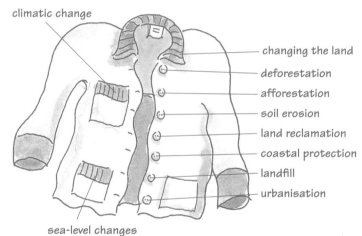

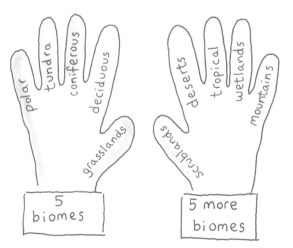

Multiple encoding

Use auditory memory

- Using a digital recorder, record yourself and then play this recording back.
- Sing an essay plan for a possible exam essay to a well-known tune. Make a list of which tunes go with each subject.
- Go over a topic with a real or imaginary friend, or your cat.
- Read notes aloud in peculiar voices. Over-dramatise to make the notes memorable.

Use visual memory

- Make page layouts clear and attractive.
- Turn your material into a film sequence that you can watch in your mind's eye.

- Assign to a topic an object such as a car, and label different bits of the object with the things you need to remember: the steering wheel with your main point; the four wheels with four main theorists; the doors with examples of practical applications of the theory; items in the boot could remind you of background information or historical development; and parts of the engine or objects on the front seat could indicate future developments.
- To remember complex lists and formulae, such as accountancy balance sheets, use a sequence of images, linked by a story.
- Use scale (size) and visually distinct images to separate out similar or confusing material, such as information about similar theories. Arrange these in a visual hierarchy.

Futures
how individuals represent their worlds

There are many views of intelligence

Spearman (1927)
One general IQ

Gardner (1993)
multiple intelligences

Hebb (1949)
inheritance & environment

Thurstone (1931)
6 types of intelligence

Past
labelling people

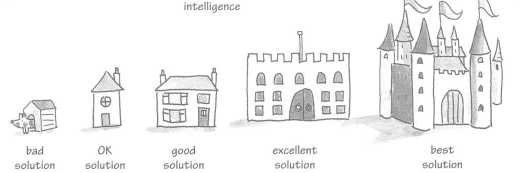

bad solution   OK solution   good solution   excellent solution   best solution

Multiple encoding

Use colour

- Assign each subject area a different combination of colours.
- You may find it useful to use a given colour for references or for formulae throughout your notes, so that you can spot them easily.
- Give each theme a different colour. As each theme appears, highlight it in the colour you allocated to it. You can then see at a glance which pages cover what, and which combinations of themes come up together. This makes reading more interactive, and finding information faster.
- Use colour on pattern notes (page 173) or in concept pyramids (page 293) to indicate information of similar types or levels. Organising your information clearly in this way can aid recall (see page 216). You may also find that you remember different colour combinations easily.
- To help you recall sequences of information, use colour combinations that are familiar to you, such as the rainbow, traffic lights, or the order of stripes on national flags.

Use verbal memory

- Reduce information to keywords.
- Organise information into hierarchies under headings (see concept pyramids, page 293).
- Write out your information in the fewest words possible – this process encourages interaction with the material, helping recall later.

Use semantic memory

- Spend time considering the *implications* of what you have found out. For example, who is affected? What would it mean for the future? What changes might arise? What theories could this information overturn? What are the moral, legal or ethical consequences?
- Think of a different way of saying what you have already written.
- Decide which are the three most important aspects of the subject, or the most important theories or ideas. Then decide which is the *one* most important.
- Consider all the ways in which one area of a subject is similar to another.

Stage 4: Recall

Good recall is linked to how much attention and awareness you bring to the process of taking in the information and encoding it.

Over-learning to aid recall

If you want to recall information at will, such as for exams or for complicated sequences that you use regularly, you may need to 'over-learn'. Over-learning is a combination of:

- active learning (see Chapter 4)
- using the techniques from this chapter
- checking back over and over again what you have learnt, without looking at prompts.

Strategy for over-learning

1   Make a set of pattern notes or an outline for an essay plan on a large index card or on paper, so that you have an overview.

2   Write names, dates and keywords for the references for each topic on index cards. Check that you can recite or reproduce the information on the card from memory.

3   If you can't, put the prompt card into a plastic folder (so it won't get smudged) and carry it around with you. Glance at it briefly in spare moments, such as at the bus stop or while doing the dishes.

4   Do this several times over a few days. Just looking at the prompt from time to time, or running the information through your head, will keep the memory fresh. Little and often is more effective than simply repeating the information over and over on one occasion.

If the information is hard to remember, there is probably a way of encoding it that suits you better, so experiment with something different.

Memory thrives on organisation

Chapter 8

Activity Organisation and memory

1 Read List A for 15 seconds, then cover it.
2 Recite a nursery rhyme (to prevent rehearsal).
3 Write down the words you remember.
4 Check List A and jot down your score.

List A

plum	elbow	giraffe	caravan
puppy	banana	foot	apple
pony	cherry	barge	bungalow

Now do the same with List B, including the underlined words. Even if you did not do well with the first list, have a go.

List B

<u>Fruit</u>	<u>Animal</u>	<u>Home</u>	<u>Body</u>
plum	giraffe	house	foot
banana	puppy	apartment	knee
apple	donkey	bungalow	elbow
cherry	pony	caravan	hand

You probably remembered many more items from List B. List B is more memorable because:

- grouping similar items together helps recall
- using group headings helps recall
- being able to see that there are only four types of information gives the task manageable boundaries
- many of the items on List B were also in List A – and going over information again helps recall.

Organising information into pyramids

Concept pyramids (see page 293) organise associated information into hierarchies. They are excellent memory aids.

In an experiment in 1969, Bower and other psychologists asked a group of people to learn 112 words. The words were grouped and linked meaningfully, as in List B above, and organised into four pyramids. People remembered 100% of the words by the third attempt.

By contrast, a second group of people were given the same words, also arranged into pyramid shapes, but this time with the words randomly assigned to each pyramid – they were not meaningfully (or semantically) linked. The second group remembered only 47% of the words by the third attempt.

This suggests the importance of both:

- linking information meaningfully, *and*
- organising ideas into hierarchies or concept pyramids.

Pyramids, pattern notes and pictures

Some people prefer to organise information as pattern notes or other images. Combining pattern notes, concept pyramids and pictures can give an even greater boost to your powers of recall.

Pattern notes and pyramids

Pattern notes work best when generating ideas and for recalling information from memory. Well organised pattern notes are easier to remember.

- Let your imagination wander when you make the initial pattern. Let the ideas flow (page 173).
- If the initial pattern shows no clear hierarchy of ideas, reorganise the words to fit into a concept pyramid. This may take some time, but it clarifies your thinking (see Chapter 11).
- Colour-code the different levels of the hierarchy. For example:
  - red for main headings
  - pink for less important headings
  - yellow and orange for intermediate-level information
  - dark green for key evidence, and light green for details about evidence
  - dark blue for specific examples, and light blue for details about examples
  - violet for references (names and dates).
- Draw rings, boxes or other shapes around crucial information, so that it stands out.

You may find it helpful to build up pattern notes as a series of concept pyramids, or to work back and forth between a pattern and

pyramids. You may wish to rework only some parts of the pattern into concept pyramids, and then to stick these pyramids back onto the original pattern with glue or Blu-Tack®. There is scope for all kinds of imaginative adaptations.

Pattern notes can be as big as you want – just keep adding and linking information.

Pictures and pattern notes

- You can select any image to anchor your memory – like the car suggested on page 213.
- Associate each part of the picture with one aspect of the topic you wish to remember.
- You can incorporate images into patterns and pyramids. Draw them, or cut images out of magazines and stick them on.
- Add small pictures to increase your interaction with the material and to make it more visually memorable. The better, brighter, odder, and more exaggerated the pictures, the more memorable the pattern.

The example below develops one section of the pattern notes on page 173. The initial ideas have been reorganised into a concept pyramid. Reworking your ideas in this way clarifies the relationship between different ideas, and sorts them into groups and sequences. It can also highlight gaps in your thinking, and suggest new ideas.

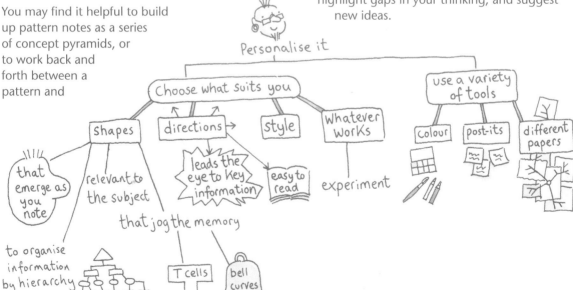

'Chunking' information

Short-term memory is the aspect of memory that allows us to store away some information for a few seconds whilst we focus on a different aspect of the problem, such as keeping a phone number in our head whilst we find a pen to write it down, or remembering to carry and add a digit to the next column when we add up numbers larger than 10.

Nobel-prize winner Herbert Simon found that we can generally hold five 'chunks' of information in short-term memory (1974). However, the 'chunk' can vary enormously in size: it could be a single word or number, or a phrase, or a whole story, or how to count up to a million. Try this out for yourself.

- Read the list under 'Small chunks'.
- Cover the list, then try to remember each phrase exactly.
- Do the same for the 'Bigger chunks' list.

You should be able to remember roughly the same number of chunks, irrespective of their size – for example, five sets of two words and five sets of longer sentences.

'Chunking' helps long-term memory

The same principle can be used to help organise information in your long-term memory. This is especially useful for exam revision. For example, if for one topic you have ten references to remember, arrange the names in the order in which you are likely to use them, and then make up a story to link them together into one chunk. Give the story a simple name. The crazier the story, the easier to remember. Good English does not matter for this purpose. In the example, the names are printed in bold.

This is a useful tactic to use whenever you have to remember information that does not link up easily. Most of your course material links up more naturally, and understanding how it fits together as a whole reduces it to a single chunk or fewer chunks.

Small chunks (2 words)

Happy Birthday
No way
Mouth-watering
Small change

No Smoking
Buckingham Palace
Photograph album
New Year

Bigger chunks (7–10-word sentences)

The rain in Spain falls mainly on the plain.

There is no business like show business.

Once upon a time there were three little pigs.

There is no escaping from your conscience.

Somewhere over the rainbow, way up high.

I hope you know what you are doing.

To be or not to be, that is the question.

Postman Pat has a very nice hat

Example

Names to revise

Gordon   Pilkington   Snodgrass
Collins   Rowbottams   Rider
Manchu   Ellis   Webster

Linking story

Bike story
Mr **Gordon**, drinking gin, shouted at glassy Mr **Pilkington**, that the **Snodgrass** needed cutting before the colicky **Collins** children slipped off their bikes onto their **Rowbottams**. The first bike **Rider** was **Manchu**-ing [chewing] a toffee and fell off because his W-**Ellis** [wellies] got caught in the spokes. He fell into a spider's **Web**ster.

What do we remember?

Flanagan (1997) argues that we remember:

- 20% of what we read
- 30% of what we hear
- 40% of what we see
- 50% of what we say
- 60% of what we do

and

- 90% of what we read, hear, see, say *and* do.

These are clearly not scientific figures, but they suggest the importance of interaction with the material and of using all your senses. This chapter has aimed to give you ideas on how to work towards that 90% – or better. Participants in Bower's research (see page 215) were able to gain 100% recall, and that was without multi-sensory involvement. By combining all of these strategies, you can greatly enhance your memory potential.

Memory is an active process. There are innumerable ways of enhancing it: if one doesn't work, try another approach which might suit you better. Work with your own learning style and memory preferences to try out new ways of remembering things. Creativity and imagination are essential ingredients. To remember well, it helps if you are relaxed, if you have fun with the memory process, and if you play with information until you find a helpful mnemonic. Be aware that what works for one kind of information might not work for another – some trial and error is involved.

You can enhance your memory by using your brain fully. Be aware of your 'left brain'/'right brain' preference, the action of the three parts of your triune brain, and the different stages of the memory process. The way you encode and organise information is particularly important.

Take charge of your conscious memories. You may achieve remarkable improvements!

Chapter 9
Confidence with numbers

Learning outcomes

This chapter offers you opportunities to:

- build your confidence in using numbers
- identify the kinds of number-related activities you are most likely to need at university
- recognise and understand the technical terms used in number-related study
- understand how to use fractions and percentages
- calculate three kinds of averages (modes, medians and means) and five-number spreads
- round numbers up or down
- understand the basics of interpreting data in graphs, tables and charts.

Most subjects at university involve using numbers – it isn't only science and maths subjects that require you to analyse and present data, and to perform numerical operations.

Many students feel uncertain about their abilities in working with numbers. They may struggle to remember what they learned at school about 'percentages' and 'averages', or feel perplexed about terms such as 'mode', 'median', or 'quartile'. If you don't feel confident with numbers, it may be tempting to skim quickly over texts that contain figures, data or mathematical terms, hoping that you can avoid thinking about them.

Gaps in basic numerical skills can make study seem unnecessarily daunting. If numbers worry you, then it may be reassuring to know:

- You are not alone!
- For most subjects, even a little knowledge about using numbers goes a long way.
- Often universities recognise that students may have difficulties with number skills and provide additional support.
- The topics in this chapter cover the basic number skills required for most study programmes.

What do I need to know?

What kind of number work is necessary?

The amount, level and type of numerical work all vary with the study programme, course or unit. Simply through practice during your programme you will probably become used to working with numbers as required.

> ### What do I need to be able to do?
>
> Find out whether you will need to do each of the following. Tick those that apply.
>
> ☐ Make sense of numerical information in texts, charts, graphs and tables.
>
> ☐ Recognise what is significant, relevant, valid or misleading about number-based information.
>
> ☐ Collect information for projects, reports and other assignments.
>
> ☐ Calculate averages and percentages.
>
> ☐ Use fractions.
>
> ☐ Identify numerical trends.
>
> ☐ Present findings from experiments, surveys, questionnaires or research projects.
>
> ☐ Use specialist statistical software.
>
> ☐ Attend training or workshops for any of the above provided by your college.

How do numbers add value?

When you are making an argument, you can generally make a better case if you can present numerical data that support what you are saying. A numerical table, for example, may sum up a great deal of information concisely and clearly, saving you thousands of words. The numbers you present must be *accurate* and *well selected*, and it should be clear why you have included them.

For example, 'Many students have jobs' is vague – it could be interpreted in different ways. Compare this vague statement with two precise numerical statements: '75% of students from the University of Aremia are employed part-time'; 'Almost 40% of students at Exford work part-time in bar work or sales.'

Note here that the accompanying words help to define the context and the meaning of the numbers. Your presentation needs to show this combination – the right numbers and the right words to explain them.

Subjects that require specialist skills

Some subjects require specific statistical methods or other specialist knowledge: if so, these are usually taught as part of the programme. If you find that you are struggling, ask your tutors for additional support or set up a student group to practise the numerical work together.

> ### Areas I want to improve
>
> | | pages |
> |---|---|
> | ☐ Building confidence with numbers | 221–2 |
> | ☐ Managing distrust of numbers | 223–4 |
> | ☐ Working with fractions | 225–7 |
> | ☐ Understanding percentages | 228 |
> | ☐ Converting fractions to percentages | 229 |
> | ☐ Rounding up and down | 230 |
> | ☐ Understanding averages | 231 |
> | ☐ Calculating averages: means | 232 |
> | ☐ Calculating averages: medians | 233 |
> | ☐ Calculating averages: modes | 234 |
> | ☐ Making five-number summaries | 235 |
> | ☐ Using graphs, tables and charts | 237–40 |
> | ☐ Collecting and presenting data | 351–6 |
> | ☐ Analysing numbers critically | 191–3 |
>
> *My priority areas are:*
>
> ....
>
> ....

Chapter 9

Build your confidence with numbers

The first obstacle many students face is anxiety. If you feel you 'can't do maths':

- Stay calm.
- Work through the steps systematically.
- Don't rush.
- Recognise your weak spots.
- Practise – then practise some more.

Overcoming your barriers

If you lack confidence in using numbers:

- Look at the barriers outlined below and on page 222. Tick any that apply to you.
- Think about how you could overcome each barrier.

1 I don't understand numbers at all ☐

A lot of basic number work is actually quite easy if you just follow a set of steps in sequence. Easy-to-use tools can also help. Maths may seem mysterious, but if you learn the steps and follow them exactly, you will get the right answer. The more you understand what you are doing, however, the more confident you will feel and the likelier you will be to spot an answer that doesn't look right.

Don't over-complicate your thinking. Most maths that you will need will build on a few simple basics such as adding, subtracting, multiplying or dividing. It is highly likely that you can do such calculations, even if you do occasionally make mistakes.

2 I make too many little mistakes ☐

- It is easy to make minor errors – don't let this discourage you.
- Many mistakes happen simply by missing a step from the correct sequence, or in basic adding,

subtracting, multiplying or dividing. The secret is to check back carefully over your maths, just as you proof-read written work.

- The more you practise, the more you will notice the kinds of mistakes you are most likely to make. You can then check for those in particular.
- If you are better with words than numbers, write out instructions in a way that makes sense to you.
- Set out the sequence of 'how to do it' for each operation. Using a layout that you can easily follow:
  - write only one step per line
  - leave space between steps
  - highlight key points in colour.

3 I can't track numbers ☐

- If you find it hard to track down columns of figures, check whether it is easier if you work on graph paper.
- If you still switch columns, colour adjoining columns or rows differently – this will help lead your eye down each column.
- Using a calculator or 'speaking calculator' may help.

4 I quickly forget how to do maths ☐

- As stress makes memory worse, focus on what you *can* do.
- Write down formulae for the mathematical operations you need, such as calculating a percentage (see page 229).
- Put these formulae where you can find them easily when you need them – in your diary, perhaps, or in a labelled file on your computer.
- Use the formulae from time to time: this will jog your memory.
- To help you recall the operations you need most often, devise personal memory joggers (see pages 212–17).

5 I'm no good at basics such as multiplication and division ☐

- Multiplication just means adding the same number over and over. '17 × 20' means adding 17 repeatedly: 17 + 17 + 17 + 17 … .
- Often there are several different ways to get the right answer: find out which way works best for you. In the example above, you could just write the number 17 twenty times in a long list, and then add up the list.
- Simple calculators make multiplication and division easy, and your computer will usually provide a calculator in its accessories.
  - *Multiplication* Enter the first number, then a multiplication sign (×) or an asterisk (*), then the second number, and press 'Enter' or the 'equals' sign (=).
  - *Division* Enter the amount you want to divide up, then the diagonal line (/), then the number you want to divide by, and 'Enter' or the 'equals' sign (=).
- You could refer to a visual table (such as that on page 399) or learn multiplication tables for speed.

6 I can't do things you're supposed to know, like calculating averages and percentages ☐

If you don't often use these, it is easy to forget how to do them. This chapter explains the common operations that many students need.

7 I don't know the technical terms ☐

Don't be daunted by technical terms in maths. The basic processes are not complicated – you can pick them up through instruction and practice. (See page 241.)

8 I don't trust numbers and statistics, so I don't want to work with them ☐

Knowing how to interpret data helps you know when to trust numbers. It also enables you to identify flaws in other people's arguments, and to detect occasions when figures are being cleverly manipulated. (See pages 223–4 and 191–3.)

9 I don't know how to interpret information in graphs and charts ☐

Graphs and charts are important not only in presenting your own work but also in understanding what you read. Practice will help. (See pages 237–40 and 191–3.)

10 I need to collect and present numerical data, but I don't know where to start ☐

The key to collecting and presenting data is to focus on the purpose of your research. What are you trying to find out? What data do you need to find the answer? (See pages 351–6.)

Reflection: Working with numbers

- What do you think are your main barriers in working with numbers?
- What would help you overcome these?
- What will you do to overcome these?

Can you trust numbers?

How useful are numbers?

Many people have strong opinions about numbers, especially statistics. It is easy to assume either that numbers 'prove' a case or that all statistics are 'lies'. In reality, numbers simply provide information, and the *value* of that information depends on what else you know about it and whether it suits your purpose.

What are 'statistics'?

'Statistics' has two meanings:

- the methods and techniques for measuring, organising, interpreting and describing numerical information (data)
- specific sets of data produced to measure a given subject.

Populations and samples

The total number of instances of something – all the plants in a meadow, for example – is the *population*. It is seldom possible to measure every individual in the population, so instead you can measure just some of the individuals – a *sample*.

If the sample is typical of the population, statements that are true for the sample are also true for the population as a whole: such a sample is said to be *representative*. If the sample is untypical of the population as a whole, however, it is said to be *unrepresentative*, or *biased*. If the samples are representative, you can use them to draw inferences about the whole population – these are known as *inferential statistics*.

Good measurements must be accurate: they should measure in full what they say they measure and should not be measuring anything else. Measurements gathered for one purpose cannot necessarily be applied in other situations – you must judge whether or not data tells you what you need to know.

The relevance of the numbers

Whether or not data are relevant depends on what is being asked of them. When considering a specific set of data, ask yourself:

- Does it provide useful insights? Does it indicate oddities I need to investigate further?
- Does it help me spot any trends?
- Does it affect how I should think about a subject?

Know the context

To interpret data, you need to know about the context in which they were collected. Suppose someone won a TV songwriting competition by gaining 56% of the phoned-in votes. Would a music producer be wise to invest in this artiste? The producer would need to know more. How many people watched the show? What proportion of them phoned in? Were they representative?

Perhaps:

- the winner was supported by people who phoned in more than once
- the winner was popular with phone voters but not with people who buy recorded music
- the phone lines were not working properly.

Questioning numbers and statistics

Do numbers provide proof?

Numbers may appear to be convincing, but they may not be as reliable as they seem. When using any set of data, be objective and critical. Consider:

- Do these data measure what they purport to measure?
- Are they likely to be accurate?
- Could they contain errors or misprints?
- How were they collected? Might this have led to mistakes or inaccuracies?
- Who wanted them collected? Why?
- When were they collected? Are they up to date? If not, does that matter?
- Are they representative? Or do they refer only to particular sets of people or particular circumstances?
- Do they cover exactly what you are looking for? Do they throw useful light on the issue you are investigating?

Are the data based on estimates?

Some data are based not on actual counting but on *estimates*. For example, a newspaper report of the size of a crowd at a public demonstration may be no more than an 'informed' guess. The estimates made by the organisers and by the police may differ – and neither may be correct.

Are the data likely to change?

Estimates may change rapidly or over time. For example, the first estimate of casualties immediately following a disaster may differ from estimates made later as more accurate information becomes available. Data about the overall impact of the disaster may change as long-term consequences, such as environmental effects, gradually become apparent.

Are the data still up to date?

Check whether there is a later or an earlier set of data that is more accurate or with which you can compare the current data. For example, if a shop claims that it won a 'Customer Satisfaction' survey ten years ago, you would probably wonder whether current customers are satisfied.

Remember, too, that it takes time to collect, analyse and publish data: some are out of date even before they are published.

What was actually measured?

Historical data need to be treated with caution. During some historical periods, whole sections of populations were simply ignored when making counts. For example, the number of casualties typically cited for the Great Earthquake of San Francisco in 1906 omits the Chinese casualties, even though the Chinese population at the time was significant. For much of history, only the views of people regarded as 'important' were counted: we cannot know what 'most people' thought if they were not allowed to vote or to register their opinions.

What kind of 'sample' was used?

We are often presented with claims about the average number of televisions in each home, how the average voter will vote in the next election, or what proportion of pets prefer a particular food. Such figures do not measure every home, every voter or every pet – that would take too long and be too expensive. Instead, a sample is taken, much smaller than the whole population, and is treated as if it were representative of the whole. For the result to be reliable, the sample must be big enough to be a fair representation of the population – if not, claims about proportions or rising or falling trends will be unreliable.

What kind of 'averaging' was used?

Different kinds of average may throw a different light on an issue. Which sort is being used? Is it appropriate? (See pages 231–4.)

For more about examining data critically, see *Critical analytical thinking*, pages 191–3.

Fractions

A fraction is part of a whole. We acknowledge this in everyday speech:

- 'Buy this at a fraction of the cost …'
- 'If you had the right tools, you'd get that done in a fraction of the time.'

In maths, a *fraction* represents one of a number of equal parts of a complete unit. Thus a fraction could be a part of a price, a time, a width, a group ('set'), or any other unit.

The language of fractions

The language of fractions is straightforward. For example, if you cut a cake into 8 equal slices, each slice would be one *eighth*. If instead you divided it into 6 equal parts, each part would be a *sixth*. If you shared it out in 20 equal slices, then each piece would be a *twentieth* of the whole cake. If you then ate 3 of those 20 equal pieces, you would have eaten *three-twentieths*. If you gave a friend 2 of 5 equal slices of the cake, you would have given *two-fifths*.

Fractions of a set

The set of stars below consists of 28 items. They are divided into 7 equal parts, or fractions: each line represents ⅐ of the total. The shaded area covers 3 of those 7 parts, or ³⁄₇.

> ### Example: fractions of 28
>
> A set of 28 items divided into 7 equal parts consists of 7 groups, each of 4 items. With the items laid out as below, you can see the relationship between the total set and the set divided into sevenths.
>
>
>
> - As you can see, ⅐ of 28 items is 4 items.
> - ³⁄₇ of 28 items is 3 x 4 items = 12 items. To check this, count the items.

One-tenth (¹⁄₁₀) of the cake

Three-tenths (³⁄₁₀) of the cake

Proper and improper fractions

In a *proper fraction*, the top number is smaller than the bottom number (e.g. ¾). In an *improper fraction*, the top number is bigger than the bottom number (e.g. ⁴⁄₃): the fraction is greater than 1. A *mixed number* combines a whole number and a proper fraction (e.g. 1⅓).

Chapter 9

More about fractions

A chart of equivalent fractions. Each column divides the same total of 24 stars:

- **1 × 24:** 1 = ★★★★ / ★★★★ / ★★★★ / ★★★★ / ★★★★ / ★★★★
- **2 × 12:** ½ (★★★★ ★★★★ ★★★★); ½ (★★★★ ★★★★ ★★★★)
- **3 × 8:** ⅓ (★★★★ ★★★★); ⅓ (★★★★ ★★★★); ⅓ (★★★★ ★★★★)
- **4 × 6:** ¼ (★★★ ★★★) ×4
- **6 × 4:** ⅙ (★★★★) ×6
- **8 × 3:** ⅛ (★★★) ×8
- **12 × 2:** 1/12 (★★) ×12

| 1 × 24 | 2 × 12 | 3 × 8 | 4 × 6 | 6 × 4 | 8 × 3 | 12 × 2 |

Comparing equivalent fractions

The chart above shows equivalent fractions. By tracking across, you can count, for example, how many one-twelfths are equivalent to two-thirds.

- The height of each column is divided so that you can compare fractions visually.
- The items in each column add up to the same total number (24), so you can also count out the relative proportions.

Comparing fractions

When fractions have the same bottom number (denominator), it is easy to compare them. For example, with $\frac{3}{12}$ and $\frac{5}{12}$ you can tell that 5 portions are more than 3 portions of the same size.

When the bottom numbers differ, however, comparison is more difficult. Which is bigger, ¼ or $\frac{2}{9}$? You need a new denominator that can be divided both by 4 and by 9. The easiest way is to multiply these two different denominators together to find a *common denominator*. In the case of ¼ or $\frac{2}{9}$ a common denominator is found from 4 x 9 = 36. Each of the two fractions can then be expressed as a number of $\frac{1}{36}$ths.

You then need to work out the equivalent number of $\frac{1}{36}$ths for each fraction. To maintain the proportion, multiply the top number (the numerator) by the same number as the bottom number (the denominator) in that fraction:

- For ¼: To get 36 at the bottom, you multiply 4 by 9, so multiply the top, 1, by 9 also. The result is $\frac{9}{36}$ (that is: ¼ = $\frac{9}{36}$).
- For $\frac{2}{9}$: To get 36 at the bottom, you multiply 9 by 4, so multiply the top, 2, by 4 also. The result is $\frac{8}{36}$ (that is: $\frac{2}{9}$ = $\frac{8}{36}$).

The question, 'Which is bigger, ¼ or $\frac{2}{9}$?', can now be answered by substituting the converted fractions. 'Which is bigger, ¼ ($\frac{9}{36}$) or $\frac{2}{9}$ ($\frac{8}{36}$)?' It is now clear that ¼ ($\frac{9}{36}$) is bigger.

Adding and subtracting fractions

Once you have converted numbers so that they have a common denominator, you can also add and subtract fractions easily. You simply add or subtract the top numbers:

$$\frac{9}{36} + \frac{8}{36} = \frac{17}{36}$$
$$\frac{5}{36} + \frac{11}{36} = \frac{16}{36}$$
$$\frac{9}{36} - \frac{8}{36} = \frac{1}{36}$$
$$\frac{30}{36} - \frac{10}{36} = \frac{20}{3}$$

Using fractions

Uses of fractions

We use fractions in everyday life:

- to share any item in equal parts
- to share out profit in proportion to the level of investment
- to work out a sale price when items are reduced by a fraction, such as '⅓ off'.

Calculating the fraction of a quantity

We can also calculate actual numbers and total amounts when we are given fractions. For example, if we know that in a survey of 800 people, three-quarters were women, we can work out how many women were questioned.

In 800 participants, ¾ were women.

1 Divide the total number (800) by the bottom number (the denominator) in the fraction (the 4 in ¾): $^{800}/_{4} = 200$.
(That is: 800 = $^4/_4$, so ¼ = 200.)

2 Multiply the result by the top number (the numerator in the fraction (the 3 in ¾):
200 x 3 = 600.
(That is: 200 = ¼, so ¾ = 600.)

Example 1

To calculate ¾ of a sample of 200:

1 Divide 200 (the total) by 4: 200/4 = 50.
2 Multiply the 50 by 3: 50 × 3 = 150.

Example 2

A shop is offering an item for ⅓ off its usual price of £120. This means that the item would cost you ⅔ of £120. To calculate this:

1 Divide £120 by 3 (bottom number):
£120/3 = £40.

2 Multiply £40 by 2 (top number):
£40 x 2 = £80.
The reduction (⅓) is £40; and the cost (⅔) is £80.

Multiplying fractions

When you multiply fractions of a whole number you are multiplying a *part* by a *part*, so the result is even smaller. For example:

- a half of a half (½ × ½) is a quarter (¼)
- a half of an eighth (½ × ⅛) is a sixteenth ($^1/_{16}$).

Top-heavy fractions

Sometimes you see a fraction in which the top number is bigger than the bottom number. This simply means that the fraction amounts to more than one whole item or set. For example, $^7/_6$ is the same as $^6/_6$ + ⅙ or 1⅙.

Activity Using fractions

1 In each case, which fraction is larger?
a ⅕ or ⅙ c $^4/_7$ or $^5/_9$
b ⅔ or $^7/_{11}$ d ⅘ or ⅚

2 Add each of the following fractions:
a ⅓ and ½ d ¼ and ⅔
b ⅙ and ⅛ e $^2/_7$ and ⅗
c ½ and ⅚ f ⅑ and ¾

3 Calculate each of the following:
a ⅔ of £750 d $^2/_9$ of 81
b ¾ of 160 e ⅗ of 620
c ⅚ of 72 f $^2/_7$ of 91

4 Calculate the total, given that:
a ½ = 100 e ¾ = 120
b ¼ = 100 f ⅐ = 10
c ⅓ = 50 g $^2/_7$ = 10
d ⅔ = 50 h ⅘ = 20

5 Multiply:
a ½ × ½ d ⅓ × ⅓
b ½ × ¼ e ⅓ × ½
c ¼ × ¼ f ⅔ × ½

Answers are given on page 411.

Chapter 9

Understanding percentages

What is a percentage?

A percentage (%) is a way of stating any fraction as a proportion of 100.

A proportion of the 'whole'

The whole of anything – the full amount of an item or a group of items – is 100%.

If you divide this total amount, 100%, into smaller parts, each part will be a proportion of the whole 100%. All the pieces together add up to 100%.

Example

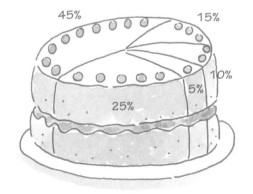

Consider this cake, which has slices of different sizes. The five slices of the cake add up to 100%.

If some of the cake is eaten, the remainder can be expressed as a percentage of the original whole cake.

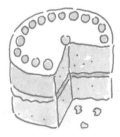 

75% remaining   25% gone

Percentages written as fractions

Percentages can be written as fractions, in which the bottom number is always 100:

$$\tfrac{1}{100} = 1\% \quad \text{(1 per cent)}$$
$$\tfrac{23}{100} = 23\% \quad \text{(23 per cent)}$$
$$\tfrac{59}{100} = 59\% \quad \text{(59 per cent)}$$

Why use percentages?

If proportions are stated relative to a standard number, 100, it becomes easy to make direct comparisons. For example, suppose you want to compare how effective two sports clubs are in attracting student members. If there are 17 students in a total of 34 members in Club A, and 13 out of 52 in Club B, it is hard to make direct comparisons between the clubs. If the figures are both converted into percentages, however, they can be compared easily on this single scale: 17/34 = 50%; 13/52 = 25%.

Reliability

The reliability of percentages depends on the sample size: see page 193.

Percentages: 'more than one cake'

Imagine two cakes of equal size. The 'whole amount' of cake, 100%, is *two* cakes. Now suppose that 75% of one cake and 25% of the other cake are eaten. Although the amount eaten is equivalent to 100% of *one* cake, it is only 50% of the 'whole amount' of cake – *two* cakes.

 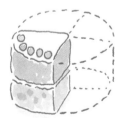

25% of Cake 1 eaten = 12.5% of the whole amount (two cakes)

75% of Cake 2 eaten = 37.5% of the whole amount (two cakes)

Total amount eaten = 12.5% + 37.5% = 50% of the whole amount (two cakes)

Chapter 9

Calculating percentages from fractions

A fraction is a part of a whole, such as a half or third. When it isn't easy to see how fractions or proportions of different items compare, then it is worth converting fractions into percentages.

Easy conversions from fractions and percentages

On page 228, the proportion of students in the membership of one club was shown to be 17/34 or 50%. This fraction is easy to convert to a percentage if you recognise that 17 is half of 34 – 'half' is always 50%. Other useful conversions are listed below.

One-half	= ½		= 50%
One-quarter	= ¼		= 25%
Three-quarters	= ¾		= 75%
One-third	= ⅓		= 33%
Two-thirds	= ⅔	= 2 x 33%	= 66%
One-fifth	= ⅕		= 20%
Two-fifths	= ⅖	= 2 x 20%	= 40%
Three-fifths	= ⅗	= 3 x 20%	= 60%
Four-fifths	= ⅘	= 4 x 20%	= 80%
One-sixth	= ⅙		= 16.7%
Two-sixths	= 2/6	= ⅓	= 33.3%
One-eighth	= ⅛		= 12.5%
Two-eighths	= 2/8	= ¼	= 25%
Three-eighths	= ⅜	= 3 x 12.5%	= 37.5%
Four-eighths	= 4/8	= ½	= 50%
One-tenth	= 1/10		= 10%
One-twentieth	= 1/20		= 5%
One-fiftieth	= 1/50		= 2%
One-hundredth	= 1/100		= 1%

It is worth playing with these basic fractions and percentages, and looking for relationships between them. For example, to find three-fiftieths, multiply one-fiftieth (2%) by 3 to give 6%.

Look for proportions that help you calculate a percentage quickly in your head. For example, '24 out of 96' is the same proportion as '1 in 4' (4 x 24 = 96) or 25%. If you know your 'tables', you will find it easier to recognise proportions.

Converting fractions to percentages

1 Divide the part by the whole.
2 Multiply the result by a 100.

Example

17/34 = 0.5 (17 = 'the part'; 34 = 'the whole')
0.5 x 100% = 50%

If you didn't recognise 17/34 as 50%, don't worry – you can use the formula above to convert any fraction into a percentage. Using a calculator, key in the operation, in order, as in this example:

$$1\ 7\ /\ 3\ 4\ \times\ 1\ 0\ 0\ =$$

Activity **Calculating percentages from fractions 1**

Turn the following fractions into percentages. For this activity, ignore any numbers that follow the decimal point on your calculator. Example: 27/134 x 100 = 20.149. Just write 20.

Activity **Calculating percentages from fractions 2**

a   In a sample, 6 of 11 plants are deciduous. What percentage is deciduous, and what percentage is not?

b   In one school, 41 out of 230 children have reading difficulties. What percentage have reading difficulties? What proportion do not?

c   Out of a population of 234,560 people, 23,456 people went to see a film. What percentage of the population saw the film? What percentage did not?

d   873 of 9,786 participants took part in the competition online, 2,314 by texting, and the rest by phone-in. What percentage participated by each method?

Answers are given on pages 411–12.

Rounding up and down

Strings of digits can be hard to read and to work with. 'Rounding' makes them easier to manage.

Whole numbers

A whole number is one with no fractions or decimal points attached to it, such as 75 or 921.

Numbers followed by decimal points

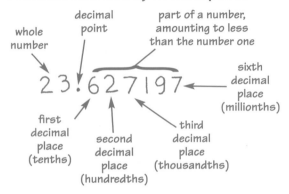

The digits that follow a decimal point represent only a *part* of a whole number. However many digits follow the decimal point, they represent less than the number 1.

When you convert a fraction into a decimal, there may be more digits after the decimal point than are useful. This is where 'rounding' helps.

Rounding money

You may be used to 'rounding up' or 'rounding down' when using money, rounding to the nearest pound, dollar, Euro, or other unit of currency. For example, if you owed a friend 4 Euros and 75 cents, you might 'round up' and repay 5 Euros, telling your friend to keep the change. Similarly, if you owed 4 Euros and 10 cents, your friend might 'round down' and accept just 4 Euros.

Rounding numbers

Example: rounding down 986.748

Rounding numbers follows the same principle as rounding money. To round 986.748 to just its first decimal place:

- The digit in the first decimal place is 7.
- If the digit immediately to the right of the 7 (in the first decimal place) is *4 or less, round down* – remove everything following that decimal place. Here the digit in the next decimal place is a 4, so round *down*, removing the 4 and the 8, and leaving 986.7.

Example: rounding up 986.752

- The digit in the first decimal place is again 7.
- If the digit in the next decimal place is *5 or more, round up* – increase by 1 the number in the decimal place you want. Here the digit in the next decimal place is 5, so you round *up*, removing the 5 and the 2, changing the 7 to 8, and leaving 986.8.

You can round up or down to whole numbers, or to one or more decimal places.

More examples

To round 756.483921 to the nearest whole number
Everything before the decimal point is the whole number: 756.

To round 756.483921 to two decimal places
The digit immediately to the right of the second decimal place is 3. For '4 or less, round down'. As 3 is less than 4, round down: 756.48.

To round 756.486111 to 2 decimal places
The digit immediately to the right of the second decimal place is 6. For '5 or more, round up'. As 6 is more than 5, round up: the 8 in the second decimal place increases to 9, giving 756.49.

Activity	Rounding numbers

Round these numbers to one decimal place.

a	41.34675	d	99.88	g	66.55
b	912.172	e	1.714	h	6.10987
c	22.222	f	10.08		

Answers are given on page 412.

Chapter 9

What are 'averages'?

Discussing a set of numbers

Many kinds of research involve collecting data by counting. For example, you might want to know:

- how many people take holidays abroad, and where they go
- how many plants and animals there are on a piece of seashore
- how many children are immunised in different communities, and against which diseases
- how much students earn.

For instance, suppose you were investigating road safety and you were measuring the traffic through a village. You might count how many people there are in each vehicle that passes through the village in a given period of the day. You might collect a set of numbers such as this:

3, 2, 5, 41, 1, 76, 1, 97, 3, 1

It would be hard to discuss this list in your report because the number of people per vehicle varies between 1 and 97. It would be even harder to make comparisons, for example with the figures at a different time of day or in another village.

Averages

One way to deal with this is to use a single number that in some way *summarises* or *represents* the set of numbers. It needs in some way to be typical of the set. It needs to be an *average* number.

- An average would help us work more efficiently with large sets of numbers.
- It would help us spot patterns and trends.
- It would help us compare numbers more easily.

Choosing the average number

In choosing one number to represent a set, we need to decide which would be the best number to use. The lowest one? The highest? The one in the middle? The one that appears most often? In discussing students' income, for example, we might choose as an average:

- the *median* – the amount that falls mid-way between £0.00 and the income of the highest earner, *or*
- the *mean* – the amount that each student would receive if their total earnings were equally divided between all of them (as if sharing out a pool of money equally between members), *or*
- the *mode* – the amount that students earn most frequently.

Calculating averages

The three averages are not all the same. For instance, for the list of numbers already given –

3, 2, 5, 41, 1, 76, 1, 97, 3, 1

– the mean is 23, the median is 3, and the mode is 1. All three averages might be useful in different contexts.

The following pages look at how to calculate these three commonly used representative averages.

Calculating averages: the mean ('equal share')

What is the mean?

Most people, when they refer to an 'average number', are talking about the 'mean' number. This is the method you would use to find out how to distribute money, objects, time or other items into equal shares or amounts.

> ### Calculating the mean
>
> Calculating a mean is relatively simple, especially with a calculator. You just:
>
> 1 Add up all the numbers in the set in order to find the grand total, or 'sum', of the numbers.
> 2 Divide the sum by the number of items in the set: that gives you the mean average.

Example 1

Consider the set of numbers given on page 231:

$$3, 2, 5, 41, 1, 76, 1, 97, 3, 1$$

To find the mean for this set:

1 Add the 10 numbers together:

$$3 + 2 + 5 + 41 + 1 + 76 + 1 + 97 + 3 + 1 = 230$$

2 Divide the total passengers (230) by the number of vehicles (10):

$$\text{Mean} = 230/10 = 23$$

'23' might seem a strange number to consider as 'representative' – most vehicles carried far fewer passengers, and 7 of the 10 vehicles each carried only 1–5 passengers. Nevertheless, this figure could still provide a point of reference when comparing overall information about volume of movement from one place to another, or at different times.

Example 2

This set of numbers records the number of US dollars held by each of 6 tourists:

$$\$34, \$31, \$200, \$11, \$19, \$88$$

To find the mean for this set:

1 Add the 6 numbers together to get the total number of US dollars held by the 6 tourists altogether:

$$\$34 + \$31 + \$200 + \$11 + \$19 + \$88 = \$383$$

2 Divide the total dollars ($383) by the number of tourists (6):

$$\text{Mean} = \$383/6 = \$63.8$$

If the tourists shared their money equally between them, they would each have $63.8.

Activity Calculating the mean

Calculate the mean number, or average, for each of the following sets of numbers.

a 1, 2, 3, 5, 6, 7, 8, 9, 11, 15, 17

b 234, 19, 1, 66, 2002, 7

c 7, 7, 6, 8, 9, 8, 11, 7, 6, 11, 2, 14, 5

d 11, 22, 33, 44, 55, 66, 77, 88, 99, 111

e 7, 14, 19, 8, 6, 11, 21, 32, 8, 19, 21, 5

f 23, 36, 42, 56, 57, 58, 59, 59, 59, 69, 69

Answers are given on page 412.

Calculating averages: the median ('middle number')

What is the median?

The *median* is the mid-way point in a set of numbers that have been put in order of increasing size.

> ### Calculating the median
>
> 1 Lay out the numbers in the set in order, from smallest to largest.
>
> 2 The median is the middle value. The way of calculating this place depends on whether there is an odd or an even number of items in the set.
>
>   *Odd number of items* Find the middle item in the ordered list: this value is the median.
>
>   *Even number of items* Find the middle two items in the ordered list. Add them together and divide by 2: this value is the median.

We represent the median height.

Example 1: odd number of items
Here is a set of exam scores:

   23, 36, 42, 56, 57, 58, 59, 59, 59, 69, 99

There are 11 scores in the set, and they have been laid out in order from lowest to highest. The median is the number that falls in the middle. For 11 numbers, the middle is the 6th place. The 6th value, the median, is 58.

Example 2: even number of items

Here is another set of exam scores:

   36, 42, 56, 57, 58, 60, 61, 69, 69, 70

Here there are 10 scores in the set, and again they have been laid out in order from lowest to highest. For 10 numbers, there is no single middle value.

- The two middle numbers (5th and 6th places) are 58 and 60.
- 58 + 60 = 118.
- The median is 118/2 = 59 (59 is the mean of the two middle values).

Activity **Calculating the mean**

Calculate the median for each of the following sets of numbers.

   a   1, 2, 3, 5, 6, 7, 8, 9, 11, 15, 17
   b   234, 19, 1, 66, 2002, 7
   c   7, 7, 6, 8, 9, 8, 11, 7, 6, 11, 2, 14, 5
   d   11, 22, 33, 44, 55, 66, 77, 88, 99, 111
   e   7, 14, 19, 8, 6, 11, 21, 32, 8, 19, 21, 5
   f   23, 36, 42, 56, 57, 58, 59, 59, 59, 69, 69

Answers are given on page 412.

When is the median useful?

The median is especially useful for small sets of numbers, as in the examples above. Other averages are often affected by extreme differences between the numbers, known as 'extreme values', such as the 99 in example 1. The median is less affected by extreme values, so it may be more representative of the set of numbers as a whole.

Calculating averages: the mode ('most frequent')

What is the mode?

The *mode* is the number in a set that appears the most frequently.

Example

Look again at this list of exam scores, sorted into ascending order:

23, 36, 42, 56, 57, 58, 59, 59, 59, 69, 99

The number that appears most frequently in this set is 59: this is the mode. In this set, 59 is the exam score that occurs most often.

When is the mode useful?

The mode is especially useful when you have a large set of data in which there is only a small range of values. For example, national data on family size would be a large data set, with perhaps millions of numbers, yet the *range* of values would be quite narrow – the number of children per family is likely to be between 0 and around 12 at most. If, in practice, most families had 3 children, it might well make better sense to use this value – the most frequently occurring number of children in a family – rather than to use a mean or a median, which would probably be a fraction such as '2.12' children. The mode can be valuable when making comparisons within large populations, as when carrying out research regionally or nationally into the effects of family size on health or income.

However, using the mode can make it harder to see trends. For example, if there were a new trend in which increasing numbers of families had 3 or more children, this trend would not be apparent if one knew only that 3 children was the most common number in a family. In contrast, the mean, a more precise decimal number, might show a rise in average family size, such as from 2.8 to 3.3.

Comparing means, medians and modes

23, 36, 42, 56, 57, 58, 59, 59, 59, 69, 99

- In this set, the mode – the number that occurs most frequently – is 59.
- The median – the number that falls in the middle place – is 58 (calculated on page 233).
- The mean – calculated by adding all of the items in the set (617) and dividing the sum by the number of items in the set (11) – is 56.

These are all accurate statistics, but they do not match. This is one reason why 'statistics' sometimes seem to 'lie'. As arguments are often based on comparisons of averages, it is important to know:

- What was included in the data set? (For example, were all the exam scores included, or were any omitted?)
- Which method of calculating the average was used? Is this kind of average suitable?

- Would a different method of calculating the average give a different outcome? (It might, depending on the numbers involved.)
- When averages are compared in an article or report, were these averages calculated using the same method, whether mean, mode or median? (Each average might be higher or lower, depending on the method used.)

| *Activity* | **Calculating averages** |

Find the mean, median and mode for the following numbers. Consider how extreme values (unusually small or large numbers) affect each average.

a   1, 1, 1, 3, 3, 4, 7, 7, 10
b   28, 14, 21, 28, 26, 62
c   19, 170, 17, 19, 19, 16, 20

Answers are given on page 412.

Five-number summaries and quartiles

What is a five-number summary?

The numbers in a set may be similar and closely related, or they may be varied with features such as very high or low scores – *extreme values* – which are quite unlike the other numbers in the set. The variety of numbers and the way in which they are clustered or spread in a set is called the *distribution*.

If you know just an average number for a set and nothing else, you cannot tell anything about the distribution of numbers in the set, and whether it is in any way unusual. Are the data reliable, or might they be distorted or unrepresentative in some way? Can they be used as they are or do they need further investigation?

The effect of extreme values

Suppose, for instance, that in a group of 12 students (a small sample), 11 students received exam marks of 64% and 1 student received just 3%. You might expect the average mark for the whole group to be 64% – after all, that is what all but one of the students received. If the average used was the *mode*, it would be 64%. If the average used was the *mean*, however, it would be around 59%.

The single mark of 3% in this set is an 'extreme value': it skews the results for the set as a whole. When data sets are small, or when means are used, extreme values can be quite misleading. In larger samples, extreme values have less impact.

The five numbers

Extreme values are just one of the possible sources of distortion when one chooses a particular number to represent the whole group. To address such problems, statisticians have found that in describing a set it is helpful to state not just one number but five numbers.

First the numbers in the set are put in sequence, from the smallest to largest. Then five numbers can be recorded:

1 *Minimum number* The first in the sequence.
2 *Maximum number* The last in the sequence.
3 *Median* The mid-point of the sequence.
4 *Lower quartile (LQ)* The value one-quarter of the way along the sequence.
5 *Upper quartile (HQ)* The value three-quarters of the way along the sequence.

Summaries and averages

The table below shows a five-number summary. Consider this information compared with that provided by averages. It may help to note that:

- The mean for the marks, by calculation, is 47.29%. The mode is 70%.
- The mean is brought down by the 2 extreme values, 2% and 3%. It would otherwise have been 51.36% (1130/22).
- Without the 2 lowest and 2 highest scores, the mean is 49.5% (990/20).

Example: a five-number summary

Below is a set of class exam scores for 24 students. These are placed in order, from lowest to highest, and the number of their place in the sequence is written below for ease of reference. The positions of the lower and upper quartiles must be calculated (as for medians: page 233).

Mark (%)	2	3	40	41	42	43	44	45	46	47	48	49	50	51	52	53	54	55	56	57	58	59	70	70
Place	1	2	3	4	5	6	7	8	9	10	11	12	13	14	15	16	17	18	19	20	21	22	23	24

Minimum	Lower quartile (LQ)	Median	Upper quartile (UQ)	Maximum
1st place = 2	The value mid-way between the 5th and 6th places = 42.5	The average of the 12th and 13th places = 49.5	The value mid-way between the 18th and 19th places = 55.5	24th place = 70

Using five-number summaries

Examples of five-number summaries

Class A

For Class A, a set of 11 exam scores is:

23, 36, 42, 56, 57, 58, 59, 59, 59, 69, 99

The five-number summary for this set would be:

1 Minimum number   23
2 Lower quartile: LQ (3rd score)   42
3 Median number   58
4 Upper quartile: UQ (9th score)   59
5 Maximum number   99

Class B

For Class B, a set of 16 exam scores is:

7, 27, 27, 27, 55, 55, 64, 65,
66, 66, 67, 68, 69, 70, 71, 78

The five-number summary for the set would be:

1 Minimum number   7
2 Lower quartile: LQ (4th score)   27
3 Median number (mean of 65 and 66)   65.5
4 Upper quartile: UQ (12th score)   68
5 Maximum number   78

Using the five-number summary

Consider Class B. If the only fact you knew about the scores for this class was that the *mode* (the most common score) was 27, you would gain a quite mistaken impression of the group's performance.

Even without a list of all the class scores, however, the five-number summary would give you a much more accurate picture. Looking at these five numbers only, you could see that the scores in the class were widely distributed, from 7 to 78, and that at least half the group must have scored 65.5% or higher.

Similarly, if you knew only that the mean was 55%, you would be unable to appreciate how well some students had done while others had struggled. The five-number summary makes the distribution clear.

The five-number summary thus gives a better 'feel' for the whole set of numbers. When you have large sets of numbers, such a summary can be very useful.

Presenting five-number summaries

Five-number summaries can be used to compare two or more sets of data. The numbers can be presented in table form so that the equivalent numbers can be compared easily. For example, the two exam scores for Classes A and B would be presented as below.

Table to compare exam scores for Class A and Class B, using a five-number summary

Scores	Class A	Class B
Minimum number	23	7
Lower quartile (LQ)	42	27
Median number	58	65.5
Upper quartile (UQ)	59	68
Maximum number	99	78

Activity ⟳ **Five-number summaries**

Draw up five-number summaries for the following sets of numbers, as in the examples above.

a Set of class scores: 10, 31, 39, 45, 46, 47, 48, 55, 56, 57, 58, 59, 61, 63, 64, 65, 66, 67, 68, 69, 71

b Number of pets per household: 0, 0, 0, 0, 0, 0, 0, 0, 1, 1, 1, 1, 1, 1, 1, 2, 2, 2, 2, 2, 2, 2, 3, 3, 4, 4, 5, 17

c Life expectancy for males in sample families (in years): 32, 39, 41, 56, 58, 64, 65, 67, 69, 70, 71, 71, 73, 73, 73, 73, 74, 77, 77, 78, 81, 84, 89, 92

Answers are given on pages 412–13.

Chapter 9

Using tables, charts and graphs

Tables, charts and graphs provide a kind of visual shorthand – they condense complex information and present it clearly.

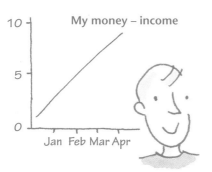

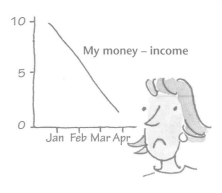

Why use tables, graphs and charts?

- Good tables and charts present information in clear, orderly, systematic ways.
- You can 'see' key information more quickly than when you read it as text.
- You can see relationships, detect patterns and trends, and draw comparisons easily.
- You may find visual information easier to interpret.
- You may see aspects to tables and charts that their authors did not see – that is, you may bring an additional interpretation.

Read the labels

Headings and labels help you to interpret the data appropriately.

- *Headings* Read the main headings carefully. Note each word or phrase, and be sure you know exactly what the graph or table is meant to represent.
- *Labels* Read the labels on rows and columns, axes and lines. These should tell you precisely what each represents.

- *Key* If colour, shading or symbols are used, look for the key that explains how to interpret these. This is usually a box above, below or to the side of the table, and tells you the meaning of each colour, shading type or symbol.

Take time; be systematic

Each table presents information differently, so take time to understand what the table is showing you.

- Familiarise yourself with the style, symbols, and measurements.
- Note dates and the source of information.
- Work your way systematically along each row, column, line, and so on.
- Keep checking back to the key and the measurements.
- Work out amounts. Look at any 'totals' that are presented – what do these tell you?

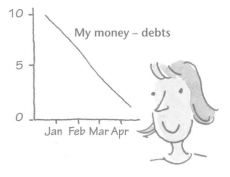

Just one word can change the meaning of the graph

Chapter 9

Interpreting graphs

Why use graphs?

Graphs are useful in indicating trends, including how one aspect, or *variable*, changes in relation to another. For example, a graph might show:

- how income rises or falls over time, or in relation to a factor such as world oil prices
- how sales vary relative to cost
- how an insect population increases or decreases with seasonal temperature or rainfall.

Drawing graphs

A graph has two axes, horizontal and vertical. Each axis is divided into equal measures and labelled to specify the scale and unit of measurement being used, such as 'Weight in grams', 'Volume in litres', 'Income in £1000s', or 'Temperature in degrees Celsius'.

Reading graphs

Read all the textual information, such as headings, labels, and units of measurement.

Follow one line on the graph. Track it in relation to measurements on the horizontal and vertical axes. From these measurements, note the changes as you move along a line.

Are there any sharp rises or falls? What do these suggest?

This graph

This graph indicates that in Aremia in 2012 women's average income was lower than men's average income, but that women's income was rising more quickly.

Heading

This should state exactly what the graph is meant to show, including dates.

Axis label

Each axis should be labelled to state exactly what it represents.

Vertical axis

This is divided into equal measures. (Here the axis scale marks intervals of $5000.)

Horizontal axis

This is divided into equal measures. (Here the axis scale marks intervals of 3 months.)

Source and date

The date and source of the information should be stated.

Labels or key

Lines are labelled or a key is used to indicate what each line represents.

Average earnings in Aremia, Jan.–Dec. 2012

Average income ($1000s)

Women
Men
Whole

Source: Aremia Official Statistics, 2013

Activity — Interpreting graphs

a What was the average salary for Aremian men in October?

b In which quarter did Aremian women's earnings rise above $20,000?

Answers are given on page 413.

Interpreting tables

The table below provides raw data for two student groups, A and B, with names, courses and test scores for 24 students. Examine the data to see what it tells you. For example, at first view, which course seems most popular? Which group does best in the test? Are these interpretations reliable?

Data set: 24 students' test scores, by subject and group (Aremia University, 2013)

Test scores for Group A

Student	Course	Test score	M/F
Belinda	Geology	67	F
Darren	Oriental Studies	41	M
Dilshad	History	54	F
Elizabeth	Maths	64	F
Femi	English	61	M
Francis	Oriental Studies	60	M
Geraint	Psychology	65	M
Omar	Geology	67	M
Patrick	Geology	72	M
Rosa	Geology	71	F
Sunjit	Geology	54	M
Thandi	Geology	58	F

Test scores for Group B

Student	Course	Test score	M/F
Assunta	Politics	60	F
Chiara	Social Work	57	F
Diane	Maths	55	F
Horace	Psychology	68	M
Joachim	Film	23	M
Joseph	Nursing	69	M
Kiran	Arabic	53	M
Natasha	Film	49	F
Niall	French	44	M
Otto	Physics	62	M
Soraya	Film	57	F
Zoe	Fine Art	31	F

A set of only 24 students is unlikely to be representative of a large university population. You probably noticed that the most popular course overall is Geology, selected by 6 of the 24 students (25% or a ¼ of students). Unless this is a specialist university, it is unlikely that a quarter of the students all study one subject.

If we looked only at the data for Group B, it would seem that Film was the most popular course and as if nobody studied Geology. Each group shows considerable variation in subject choice. With only one or two students taking each subject, in most cases, the sample size is too small for us to make generalisations about subject popularity.

This data on programme choices is unstable – if we were to add data about additional groups, it is likely that the proportions who had chosen each subject would change.

The mean test score overall for each group would allow one comparison between the groups. The total number of marks for Group A is 734 and in that group there are 12 students, so the mean score is 734/12 = 61 marks. The total marks for Group B is 628: the mean score is 628/12 = 52 marks.

This is a big difference between the two groups. To interpret this data, you would need to know more. For example:

● How were these two groups selected?
● How do marks for these groups compare with those for the university overall?
● Does the high number of geologists in Group A distort the data?
● Are there other particular differences between the two groups, such as the proportions of men and women or the proportion in part-time employment? Do these differences affect group marks?

You would also want to know what was being tested. For example, if the test were in geology, we would expect the geologists' scores to be higher!

Interpreting charts

Showing relationships

Tables, graphs and charts can be used to present two or more sets of information in a way that makes it easier to see how one set of information relates to the other, to find patterns and trends, and to draw comparisons.

Bar charts

Bar charts contain less detail than tables, but summarise data in a way that makes it easier to read.

For example, the chart below presents the average marks for two student groups, A and B (page 239), and for their university as a whole. It breaks the data down to show the mean figures for whole sets, and also separately for men and women. Note that the marks are shown from 50 upwards.

Mean test marks by group 2012–13

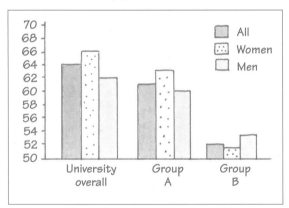

Source: Aremia Assessment Report, July 2013

Activity　**Interpreting bar charts**

From the bar chart above, is Group A or Group B more representative of the university as a whole?

How do mean average scores for these groups compare with those for the university overall?

Answers are given on page 413.

Pie charts

Pie charts are useful in indicating the *relative proportions* of the various components that make up a whole. They cannot provide statistical precision, however.

Consider the information about recruitment to two groups on different programmes (page 239). The pie charts below compare the data for the 24 students with data for the university as a whole.

Distribution of students by subject, 2012–13

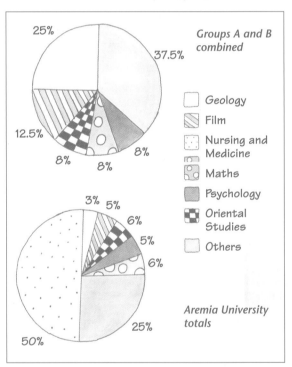

Source: Aremia Official Statistics, 2013

Activity　**Interpreting pie charts**

Examine the two pie charts. In what ways were the 24 students representative or unrepresentative of the whole university?

Answers are given on page 413.

Technical terms

Average A number that is in some way 'typical' of a group of numbers, and that can be used to 'represent' them. What is meant by 'typical' depends on the context, and three kinds of average are commonly used: *mean*, *mode* and *median*. (See below and pages 231–4.)

Data 'Data' is the plural of the Latin word *datum* (meaning 'something given'). Data are facts, observations and measurements; collectively data provide information. Numerical data are collected by sorting, measuring and counting. For example, measurements of people's heights and weights, or of sales or industrial production, or even of conditions on Mars, all provide numerical data.

Data set A complete collection of information on a particular topic. For example, all the data collected in a survey of transport in London, Zagreb or Jakarta would together provide the data set for that survey.

Denominator The bottom number in a fraction (see pages 225–6).

Elements The basic categories of data used for collection, counting and analysis, such as 'Income', 'Pieces of broken pottery', 'Respondents to the survey about font styles'.

Extreme values Numbers that are much lower or much higher than the rest of the set. For instance, in the set 16, 55, 56, 56, 56, 57, 59, 61, 61, 63, 64, 68, 88, the numbers 16 and 88 would be 'extreme values'.

Mean The middle point of a sequence. This is the usual meaning of the word 'average' in everyday conversation. (Calculation of the mean is explained on page 232.)

Median The middle number in a sequence: one way of expressing an average. (Calculation of the median is explained on page 233.)

Mode The number in a set that occurs most often: one way of expressing an average. (Calculation of the mode is explained on page 234.)

Numerator The top number in a fraction (see pages 225–6).

Percentage The number of occurrences in each 100 instances. For example, suppose 25 out of every 50 people are able to swim. The same proportion can be given as 50 people in each group of 100 people: '50 per cent' or '50%'. (Calculation of percentages is explained on page 229.)

Prime numbers Numbers that, without resulting in a fraction, can be divided *only* by themselves or by the number 1. For example, the number 7 can be divided only by 1 or by 7 – division by any other number gives a fraction. The same is true of 3, 5, 11, 13, 17, etc.

Qualitative data Information that comprises subjective descriptions rather than objective measurements. For example, a survey of pets might record owners' reasons for choosing a particular animal, and how they feel about their pet. (See page 312.)

Quantitative data Information that comprises objective measurements rather than subjective descriptions. For example, a survey of pets might count the number of each kind of animal, and the annual cost of keeping it. (See page 312.)

Raw data The basic information as collected, with no interpretation. (See page 239.)

Rounding 'up' or 'down' Replacing a number with a simpler number that is no longer as accurate but is easier to work with. (See page 230.)

Statistics Sets of data, and techniques for working with them. (See page 223.)

Variables The aspects of the elements (or countable items) that may differ from one item or group to another. For example, a shopping survey might consider the kinds of product bought, the quantity of each, the number of shopping trips each week, the amount spent, the age and gender of the shopper, and so on.

Vulgar fraction Another name for a fraction (see page 225).

Review

This chapter has provided information about, and practice in, several aspects of working with numbers. The areas covered – such as working with fractions, calculating averages, and interpreting graphs and charts – challenge many students at times, even when they are good at other aspects of number work. Although the necessary mathematical operations are not particularly difficult to learn, they are easy to forget if you do not use them regularly.

Here are some key messages from the chapter:

- You can overcome obstacles and barriers to using numbers, even if you have found these difficult in the past.
- Numbers must be *interpreted* – in themselves, they provide no authority.
- In using numbers to find answers or make interpretations, you can be much more confident if you:
  - don't rush at the task
  - take time to absorb what is required

  - work systematically through a sequence of steps or rules for working out the right answer
  - check your answers repeatedly
  - practise often the numerical operations and tasks that are relevant to your course.

- If you are providing data in charts, tables and graphs, present these clearly. Use precisely worded headings and labels.
- Words can be just as important as the numbers themselves. Make sure you read the instructions, labels, headings, explanations and any other verbal information carefully.

If specialist techniques or statistical software packages are required for your course, your university or college is likely to provide sessions that explain how to use these. To cope with these more specialist areas of your programme, however, you will probably need first to be able to understand and perform the basic numerical functions outlined in this chapter.

Part C
People skills

10 Working with others: Collaborative study

Although 'people skills' may not seem to be an obvious study skill, on most courses you will be expected to interact with others as an integral part of the learning experience. This can be true of both distance learning courses as well as those based on campus or in the workplace.

As academic work in Higher Education is developed within a learning community, you need to understand how to work alongside others, to give and receive support and share ideas whilst also maintaining the academic integrity of your own work. As a student, you will benefit from understanding how groups work, and how you can play an effective role as a team member.

Depending on your course, you may need to demonstrate good communication skills in listening and in making your point, to be able to give and receive criticism, and to take part in group tasks in class or for group projects. In some instances, your input to the group, or to group outcomes, may contribute to your overall marks and grades.

This section covers, in brief, a range of people skills that will help you as a student. These range from in-class participation through to skills needed for specific tasks such as making presentations and managing group projects.

Chapter 10
Working with others
Collaborative study

Learning outcomes

This chapter offers you opportunities to:

- consider the advantages of working with others
- develop your communication skills
- build your confidence in participating in discussion groups and seminars
- understand what makes groups work and how to be an effective team member
- develop strategies for particular aspects of collaborative study, such as peer support, offering constructive feedback, contributing to seminars and group projects, and making presentations.

Academic study at university level generally focuses on the achievements of individuals. In part, this is to ensure that each person is awarded a qualification purely on the strength of his or her own work. Increasingly, however, courses require collaborative working in groups or teams. Such activities vary, but typically include: peer support groups, making presentations in seminars or group tutorials and contributing to the discussion, providing constructive feedback on other students' ideas or work, and undertaking and presenting group projects.

There are a number of reasons for encouraging students to undertake collaborative working.

- *Learning community*: to enable students to learn from each other, sharing knowledge as active members of a learning community.
- *Diverse viewpoints*: to encourage an appreciation of what can be gained through taking multiple perspectives on board.
- *Learning styles*: to provide varied teaching methods, in recognition that students learn in different ways, including through social learning, groupwork and discussion.
- *Cohort effect*: to provide opportunities for group bonding and mutual support; these tend to lead to whole groups achieving well.
- *Graduate skills*: to prepare students for life after their degree, whether in research teams

or in employment; good interpersonal skills are essential to many graduate jobs and are highly valued by employers.

This chapter looks at skills and general principles for working well with others, whether face to face or online. It looks at such issues as:

- being open to what others have to offer
- getting your own message across clearly
- giving and receiving constructive criticism
- giving and receiving support from others, whilst retaining your own academic integrity
- playing a useful role as a group member, contributing to group effectiveness.

Studying collaboratively

Contexts

Using the course material provided to you, find out which of the following contexts are likely to arise for collaborative study on your course.

- [ ] seminars
- [ ] chat rooms
- [ ] group projects
- [ ] class wiki
- [ ] lab groups
- [ ] discussion groups
- [ ] work placements
- [ ] support groups
- [ ] mentor schemes
- [ ] art 'crit' groups

Others:

The challenge of collaborative working

In collaborative study tasks, you gain a chance to hone skills that are valuable to being part of a research team as well as more generally. These include awareness and understanding of group dynamics, of how others think and feel, of what motivates others, and of how to deploy a team's skills and time to best effect. It means thinking about how you can help others to contribute well, whilst taking on board what others say about your own role.

Developing such attributes can be challenging as this requires greater self-awareness, which can be unsettling. It can also mean putting group interests before your own.

Reflection: Skilful collaborative work

Identify one occasion when you were in a group that worked particularly well.

- What made the group successful?
- How did that group differ from others?
- What skills and qualities do you think are important to effective collaborative working?

The value of collaborative working

Which of the following aspects of collaborative working do you value? Select ✓ all that apply.

- [ ] 1 Enjoying a sense of group solidarity
- [ ] 2 Sharing ideas and stimulating each other's thinking, so everyone gains more ideas
- [ ] 3 Gaining new and diverse perspectives
- [ ] 4 Tapping into a wider pool of experience, background knowledge and styles of working
- [ ] 5 Developing skills relevant to employment
- [ ] 6 Learning to stay on task even when working with people whose company I enjoy
- [ ] 7 Achieving greater outcomes than I could alone
- [ ] 8 Having a chance to take on responsibility
- [ ] 9 Having a chance to take on different team roles
- [ ] 10 Learning 'give and take', rather than dominating a group or being dominated by others in it
- [ ] 11 Clarifying my own thoughts through discussion
- [ ] 12 Gaining confidence in asserting my viewpoint
- [ ] 13 Learning to work with people I find difficult
- [ ] 14 Learning to deal with challenge and criticism
- [ ] 15 Receiving support when I need it
- [ ] 16 Helping and supporting others.

Reflection: The value of collaborative study

Which of the above do you value most, and why?

How would skills in these areas help your future career or life ambitions?

Collaborative working: what students say

Studying can be quite a solitary activity – you are on your own with your thoughts or books or your essay a lot of the time, so it was actually a really nice change working in a group.

My group bonded very well. We got very close and had a laugh. I worked so hard on that project because I knew others were relying on me and I didn't want to let them down. I even worked harder on my other assignments because the group members kept asking how they were going and texting me with encouraging comments.

The most useful part was getting feedback on my ideas. I often make judgements very quickly about where I think an idea is leading. The others saw things that I hadn't spotted. I recognise now that there is value in not rushing to the first solution … . I am also a bit less impatient now, which helps me get on with people at work.

Our project group is brilliant. We all have a lot going on in our lives so we just keep each other going. I was going to leave the course at one point and everyone just got me to think about ways of staying.

I really don't like discussion groups much but we had to be in one. I am very focused and I hate it when groups wander off point. The turning point for me was when some of these meanders went in directions I wouldn't have thought of. Some were really unexpected, really good. This made me a bit less vain about my own thinking, which was probably a good thing.

I can't say I enjoyed groupwork. It wasn't my thing. I found it slow and I hated wasting time. I am competitive and didn't like sharing my ideas. That said, I came to terms with it because I can see how the skills you use help my CV. I wouldn't have thought I could be a good leader as I am not a very sociable type but I like to get things done. I found out that I am good at seeing what a group needs to do, explaining this to others, and seeing everything gets organised. I am interested in developing leadership skills further, so I look on groupwork differently.

Doing group evaluation was a bit of a shock to me as I think of myself as a people person. I am very chatty so it was quite hard to hear that the group felt I should, basically, talk less and listen to others. I thought I was listening, but the group said I didn't actually take on board what people were saying and act on it. I can't say it was easy to hear this but it was something I needed to know, it was one of the most useful parts of the course.

The thing that used to annoy me about collaborative working was people not pulling their weight. I have learned that, right at the start, you need to spell out the ground rules, who is doing what, and what will happen if someone doesn't do what is agreed. If you do that, then you can get a really good group going.

Self-evaluation: studying with other people

Rate yourself on the following aspects of studying with others.

Aspect	very weak	weak	OK	good	excellent	See page
1 Appreciating the value of collaborative work						248
2 Creating a supportive environment for groupwork						249
3 Creating an effective environment for groupwork						249
4 Setting ground rules for groups						249, 259
5 Sharing out roles and responsibilities						249–50
6 Getting the most out of discussion						251
7 Knowing how to be an effective group member						251
8 Knowing how to deal with difficulties in a group						249, 254
9 Listening to what other people say						252
10 Making a point effectively in groups						253
11 Giving criticism effectively						255
12 Receiving criticism effectively						255
13 Understanding how to deal with unfairness in groups						256
14 Setting up study groups						257
15 Knowing how to share study without cheating						258
16 Managing group projects						261–4
17 Contributing effectively to seminars and taught sessions						269
18 Making an effective oral presentation						265–8

Reflection: Working collaboratively

Which of the above skills would it be helpful for you to develop further?

Making a group work

Although there are many benefits to working in groups, it isn't always easy. Dealing with the challenge of the group develops a range of skills. The following guidelines are helpful for varied types of groupwork, from class and seminar groups to study groups and online project groups.

Create a supportive group atmosphere

Be aware of people's feelings

People are often more anxious than they seem, and worry about being criticised or found wanting. Be constructive in your comments. Aim to be kind, rather than to score points.

Address anxieties directly

Groups work best when members bond. In the first session, give time to checking how everybody feels about the group or the course. What were their concerns before arriving? Did others feel the same way? It helps to know that you are not the only person who has concerns. Discuss how the group could turn anxieties into opportunities.

Make ground rules

This is especially important if you are forming a study or project group. Ground rules should address directly the anxieties raised by the group. Also include:

- expected attendance, punctuality and commitment
- behaviour or comments that would be unacceptable
- what the group will do if someone dominates, does not pull their weight or ignores the ground rules. See page 259.

Set clear boundaries

Be clear what the group will or won't do to support those in difficulty. Be supportive and encouraging, but avoid being drawn too deeply into others' personal difficulties or trying to 'rescue' them. Help them find the appropriate support services.

Plan to prevent difficulties

If you are going to work collaboratively with one or more people over a period of time, think through what you hope to gain from working together and what might go wrong. Write down your considerations under three sets of headings:

- 'Advantages'
- 'Potential difficulties'
- 'Ways we could deal with these difficulties'.

Go through all the advantages together. Consider each potential difficulty and brainstorm ways of dealing with it. Be creative in looking for strategies. If you are truly stuck, speak to a tutor.

Create an effective group environment

Clarify the group's purpose

Keep the group focused on its purpose and on what it was set up to achieve. This might be:

- a particular product or outcome such as a report, wiki, research project results?
- to develop interpersonal skills?
- to gain personal insights?
- emotional support?
- social interaction?
- solidarity?

Set clear agendas

- Be clear about the purpose of each meeting.
- Set an agenda for meetings, decide how long to spend on each item, and stick to this.
- Meet in a suitable venue. If it isn't a social group, avoid social venues.
- Arrange meeting times and venues well in advance, so that everyone can attend.

Check progress

If the group does not seem to be working well, address this directly. Each person in turn should say what they think could be done to improve matters, including what they personally could do differently. Consider:

- Does the group need to bond through a social activity, or meet earlier to socialise?
- Are tasks shared fairly?
- Is somebody dominating?
- Are you considerate enough about each other's feelings and ideas?

Aim to avoid negative criticism or allocating blame.

Making a group work

Taking responsibility

The responsibility for the group lies with each member. Everyone needs to play an active part. If a problem arises, even if it seems to be the fault of one person, everyone has responsibility for sorting it out so that the group can function.

Investigate group strengths

Find out the range of skills and experience in the group. Who prefers to organise, run meetings, write? State clearly what *you* would like to do. If several people want to do the same thing, rotate roles or share tasks out. Ensure everyone has a role.

Task allocation and group roles

For each session, decide who will take which role.

- Be clear who will do what.
- Set clear deadlines for completion.

Chairperson

Although everybody should help, the chair helps the group to draw up an agenda and keep to it, ensures that everyone gets to speak and that their views are heard, keeps the group focused on the point being discussed and sums up the main points.

Timekeeper

The timekeeper ensures the group keeps to time schedules. Sometimes, in meetings, they allocate each person a set time for contributions.

Record-keeper or secretary

The record-keeper notes who is going to do what and when, and any other decisions made.

Task or project manager

The task manager checks, between meetings, that everyone is doing what was agreed.

Sharing groupwork fairly

Consider what is fair in the circumstances, and what to do if someone really cannot do what was agreed. Be clear what the group will do if someone doesn't pull their weight. Talk through whether, for this group, it is better to assign tasks according to individual strengths – useful if the group needs to produce an outcome at speed or in a competitive context. Alternatively, if a key aim is to learn to work collaboratively, consider rotating roles so that everyone has a chance to develop a range of skills and experience.

Manage potential 'saboteurs'

Be alert to individuals or groups that seem to want to divert time and attention by complaining about the nature of the group or shortcomings of the task set. Avoid being drawn into this. Keep bringing the group back to task. Consider what next step the group can take towards achieving its purpose. Focus on potential solutions rather than problems.

Group sabotage

It is quite easy to sabotage a group. Often this happens unintentionally, because people are nervous or worry about being judged by others.

Reflection: Sabotage

How might you sabotage a group unintentionally – for example, by being late, not preparing, whispering or chatting? What could you do differently?

Being effective in group discussion

Getting the most out of discussion

Before

- Ensure you have done any tasks agreed for the group.
- Read around the subject. Think about it.
- What questions do you want answered?

During

- Check that everyone can see and hear everyone else.
- Be open to hearing something new.
- Jot down useful information.

- Jot down questions to ask.
- If you don't understand something, ask.
- Link what you hear to what you already know.
- Make contributions – for example, raise points that interest you.

After

- Go over your notes and summarise them. Add any new details and thoughts.
- Check that you know exactly when you will do activities arising out of the group. Are they in your diary?

Enabling good discussion

Be encouraging
Encourage others. For instance, you might say, 'I found it interesting that ...'.

Include everyone
Speak to everyone in the group, not just particular individuals. Make sure that everybody has a chance to speak.

Use 'body language'
As you listen, show your attention by smiling, by nodding agreement, and so on. If you want to speak, make clear signals.

Listen to other students
Your fellow students deserve your respectful attention as much as does your tutor – just as you deserve theirs.

Indicate when you agree
Express your agreement: 'So do I ...'; 'Yes, that's true ...'

If you disagree
Instead of just rejecting the other person's ideas, explore them: 'What makes you think that?' 'Have you thought about ...?'

Help the flow
- Contribute to the discussion – but don't dominate it.
- Ask questions – but not too many.
- Take responsibility: don't leave everything to one person.
- Encourage the group to keep to the subject.

Admit mistakes
Acknowledge your errors, and apologise: 'Sorry, my mistake'; 'Oh, I see! I misunderstood ...'

Make suggestions
Share your ideas: 'Why don't we ...?'

Offer information
Share your knowledge: 'There's some useful information on that in ...'

Sum up for the group
'Well, have we agreed on these two points so far? First, ...? And second, ...?'

Build on other people's ideas
'That's an important point you made, for several reasons ...'

Be willing to share ideas
Let others know if you have found a good source or if you have a different perspective on the issue. Have the courage to ask the group for their input on ideas that you are working on.

Speaking and listening skills

Good communication is a two-way process. It requires both good listening skills and participation in the discussion.

Do you talk *to* people, or *at* people, or *with* people?

- People who talk *at* you are listening to themselves. They leave no space for a response.
- People who talk *with* you are keen for you to join in.
- People who talk *to* you consider you, and your response, carefully.

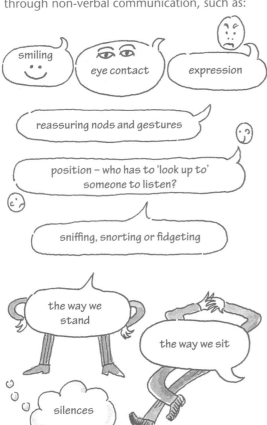

Non-verbal communication

We indicate to other people how well we are listening through our verbal responses, and also through non-verbal communication, such as:

smiling

eye contact

expression

reassuring nods and gestures

position – who has to 'look up to' someone to listen?

sniffing, snorting or fidgeting

the way we stand

the way we sit

silences

How well do you listen?

- Ask someone to watch you while you are listening in a group.
- Ask for comments about your non-verbal signals to various group members.
- Are you surprised at this feedback?
- Do you come across to others in the way you imagined?
- If not, what would you like to change?

Reflection: Listening skills

In your journal, consider how well you listen to others. Do you:

- take in what other people say?
- give other people room to speak?
- let other people finish before you start?
- use encouraging non-verbal signals?
- 'switch off' when bored or if you dislike the person?

Could you do anything differently to put others more at ease when they are speaking? Which non-verbal communication are you sensitive to? What do *you* find encouraging? What do you find *discouraging*?

 ## Better listening

Make a conscious effort to tune in to speakers. Some of these techniques may help:

- consider the speakers' feelings
- find ways of encouraging them
- focus on the content – think of some way this could be of value to you
- listen for key words and jot them down
- think of a question you could ask (when they have finished speaking)
- link what they are saying to something you already know
- find one positive comment you could contribute.

Speaking up

Playing your part

Discussion sessions in class or within groups are most effective when everyone makes a contribution. This requires each student to take personal responsibility for:

- creating the kind of environment where everyone has the chance to contribute
- having the courage and making the effort to contribute.

Professor Locke's discussion group wasn't an instant success

Reflection: Taking your space

Are you someone who needs to focus more on:

- creating the space for yourself to speak, and making more of a contribution in class/groups?
- leaving more space for others to speak?

Speaking in a group

If you are anxious at the idea of speaking out in a group, the following may help.

Before the group

- Make a decision to speak at least once during the group – even if it is only to hear yourself say 'yes' out loud. Build up from a small base.
- Get to know other group members, if possible, so that you feel more at ease.

During the group

- Sit next to somebody you find reassuring.
- Write down what you want to say – if necessary, read it out.
- Think of an example, or evidence, or an illustration to support your point.
- If you are nervous, breathe out slightly more slowly than usual.
- Take your time when speaking – aim to speak more slowly than you would usually.
- Make eye contact with at least one person in your audience.
- Be brief. When you have made your point – *stop*. Avoid going back over what you have already said.
- Be clear. If something sounds confused, say 'I'll make that clearer', or check people have understood.
- Speak up so everyone can hear. If people have to strain to hear you, they will be less sympathetic to what you are saying – and you may have to say it all over again.
- Act as though confident, even if you don't feel it.
- Don't apologise – smile!

After the group

- Congratulate yourself on any progress.
- Keep any mistakes or stumbling in proportion – it is not the end of the world.
- Decide what you will do next time.

Being judged by your voice

Many people feel self-conscious about the way they speak, or about their accent. If you feel anxious about your voice, remember:

- your voice is an important part of you – everybody has an accent, and no accent is better than any other
- your voice, or accent, is less important than your ideas and opinions
- other people may be just as self-conscious about the way they speak
- concentrate on getting your message across and making sense, rather than on pronunciation
- there are many successful people with all kinds of accents.

Dealing with difficult moments in the group

Strong emotions in a group

When strong emotions are expressed, people may feel nervous – yet these emotions are often honest expressions of what someone is feeling.

Emotions arising from strong opinions

A strong attack on somebody's views can be distressing; people often identify themselves with their own opinions. If you reject the *opinion*, the *person* may feel rejected. The group may need a ground rule that *opinions* can be challenged, but not the person who holds them.

Emotions arising from group problems

If the emotion arises out of the group not working properly, then address how the working of the group could be improved.

For example, it might be that some people feel their views are ignored. What would make them feel they were being heard? Would that be realistic? Can a compromise be found?

Emotions arising from outside the group

People bring into any group events or emotions from everyday life. This can be disrupting, as it is not clear where sudden strong emotions are coming from.

It may help to take a minute or two at the start of each session to say what has been going on for group members. You may also need ground rules about strong emotions – such as, 'If one person is aggressive towards another, the rest of the group will intervene.'

Tears

If people are distressed, for whatever reason, let them have a few minutes' quiet or some space to express their emotions. Don't worry about tears – crying can release pent-up stress. Distressed people may need to be alone, or to speak with just one other person quietly for a few minutes. Show kindness. Ask the person what he or she needs.

Silences

Silences often seem longer than they really are. This is because we so rarely experience silence. Silence can be very productive, however. Sit with it and value it, especially if the group needs to discuss something of weight. Don't feel obliged to fill silences with questions or jokes.

Dead-ends

If silences suggest stagnation or stalemate, try a new approach.

- Think of several different ways to break the task into smaller parts.
- Is there a way of turning the problem on its head?
- Brainstorm ideas – might one work?

Imbalances in group interaction

Group discussions can easily become unbalanced if:

- one or two people dominate
- two people are locked into an exchange
- there are no spaces in which quieter people can get into the discussion.

The chairperson or group members can address these imbalances directly:

- by thanking dominant members for what they have contributed, and reminding them that others may wish to speak
- by asking if anybody who has not spoken would like to
- by pointing out any imbalance so that the group can discuss it and deal with it.

Some contributions – such as updating the group at the start of a session about your day or week – are important, but can drift on too long. Set time limits in such cases.

Chapter 10

Giving and receiving feedback and criticism

One of the most difficult aspects of working collaboratively is offering constructive feedback/criticism on other people's work or contributions to the group. You may be asked to do this either formally or informally.

What is meant by constructive?

Constructive criticism is feedback to others that:

- provides insights or suggestions that benefit them, that encourage them in the right direction and that they can apply to improve their work or achieve their goals
- is offered in such a way it does not belittle or undermine the recipients.

Reflection: Giving criticism

How skilled are you at giving criticism in this way? What, if anything, could you do better?

Receive criticism in a constructive way

It can be hard to hear any criticism, whether positive, in the form of compliments, or as areas for improvement. However, we can learn a great deal if we are prepared to listen to feedback. This is now a requirement of many courses and in the workplace.

- Be open to hearing what people say, even if you find it difficult to sit through.
- Assume that the person giving feedback wants to be constructive and is on your side, even if it doesn't feel like it.
- Listen attentively. Take time to think about what has been said. Look for the truth in it.
- Hear the main message, rather than questioning whether the speaker has understood everything about your intentions or the issue.
- Ask questions to clarify anything you do not understand. Ask for examples if you are not sure what is meant.
- Thank people for their feedback: they may have found this challenging to do.

Offer constructive criticism

When to offer constructive criticism

- if you are asked to do so by the recipient
- if it is a requirement of your course to do so
- if it is a ground rule set by the group
- if you have something worthwhile to offer that you consider that the recipient is willing and able to hear.

How to offer constructive criticism

1. Be sensitive: comment on behaviour, actions, products or outcomes, not on people.
2. Be current: refer to what is going on now, rather than delving back into history.
3. Be balanced: point out what is good, as well as what could be improved. It is important that the recipient knows what is good, so that they can build on their strengths.
4. Be honest: don't say things you do not believe. When listening, jot down a list of positive points and ways of making improvements, so you have something concrete to refer too.
5. Be productive: start with what you can praise. This may help the recipient to be open to relatively negative comments later.
6. Be selective: choose one or two areas for improvement that would make a real difference.
7. Be helpful: phrase your suggestions in ways that can lead to practical outcomes. Suggest ways forward, rather than just stating what is wrong.
8. Be realistic: only suggest changes that can be achieved.
9. Be precise: give a clear example of what you mean.
10. Be kind: use a voice and a manner that help others accept your criticism.

Being fair to everyone in the group

When groups don't act fairly towards all members, everyone loses out. The group isn't working to the best potential of the whole team. Individuals may experience stress, or ill health, and be unable to contribute to the best of their abilities. It can also produce tensions and anger, which affect the study of everybody in a group or on a course.

Avoiding unintentional unfairness

Some people set out to hurt others deliberately, but a great deal of unfairness and discrimination is unintentional, caused by thoughtlessness, awkwardness or not being aware of the issues. Many people are concerned to find out they have unintentionally caused distress to somebody else.

The atmosphere may become very tense

Unfair treatment

This may take the form of:

- not being given the chance to undertake certain group roles
- not being listened to
- contributions being ignored or not heard – especially if another person makes that point a few minutes later and gains the credit for it
- being overlooked or left out of activities
- experiencing discrimination on the grounds of colour, ethnicity, appearance, disability, age or other such reasons.

Reflection: Experience of unfair treatment

Think about an occasion when *you* were treated unfairly, because of somebody else's attitudes. For example, can you recall an occasion when you were blamed for something you did not do, or when people tried to embarrass you for no good reason?

What were your feelings and attitudes then?

Did the incident have any longer-term effects, such as on your trust and confidence?

Activity **Awareness of fair play**

- There are dozens of ways in which members of a group could be unfair to its members, maybe without anybody realising. Jot down as many such situations as you can think of, drawing on experiences of previous groups or things you have seen on TV or read about.
- What questions could you ask yourself to help you monitor whether everybody in your group is being included, or whether someone is being left out?

When you have completed this exercise, compare your ideas with those on page 413.

- What could you do to involve everyone in a fair way?

Chapter 10

Study groups

Types of study group/support network

Some courses organise a study group or network. This may be led by a 'mentor' – a student from the year above. If no such group exists, you may like to set one up yourself. You could communicate by telephone or online, or meet after class in a study area, café or somebody's home. Follow the principles outlined above for other groups.

What a support group can do

The work of the support group is limited only by your imagination, but the following activities are generally helpful to most students.

✓ Select aspects that interest you. Decide when and how you could arrange these activities with others.

Encourage each other

☐ Arrange to ring, text or Skype each other to encourage work on a particular activity.

☐ Talk through your difficulties and concerns – others may feel the same way. Help each other to find solutions.

☐ Comment on each other's blogs.

☐ Let others know what they do well. If you appreciated a particular contribution, tell them!

Befriend each other

Simply listening to each other can be very helpful – don't underestimate its value.

☐ Meet up for coffee, suggest a group goes out for a meal, or organise a social event such as a trip.

☐ Befriend each other on social networking sites. Send supportive texts or tweets. Leave comments in group members' social networking accounts.

☐ Set up a support group, chat room, or discussion board for students in your subject, year, college or club, or for mature students, work-based students, or for those studying on a particular project.

Review lectures

☐ Go through your lecture notes together. See if you picked out different points. Each person notes different things, so by sharing information you each gain a fuller set of lecture notes.

Share ideas and study tasks

☐ Share ideas about how to tackle assignments and strategies for coping with work, study and life.

☐ Divide different aspects of your study between you: for example, you could each check a different library or organisation for information, or act as guinea pigs for each other's project questionnaires.

☐ Share background reading. Read different texts and summarise verbally the main points.

☐ Discuss your ideas about what you read.

☐ Help each other to revise material for exams.

Signpost each other to good resources

☐ Let each other know about helpful learning resources, workshops, services, places to study, discounted products, and local events.

Learn from each other's marked work

☐ Share essays once these have all been marked. What differences do you notice?

Action Learning approaches to study

- Give one person, 'person *A*', 5 minutes to describe a current study problem while the rest of the group listen without interrupting.
- As a group, spend ten minutes clarifying the issues. Brainstorm ideas for dealing with the problem, whilst *A* listens without interrupting.
- Person *A* has 5 minutes to use the suggestions to identify action to take, set a timescale for doing this, and negotiate support from the group.
- Repeat the process for each group member. At the next meeting, check that you all carried out your actions, and set new ones.
- See Beaty and McGill (2001).

Sharing work without cheating

Some kinds of work can be shared with other people, whereas sharing other activities would be considered cheating. Below are some guidelines. If you are in any doubt, however, always check with your tutors.

All in your own words …

In general, any writing you submit should either be in your own words, or referenced as described on pages 179–81.

● When you discuss ideas in a group, write them down as notes with bullet points. Avoid writing sentences you have heard – others might write down the same sentences and copy them into their assignments, and this would be seen as cheating.

● If you record discussions, do not type out what is recorded. If you do, you may accidentally copy someone else's words into an assignment – this too would be cheating.

● You may be asked to work as a group to design a project and collect data together. In such cases, always make your own notes about the design, methods, data collection, results, discussion, and conclusions. Write the final account from your own notes – not from anyone else's.

● Don't share out writing tasks between group members. It is usually a requirement that the whole of an assignment is written entirely in your own words.

● If text is sent to you by other group members, never copy and paste it into an assignment – this would be cheating. The person who sent it might also use the text in their own assignment, and this would be noticed.

● Don't let anybody see your writing before the tutor has marked and returned the whole group's assignments. If someone copies your work and hands it in as their own, you may also be held responsible.

● Always write your own references. Mistakes easily creep into references, and tutors are usually good at detecting copied errors.

Accidental cheating?

Tutors are usually adept at finding identical and near-identical sections in students' work. Software is available which can help them to find work copied from the internet or from other students.

If your tutors find the same wording in more than one assignment, they will suspect that cheating has occurred. This could mean that you would have to retake the whole module. You might even be asked to leave your course. Cheating is a very serious academic offence.

Tasks that can be shared

There are many tasks that *can* be shared out amongst friends, support groups or project group members. These include:

● deciding on the group project title

● clarifying each other's understanding of course material, by discussing lectures, notes, texts, cases, experiences, ideas

● discussing new ideas and publications

● sharing administrative tasks, such as booking rooms, keeping agendas of meetings, or writing for permission to interview people

● undertaking a literature search, and then identifying key texts and sections that everyone should read

● discussing and deciding on a methodology

● checking out useful websites

● collecting data

● discussing data, and what it means

● helping one another to use software packages

● encouraging each other to succeed.

Communicating as a group

Deciding on group communications

Good communication is essential to effective group-working. For some groupwork, you will need to negotiate the following factors.

Access: How long will it take for members to travel to face-to-face meetings? Which forms of communication can all group members access? Do they all have home Internet connections?

Group knowledge and skills: Do some students need more encouragement to speak than others? Does everyone know how to use the preferred apps? Do they all use Dropbox or Google Docs? Can you share these skills within the group?

Shared interests and understandings: Do members have the same attitude towards meeting up or using social networking sites? Do they share the same values for privacy, use of texting or Skype, or speed of responding to messages?

Using a group moderator

Page 250 looked at the roles typical of face-to-face groups. For online discussion groups, it can also be useful for a group member to have the role of 'moderator' to facilitate interactions, such as the following.

Set up the group

- Set up the chat room or discussion board.
- Let group members know that it is there.
- Invite the group to set ground rules and to decide actions to take if these are not followed.

Help generate discussion

- Stimulate debate by asking key questions, making comments or offering useful prompts.
- Summarise the discussion so far.
- Respond to comments.
- Bring out links between contributions.
- Encourage new discussion threads.

Keep it live

Archive material that is not in use.
Allocate tasks to group members.
Check that ground rules are being followed.

Setting ground-rules

For all kinds of group interactions, it is worth setting ground rules for a group's communications, and renegotiating these as the group takes shape. Be clear for yourself what you would want addressed as ground rules. Select ✓ any that apply.

- ☐ The group's staying focused on its core purpose and/or on the subject of the discussion/chat room)
- ☐ Use of the group's meeting time to arrange outside meetings or to discuss other items
- ☐ Punctuality for logging in or arriving at meetings
- ☐ Attendance, including leaving or logging off early
- ☐ Contributing fairly to activities and discussion
- ☐ 'Lurking' (reading messages but not contributing)
- ☐ 'Small talk' and socialising
- ☐ Making personal comments
- ☐ Showing respect towards other participants
- ☐ Unacceptable behaviours such as aggression, belittling, flaming, trolling and cyber bullying
- ☐ Managing disagreements
- ☐ Spelling, grammar and use of 'text-speak'
- ☐ Other netiquette and security (e.g. protecting each others' online identities; agreeing who has access to the group's personal information and project materials; keeping anti-virus software up to date if sharing files).

Other:

Group projects

Student projects

You may be asked to undertake different kinds of group project throughout your course. These can vary in size and length but, typically, you need to:

- investigate a topic, for which you may have a choice of the topic and title
- decide a method for your investigation
- gather information and data together
- share your findings with each other as a group
- report as a group, such as through a presentation in class or a seminar session, or through a group report, wiki, blog or poster
- write up the details of your project either as an individual or as a group.

Managing your project

Effective project management draws on the skills covered throughout the book, and especially:

- the collaborative working skills referred to in this chapter, and
- research project skills covered in Chapter 13.

Group project 'To do' List

1 **Communications**: Decide how you will communicate as a group (see page 259). Decide whether you will use tools such as a wiki, blogs or social networking to support the group's work.

2 **The project brief**: What learning do you have to demonstrate? Does this relate only to subject content or are you required to demonstrate how effectively you functioned as a group?

3 **Roles**: Decide the range of roles needed, how these will be allocated, and who will fill each (and for how long, if relevant). See pages 250 and 261.

4 **Planning timetable**: Make a detailed list of all the things to do. Draw up a timetable detailing clearly what will be completed by when and by whom.

5 **Reporting**: Be clear how you are intended to report on the group project. Leave plenty of time to write up your report and, if relevant, prepare and rehearse the group presentation.

Using a group wiki

A wiki is a website containing information that multiple users can edit. You can add your own contributions to other people's ideas, and they can add theirs to yours. Using wikis can develop useful collaborative working and team skills in researching, negotiating, and co-writing.

Your group may wish to create a wiki:

- to draw together information on the topic
- as a resource for students on your course
- to build knowledge of a topic that group members find challenging
- to build understanding and critiques of a difficult text or theory
- to develop the group report together
- to publish the results of a project or to communicate this to others in the class.

> For more information, see:
> http://en.wikipedia.org/wiki

Using a group blog

A blog is a web-based log or electronic journal written by an individual or a group, which others can read online. You might opt to use this:

- to maintain a research diary, recording group methods and findings as these arise
- to keep team members up to date about the progress of those aspects of the project for which you each have responsibility
- for mutual support, to share experiences with other group members, especially if the assignment brief encourages reflective analysis of your project work
- as a group, to communicate with others about your project.

Chapter **10**

Managing a group project

1 Communications

Agree what combination of communication methods will best suit the group. Check whether anyone has a disability or other difficulty that prevents them from making full use of any methods. Select ✓ methods that suit your group.

- ☐ Face to face
- ☐ By phone
- ☐ Email
- ☐ E-messaging
- ☐ Blog
- ☐ Shared electronic space
- ☐ Chat room
- ☐ *Other:*

Ground rules and processes

Discuss the following. Select ✓ when completed.

- ☐ Setting ground rules (see page 259 above).
- ☐ How will you allocate roles?
- ☐ What do you expect from one another?
- ☐ Have group members any concerns about working together on the project? If so, how can you resolve these?
- ☐ What agreements about communications are needed? How often should members log in?
- ☐ Do you all wish to assign someone to manage communications for the group.

2 The project brief

Check the project brief carefully. Discuss the following. Mark off ✓ once completed.

- ☐ What are you required to do as a group?
- ☐ What will be assessed, and how?
- ☐ What are the marking criteria?
- ☐ What must be produced collectively?
- ☐ What must be contributed individually?

Outputs

Select ✓ the required outputs from your project.

- ☐ Report
- ☐ Website
- ☐ Database
- ☐ Newsletter
- ☐ Blog
- ☐ Group presentation
- ☐ Wiki
- ☐ Poster
- ☐ *Other:*

3 Roles and responsibilities

Decide which roles are needed and who will fill them. Some possibilities are listed below. Select ✓ those that apply for your project.

- ☐ Project leader
- ☐ Fundraiser/ treasurer
- ☐ Secretary
- ☐ Chair
- ☐ Deadlines manager
- ☐ Timekeeper
- ☐ Website manager
- ☐ Record keeper
- ☐ Blog manager
- ☐ Design aspects
- ☐ Wiki manager
- ☐ Moderator
- ☐ Technical aspects
- ☐ Research manager
- ☐ *Other:*
- ☐ Data manager
- ☐ Communications manager

Managing your group project

Project name		
Project team		
Name	Phone	Email

Tutors		
Name	Phone	Email

Project communications			
Email address		Chat room address	
Blog address		Wiki address	
E-messenger address		Website	
Other		*Other*	

Roles and responsibilities			
Role	**Who**	**Role**	**Who**
Project Manager			

Project brief

Project outputs

Project outputs (e.g. project website, reports, posters, leaflets, presentations)			

Ground rules for the project team

1
2
3
4
5
6
7
8
9
10

Project resources: websites

Web address	Useful for	Web address	Useful for

Project timetable

Task	Details	By whom	Deadline

Chapter 10

End of project: date	
Group presentation	
Order of presenting	Material to present

Order	Name of group member (s)	

Chapter 10

Making a presentation or giving a talk

What is the purpose of a presentation?

Students are often asked to give presentations, alone or in groups, in order to:

- start off class discussion
- produce a variety of perspectives
- give opportunities to those who are stronger
- develop a skill required in many occupations.

How are presentations assessed?

Find out from your tutors which criteria will be used. In general, the important feature of a presentation is that you have an *audience* – and you need to communicate information to them. This means that the talk should be very focused on audience needs. Group presentations should be well coordinated with everyone contributing.

- Make a few main points. Don't swamp the audience with everything you know.
- Select a few concrete examples which are easy for the audience to visualise.
- Structure the talk very clearly, using just a few headings. Know who is presenting points, for how long, and in which order.
- Repeat main points, and summarise what you have said. When people take things in by ear they need to be reminded of the direction your talk is taking, and how the major points link up. Use a handout or overhead projector, numbering three or four main areas you are going to address.

Preparing your talk

It always takes longer to *say* something than it does to read through it in preparation. Also, you need to speak slowly in a presentation so that people can take in what you say.

- Prepare only what you can deliver at a reasonably slow pace.
- Divide your material into the *essential* points that you definitely want to make, and *extra* material you can use if there is time.
- Prepare a strong closing summary.

The postcard technique

- Break your talk into sections.
- Give each section a heading.
- Write one heading, and a few easily-read prompt words, onto each card.
- Number the cards in the order that you want to introduce those points.
- These will give you confidence that you have structure and content for your talk.

Using audiovisual aids

Slide presentations

If you use *PowerPoint*® or similar software:

- Use large text: at least 28-point.
- Introduce new slides from the same direction.
- Use only one *PowerPoint*® slide for every 2–3 minutes of the talk.
- Avoid animations, sound effects and flashy graphics, unless these are really essential.
- If you use video clips, keep these very short, typically under 2–3 minutes.

Posters

If you are using posters:

- Make these large, bright and informative.
- Use blocks of text beneath large, numbered headings.
- Avoid overloading the poster.
- Use a simple, clear structure so that it is obvious which order to read the information.

Practising

Practise your talk several times, going slowly and timing yourself. If it is too long, edit it down. For group presentations, plan what each person will say, for how long, the transition from one person to the next, and the agreed cues for each speaker.

Overcoming nerves

Many people spend so much time worrying about giving a talk that they leave no time to prepare what to say. You can reduce nervousness in the following ways.

- Prepare carefully – be confident about what you are going to say, and how you are going to say it.

- Make a conscious effort to relax (see page 381), especially 2–3 hours before the talk.

- Arrive early so that you do not need to worry unnecessarily about the journey.

- Be in the room before everybody else. Instead of suddenly being confronted by a sea of faces, it's your space. Smile at your audience as they arrive.

- Have water to drink.

- Don't apologise for anything you feel could be better. Act as though you are quietly confident that your talk is excellent, and you will be halfway to convincing your listeners.

- Look up. Make eye contact with at least two people in your audience.

- At the beginning, summarise what you are going to say – and in which order.

- Go through your cards or overheads in turn. Make each point clearly.

- Pause and take a breath after each point. This gives your audience time to absorb the point. It also makes you look more professional.

- At the end, briefly sum up what you have said.

- Prepare a good line to end with. If you're not sure how to end, simply smile and say 'Thank you'.

Giving the talk

- Read the section *Speaking up* (page 253).

- Use a clock to time yourself.

- Wait until everybody is settled and quiet before you start speaking.

- Tell the audience whether you would prefer questions at the end or during the talk.

- If possible, speak from your postcards, from a poster or from memory, rather than reading. The talk will flow better and will be easier to listen to. However, if you are unable to give the talk in any other way, write it out in full and read it.

- Remind yourself to speak more slowly and loudly than you would usually.

How effective am I in giving presentations and talks?

Aspects of giving a talk	Rating		How could I improve this aspect?
	low	high	
1 Was my main argument clear?	1 2 3 4 5		
2 Did I begin with a brief outline?	1 2 3 4 5		
3 Did I stick to my outline?	1 2 3 4 5		
4 Did I sum up at the end?	1 2 3 4 5		
5 How good was my opening?	1 2 3 4 5		
6 How well did I finish?	1 2 3 4 5		
7 How appropriate were my handouts or audiovisual aids?	1 2 3 4 5		
8 Did I move logically from one point to the next?	1 2 3 4 5		
9 Did I give good examples to support my points?	1 2 3 4 5		
10 Did I answer questions well?	1 2 3 4 5		
11 Did I make eye contact with most of those present?	1 2 3 4 5		
12 Did everybody feel included?	1 2 3 4 5		
13 Did I respect the different viewpoints of those present?	1 2 3 4 5		
14 What feedback did the audience give me?	1 2 3 4 5		

Being aware of your audience

The more talks and presentations you give, the more you will gain confidence in adapting the talk to suit the audience. Here are some useful things to remember.

- Your audience's attention will tend to drift: key points may be missed. State essential points more than once, using slightly different words.
- Your audience's attention span may be short. Break up your talk into a few clear sections. Make planned brief pauses between sections.
- Focus on the key points. Avoid unnecessary details, and don't go off at tangents – you may confuse your audience.
- It is harder to follow a complex argument or a sequence of points when listening rather than looking. A clear chart or handout will help your listeners follow you.
- If you run short of time, don't gabble to fit in more material or more overheads. Instead, edit the talk to fit the available time. (You can plan such reductions when you practise your talk.)
- Audiences usually like 'stories'. Use a strong structure and relevant examples, images and case studies to engage their attention.

Reflection: Speaking formally to an audience

- How aware am I of my audience when I make a presentation or give a formal talk?
- Which techniques suggested in this chapter would help me to interact better with my audience?
- Which three things would be most useful to try out first?

Seminars and class-based audiences

The most typical audiences that you will face as a student are likely to consist of other students, particularly in seminars, workshops, larger tutorial groups or other class-based groups.

These tend to occur on a frequent basis throughout your course, offering you many opportunities to gradually hone your skills in working with, and communicating with, others. Whenever you speak in these contexts, you also have an audience.

Speaking and contributing in seminars and class gives you opportunities to:

- practise speaking to different kinds of audience
- make both formal and informal contributions
- gain valuable feedback from people who may be observing you over several weeks, months or years
- observe group dynamics, so you can gain insights from how other people interact with an audience and then apply these to your own group contributions.

Reflection: Speaking informally to an audience

Drawing on the information that you have covered in the chapter so far, complete the evaluation on page 269. Use this to stimulate your thinking about how strong a contribution you make to seminars and classes.

- When in class, how aware are you that you are speaking to an 'audience'?
- How well do you bring in other people, or leave space for them to speak, during class-based sessions?
- How much of the classes' time do you take up, compared with others in the group?
- How do you think other members of the group, as your audience, view your contribution to the group?

What changes, if any, would you like to make?

Discuss your performance with a friend or other group member. Ask this person to tell you three things you do well, and three things you could improve.

How well do I contribute to seminars and groups?

Unit/module:	Seminar:

Aim of this evaluation	*Strategy*
<ul><li>To make seminars and groups work more effectively, both for me and for others.</li><li>To ensure that everybody feels included and safe in contributing.</li><li>To ensure that, as a group, we cover the material we need to cover.</li></ul>	<ul><li>To evaluate my contributions using this chart, discussion and reflection.</li><li>To compare my self-evaluation with a colleague's evaluation of me.</li><li>To use our evaluations to develop a joint strategy for better seminars.</li></ul>

Self-evaluation chart

1: considerable room for improvement   5: excellent

1 Had I done the necessary preparation for the group or seminar?	1	2	3	4	5
2 Did I make contributions during the session?	1	2	3	4	5
3 Did I speak for more than my fair share of the time?	1	2	3	4	5
4 Were my questions and comments relevant to the discussion?	1	2	3	4	5
5 Did I listen to, and consider, points raised by other people?	1	2	3	4	5
6 Was I encouraging to the main presenter or other speakers?	1	2	3	4	5
7 Was I as encouraging as I could have been to the less confident people in the group?	1	2	3	4	5
8 Did I take a full part, or was I shy or withdrawn?	1	2	3	4	5
9 Did I take relevant notes and references?	1	2	3	4	5
10 Did I keep my attention on the session or did I get distracted?	1	2	3	4	5
11 Did I make all my contributions to the group, or were some to my neighbour only?	1	2	3	4	5
12 Am I clear what I have to do for the next seminar/group session?	1	2	3	4	5

Chapter 10

Review

It is likely that you will be expected to work with others during your time as a student, whether in seminars, support groups or project groups, and in any case you will find yourself in groups just by being around other students on campus. This may be on an informal basis although, increasingly, skills in collaborative groupwork form are assessed as part of graded assignments.

Overall, it is easier to work with others if it is clear what the boundaries are, what is expected, who is doing what, and when, and if everyone acts with everyday consideration for the feelings of others.

Nevertheless, it is quite natural for groups to present challenges. For example, they can bring out people's anxieties, some of which may appear as aggression or failure to contribute. In dealing with such difficulties you will develop a wider range of interpersonal and problem-solving skills.

As in other areas of study, there are strategies which can both be applied to study and which are valuable in life more generally, such as listening skilfully to others, getting your point across clearly to an audience, planning out project work in an organised way, and being able to offer and receive feedback constructively. Reflection on, and self-evaluation of, your own contributions are especially important in developing and fine-tuning your skills in working collaboratively with others.

If the groups you are in work well, you will gain. You will benefit from different perspectives and views. Your own thinking will be stretched, your ideas refined, and you will gain good sources of support. You will also be able to develop skills that you will find essential in the workplace once you graduate. Whatever groups you are in, it's in your interest to help them function at their best.

Part D
Task management skills

11 Writing at university level

12 Developing academic writing

13 Research projects, case studies and dissertations

14 Revision and exams

For most courses of Higher Education, students are required to complete written assignments in order to demonstrate their understanding of some or all of their course material. These assignments tend to consist primarily of essays, reports, case studies or exam answers in the earlier years, and longer pieces of work such as larger research projects or dissertations in the final year.

To complete such assignments, you need to combine basic academic writing skills with an understanding of the relevant writing conventions. Thinking about academic assignments as tasks that can be managed helps you to identify a range of skills that can be applied to non-academic contexts, from interpreting briefs to project management.

This section looks at assignments and exams from all three angles. It looks at ways of:

• developing academic writing skills
• within the conventions of Higher Education
• and as tasks to be managed.

Chapter 11
Writing at university level

Learning outcomes

This chapter offers you opportunities to:

- become better at managing writing tasks
- become more aware of any writing skills that you need to improve
- develop the writing habit if you have been away from formal education
- get started on a piece of writing and overcome writer's block
- understand how to examine assignment titles
- develop a procedure for writing essays and other assignments
- recognise what is meant by concepts and 'concept pyramids' and how you can use these to help you in your study
- develop strategies for organising your ideas, planning your writing, and structuring assignments
- consider how to complete the basic steps of writing an assignment, such as writing drafts, editing, and presenting your work.

Academic writing

Writing a good assignment is both a challenge and one of the most rewarding aspects of study. Almost all students find their writing skills develop significantly at college. This is due partly to the additional practice, and partly to an increase in critical awareness developed by analysing issues from many perspectives.

Writing tasks cannot be separated from other processes such as reflection, goal-setting, organisation and research. Although this *Handbook*, of necessity, addresses these skills in separate chapters, in practice you will find that they are interrelated. You will make best use of this chapter if you are already confident about the material in Chapters 4 and 6. Before you complete your next piece of writing, you may find it helpful to look at Chapters 7, 12 and 13 too.

This chapter looks at skills and stages common to many types of academic writing assignment. It takes you step by step through the different processes involved in writing a piece of course work such as an essay or report.

As your writing skills develop and you become more aware of what is required, you can be more flexible and creative in your approach to writing tasks. However, be wary of tutors who say they value 'individuality': this often means 'be individual within the conventions of our subject area'. Make sure you know what is acceptable, and what is not, in each subject.

How good am I at managing writing tasks?

On the chart below, tick the appropriate box and rate how you well you perform the skill now (9 = excellent, 1 = weak/needs a lot of work).

Do I know how to …	Yes	Rating	I just need practice	Not sure	No	See pages
● get into the habit of writing?						275–6
● get started/overcome writer's block?						278–80
● write an essay?						281; 325–38
● analyse assignment questions?						284–5
● organise information?						288–9
● use and organise concepts?						293–6
● structure an essay?						290
● structure a report?						358
● plan assignments, organising ideas?						289–93
● write good paragraphs?						298–301
● write a persuasive argument?						317–18; 196
● use critical analysis?						188; 197–9
● use academic writing styles?						287; 315–22
● use personal experience in writing?						322
● draft, edit and proof-read?						297; 302–3
● present my writing?						304–5
● get good marks?						323
● use feedback to improve my marks?						324

Reflection: Improving your written assignments

What are the two main priorities for improvement in your next written assignment? Highlight these two in colour.

Repeat this self-evaluation when your next piece of writing is returned, using the tutor's feedback.

Writing for the fearful

Make any mark rather than worry about a blank page

If your writing skills are *very* rusty, try some of the following short exercises. If you are more confident, skip forward to the next section that you find useful.

Get the writing habit

- Write one word ten times, in different handwriting styles. Which is most comfortable?
- Write out a story you enjoyed as a child.
- Write to a friend saying what you hope to get out of being a student.
- Jot down ten words you like the sound of. Write a short piece which includes all those words. Be as crazy as you like.
- 'Just a minute': give yourself one minute to write about one of the following:
  (a) The worst thing I ever ate …
  (b) The most embarrassing thing that ever happened …
  (c) I'm lucky because …
  (d) What gets on my nerves is …
  (e) Anything you like.

Write for five minutes

1 Choose any subject.
2 Don't stop to think. The idea is to get used to writing continuously, whatever the content. Just write as much as you can.
3 When you can write for five minutes, extend the time to ten minutes and build up your limit.

Write from prompts

pictures   photographs   music

dreams   things you see in the street

conversations with friends   reading   YouTube videos

Let yourself be inspired by what you see, hear, think, or dream.

Make a life chart

- Include important events in your childhood, family, education, interests, work, and so on.
- Write a few lines about each item.
- Choose one item and write about this in more detail. Describe what happened, how you felt about the episode at the time, how it affected you in the long term, whether what happened was unusual, and so on.

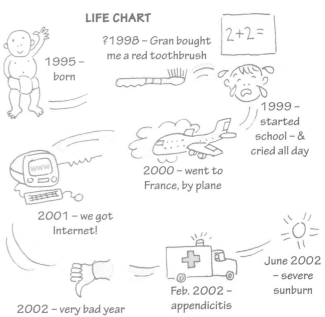

LIFE CHART

?1998 – Gran bought me a red toothbrush

1995 – born

1999 – started school – & cried all day

2000 – went to France, by plane

2001 – we got Internet!

Feb. 2002 – appendicitis

June 2002 – severe sunburn

2002 – very bad year

Developing your writing

Most experienced writers rewrite their work over and over, refining their thoughts, finding a better way of saying something, making a long-winded section a bit briefer, or adding more details to develop an idea.

Rewrite 1
Filling out the writing

- Take one piece of writing you have done.
- Jot down a list of five extra details you could add to give a fuller picture.
- Add something you know about someone else's ideas: from television, radio, or reading.
- Add a personal opinion about some aspect of what you wrote.
- Rewrite the piece, adding the new detail.

Rewrite 2
Playing with your ideas

Play around with what you have written. For example, you could:
- change the order of the sentences around
- change some of the words
- add more details
- change the order of the paragraphs
- ask a question and turn what you have written into the answer
- write from the opposite point of view.

Rewrite 3
Organising your material

- Select one of your pieces of writing.
- Read through it, underlining each major idea in a different colour. For each change of subject, change the colour. If a subject comes up again, use the colour you used before.
- When you have finished, check how often the colour *changes*.
- Rewrite the passage so that all the parts underlined in a given colour are grouped together.

Anxieties about writing

Typical comments from students

Anxiety about writing is very common at university level.

> 'I start a sentence, cross it out, start it again, cross it out, throw the paper in the bin, start a sentence, cross it out …'

> 'I just see the essay title and panic. I think, "I don't know anything about that!"'

> 'I can't get down to it – I keep putting it off and then I'm in a huge rush to finish it.'

> 'Some people just write out a report in a night – I have to write it over and over again.'

Maybe some of these comments strike a chord with you? What do you find difficult about getting started on a piece of writing? The list below may clarify your thinking.

What stops me from writing?

- [ ] The blank page/screen is very off-putting.
- [ ] My mind goes empty.
- [ ] I don't know where to begin.
- [ ] I just can't get down to it.
- [ ] I am not as good as other people.
- [ ] The ideas go round and round in my head.
- [ ] I am embarrassed about my handwriting.
- [ ] I am embarrassed about my spelling.
- [ ] I worry about grammar and punctuation.
- [ ] Other reasons.

Reflection: Getting started

In your journal, note down your thoughts and observations about any difficulties *you* have in getting started with writing tasks.

Similarities between academic writing tasks and other activities

Every day you are involved in situations that require you to plan and to make decisions. Think of one activity you completed recently, such as planning a holiday, choosing this course, or organising a party. Write down what you did, from start to finish.

The activity probably involved six stages. In the box opposite, tick ✓ the stages you went through to complete your activity.

Getting organised

☐ 1 Deciding in general what to do.

☐ 2 Collecting relevant information or materials to complete the task.

☐ 3 Planning the order to do things.

☐ 4 Carrying out the plan.

☐ 5 Checking that you were going about the task in the right way.

☐ 6 Reflecting on how you would do it better next time.

Academic writing follows a similar pattern of planning and decision-making. Suppose you were asked to write about 'The influence of theories on cloning animals'. You may know very little about the subject, and you may have no clear opinion. But you can approach the writing task much as you did with the activity you analysed above.

Activity **Approaching a writing task**

To plan a piece of writing you would probably take the steps shown in the table, but not in the order given.

- Rearrange the steps in the order you would be likely to carry them out.
- Consider a second order you could use.
- Then look below and compare your responses.
- Would your own suggested order suit you better?

Possible sequences

1 9 12 11 10
5 4 8 7 3 13 6

1 10 9 11 12
5 4 7 8 3 13 6

Steps taken		Order
1	Decide how you would do better next time	
2	Make an outline plan	
3	Put the ideas in order	
4	Research the subject (reading, interviews, experiments, etc.)	
5	Examine the assignment question and decide what is required	
6	Write a rough draft	
7	Take notes from your reading (or interviews, experiments, etc.)	
8	Select the relevant information to include	
9	Write the final draft	
10	Write out the references (books and other sources of information)	
11	Read through the writing, checking for sense and small errors; make corrections	
12	Check if your text is within the word limit	
13	Separate main ideas from supporting detail and examples	

Overcoming writer's block

The following activities can help to overcome writing blocks. Which would be most useful for you?

☐ Scribble

Scribble ideas fast, in any order – whatever comes into your mind – then rearrange what you have written and rewrite it.

☐ 'It's only a draft'

Think of each piece of writing as something you will develop through several drafts. As it's just a draft, it doesn't have to be good – it's just something to work on.

☐ Write in pencil or type in an unusual colour

This will remind you that your draft is a rough one – mistakes are allowed!

☐ Write on loose paper – not in a book

If you don't like what you have written, you can throw it away. Alternatively, you can cut it up and rearrange it.

☐ Ignore mistakes in early drafts

Don't worry about minor corrections, such as spellings – you can sort those out in the final draft.

☐ 'For your eyes only'

Remind yourself that nobody but you needs to see early drafts. Handwriting, untidiness and mistakes don't matter at this stage.

☐ Experiment

Try out different starting methods – see *Tricks for getting started* (page 279). Which ones work best for you?

☐ Start anywhere

Write things in any order that suits you – you can rearrange them later. For example, it may be easier to write the introduction last.

☐ Mark the paper

If blank paper puts you off, make any mark or doodle on it so that it's *not* blank. The paper is only a tool – it can't judge you.

☐ Write by talking

If you find it hard to express yourself in writing, say it out loud and record yourself. Then copy this out and redraft it.

☐ Take one step at a time

Break the task into manageable steps. Look back to the C·R·E·A·M strategies (Chapter 4), such as setting mini-goals.

☐ Word process it

On a computer or mobile device, it is easy to change what you have written. You can use a spellchecker, and nobody sees your handwriting!

☐ Quick fire headings and bullet points

Brainstorm a series of possible headings. For each, jot down a set of possible areas to follow up. Rearrange on screen in the best order, editing or adding further points. Alternatively, jot ideas down fast onto sticky notes and rearrange these on a large board or piece of paper under headings. Rewrite the bullet points as continuous text.

☐ Use specialist software

Use software (such as *Inspiration*®) which allows you to brainstorm and organise ideas both as pattern and linear notes. You can colour-code ideas on screen and print them out. This can be useful if you find it difficult to organise your writing.

☐ Rest and relax

If your mind goes blank, you may be tired or stressed. See *Managing stress* (page 380).

Tricks for getting started

Here are some ideas for getting started on a piece of writing.

- You can combine several of these.
- Which ones do you want to try?
- In your journal, keep a record of which work best for you.

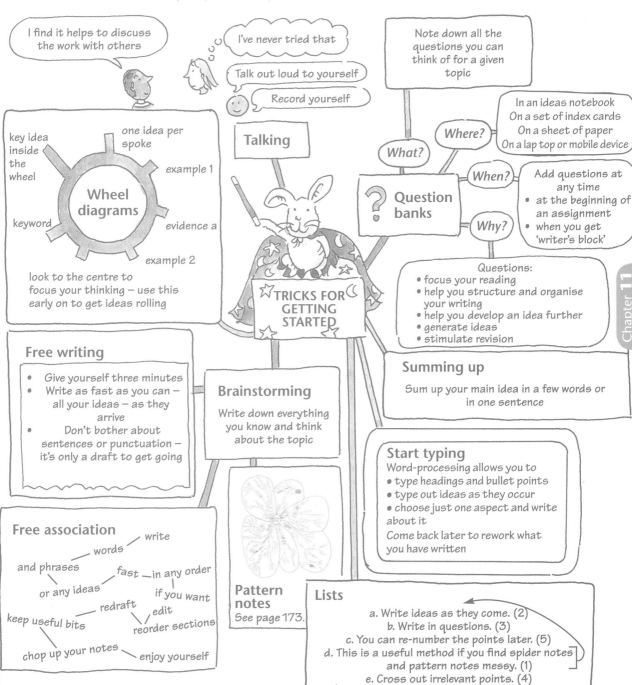

I find it helps to discuss the work with others

I've never tried that

Talk out loud to yourself

Record yourself

Talking

Note down all the questions you can think of for a given topic

What? **Where?** **When?** **Why?**

In an ideas notebook
On a set of index cards
On a sheet of paper
On a lap top or mobile device

Add questions at any time
- at the beginning of an assignment
- when you get 'writer's block'

? **Question banks**

Questions:
- focus your reading
- help you structure and organise your writing
- help you develop an idea further
- generate ideas
- stimulate revision

Wheel diagrams

key idea inside the wheel

one idea per spoke

example 1

keyword

evidence a

example 2

look to the centre to focus your thinking – use this early on to get ideas rolling

★ TRICKS FOR GETTING STARTED ☾

Free writing

- Give yourself three minutes
- Write as fast as you can – all your ideas – as they arrive
- Don't bother about sentences or punctuation – it's only a draft to get going

Brainstorming

Write down everything you know and think about the topic

Summing up

Sum up your main idea in a few words or in one sentence

Start typing

Word-processing allows you to
- type headings and bullet points
- type out ideas as they occur
- choose just one aspect and write about it

Come back later to rework what you have written

Free association

write
words
and phrases
or any ideas
fast — in any order
if you want
keep useful bits
redraft
edit
reorder sections
chop up your notes
enjoy yourself

Pattern notes
See page 173.

Lists

a. Write ideas as they come. (2)
b. Write in questions. (3)
c. You can re-number the points later. (5)
d. This is a useful method if you find spider notes and pattern notes messy. (1)
e. Cross out irrelevant points. (4)

Students' solutions to writing blocks

Here two students describe how they incorporate some of the ideas mentioned in this chapter into their own way of working. How would you adapt their methods to suit you?

Marco

WHAT I USED TO DO

I used to find myself staring at the blank page, not knowing where to begin. I had done the reading. I knew in my head what I wanted to say. Nonetheless, getting started on a piece of writing seemed harder than climbing Everest. The page was too empty. Whatever I wrote seemed wrong. I used to write the first line and cross it out twenty or thirty times – maybe more – get a fresh piece of paper, and do the same thing again.

WHAT I DO NOW

I realise now that I used to aim at writing my good draft long before I was ready. My plans were too skimpy to be useful. I was actually trying to develop my ideas, organise information, write a final draft and compose good academic English all at the same time. No wonder I found it hard.

The first thing I do now is draw a face smiling up at me. It reminds me that this is only a draft – not my best copy, so it does not matter if I make mistakes. Next, I look away from the page or screen, and stop writing. I think of a few things I want to include in my writing and jot them down in a list. When the list is getting long, I turn it into a map or chart of all the ideas – I think other people do it the other way round but it seems to work OK for me like this. I push each part of the map as far as I can take it by asking questions (*who? why? how often? always? everywhere? example? how do I know this?* etc.) As I read or go through my lecture notes, I add bits to the map.

When I have all the information I need on my map, I look at the main themes and number them in the order they should be in my writing. I do the same with the topics I will cover under each theme, and any other material – so I know exactly where everything fits. I draw a different-coloured ring around each theme on the mind-map so it stands out. Sometimes I turn the mind-map back into a list to be clear what I am doing.

I then start with whatever topic looks easiest and just write the basics – not being too fussy at this stage about whether it sounds good – it's just a starting place. I remind myself that I am free to write any sentence or bits of sentences in any order that I find easiest to do. I can always correct and edit and move things around later. When I come to rewrite it, lots of ideas and obvious corrections come quite easily, because I have something to look at.

By the time I write my best version, I am already nearly there. By working in stages, there is not that awful moment when writing actually 'begins' – it has developed bit by bit.

Ayeesha

I have revolutionised my writing. I am a 'headings and points' (1, 2, 3) person. I type these out first. This organises everything easily. Then it's like joining up the dots. I write a sentence or two about each point. Everything under one heading is a paragraph. Then I write my conclusion, and the introduction. I keep correcting tiny bits as I go along – I am a perfectionist, I suppose. At the end, if it's an essay, I erase the headings, and find a hundred things to correct – mostly quite small. Then I print it out to read the hard copy, and this usually shows up different things to correct. I might do this many times. I feel like an artist fine-tuning my work until I am happy with it. Well, I am never a 100% happy. No piece of writing is perfect. You just have to make a decision at some point that 'that's it', the best you can do for now, and make sure you submit it on time.

Essays and other academic writing

Academic writing

The following pages look at the basics of:

- what an essay is
- a seven-point procedure for approaching writing tasks
- analysing the title
- structuring your writing
- drafting, editing, and proof-reading.

The next chapter looks at more advanced features of academic writing tasks: aim to read the two chapters quite close together.

What is an essay?

An essay is a piece of writing which is written to a set of writing conventions. The diagram below gives some brief answers to questions many new students ask.

- An essay is a piece of writing with a particular structure and layout (see page 290).
- Usually it is written in a formal, academic style: the language is different from the way you speak, or the way you would write letters to a friend – it is not conversational (see page 315).
- You are expected to keep very strictly to the task set. You are usually given an essay title: often this is referred to as 'the question', even if it isn't actually worded as a question.

In each essay you can:

- explore a topic in detail
- develop and organise your own ideas through writing
- develop your writing skills
- express your views about a topic
- engage with critical debates in your subject.

Essays also help tutors to assess your progress, and to assess and grade your work.

Ask your tutors why they give you essays to write – they may have additional reasons.

What?

Why?

Writing essays

How often?

Where?

For whom?

- Typically, you may write between two and eight essays each term, but this varies from course to course.

Write wherever suits you, or as required:

- at home
- in the library
- in the exam room.

You write essays for:

- your tutors
- yourself
- examiners
- (sometimes) other students.

A seven-point procedure for writing assignments

Until you develop your own method of writing essays and other assignments, you may find this seven-point procedure helpful.

1 Clarify the task

Before you start research, make sure you know what you are looking for.

- Examine the assignment brief carefully (page 284). What exactly is required? See page 95. Ask your tutor early on if you are unsure.
- Write one line to sum up your basic opinion or argument. Adapt it as you proceed.
- Jot down what you know already.
- What do you need to read or find out?

2 Collect and record information

- Be selective – you can't use everything.
- Write a set of questions to guide your research – and look for the answers.
- Check the word limit to see how much information you can use for each point.
- Keep a notebook nearby to jot down ideas.

Sources

Many sources of information are available to you. Select from what is considered relevant for academic assignments in your discipline:

- books, articles, conference papers, academic blogs, webpages
- official records, reports and surveys
- lecture notes, data from laboratory work and projects
- case studies, interviews

3 Organise and plan

Organise your work as you go along (see page 289).

- Make a big chart to link ideas and details.
- Make a rough outline plan early on – you can refine it as you go along.

Planning

Keep checking what you are doing. Careful planning:

- helps to prevent repetition
- clarifies your thinking
- helps you organise your material.

- documentary evidence, artefacts
- television, radio, newspapers, videos, podcasts
- experience and opinion (in some subjects).

Selecting

Keep asking yourself:

- Is this good quality information?
- Is it the most up-to-date and reliable?
- Is it the best example?
- How will I use it?
- Do I really need it?

Recording

Record information as you go along (see page 176):

- where you found information/inspiration – for citations and references (see page 181)
- notes of themes, theories, dates, names, data, explanations, examples, details, evidence, page numbers (see page 171).

4 Engage, reflect, evaluate

When you have gathered the information, think about where you have got to.

- What have you discovered?
- Has your viewpoint changed?
- Have you clarified your argument?
- Have you enough evidence/examples?
- What arguments or evidence oppose your point of view? Are they valid?
- Is it clearer to you why this task was set?

5 Write an outline plan and first draft

Now structure your writing.

- Refine your plan. Work out the order to introduce each point, using numbered headings and lists of points, as in the plan opposite.
- Work out how many words you can write on each point. What must you leave out?
- Write a first draft. Write quickly: it is only a draft. You may find it easier to type headings onto the computer first.
- Start with whatever seems easiest.
- Keep going: don't worry about style at this stage.
- To begin with, state things clearly and simply in short sentences.

```
Outline plan
1   Title
2   Introduction
3   Main argument – notes Q (red)
       evidence for – notes Q, p. 3–4
       evidence against: Q, p. 5 (orange)
       evaluation of evidence
4   Alternative theory: notes R (yellow)
       example of application
       evidence for
       evidence against (lemon)
       why not convincing
5   Alternative theory 2: notes S (green)
       evaluation of evidence
       why not convincing
6   Underlying issues – notes T (blue)
7   Conclusions
       a
       b
       c
```

6 Work on your first draft

Develop your first draft. You may need to do this several times, improving the assignment with each version. Leave time between drafts for your ideas to simmer.

- Rewrite your early draft (see page 297). Adapt the structure (pages 290, 358) and organise the writing into paragraphs.
- Make sure your argument is clear to readers.
- Check that you have included evidence and examples to support your points.
- Check that you have written in a succinct style such that you make best use of the word limit
- Check you have included citations for every source you drew upon for information and inspiration.
- Write out a list of references, covering each citation in your assignment.

7 Final draft

Edit and check your final draft (see page 303).

- 'Fine-tune' your drafts to see where you can rewrite sections, add further points, correct errors and improve the flow of the writing – this is where you can really gain marks.
- Read it aloud to check that it is clearly written.
- Keep redrafting until you are happy with the text.

Analysing the question

Pick the assignment title to bits

However they are worded, all assignment titles contain a central question which has to be answered. Your main task is to apply what you know to a particular problem. It is *not* to show how much you know – however brilliant your piece of writing, if it does not 'answer the question' you may get no marks at all.

You are marked partly on how well you select and organise information to meet the requirements of the question or problem – even in exams. Use the question to guide you in selecting what to read and note.

Focus on the question

It's essential to take time making sure you understand what is required.

- Read the title aloud slowly three times.
- Underline or highlight words which tell you the *approach* to take (see page 285).
- Underline words which guide you on how to select the *subject matter* of the assignment.
- Write out the title to help you take it in.
- How many sections are there to it?
- Write it out more fully, putting it in your own words. What is the assignment really looking for? What are the central questions?
- How does the title link to what you have read or heard in lectures?
- What topical issues does it refer to?
- Discuss the title with someone else to check for alternative interpretations.

Make notes

Write down in your own words exactly what the question requires. It may form a useful part of your introduction later. To help identify the question do this:

- Note obvious questions implicit in the title, such as 'Why did this happen?' 'How effective …?' or 'Which was more successful …?'

Pick the title to bits

- Consider why this question was set. Is there some public or academic controversy you should know about? Or a recent publication on the topic? Are there important issues to include?
- Jot down your reflections about it.
- What do you already know? Do you have evidence to back up your opinions?
- What do you not know yet? Where or how can you find out more?

Use the title

Keep focused on the title

Put the title where you can see it easily.

Keep checking the exact wording

As you research and write, remind yourself of the *exact wording* of the title. It is easy to forget the focus of the title and drift off on a tangent.

Introductions

In your 'Introduction' (the first paragraph of your writing), refer directly to the title in order to focus your reader. Indicate how you interpret it, such as by rephrasing it in your own words. (If you misunderstood the question, at least the reader will be aware of what has happened.)

Conclusions

In your conclusion, refer back to the title to demonstrate to your reader that you are still answering the set question. Link your final sentence to the question contained in the title.

Academic keywords used in titles

These words indicate the approach or style expected for the piece of writing.

Account for Give reasons for; explain why something happens.

Analyse Examine in very close detail and in terms of component parts; identify important points and chief features.

Comment on Identify and write about the main issues, giving your reactions based upon what you have read or heard in lectures. Avoid purely personal opinion.

Compare Draw out the similarities or common features, indicating the relevance or consequences of these similarities.

Consider *As in 'Consider the implications of ...' (or similar)* Analyse the key issues, reflecting on the different viewpoints in a balanced way.

Contrast Set two or more items or arguments in opposition so as to draw out differences. Indicate whether the differences are significant. If appropriate, give reasons why one item or argument may be preferable (see Chapter 7).

Critically evaluate Weigh arguments for and against something, assessing the strength of the evidence on both sides. Use criteria to guide your assessment of which opinions, theories, models or items are preferable.

Define Give the exact meaning of. Where relevant, show that you understand why the definition may be problematic.

Describe Give the main characteristics or features of something, or outline the main events.

Discuss Write about the most important aspects of (probably including criticism); give arguments for and against; consider the implications of.

Distinguish Bring out the differences between two (possibly confusable) items.

Evaluate Assess the worth, importance or usefulness of something, using evidence. There will probably be cases to be made both *for* and *against*.

Examine Put the subject 'under the microscope', looking at it in detail. If appropriate, 'Critically evaluate' it as well.

Explain Make clear why something happens, or why something is the way it is.

Illustrate Provide examples or evidence to make a point or clarify a position on an issue.

Interpret Give the meaning and relevance of data or other material presented.

Justify Give reasons, supported by evidence, to support a particular argument, point of view or action; address objections that others might make.

Narrate Concentrate on saying *what* happened, telling it as a story or chronology of events.

Outline Give only the main points, showing the main structure.

Relate Show similarities and connections between two or more things.

State Give the main features, in very clear English (almost like a simple list but written in full sentences).

Summarise Draw out the main points in brief (see 'Outline'), omitting details or examples.

To what extent Consider how far something is true, or contributes to a final outcome. Consider also ways in which the proposition is not true. (The answer is usually somewhere between 'completely' and 'not at all'.)

Trace Follow the order of different stages in an event or process.

Devising your own essay title

A short history of the world in five succinct paragraphs

Some programmes will require you to devise your own essay titles. There is an art to this, as a good title can help you to produce a forceful piece of work. In choosing your title, consider each of the following elements.

Core questions

Good essay titles usually contain one or two key questions which the assignment should answer. The title may contain a question, such as:

> To what extent are interest rates affected by consumer spending?

However, the question is not always obvious. For example:

> Compare and contrast the effects of consumer spending and stock market variations on changes in interest rates.

Although the wording is different, the core questions in both cases are 'What affects interest rates the most? What else affects interest rates to some extent?'

In addressing each title, you would be expected to compare and contrast the effects of different factors on changes in interest rates, and to include similar material in each essay.

Factors to contrast

Choose a title that allows you the opportunity to analyse, to compare, to contrast and to evaluate different perspectives, research findings and/ or theories. This will help you develop a strongly structured argument and make the essay more interesting to read.

Aim for clarity

- Avoid long, complex titles.
- Avoid using several questions within the title.
- If you use a quotation, keep this short and follow it with a typical assignment question.
- To check whether your title is clear, ask a non-expert whether she or he understands it.

Research evidence

Ensure that you can:

- find published research to support the topic
- access this material easily
- collect any new data you need easily.

Scale: keep it manageable

Ensure that the title:

- is narrowly defined – select a specific topic, issue or timescale rather than trying to cover everything on the subject
- can be researched within the time limits
- can be discussed in reasonable detail within the word limit.

Issues for debate

Select an area in which you can debate issues relevant to your subject. Devise a title that allows you to discuss these issues and differences of opinion about them. This will help you to develop a good line of reasoning (see Chapter 7).

Activity **Essay titles**

Read the following titles. What do you think are the weaknesses in each?

1 Reptiles.

2 'The world is a safer place today than it has ever been.' J. K. Moody (2013). Is this really true?

3 What were the main changes in the use of technology within the British home during the twentieth century? What was the incentive behind innovation? Who promoted change? Did these affect women differently from men? What forces have hindered change?

4 The negative effects of violence on TV.

5 Describe how placebos work.

For a discussion of these titles, see page 413. For guidance on devising titles for projects and dissertations, see page 348.

Common features of all academic writing

Although the wording of essay or other assignment titles may differ, almost all academic writing tasks require you to do certain things.

Draw on good source materials

Do not simply state your personal opinion or what first comes to mind. Draw on good quality material to develop your thinking and to support your case. Use these to provide reasons, evidence, examples and case studies.

Compare and contrast

Most assignments require some element of comparing and contrasting, especially of theories, models or research findings. You would normally evaluate several perspectives, theories or schools of thought, weighing these against each other.

Use criteria to evaluate

It should be clear from your writing which criteria you have used to evaluate evidence. This is often indicated through phrases such as 'the most recent data' (giving dates), or 'data from the largest survey'.

It should be evident that you have really thought about whether the evidence base is convincing, and that you are not over-impressed by material just because it is in print or on the Internet. (See Chapter 7, *Critical analytical thinking*.)

Show awareness of complexities and nuances

Demonstrate that you are aware that answers are not always clear-cut and that there may be some weaknesses even with an overall strong case. For example, although experts you quote might sound convincing, they may:

- base their conclusions on a very small number of examples
- refer to a large survey or database, but not all the data might be directly relevant to the question.

Similarly, be prepared to acknowledge weaknesses in your own arguments and strengths in potential counterarguments. State clearly why there are difficulties in coming to a firm conclusion one way or another.

Provide a well-structured argument

In your writing, provide a line of reasoning which gives direction to your writing: each point should follow logically from another. (See Chapters 7 and 12.)

Make a decision

Don't sit on the fence. Indicate which side of the argument, or which model or theory, you believe is best. Even though the case may be fairly evenly weighted, show that you are able to make a decision on the basis of the evidence.

Synthesise

Look to see if you can draw together the best of several different points of view. Combining these may provide a new overall perspective.

Follow a set structure

There is likely to be a set structure for the type of assignment and a particular style for your subject discipline. (Different styles are considered in the next chapter.) *All* academic writing requires that you group similar points together in one paragraph or section, rather than scattering them through the text.

Be 'discursive'

Link your points so that they feed into sentences and paragraphs, and so that each paragraph follows naturally from the previous one. All should contribute to a central guiding line of reasoning. (This is different from presenting a random set of points, for example, or headings with bullet points under them.)

Be emotionally neutral

Most academic writing requires you to stand back and analyse dispassionately, as an objective onlooker.

Structuring your writing

The structure and organisation of your work is just as important as the content. What matters is not just what you know but the way that you organise it.

How do you structure academic writing?

Like a building, a piece of academic writing gains its structure and shape from several elements.

Design: your argument

What you are trying to say (your argument) should provide the structure for the whole piece of writing. Your reader should be able to follow your line of reasoning easily: how it moves from *a* to *b* to *c*. (See page 317 and Chapter 12.)

Scaffolding: organising and planning

Organise and plan your work before you start.

- Group ideas together, in files or on paper.
- Devise a working plan to guide your research.
- Make an outline plan for your writing. (See pages 289 and 291.)

Central framework: formal structure

Different formal structures are required for different kinds of assignment, such as essays or reports – see pages 290 and 358.

Bricks: paragraphs

Writing is organised into paragraphs, and each paragraph itself has a structure. Clear paragraphing assists the reader. (See pages 298–300.)

Cement: wording

You can use language, such as linking words and emphasis, to highlight your point and show the direction of your argument. (See page 301.)

Organising information: grouping things together

First try this …

For each box, work out:

- How many circles are there?
- How many triangles?
- How many *types* of triangle?

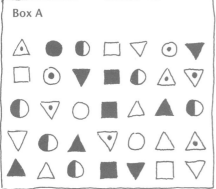

Box A

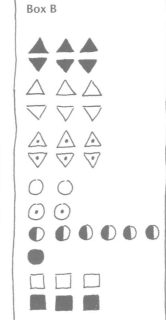

Box B

Comment

You probably found it quicker and easier to find the answers for Box B. If so, why was this the case?

Why group information?

Grouping ideas and points has several advantages.

- You will be able to find things more easily.
- You will find it easier to draw up your writing plan and follow it.
- Your thinking will be clearer.
- Your readers will be able to follow your argument more easily.
- You will get in a mess if you don't.

See pages 176 and 289.

Chapter 11

Organising information: planning your writing

Below are four steps you will need to take in organising information for an assignment. Each step makes the next one easier. (See also *Recording and using information*, page 176.)

1   Divide the work into topics

When making notes, it may be easiest to use a separate file or sheet for each main point or topic. You could use a large sheet of paper, writing out points so you can see them all clearly.

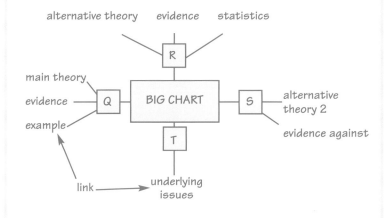

2   Rearrange your notes

- Either spread out hard copies of notes so that you can see them, or compare on screen.
- Group related information in one place.
- Arrange the material in the best order.

notes about Q (red)	notes about R (yellow)
notes about S (green)	notes about T (blue)

3   Write an outline plan

When making notes, it may be easiest to use a separate file or sheet for each main point or topic. You could use a large sheet of paper, writing out points so you can see them all clearly.

> Outline plan
> 1   Title
> 2   Introduction
> 3   Main argument – notes Q (red)
>   evidence for – notes Q, p. 3–4
>   evidence against: Q, p. 5 (orange)
>   evaluation of evidence
> 4   Alternative theory: notes R (yellow)
>   example of application
>   evidence for
>   evidence against (lemon)
>   why not convincing
> 5   Alternative theory 2: notes S (green)
>   evaluation of evidence
>   why not convincing
> 6   Underlying issues – notes T (blue)
> 7   Conclusions
>   a
>   b
>   c

4   Organise information into paragraphs

Colour-code each set of notes. Give each topic or paragraph a colour: underline the main points using this colour. The plan opposite uses the sequence of colours of the rainbow, to assist memory. Be consistent in using this colour-coding onto pattern notes, outline plans, and rough drafts. Divide hard copy files of notes using coloured dividers.

Once you start writing, each paragraph should have one main idea – with supporting detail or evidence, and relate to one set (or page) of notes. (See page 298.)

Structuring an essay

1 Title/question

As stated on page 284, every essay title contains an actual or implied question. The whole of your essay must focus on the title and address that question.

2 Introduction

In your introduction, explain what the essay is going to do.
- Explain how you interpret the question, and summarise your conclusion.
- Identify issues that you are going to cover.
- Give a brief outline of how you will deal with each issue, and in which order.

Length: about one-tenth of the essay.

3 Develop your argument or line of reasoning

Paragraph 1
- This paragraph covers the first issue your introduction said you would address.
- The first sentence introduces the main idea of the paragraph.
- Other sentences develop the topic of the paragraph. Include relevant examples, details, evidence, quotations, references.
- Lead up to the next paragraph.

Paragraph 2 and other paragraphs
- The first sentence, or opening sentences, link the paragraph to the previous paragraphs, then introduce the main idea of the paragraph.
- Other sentences develop the paragraph's topic.

(For more about paragraphs, see pages 298–300.)

4 Conclusion

The conclusion contains no *new* material.
- Summarise your argument and the main themes.
- State your general conclusions.
- Make it clear why those conclusions are important or significant.
- In your last sentence, sum up your argument very briefly, linking it to the title.

Length: about one-tenth of the essay.

5 References and/ or bibliography

References and bibliography

List all the books, articles and other materials you have referred to within the essay. (See page 181.) If a bibliography is required, list relevant texts, including those you read but did not refer to in the essay.

The structure given here is a basic outline but it is core to many types of writing. The structuring of different types of essay is discussed in Chapter 12.

Planning your writing assignments spatially

It can sometimes be difficult to gain a sense of what the word limit means in terms of how much you will actually write.

Before beginning any work on an assignment:

● Work out roughly how many words you type on one page of A4 paper. (This may be about 300 words.)

● Check the overall word limit for your assignment. (This may be 1200 words.)

● How many pages of your writing or typing will your essay occupy? (For instance, 1200 words at 300 words per page will occupy 4 pages.)

● Take that many pieces of paper. Draw out in pencil how much space you will give to each section, item or topic, as in the sample essay below. How many words can you allocate to each section? Or to each topic or example?

● It may take a few attempts to get the balance right. Note how little or how much you can write for each topic or example.

● If you wish, continue to plan out your essay, point by point, on these sheets. Notice how much space each item can take.

With this spatial plan, can you now see:

● how many pages of your writing your assignment will take?

● where sections or topics will be on the page?

● how your word limit divides up?

● how little or how much you need to read and note for each item?

An outline plan for the essay on pages 325–7 (1000 words)

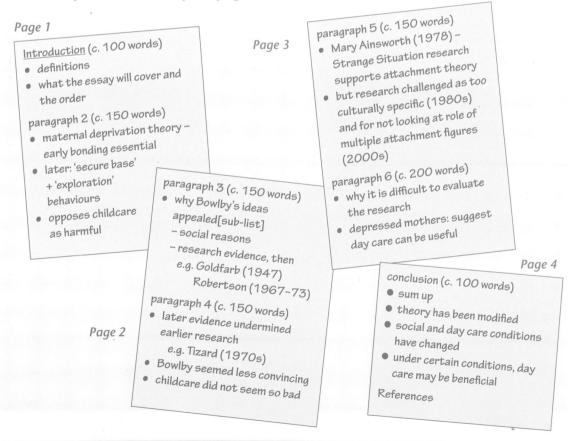

Page 1

Introduction (c. 100 words)
● definitions
● what the essay will cover and the order

paragraph 2 (c. 150 words)
● maternal deprivation theory – early bonding essential
● later: 'secure base' + 'exploration' behaviours
● opposes childcare as harmful

Page 2

paragraph 3 (c. 150 words)
● why Bowlby's ideas appealed [sub-list]
  – social reasons
  – research evidence, then e.g. Goldfarb (1947) Robertson (1967–73)

paragraph 4 (c. 150 words)
● later evidence undermined earlier research e.g. Tizard (1970s)
● Bowlby seemed less convincing
● childcare did not seem so bad

Page 3

paragraph 5 (c. 150 words)
● Mary Ainsworth (1978) – Strange Situation research supports attachment theory
● but research challenged as too culturally specific (1980s) and for not looking at role of multiple attachment figures (2000s)

paragraph 6 (c. 200 words)
● why it is difficult to evaluate the research
● depressed mothers: suggest day care can be useful

Page 4

conclusion (c. 100 words)
● sum up
● theory has been modified
● social and day care conditions have changed
● under certain conditions, day care may be beneficial

References

Planning stages

Develop your outline plan

Make a first outline plan

Make pattern notes or a structured outline plan showing what you know, what at this stage you think are the main issues, your questions, and things to find out.

Action plan

Convert your list of things to find out into an action plan with priorities (pages 134–5).

Plan your time

Use *Working backwards from deadlines* (page 139) and your diary or planner to map out when and where to complete each stage of the writing process. (This becomes easier after a few assignments, when you gain a feel for your own pace of working.)

What is the *minimum* you can do? What additional research would you *like* to do, if you have time? Depending on how well you proceed, you can adapt your reading and note-taking to suit.

Rework your plan

If necessary, rework your outline plan as you proceed. You may rework your plan several times as your thinking becomes more sophisticated. This is part of the process of understanding the topic.

Make a clear final outline plan

Clarify your final plan. Use colour to highlight certain areas, or rewrite untidy parts afresh. Take note of whether you are using the excuse of 'neatening' or 'updating' the plan' to put off writing the first draft.

From pattern notes to linear plan

It's essential to be really clear about the structure of your assignment before you start writing your final drafts. If you're not, your writing and thinking may appear muddled.

Advantages of pattern notes and 'mind maps' Pattern notes illustrate connections and resemble the way the mind organises information in networks, so can be a helpful starting point for generating ideas.

Limitations of pattern notes and 'mind maps' It can be difficult to write assignments directly from them as they show interconnected webs of ideas as a whole, whereas writing is linear and sequential – one point follows another. Also, pattern notes lay out information but tend to be less effective for the kinds of analysis, evaluation and comparing and contrasting needed for academic assignments.

From pattern notes to linear plan

- *Generate*: Use the pattern notes to brainstorm what you know and to generate ideas rather than worrying about organising information at this stage.
- *Find connections*: Use colour, numbers and connecting lines to link related information in the pattern notes.
- *Group*: Rework the pattern notes, placing together all connected information.
- *Create a hierarchy*: As a half-way stage between making pattern notes and sequential writing, it helps to organise your ideas hierarchically so that key points stand out from underlying details. (See page 293.)
- *Create headings and points*: Give each area of your pattern notes a title or heading. Type out a list of the headings, then type a list beneath it of all points that relate to that heading. Use the colour-code you used in your pattern notes to guide you in what belongs to each paragraph.
- *Relate to plan*: Position these lists on your spatial plan (page 291). (For software that helps with this, see Appendix 2.)

Concept pyramids organise ideas

What is a concept?

A *concept* is a mental representation of a group of items which are similar in some way. For example, the concept 'cutlery' includes objects as different as a four-pronged fork, a hollowed, round-ended spoon, and a sharp-edged knife. Conceptually, these all share the characteristic of being tools used in eating food. Sometimes the phrase *conceptual category* is used instead of 'concept'.

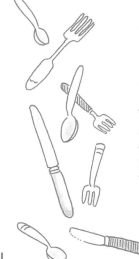

Why concepts are useful

When we come across a new object, the brain matches the main features of the new experience against those of previous experiences. It can then make a good guess at what kind of thing the new object is – its concept category:

'Branches, trunk, leaves, bird's nest: must be a tree'

Once it has identified the category, the brain can second-guess, or infer, other information:

'If it's a tree, it must have roots and sap. It won't leave the area. I don't need to take it for walks. Sorted!'

This ability to identify and share conceptual categories enables us to communicate more easily

with other people: we don't need to describe everything in minute detail whenever we speak. In academic writing, if ideas are well organised, the reader can second-guess meaning and other information more easily.

Concept pyramids organise ideas

We can organise concepts into hierarchies – shaped like a triangle or pyramid, as in the simple one for 'tree' below. You don't *have* to use concept pyramids – but they give you an extra analytical tool.

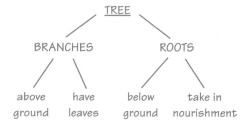

The most general information, or the most inclusive heading, is placed at the top of the pyramid. Aspects of the tree are placed below. Details of those aspects are placed below again – and so on.

Each level of the pyramid shows information of a different category. There are technical names for different category levels, but everyday terms work just as well.

Technical term	Everyday term
Superordinate category	Upper level (*tree*)
Intermediate or basic category	Intermediate level (*oak tree*)
Subordinate category	Lower level (*red oak tree*)
Exemplar	Example (*this red oak tree*)

On another pyramid, *plant* might be the upper-level concept, and *tree* would then be at the intermediate level.

Concept pyramid for contrasting birds and mammals

The example below is of a more detailed concept pyramid, showing how different levels of information about animals can be arranged.

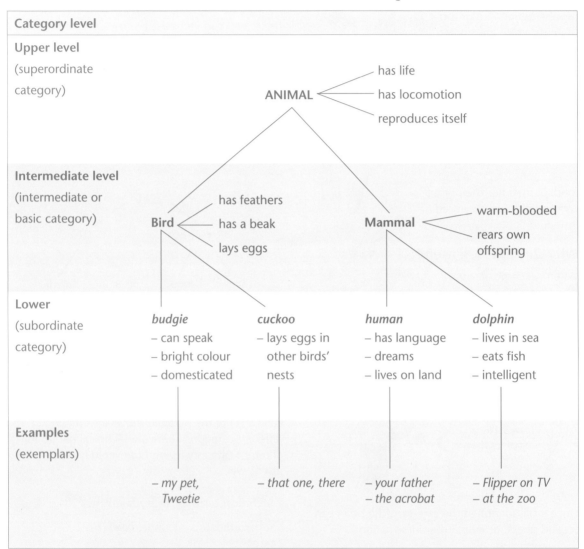

Category level

Upper level
(superordinate category)

ANIMAL
- has life
- has locomotion
- reproduces itself

Intermediate level
(intermediate or basic category)

Bird
- has feathers
- has a beak
- lays eggs

Mammal
- warm-blooded
- rears own offspring

Lower
(subordinate category)

budgie
– can speak
– bright colour
– domesticated

cuckoo
– lays eggs in other birds' nests

human
– has language
– dreams
– lives on land

dolphin
– lives in sea
– eats fish
– intelligent

Examples
(exemplars)

– *my pet, Tweetie*

– *that one, there*

– *your father*
– *the acrobat*

– *Flipper on TV*
– *at the zoo*

Examples at different levels

If the upper level were *painting*, an intermediate level could be the style, *Impressionism*. A lower level would be painters, such as *Monet*, and examples could be Monet's paintings *Water Lilies*, *Wisteria*, and *Poplars*. You might have separate hierarchies of details of the paintings – with *size*, *colour*, *design*, or *brushwork* as category headings.

If the upper level were *instrument*, an intermediate level could be *drum*, and a lower level might be a *timpani drum* or *African drum*. Specific examples would be *that drum on the table*, or *Gino's new drum-set*.

Essay plans as pyramids

Essay structures consist of several concept pyramids combined into one piece of continuous writing. A halfway step between pattern notes and linear writing, the concept pyramid incorporates more structure and linear development. Unlike pattern notes, it enables you to evaluate the weight (or level) of one kind of information against another – and to see this visually.

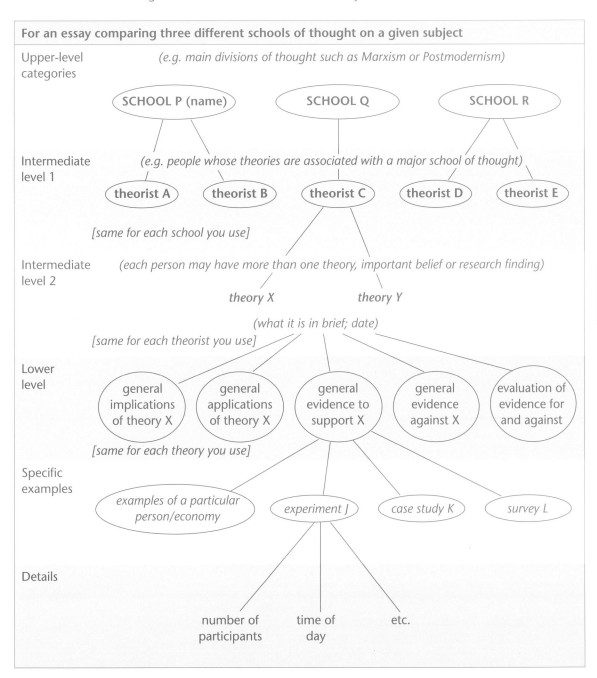

For an essay comparing three different schools of thought on a given subject

Upper-level categories — *(e.g. main divisions of thought such as Marxism or Postmodernism)*

SCHOOL P (name) · SCHOOL Q · SCHOOL R

Intermediate level 1 — *(e.g. people whose theories are associated with a major school of thought)*

theorist A · theorist B · theorist C · theorist D · theorist E

[same for each school you use]

Intermediate level 2 — *(each person may have more than one theory, important belief or research finding)*

theory X · theory Y

(what it is in brief; date)

[same for each theorist you use]

Lower level — general implications of theory X · general applications of theory X · general evidence to support X · general evidence against X · evaluation of evidence for and against

[same for each theory you use]

Specific examples — examples of a particular person/economy · experiment J · case study K · survey L

Details — number of participants · time of day · etc.

Use pyramids for planning assignments

Use pyramid questions

Ask yourself key questions to search for or organise the information at each level.

Upper level

- How many major schools of thought or key theoretical perspectives are there on this question?
- Which are the most relevant for your assignment? (If unsure, go down to the intermediate level and check who said or wrote what.)

Intermediate level

- Which theorist (or judge, writer, or similar) said what, when?
- How can you sum that up briefly?

Lower level

- Overall, how good is the general evidence to support this position or theory?
- What are the general implications of the position or theory?
- What are the general applications of the position or theory?
- What is the general evidence against the position or theory?
- Overall, how good is the evidence for or against?

Exemplar level

- Do you need to include specific examples of applications, implications or evidence? Which are the best examples?
- Given the word limit and the time available, how much detail should you give? For instance, have you space only to mention the name and date and one line about this research? Or are you short of words, in which case you could give more details?

Use pyramids to help with word limits

Having mapped out your information as a pyramid, do you have the right amount for your word limit?

Too much information

If you have too much, you will need to leave something out.

- If you have several examples at any one level, select just one or two examples of them. Do the same with the other levels.
- If you have already used most of your word limit, you may be able to refer to specific examples by name without going into detail. (This depends to some extent on the subject.)

Too little information

If you have too little, you can build up to the word limit.

- Add more examples at the middle or lower levels.
- Write more about your specific examples. Evaluate the significance of the examples for the overall assignment.

Balancing the pyramid

In general, it is more important to explore ideas at the middle and lower levels than to give a lot of detail for specific examples. (See also page 216.)

Writing drafts

The art of writing is in the craft of redrafting

Professional writers redraft many times before they are happy: writing rarely flows out 'all at once' in its final version. You would expect to write several drafts of an assignment to shape and fine-tune it.

Draft 1: A quick draft to get ideas down

Use your plan. Don't worry about style or good English at this stage – just get started.

Focus on the assignment question. Write out your interpretation of the title.

Clarify your core points. Write out your central ideas, hypotheses, conclusions or the main direction of your line of your reasoning.

Write headings and subheadings. Use your plan (or the pyramid you have created) to identify these. You can retain these headings and sub-headings in most reports and some dissertations, but leave these out of the final draft of an essay. This provides your structure.

Add in supporting details below each heading.

Link it up. Write your headings and points into sentences.

Stick to your plan. Keep looking back to it after writing each paragraph. Go back to the assignment title and its central questions: check that you haven't gone off on a tangent. If so, put a line through anything irrelevant. Be a harsh critic of your own work.

Draft 2: Fine-tune the structure

Check that information is grouped and ordered – especially into paragraphs (page 298). If not, rearrange it.

Check that the line of argument is clear from one paragraph to the next. If necessary, add in sentences to link ideas. You may need to do this more than once. Look for places where you could summarise points so that you use fewer words, and consider adding further points. Rewrite sections.

Draft 3: Fine-tuning and style

Read what you have written aloud. How does it sound? If you are stumbling as you read, this may indicate poor flow. Look for where you can improve continuity, links, sentence lengths, and overall style. Add sentences or phrases to clarify points. If you have a screen-reader, you could use this to read your text aloud. Listen for meaning, and for punctuation pauses.

Draft 4: Finishing touches

Aim to leave at least a day between drafts. Your mind will go on working on your ideas. After a break, you will find it easier to spot passages that need rephrasing. See *Editing your draft*, page 302.

Saving your drafts

- Save your first draft as draft 1 and type that and the date in the footer.
- Save each new draft as a separate file, draft 2, draft 3, etc., dating each draft.
- Alternatively, use a tool such as Google Docs that enables you to return to revised edits (see page 182).

Check using a hard copy

It is easier to identify some errors on hard copy. Print out final drafts and read carefully for errors.

Paragraphs

Paragraph structure

Paragraphs are made up of sentences and are, typically, several sentences long.

A paragraph groups similar ideas and material together, all organised around a central idea or theme, which is usually made clear in its first sentence. All sentences relate to the main idea of the paragraph.

First sentence

The first sentence of each paragraph:

- is usually the 'topic sentence' that introduces the subject of the paragraph
- starts on a new line
- is preceded by a gap – either an indent on the same line, or a blank line before.

Later sentences

Other sentences of each paragraph:

- develop the theme of the paragraph's 'topic sentence'
- follow each other in a logical order – one sentence leading to the next.

Last sentence

The last sentence sums up the paragraph, or leads into the next paragraph.

Paragraphs help the reader

 Paragraphs break up the text into manageable portions. A page is easier to look at when divided into three, four or five sections.

Successive paragraphs follow each other in a logical order, taking the reader from *a* to *b* to *c*. Words or phrases within them link them to earlier or later paragraphs.

Paragraphs also organise meaning. They help your readers to think clearly about what you have written.

 Activity **1 Analysing paragraphs**

Choose two or three pages from one text.

- Read the topic sentences – the ones that sum up the main theme of each paragraph. These are often, but not always, the opening sentences.
- How well do the topic sentences sum up the main ideas of those paragraphs?
- How are the paragraphs linked?
- If paragraphs lacked a clear topic sentence, were they more difficult to read?

 Activity **2 Paragraphs and sentences**

Separate this passage into paragraphs and sentences with correct capital letters and punctuation.

A Life of Adventure

mary seacole was born in 1805 in kingston jamaica her mother practised as a 'doctress' using medical knowledge which women had brought from africa and developed in the tropics from her mother mary inherited her medical skills as well as her ability to run a boarding house from her father a scottish military man she inherited her fascination with army life marys own medical reputation was established during a series of cholera and yellow fever epidemics she made her own medicines and emphasised high standards of hygiene as well as enforcing strict quarantine on victims by these methods she saved many lives on the outbreak of the crimean war mary volunteered her services to the british army although she had worked for the army before at its own request this time she was turned down undaunted mary made her own way to the war zone once in the crimea she not only nursed the soldiers but also ran a hotel and sold food wine and medicines after the war mary was treated as a celebrity she was decorated by the governments of four countries in england a poem in her honour was published in punch and even the royal family requested her company and medical expertise

---

 Activity **3 Identify the theme**

- Re-read the paragraphs for Activity 2.
- Decide the main theme of each paragraph and sum it up in 1–4 words.

See opposite for answers.

Writing paragraphs

Writing paragraphs

If you have difficulties with paragraphing, divide your page into three columns:

1 Arguments	2 Main information	3 Supporting detail

- In column 1, jot down the ideas, theories, opinions and line of reasoning that you want to include in your writing.
- In column 2, jot down the main examples and types of evidence that support your line of reasoning.

- In column 3, write down lesser details, facts, names, statistics, dates and examples that support your main argument.
- Each paragraph should have:
  - one item from column 1
  - one, two or three items from column 2
  - several items from column 3.
- Items selected for each paragraph should all help to make the same point.

Alternatively, using a concept pyramid:

- Each paragraph is likely to need one item at the intermediate level, one at the lower level, examples, and a few details.

Suggested answers

Activity **2 Paragraphs and sentences**

A Life of Adventure

Mary Seacole was born in 1805 in Kingston, Jamaica. Her mother practised as a 'doctress', using medical knowledge which women had brought from Africa and developed in the Tropics. From her mother, Mary inherited her medical skills as well as her ability to run a boarding house. From her father, a Scottish military man, she inherited her fascination with army life.

Mary's own medical reputation was established during a series of cholera and yellow fever epidemics. She made her own medicines and emphasised high standards of hygiene as well as enforcing strict quarantine on victims. By these methods she saved many lives.

On the outbreak of the Crimean War, Mary volunteered her services to the British Army. Although she had worked for the army before, at its own request, this time she was turned down. Undaunted, Mary made her own way to the war zone. Once in the Crimea, she not only nursed the soldiers, but also ran a hotel and sold food, wine and medicines.

After the war, Mary was treated as a celebrity. She was decorated by the governments of four countries. In England, a poem in her honour was published in Punch and even the Royal Family requested her company and medical expertise.

Activity **3 Identifying the theme**

The main themes of the paragraphs are:

1. general information: birth and background
2. early medical reputation
3. the Crimean War
4. after the War.

Reflection: The value of paragraphing and punctuation

Did you find it easier to read the text for Activity 2? If so, did this increase your appreciation of the value of good paragraphing and punctuation?

Did you have difficulty adding in the punctuation? If so, you could ask your tutors whether any additional support is available.

Checking your paragraphs

If paragraphing isn't your strong point, then when you have finished your early drafts, you can check your paragraphing by doing the following exercise.

1 Read each paragraph

Read each of your paragraphs in turn. Decide what is the main topic of each.

2 Sum up the topic

Sum up that topic in about 1–4 words.

3 Give the topic a name and colour

Write the topic in the margin. Give it a colour.

4 Which is the topic sentence?

Which sentence is your topic sentence – the one that sums up the topic? Highlight it. Is it at the beginning of the paragraph? If not, would it be more powerful there?

5 Is everything relevant?

Check whether everything in each paragraph relates to the topic sentence. If you're unsure about something, underline it and check whether it would be better placed in a different paragraph. Is anything superfluous? If so, cross it out.

6 Is everything in the right place?

Once you have assigned a different colour to each topic (see 3 above), search for each topic in turn throughout your writing to see whether any material on that topic has wandered into other paragraphs. If so:

- highlight it in the topic colour – using colour will show up whether your material is well organised or scattered
- cut separated items of the same colour and then paste them together into one paragraph
- rewrite the paragraph, integrating the bits you have moved so that the paragraph flows well.

7 Are sentences in the best order?

In each paragraph, are the sentences in the best order? Is it clear how each sentence leads on to the next?

8 Is the line of argument clear?

Is it clear to the reader how the topic sentences of each paragraph relate to each other? Is it clear how the material in each paragraph builds on that in previous paragraphs in order to establish an argument with a clear direction?

9 Are paragraphs well-linked?

Is it clear how each paragraph leads on to the next, such as through phrases that link the ideas in one paragraph to that in the one that either precedes it or follows on from it? See pages 298 and 301.

10 Is every paragraph relevant?

Is every paragraph relevant to the title? Are they all needed in order to make the argument?

Make time for relaxation and exercise – you can go on thinking about your assignment!

Linking ideas together

Certain words are used to link ideas and to signpost to the reader the direction your line of reasoning is about to take, such as adding more emphasis, or introducing an alternative viewpoint. Below is a selection of words used to link ideas, depending on the direction of your argument.

Adding more to a point already made

- also; moreover; furthermore; again; further; what is more; then; in addition
- besides; above all; too; as well (as)
- either; neither … nor; not only … but also; similarly; correspondingly; in the same way; indeed
- in fact; really; in reality, it is found that …
- as for; as to; with respect to; regarding

Writing in lists

- first(ly); second(ly); third(ly)
- another; yet another; in addition; finally
- to begin with; in the second place
- moreover; additionally; also
- next; then; and to conclude; lastly; finally

Putting the same idea in a different way

- in other words; rather; or; better; in that case
- to put it (more) simply
- in view of this; with this in mind
- to look at this another way

Introducing examples

- that is to say; in other words
- for example; for instance; namely; an example of this is
- and; as follows; as in the following examples; such as; including
- especially; particularly; in particular; notably; chiefly; mainly; mostly

Introducing an alternative viewpoint

- by contrast; another way of viewing this is; alternatively; again; rather; one alternative is; another possibility is
- on the one hand … on the other hand
- conversely; in comparison; on the contrary; in fact; though; although

Returning to emphasise your earlier viewpoint

- however; nonetheless; in the final analysis; despite x; notwithstanding x; in spite of x
- while x may be true, nonetheless
- although; though; after all; at the same time; on the other hand; all the same; even if x is true; although x may have a good point

Showing the results of something

- therefore; accordingly; as a result
- so, (then,) it can be seen that
- the result is; the consequence is
- resulting from this; consequently; now
- we can see, then, that; it is evident that
- because of this; thus; hence; for this reason; owing to x; this suggests that; it follows that
- in other words; otherwise; in that case; that implies

Summing up or concluding

- therefore; so, my conclusion is
- in short; in conclusion; to conclude; in all; on the whole
- to summarise; to sum up briefly; in brief; altogether; overall; thus; thus we can see that

---

 Activity **Check for linking words**

How are these words used in the sample essays on pages 325–9 and 331–3?

Editing your draft

'Editing' is working on your draft in order to improve it. When you edit, you can …

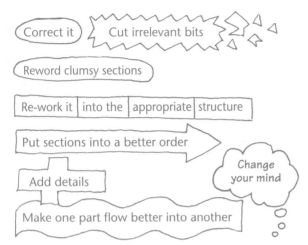

Correct it
Cut irrelevant bits
Reword clumsy sections
Re-work it | into the | appropriate | structure
Put sections into a better order
Add details
Make one part flow better into another

Change your mind

Different kinds of editing

Typically, you would need to go through your work at least several times, with a different focus each time.

1 Meaning

- Does it make sense? Read it aloud slowly.

2 Organisation and structure

- Have you used the appropriate structure?
- Is connected information grouped together?
- Is information presented in the best order?
- Is the work well paragraphed? (See pages 298–300.)

3 Evidence

- Have you backed your argument with evidence, examples, details, and/or research?

4 References

- Is the source of your information clear?
- Are your quotations accurate?
- Are citations and references written correctly? (See pages 179–82.)

5 Style

- Is the text easy to read?
- Is it too chatty? Or long-winded? Or pompous?
- Are any sections confused?
- Is it precise and succinct? (See page 309.)
- Is the style appropriate? (See Chapter 12.)

6 Punctuation, spelling and grammar

- Have you written in sentences? (See 'Proof-reading', below.)

7 Presentation

- Is the text legible?
- Does it look neat and well presented?
- Does it follow any presentation guidelines you were given?

> **Reflection: Editing your drafts**
>
> Which aspects of editing do you need to spend most time on?

Proof-reading

Edit your draft until you are happy with it. Then do some final proof-reading. You may find a different set of corrections if you do this using hard copy.

- Read it once again aloud – does it make sense?
- Look for mistakes such as typing and spelling errors. Look up doubtful spellings or ask someone.
- If you used a spellchecker, check for words that are not misspellings in their own right, but which are not the words you want to use, especially homophones such as 'there' and 'their'.
- When proof-reading for grammar, punctuation and spellings, it can help to work backwards through your writing (word by word for spelling), to avoid drifting into skim-reading.
- Everyone has their own pattern of errors. If there are certain mistakes you make repeatedly, note these down and be particularly careful in checking for them.

Editing final drafts

Tick each box below when you have finished checking that point.

Content and argument

☐ I have followed the assignment brief to the letter

☐ The text answers the central question(s) posed by the title (page 284).

☐ Sufficient space has (or words have) been given to the most important points.

☐ All the information included is relevant to the set question.

☐ The main line of argument is clear, not lost in a sea of detail.

Research material

☐ There are sufficient examples and evidence to prove or illustrate my points.

☐ My own ideas and opinions are clear to the reader.

Structure and grouping

☐ The text is in the appropriate structure or format.

☐ Ideas are suitably linked.

☐ Each paragraph is well structured.

☐ Ideas are presented in the right order.

☐ It is clear how each paragraph links to the others (page 301).

Style

☐ The style is appropriate for my course (Chapter 12).

☐ The text is not too chatty or flippant.

☐ It is free of slang and colloquialisms.

☐ Technical vocabulary is used correctly.

☐ I have written succinctly, making best use of the word limit.

☐ The words used are my own. (There is no plagiarism.)

☐ The text is not repetitive.

☐ The text can be read aloud easily.

Clarity

☐ There is nothing the reader will find confusing.

☐ The language is clear and straightforward.

☐ The reader will follow the line of reasoning easily (Chapter 7).

☐ It is clear which sentence in my introduction summarises my viewpoint or argument.

☐ Sentences are of reasonable length and are uncomplicated.

General

☐ The introduction is suitable.

☐ The conclusion is suitable.

☐ Spelling, grammar and punctuation are correct.

☐ Every source that I have used to build my argument or make a point is correctly cited within my writing.

☐ My list of references includes every source that I have cited in my writing.

☐ I have written out citations and referencing correctly and in full.

☐ The bibliography (if needed) is accurate.

☐ I have taken account of feedback I received for earlier work (page 324).

Presenting your writing

For all assignments

Typically, you will be required to hand in work electronically. Often, this is then put through software that helps to check that this is all your own work.

Complete and well-organised work

- If you saved several drafts, make sure you submit the right one.
- Complete and attach cover pages, if required. These may include a confirmation that the work is all your own.
- If you have collated references in dedicated software, ensure these are included within your assignment.
- Number your pages.
- Remove all colour coding, underlining, inserted comments, links and tracked changes that you used to help the process of writing your work.
- Leave space to one side or between lines so that your tutor can add comments and feedback easily.

Anonymity and confidentiality

- If work must be handed in anonymously, be careful not to include your own name on your work.
- Include your student number on every page.
- Write the short title of the assignment in the footer, as well as any code number you are given.
- Check that any confidential material is removed. This includes avoiding giving thanks and acknowledgements to individuals and organisations at the start or end of the material, as well as in citations, if they gave you material to use confidentially.

Hard copy

- If you are required to hand in a hard copy, your final text should be neatly presented.
- Print on one side of the page only.
- Occasional minor corrections made neatly by hand are acceptable, otherwise type in corrections and print out a good copy.

For essays

- Write the title at the top of the first page.
- Remove any sub-headings that you have used to help organise your work.
- Use any guidance provided about securing pages or using folders if handing in hard copy.

For reports and dissertations

- Write the title on a cover page.
- Use appropriate section headings, all in the same format.
- Number sections and paragraphs.
- Insert charts, tables and appendices. Provide clear headings. Check that headings and numbering for charts and appendices match those used in references to them within the main body of your report.
- Remove any unnecessary appendices – such as anything not referred to within your report.
- If you are given instructions about binding projects, follow them carefully.

Format

Adapt to purpose

It may suit you to use one font or size while working, and another for the final printout to hand in. For example, you might use very large type on the screen, making it easier to proof-read, and then reduce the size before printing it out.

For your final copy

- Use only one type size for your main text.
- Use one clear, simple font for your final draft – not script designed to look like handwriting.
- Vary type size for headings and sub-headings. Be consistent in the way you use them.

Lecturers' preferences

Your tutors may have preferences about the technical and stylistic aspects of presentation listed below.

Tutor/Subject:	
Aspect	**Requirements**
● Electronic submission or hard copy also required?	
● Is a cover sheet required? What information should it contain?	
● For hard copy, print on one side or both?	
● Begin each section of a report on a fresh page?	
● Use sub-headings?	
● Number paragraphs?	
● Leave a wide left-hand/right-hand margin?	
● Write my student number on each page?	
● Write the assignment title and/or code on each page?	
● Write as 'one', 'I' or 'we'? (Address the reader as 'you')?	
● Use passive or active voice? (Passive: 'The essay was written'. Active: 'I wrote the essay'.)	
● Which style should be used for references? Any special layout for references?	
● Bibliography needed? Any special layout?	
● Anything else? (E.g. Use of diagrams, charts, graphs? Standard keys on maps? Use colour in diagrams? Is annotation needed?)	

Chapter 11

Review

Although all students will be familiar with writing tasks to some extent, most students struggle at times with getting down to writing their assignments and with getting to grips with what is really required. Even talented students working at the highest levels can face writer's block, procrastinate with starting new sections of their assignments, or find they are grappling to translate good ideas into writing.

This chapter has looked at how to develop your writing from small beginnings, so as to build your confidence and familiarity with writing. Although academic writing is a distinct kind of writing, you will profit from making *any* kind of writing a daily activity. You will build up speed, become more able to think and write simultaneously, become more aware of how you can improve your writing, and grow in confidence.

The chapter also looked at how to approach a piece of academic writing as a task with:

- sets of manageable steps that you can follow
- sets of given conventions that you can adopt
- sets of requirements that you can meet.

The more you write and the more organised you are in following these steps, conventions and requirements, the sooner you start to use them automatically. With practice, you will find that you combine separate stages quite easily and that you find faster ways of doing things.

The following chapter looks in more detail at what is expected for academic writing at undergraduate level. It looks at general expectations and provides annotated examples of essays. Chapter 13 draws on the points covered in Chapter 11, and also looks at other kinds of written assignment such as case studies, project reports and dissertations. The critical analysis that you would need to apply within most kinds of written assignments is covered in Chapter 7.

Check your learning outcomes

- Look carefully at feedback from your tutor. If it is not clear where you have lost marks, ask for an appointment to discuss this. If you take with you a copy of the self-evaluation questionnaires on pages 274 and 303, you can use these to help provide structure to the session.

- Using your tutor's feedback and advice, complete the self-evaluation questionnaire on page 274 again. Notice which areas you now feel confident about, and which you would still like to improve.

Basic English skills

It is difficult to get the highest grades at college if your basic English skills, such as grammar and punctuation, are weak. It is worth investigating any language workshops at your institution or at a local College of Further Education.

Chapter 12
Developing academic writing

This chapter offers you opportunities to:

- consider further requirements of academic writing including:
  - stylistic conventions
  - precision
  - distinguishing fact and argument from opinion
- be aware of how different approaches to research impact upon academic writing
- understand the influences of the scientific model on most areas of academic writing, including non-science subjects
- understand better what is meant by terms such as 'subjectivity' and 'objectivity', 'quantitative' and 'qualitative'
- learn to use the four main writing styles used in Higher Education:
  - descriptive
  - argumentative
  - evaluative/analytical
  - personal/experiential
- know what gains good marks for an assignment, and how to use tutor feedback constructively
- develop insights into what makes a good essay through evaluating these for yourself.

Writing improves through practice and informed reflection. As you progress through Higher Education, your tutors will expect your writing style to continue to improve. In particular, your writing should demonstrate that you are aware of academic conventions and when to use them.

You will also be required to move flexibly between different writing styles, moving from precise description to critical analysis to evaluative summary, depending on the task.

This chapter helps you to build your awareness of what is expected in academic writing. Browse through it before doing your first assignment. Return to look at it in more detail, along with Chapters 7 and 13, before writing up your assignments.

Stylistic conventions for academic writing

Would that more of the youthful populace were so moved as to indulge in the daily pursuit of informative literary input such as might raise the accuracy of their perceptions regarding their health.

Studies by World Youth (2009) reveal that young people benefit from reading about their health.

So basically, you need to go read more, man!

There is no single style that can be used in all academic writing. Each discipline has developed its own particular styles, and in some subject areas you may find that even various branches of the discipline use quite distinct writing styles.

The following conventions apply to *most* academic writing. Nevertheless, if your tutors offer specific guidance, follow their directions.

Use formal English

Academic English is more formal than the language used in everyday conversation, emails, letters, magazines and most newspapers. It shouldn't sound 'chatty'. It also avoids slang and colloquialisms such as these:

- 'The writer is *out of order* when he suggests …'
- 'The new plans were *just the stuff.*'
- 'These findings need to be *taken with a pinch of salt.*'
- 'The argument was *a bit over the top.*'

Aim for clarity

Write so that your reader can easily follow what you are trying to say. Do not use long words and technical jargon simply in order to sound impressive. Check whether your sentences are so long and complicated that they are hard to follow. Avoid antiquated language, convoluted sentences

or mannerisms – as well as using up your word limit and obscuring your argument, these could be off-putting to your readers.

Learn how to use specialist vocabulary

It is important to learn the specialist styles and technical terms used for your subject, and also to extend your vocabulary.

- If you are not familiar with specialist terms, look for explanations of these terms in introductory textbooks or glossaries.
- Pay attention to how such terms are introduced in books and articles – note the different forms used, such as noun and verb forms, and past tenses.
- Do not litter your writing with terms that you yourself do not understand – it is better to write in your own words than to sound as though you do not understand the words you are using.

Reflection: Writing in the discipline

Browse through several articles for your own subject, looking just at the writing style.

- What features do each of the pieces share?
- Are these features of your own writing?

Avoid abbreviations and contractions

Write words out in full:

- 'dept.' as 'department'
- 'e.g.' as 'for example'
- 'didn't' as 'did not'
- 'they're' as 'they are'
- 'isn't' as 'is not'

Be impersonal

Most courses prefer you to avoid personal pronouns such as 'I'/'we' and 'you'. Instead, sentences begin in impersonal ways such as:

- It can be seen that …
- There are a number of …
- It has been found that …

Be cautious

Academic writing generally sounds cautious. Writers indicate that they are aware that nothing is completely certain. They use words that express this lack of certainty, such as:

- appears to; seems to; tends to; may; might; possibly; probably; apparently; generally; seemingly.

They may use phrases such as:

- in some cases, this …
- the evidence suggests that …

Avoid misplaced conjunctions

The following words are not used at the start of sentences: *or*, *and*, *but*, *yet*.

Numbers

Numbers below a hundred are often written out in full, such as:

- thirty-one per cent
- nineteen members.

However, figures are retained in statistical and scientific work:

- 31 per cent
- 15°C
- 7.3 newtons.

Be objective

Academic writing avoids personal, subjective words such as 'nice', 'wonderful', 'worthwhile', 'usual' or 'natural', because the reader's understanding of these words may be very different from your own.

Avoid apologies

Don't apologise to the reader for any weaknesses you think there may be in your research or writing, such as that you found the subject difficult or that you had no time to write a conclusion. Write as if you are confident of what you are saying – even if you don't feel it!

Addressing the reader

Avoid asking readers questions or telling them what to think.

Be concise

Edit out unnecessary words:

A man called Jay Singh invented …
In a book called *Scottish Pathways*, …

Use continuous prose

Write in full sentences, grouped together into paragraphs (see page 298). For essays and dissertations, avoid lists of points: incorporate the points into sentences. Lists and headings may be acceptable in reports and projects.

Being precise

Example of a vague sentence

> Some people did not like the idea at the time and made the politicians stop it but then he attacked him publicly.

Why is it vague?

- 'some people' – who exactly?
- 'the idea' – which idea?
- 'at the time' – when? date?
- 'the politicians' – all politicians? or a certain group? or a political party?
- 'made the politicians' – how did they 'make' them?
- 'stop it' – stop what? how was it stopped?
- 'people did not like the idea' – why not?

It can be confusing to have more than one pronoun (such as 'he', 'she', 'it', 'this' or 'that') in a sentence.

Activity		Precise wording

Which of the following is most precise?

1. A woman ruled the country.
2. Mrs Thatcher served as Prime Minister in Britain between 1979 and 1991.
3. A woman ruled Britain during 1979–1991.
4. Mrs Thatcher ruled Britain for several years and introduced many policies which affected various aspects of people's lives.

Answer

Response 2 – the others all contain vague information.

> … rather than sort of not saying quite what you mean, if you know what I mean …

Using facts, opinions or arguments

> I think there should be fewer adverts on TV.

Opinions

Opinions are personal beliefs. These are not always based on good evidence, and may even run *contrary* to the evidence.

> Adverts for toys should not be shown on TV because research by Dr Meehan (2013) suggests that they …

those gathered and recorded in some formal way, such as in journals or official records.

What is considered 'natural' or 'normal', for example, is generally a matter of opinion. Even if most people agree with you, it is still opinion, unless you can give *evidence* that what you think is likely to be true.

> There were an average of 35 adverts an hour on channel X, on 25th July 2013.
>
> SURVEY

Facts

Facts can usually be checked against evidence. Facts used in academic writing are generally

Arguments

Arguments are *reasons* (which can include facts) given to support a point of view.

As you write, question what you write

As you write, keep checking for precision. Ask yourself questions, such as 'when exactly?', 'why exactly?' or 'who?' Check that you have given your readers enough detail for them to know exactly what you are talking about.

Writing for different subjects

Different approaches

Each academic subject has a slightly different approach regarding:

- *research methodology* – how to conduct research
- *evidence* – what is regarded as appropriate and sufficient
- *writing genre* – the preferred writing styles and conventions
- *objectivity* – how far your approach should be objective or subjective, quantitative or qualitative, scientific or personal.

As a student, you will need to identify the approaches taken by your subject and produce work appropriate to that subject. You will need to be particularly aware of this if you take a 'joint' or 'combined' honours degree, but even *within* a subject, approaches can vary depending on the area of study.

The influence of the 'scientific' model

Academic writing has been heavily influenced by the notion of being 'scientific' – even when the subject is not obviously about science. Although this view is changing, the approach you are expected to take is likely to be affected by some of the principles of the scientific model, so it is helpful to know what it involves.

The main features of the scientific model are:

- objectivity
- a testable hypothesis
- replicated results
- controlling for variables
- quantitative analysis
- accurate description
- qualitative analysis.

Objectivity

The scientific model values objectivity. This means that instead of relying on personal opinion or common sense, scientists test possible explanations against the available evidence. If data is objective, two people undertaking the same research in the same way should arrive at the same results and conclusions.

A testable hypothesis

A hypothesis is a possible explanation of why or how something occurs, consistent with available evidence. The hypothesis is formulated in a way that can be tested.

A hypothesis cannot be proved true, but it can be proved *wrong*. If a hypothesis survives many attempts to prove it wrong, increasingly it may be considered reliable and trusted as a 'theory'.

Replicated results

For a piece of scientific research to be taken seriously, another researcher needs to have repeated the research with similar results. This 'replication' indicates that the first results

were reliable, and not just a 'one-off' or due to individual opinion or bias. (However, it is still important to think hard about whether bias may be built into the research method itself.)

Scientific approaches

Controlling for variables

Scientists need to know that what they *think* they are testing is what they are *actually* testing. They need to make sure that 'variables' – all the things that can change, such as the weather, or the time of day, the people involved or the materials used – have not influenced the results unexpectedly.

Usually, research experiments are run many times to check the effects of different variables. The researcher tries to change only one variable at a time, keeping everything else constant. This is known as 'controlling for variables'.

For example, researchers comparing the effect of blue light or red light on plant growth would check that everything *apart* from the colour of the light was identical. For each light colour they would use the same type and size of plant, the same amount of water, the same levels of nutrients, the same temperature, and the same air source.

Quantitative analysis

Scientific research relies heavily on quantitative data. This means it focuses on changes or differences that can be *measured*. Standardised measurements are used – such as number, time, weight and length – so that results are easy to compare objectively. Thus experiments might investigate:

- whether the height (measurable) to which a particular kind of plant grows depends on the temperature of the environment (measurable)
- whether fruit yield (measurable) depends on the amount of light (measurable)
- whether how many words somebody can read in a given amount of time (measurable) depends on the size of print (measurable) or the age of the person (measurable).

The approach is: 'If *this* changes while everything else stays the same, does it have an effect on *that*?' This could also be stated as: 'If *X* changes while *A*, *B* and *C* stay the same, does it have an effect on *Y*?' Quantitative analysis involves analysing the relationship between changes in one variable and changes in another.

When changes in *X* exactly match changes in *Y*, the changes are said to be 'correlated'. It is important to understand, however, that correlation does not prove that changes in *X cause* changes in *Y*, or vice versa. Correlation may be due to chance, or both *X* and *Y* may be affected by a third variable, *Z*.

Accurate description

When writing up research, scientists describe their methodology, research conditions and results exactly, so that anyone who wishes to replicate their research can set up near-identical conditions. You will be expected to write accurate descriptions in the same way, such that someone else could replicate your research.

Descriptive writing for reports is very precise: no unnecessary words are used. (See pages 316 and 197–9.)

Qualitative analysis

In qualitative research, the data used are not easily measurable. The research is not completely objective: some judgement and interpretation are involved. It is acknowledged also that the researcher is in some way part of the research itself and may unintentionally influence its results – for example, by having a role in making sense of the findings.

Scientists use qualitative analysis in the 'Discussion' part of a report, where they make sense of their results and offer possible reasons why things did not go as expected. Here they evaluate strengths and weaknesses, such as in the way they designed the experiment or worded the experimental hypothesis.

Nevertheless, science generally regards subjectivity as a 'problem', and often uses language which makes it sound as if no scientists were involved – as if the experiment just happened on its own:

> The experimental design could have been improved by …

rather than:

> I could have improved the design by …

Alternatives to the scientific model

Most academic disciplines are influenced by the scientific model. However, subjects vary in how far they value the different aspects of the model. The main differences are in varying attitudes to subjectivity and to qualitative data.

Subjectivity and objectivity

Subjectivity simply means bringing yourself, your own views, opinions, experiences or value judgements into your research or writing. In counselling or fine art, a high value is placed upon subjectivity – that is, upon personal emotions, feelings, intuitions and experiences. It is the opposite of *objectivity*, the aim of the traditional scientific model.

In many subjects, however, you need to combine the two: to analyse both objective criteria, such as the results of independent surveys, market research or case studies, and your subjective response – your feelings, tastes, interests or intuitions.

(See also *Using personal experience*, page 322.)

Quantitative approaches in non-science subjects

Science subjects tend to avoid research where it is difficult to control for variables or to quantify results. For example, issues such as gender, romance or childhood change over time, but as these changes are not easily measurable they would not usually be studied by scientists.

Non-science subjects often find ingenious ways of categorising such information, however, so that it can be roughly standardised according to set criteria. This enables a wider range of issues to be studied in relatively objective ways.

Example: attitudes to children

A researcher interested in how attitudes to children changed over time would aim at finding an objective way of analysing data rather than simply relying on her opinion. She might choose to focus on how often popular magazines referred to themes of 'childhood innocence' and 'goodness' compared with themes on 'disciplining bad children'. One approach could then be to count how often a popular magazine included each theme, and compare data over ten-year intervals to see whether the number of references changed significantly over time. This would give quantitative data.

The researcher here would also have to classify her information carefully to be clear what type of material should be included under her chosen themes ('innocence' and 'discipline'). Classification of words and themes involves some subjectivity, as people mean different things by the same words. For example, someone quoted in one of the magazines as saying 'A good child does as his mother says' might have meant that he obeyed because he was well disciplined, or that he obeyed because he was naturally virtuous – or something else entirely.

Qualitative analysis

It is not always easy to draw a line between what is quantitative and what is qualitative – as you can see from the example above of attitudes to children. In that instance, the researcher needed to make subjective judgements about what was *meant* by innocence or discipline. Usually social science researchers acknowledge their subjective role in the experiment as interpreters of the evidence. Social science and arts subjects may aim at objectivity and quantification where this is possible, but are also interested in the subjective – how decisions and interpretations are arrived at. They are more accepting of overlaps between objectivity and subjectivity.

As a student, you may be asked to make qualitative evaluations about project evidence, about decisions made during work placements, or about art or literature. Your lecturers will look for:

- the relevance of the detail you select
- the criteria you use in making decisions
- the aptness of your interpretations.

Polar opposites in academic approaches

For each of the aspects numbered below, find out whether it is the convention in your subject area to be nearer the North or the South Pole. This may vary depending on the type of assignment.

Consider how far each dimension is important for your assignment. You could indicate this by making a tick on the dotted line.

North Pole

South Pole

1 Every attempt is made to control the conditions under which the research takes place, so that the researcher can decide which variables to manipulate and measure

....

1 Every attempt is made to keep the research true to real life – that is, to give it 'ecological validity'

2 Results can be generalised – that is, they would hold true if the research were repeated

....

2 The unique is considered worthy of study – results may be impossible to repeat exactly

3 Numbers and standardised measurements make it easier to generalise results

....

3 Creative interpretation is highly valued

4 Objective views are formed, based on evidence and facts rather than personal opinion

....

4 Subjective responses, feelings, intuition and creativity are regarded as valuable resources

5 The role of the scientist in the research is minimised and rarely discussed

....

5 The role of the researcher is made explicit – it is considered useful to discuss how the researcher's presence influenced the results

6 Individual differences are not important – generalised findings are valued

....

6 Individual instances, and opportunities for detailed interpretation, are valued

7 Personal experience is regarded as individual and irrelevant: it is not referred to

....

7 Personal experience is highly valued as giving insight and a deeper understanding

8 The language is clinical, neutral, impersonal and dispassionate, even if the researcher is passionate about the subject

....

8 The language used allows the personality and feelings of the writer to shine through

PLANNER

Different styles

Compare the following two styles of writing. The first is conversational:

> Mount Pepé is going up – it's going to take everything with it when it goes. And I mean everything – villages, farms, trees, the lot. It's frightening to think of how powerful a volcano can be. Think of the damage they cause! Remember Pompeii and Mount Etna!

The second is in a general academic style:

> In order to assess whether it is necessary to evacuate the villages on Mount Pepé, three main factors need to be taken into consideration. The first, and most important, of these is the element of safety. According to seismic experts currently working on the volcano, there is likely to be a major eruption within the next ten years (Achebe 2012). According to Achebe, the eruption is likely to destroy villages over a radius of 120 miles (Achebe 2013, p. 7).

Notice the differences between the two examples. For each piece, consider questions such as these.

- Does it use full sentences?
- How formal does it sound? (What is the writer's 'voice'?)
- How is emotion expressed?
- Is personal opinion expressed? If so, how?
- How are other people's views included?
- Is the sequence logical?
- Does the piece observe the conventions listed on pages 287 and 307–12?

Styles of academic writing

Although academic writing is distinct from other kinds of writing, it isn't all the same. There are different styles *within* academic writing, including:

- descriptive
- argumentative/analytical
- evaluative/analytical
- personal, drawing on the writer's own experience.

These are explored in more detail below.

Finding the appropriate style

When writing an assignment, it is important to choose the appropriate writing style.

Look at the two examples below, of draft introductions to an essay in response to the questions, 'What problems faced Henri IV on his accession to the throne? How successfully did he solve them?' The first follows the guidance for introductions given on page 290, and analyses the problem set. The second uses descriptive writing, giving background details not relevant to the question.

The first example is of a good introduction:

> In 1598, Henri IV was anointed king of a war-torn France, the country having been split by religious and political wars since the death of Henri II almost half a century earlier. The problems Henri IV faced were essentially threefold. He needed to resolve Catholic–Protestant divisions within the country; to curb the power of the Guise, Montmorenci and Bourbon factions which threatened to subvert royal power; and he needed to restore the French economy. This essay will look at the three areas in turn, but will also show how they were interrelated. It will demonstrate how Henri IV tackled each, and argue that ultimately he was extremely successful in solving what had seemed intractable problems.

The second is an example of interesting but irrelevant description (for a *history* essay):

> Henri was brought up by his grandfather in the mountains of Navarre. His grandfather was a very religious man and brought his grandson up as a Protestant. Because of his religion, he wanted Henri to appreciate the simple things in life – the fields, the flowers, good wholesome food such as bread and local cheese, and the beauty of the natural surroundings. Henri was allowed a great deal of freedom, and was allowed to roam barefoot in the mountains, and to play with animals …

Compare each example with the conventions listed on page 287.

Which writer might find it easier to write a good observation case study (page 316)?

Descriptive writing

You are likely to include descriptive writing in most assignments. In some ways it is the easiest style, as we are used to describing things in everyday life. On the other hand, it is easy to give too much detail and forget the underlying purpose of the description. In Higher Education, you are unlikely to be asked to describe anything just for the sake of describing. There will usually be another purpose, such as:

● being precise about methods used in an experiment

● giving essential background information so that you can analyse significant features in more detail later.

You may be required to:

● *describe what happened* – for example, outlining the main events in a history essay, or your methods and results in a project report

● *describe main features or functions* – for example, of different bodily organs in a biology essay

● *summarise the main points of a theory or an article you have read* – for example, in reviewing a book or in introducing the ideas of another author within an assignment.

What gains marks

You will gain marks for:

● identifying relevant themes to include

● identifying the *most* relevant facts in what you include

● clarity, precision and accuracy

● presenting items in the best order

● keeping to the point

● indicating the significance of what you describe.

Examples of descriptive writing

Note the differences between the two following types of descriptive writing. The first is from a cognitive psychology report.

> ### METHODOLOGY
>
> **Participants**
> There were twenty English first-language speakers in each condition, forty subjects in all. These were matched for age and gender across conditions.
>
> **Procedure**
> (See Appendix 1 for instructions.) Each participant was tested separately. They were asked to indicate whether each string of five letters (such as *yongt*) presented on the computer screen was a real word. For real words they pressed the 'y' key on the keyboard; otherwise they pressed the 'n' key …

The second example is from an observation case study from the social sciences.

> The man did not appear to be interacting with the child. The train entered Ely station, and he looked to the pushchair, perhaps to see if it was obstructing the exit. He looked out of the window. The child pointed to the door, and leaned towards him; he instantly leaned towards her to listen.
>
> She said, 'Get off soon?'
>
> He replied, 'Not now. In five minutes we're getting off.' The child still leaned towards him, but he didn't say anything else, and looked away. The child turned away and put the teddy on the seat. The man leaned across her, picked up the teddy, and returned it to her lap, saying 'Hold it.' They looked at each other for a moment. The child half-smiled, and they both looked away, so they were looking in opposite directions.

From this you will see how descriptive writing can vary depending on the subject. Look carefully at journal articles and other examples from your subject area to find the appropriate style for your subject. (See also pages 360 and 197–9.)

Argumentative/analytical writing

Most tutors want essays to be analytical, examining 'What exactly?' and 'Why exactly?' in detail. Chapter 7 looks in more detail at argument as part of critical analytical thinking.

They also want essays to be 'discursive' – to discuss ideas and opinions, and to show reasoning. In a persuasively argued essay, the writer – that is, you – tries to influence the opinion or thoughts or actions of the reader.

Reflection: Persuasive writing

Find the 'Editorial' section in two quality newspapers. How do the writers try to persuade you to their points of view?

What makes good argumentative writing?

To argue a point of view effectively, you need to do the following.

- State a point of view or opinion, and a clear line of reasoning to support it.
- Offer evidence or examples to support your argument.
- Show where the evidence comes from, and that it is reliable. (For example, it should not *all* be personal experience nor what you have heard somebody else say.)
- Show that you have considered any possible arguments which might *contradict* your case or opinions.
- Be able to demonstrate convincingly why your argument or position is the best (that is, why you think you are right).

Your case will not look very convincing if you merely argue, 'Well, that's my opinion' or 'That's my experience' and fail to consider any alternatives seriously.

Writing the argument

1   State your position

- Sum up your argument in one brief, clear sentence.
- Don't be tempted to sit on the fence. You can sound cautious, and show that there are strong arguments on more than one side, but indicate which side *you* find most convincing.

2   Support your argument

- Show why your point of view is a good one.
- For each main point, give evidence (dates, names, statistics, examples, opinions from other sources).
- Consider: 'Would the evidence stand up in court?' Is it really convincing?

Here is the evidence, my Lord …

3   Consider the opposition

Assume that your reader disagrees with you: you have to convince the reader with good evidence and examples.

- What could your opponents argue?
- What evidence might they have?
- How could you persuade a neutral party that your case and your evidence are better?

Activity **Develop an argument**

- Choose a subject about which you feel strongly.
- What is the debate? Engage in it.
- What is your own case or position?
- List your reasons for taking that position.
- List possible arguments *against* it.
- How could you reply to each of them?
- Use the planner on page 318 to write out your argument.

Framework for an argumentative essay

Main proposal/hypothesis/argument:

Reasons or arguments in favour	Evidence and examples
1 _____	1 _____
2 _____	2 _____
3 _____	3 _____
4 _____	4 _____

Opposing arguments	Reasons and evidence
1 _____	1 _____
2 _____	2 _____
3 _____	3 _____
4 _____	4 _____

Reasons why my arguments are stronger; weaknesses in the reasoning or evidence for the opposing arguments

1 _____

2 _____

3 _____

Conclusions (including drawing together or synthesising, if appropriate, the best of all perspectives)

Evaluative/analytical writing

Most academic writing will also include an element of evaluation, even if this is not obvious from the title of an assignment. You may be required to evaluate:

- two or more schools of thought
- two or more theories or theorists
- which of several items, models or ideas is best for a purpose
- how well another writer has analysed a subject.

Features of evaluative writing

Evaluative writing involves the following:

Comparing

Find the points of similarity, and show that you are aware of any minor points of difference within areas of overall similarity.

Contrasting

Set items in opposition, in order to bring out the points of difference.

Evaluating significance

Evaluate the *significance* of any similarities or differences. Do they matter? Do they have important implications for which model should be used? Or for probable outcomes (which animal is likely to survive, which treatment should be offered, and so on)?

Making a judgement

Indicate which theory or side is preferable. Give the reasons for your opinion, based on an analysis of the evidence.

Showing your criteria

Show the criteria you used in arriving at your opinion, such as that you used data or research evidence as the basis of your decision.

Synthesis

Draw out potential ways of combining the strengths of different approaches so as to arrive at an alternative way of looking at the issue.

Get the balance right

In evaluative essays – such as 'compare and contrast' essays – it is important to be balanced in the kind of information you use to make a comparison. You need to compare like with like.

'Compare and contrast' at the same category level

Suppose you are asked to compare and contrast two animals in terms of their habitat. First you need to compare them at the basic category level, making it clear you are comparing, for example, birds with mammals (see diagram, page 294). You could then compare cuckoos with dolphins, as these are at the same category level (on this diagram, the lower level). You should not compare cuckoos to mammals, as these are not equivalent concepts – they are at different levels on the pyramid.

Balance for bias

If you go into detail about one point of view, such as by drawing on the best case studies that support the case, then this should be balanced by similar exploration of the best case studies that support alternative perspectives.

Check your content for balance

When you have completed a draft, make a plan of what you have actually written, using a concept pyramid. You may find that you have spent a disproportionate amount of time on one area, such as one middle-level subject (birds), and included too many examples from a lower level (cuckoos, chaffinches, peacocks). By contrast you may have said very little about mammals as a basic category but referred to ten pieces of specific research on dolphins.

This essay would show imbalance: it would not balance like with like. Use your pattern notes (page 173) or pyramid (page 296) to plan your piece of work, selecting a similar number of examples at each level.

Organising information for 'compare and contrast' essays

One easy way of organising information for 'compare and contrast' essays is by making a grid and writing information in the appropriate columns.

- Use one column for the information about one theory or item.
- Group similarities together.
- Group differences together.
- At the end, jot the main points in the boxes for the introduction and conclusion.

Introduction: Main themes:		
Areas to be compared and contrasted	A Birds	B Fish
Similarities 1 group behaviours 2 3 4 5	flocks	shoals
Differences 1 respiration 2 locomotion 3 4 5	flies (wings)	swims (fins)
Significance of similarities or differences. (How did I decide whether something was significant?)		
Conclusion. (Draw the reader's attention to the main points.)		

An empty grid for use is printed on page 321.

Three ways of writing out the essay are given below. Whichever one you use, be consistent with it for that essay. Before you begin writing from the grid, it is a good idea to map out your points spatially (see page 291).

Method 1

This method is straightforward, but tends to use more words than the others.

- Work down the chart.
- Write out all your points for column A.
- Write your points for column B, in the same order as for column A. Highlight the point of similarity or contrast.
- Do the same for any other columns.
- Draw together the significance of the similarities and differences.

Method 2

- Work across the chart.
- Select one item from column A and 'compare and contrast' it with column B (and any other columns).
- Go on to the next item in column A and compare that with column B (and any others). Continue until all points are covered.
- Draw together the significance of the similarities and differences.

Method 3

If the similarities are so strong as to make the items almost identical, state in the introduction that you will look at similarities together, and then at points of contrast separately.

- Describe one way in which A and B are similar.
- Continue until all points of similarity are covered.
- Continue with points of contrast as for either method 1 or method 2 above (depending on which is clearest to read).
- Draw together the significance of the similarities and differences.

Framework for a 'compare and contrast' essay

Introduction: Main themes:		
Areas to be compared and contrasted	A	B
Similarities 1 2 3 4 5		
Differences 1 2 3 4 5		

Significance of similarities or differences. (How did I decide whether something was significant?)

Conclusion. (Draw the reader's attention to the main points.)

Developing academic writing

Chapter **12**

Using personal experience

It is often useful to call upon personal experience in order to make your learning concrete. Reflection on what happened to you, or how you dealt with a similar situation, can help your thinking – even if you don't make a direct reference to it in your writing.

Find out whether your course expects you to write about personal experience. Some subjects expect you to do so, whereas in others it will be inappropriate.

And then I thought that as I had been living in the same address for two years it was time for a change. So, in 1967 I moved down to Essex. I lived in Barr Road, but I soon moved to Small Street ...

Writing from experience

Use your personal experience as a starting point. Consider what lessons can be drawn from your experience, then start your research. Personal experience should not be your main evidence – unless your tutors specifically ask for this.

- If you include personal experience in your writing, consider how typical it is. Has any research been done. Do you know of relevant reports or articles which show that *your* experience is true more generally?
- Compare your experience with other people's. If theirs is different, why is that?
- Keep your description short. Avoid long lists and detailed accounts of events.
- Be careful what you say about anyone you mention (by name, or if it is obvious to whom you are referring). Check that they do not mind being included – especially if they are known to those who will read your essay.

Analyse your experience

- How is it relevant to your course?
- How does it link to theories you have studied?
- How does your experience support or contradict the views of a writer or theorist you are covering on the course?
- Can any lessons be drawn from it?
- Can generalisations be drawn from it?
- What evidence is there to show that your experiences are typical or unusual?

Example

Suppose you wrote about your own experience, saying:

> Working this way, I found that I was less stressed and my work improved.

You could generalise this provisionally:

> It would appear that the absence of stress can produce more effective results.

You would then need to ask questions such as:

- How valid is this generalisation?
- Do other people feel the same way as you?
- Are there circumstances where stress can produce *better* work?

Personal writing and academic writing

There are some general differences between personal writing and academic writing.

Personal writing	Academic writing
emotional	logical
can be intuitive	uses reasoning
active voice: 'I find that...'	passive voice: 'It was found that ...'
anecdotal	uses evidence
data from one person	wider database
subjective	objective
tangents may be important	keeps to a logical sequence

What gets good marks?

To get good marks, you do not necessarily have to work longer hours. You *do* need to:

- identify the task or problem correctly
- discover the underlying issues
- find out exactly what is expected of you.

Although all subject areas have their own assessment criteria, the following general requirements provide a good guideline as to how marks are allocated.

Activity 6   Use the clues provided

Level descriptors

Find out whether your university or your college provides details of the characteristics of each level of study. These may be outlined in your course handbook or on the department website. If so, make sure that you understand what these mean, as them tell you what tutors expect of students in your level or in your year.

- What do the level descriptors for your year mean for your current assignment?
- What is expected at the next level up – are you working towards that level yet?

Marking criteria

- If your college provides marking criteria, check these before you start your assignment, and use them as you work on it.
- Go through drafts of your assignments, checking them against the marking criteria.

Lowest marks

The lowest marks are awarded for work which:

- has weak structure
- shows little research, thought or reflection
- is mostly descriptive, with little analysis, synthesis or argument
- considers only one point of view.

Tutors' comments may resemble these:

> 'You have just written out my lecture notes and paraphrased a few lines out of books, without considering why this is such an important issue.'

> 'The student seems to have written out everything he knows about the subject, in any order, with lots of mistakes, and has not answered the question he was asked.'

Better marks

Better marks are awarded for work which:

- meets the set criteria and follows appropriate conventions
- shows understanding of the key issues
- is focused on answering the question
- is well structured and organised
- demonstrates good background reading
- develops a strong argument and presents a clear position on the issue
- uses evidence and examples to support arguments, points and conclusions
- indicates the relationship between issues or concepts within the subject area
- reveals some thought and reflection
- is succinct, well-expressed, properly referenced and error-free.

Highest marks

Highest marks are awarded for work which is strong in all the features required for 'better marks' and, in addition:

- engages actively with subject-related debates in a thought-provoking way
- demonstrates a deeper and more subtle understanding of the significance of the issues and evidence, drawing out complexities or nuances
- synthesises material well.

Using feedback from tutors

'What if I get bad marks for my work ...?'

Although 'marks' such as 'B' or '64%' can be an indicator of how well you are doing, the *comments* you receive are more important. You may feel discouraged and feel inclined to throw your work in the bin if it is returned covered with your tutor's handwriting, but do read the comments – they are likely to be your passport to better marks.

 No, no, no!

 This is gobbledegook!

It can be distressing if tutors seem insensitive in their comments. Sometimes this is due to bad tutoring on their part, but try not to be oversensitive to their remarks. It is best not to take any harsh comments personally. Focus instead on the issues behind the words.

It is also quite usual to have strong feelings about your marks – especially if the amount of effort you put in does not seem to be reflected in the mark. You may feel angry or disappointed, or want to give up altogether.

Don't give up. Wait a day or two, then start an action plan.

Action plan for using tutor feedback

Read through your work and the tutor's comments. Be constructive. Keep asking yourself, 'How can this help me to improve my work?'

1 After each comment, check whether you understand what it was that made the tutor write it. Highlight any comments that you feel are useful to you for your next piece of work.

2 Create a table or divide a page into sections to show:
   – major issues: areas which lose a lot of marks, such as not answering the question, lack of evidence, poor argument, weak structure
   – minor errors: spelling, punctuation, grammar.

3 Go through your tutors' comments, listing them under 'Major issues' or 'Minor errors'.

4 Compare this with lists you completed for any previous work. Which comments appear more than once?

5 Number the items in order of priority (with '1' for the most urgent matter to work on), or use the *Priority organiser* (page 135).

Action plan	
Major issues	**Minor errors**
2 paragraphing	①spelling authors' names
3 referencing	3 commas
①structure	2 '-ed' endings for past tense

Making improvements

1 Select one, two or three priority issues from each list to work on in your next piece of work. Set yourself realistic targets.

2 Consider how you will deal with each item on your list. Don't panic! Think constructively.

3 Make sure you understand *why* you received that feedback.

4 Re-read any relevant sections in this guide.

5 If there are comments or marks you do not understand, ask your tutor.

6 If you do not know how to improve your 'priority areas', ask your tutor for advice.

7 Find out what gets good marks – *ask*!

8 Ask your tutor for examples of the kind of work she or he would *like* you to produce.

Reflection: Using advice and feedback

● How well do you use your tutors' feedback?

● Apart from comments on your work, is any feedback provided to the whole class or on the department website?

● How could you make better use of the totality of advice and feedback provided by tutors and other students?

What is an essay like?

Essay 1

Below is a sample first-year essay for an assignment of 1000 words.

1 Read through it. Essays should be addressed to an 'intelligent reader' who does not know much about the subject, so it should not matter if this is not your area.

2 Once you know what the essay is about, put yourself in the role of a tutor marking it. This will give you a better sense of what your tutors are looking for.

3 Even though you may not know the subject, you can still evaluate it according to the criteria set out on the *Editing your draft* checklist (page 303) or the *What gets good marks?* list (page 323). Add your comments down the side of the essay or in your journal.

4 Compare your own comments with those on pages 327–8.

5 Has reading these comments changed your view about how *you* marked the essay?

The question set

How has Bowlby's Attachment Theory been modified by the findings of later research? How have theories about attachment affected ideas about child care?

The essay

Page 1

Parag 1 Attachment theory originated in the work of Bowlby (1907–90). The theory was that an infant's ability to form emotional attachments to its mother was essential to its survival and later development. This raises important questions about what circumstances could affect the mother–child bond, and the effects on the child of different kinds of separation. This essay looks in particular at Bowlby's work on maternal deprivation, and at how early research and the later work of Mary Ainsworth seem to support Bowlby's Attachment Theory. It also looks at later challenges to that evidence, which suggest that short spells of separation may not have negative effects upon attachment nor on the child's development. The impact of these theories on attitudes towards day care will be explored throughout the essay and brought together towards the conclusion.

Parag 2 Bowlby's Attachment Theory originally claimed that if bonding was to occur between a child and its carer, there must be continuous loving care from the same carer – the mother or 'permanent mother substitute'. Without this, he argued, chances of bonding were lost forever, and the child was likely to become delinquent. Originally this was formulated as a theory of 'maternal deprivation'. Later Bowlby focused more specifically on the first year of life, which he called the 'critical period'. During this time, he believed, the child organises its behaviours to balance two complementary predispositions. These predispositions are firstly 'proximity-promoting behaviours', which establish the mother as a secure base, and secondly 'exploration', away from the mother. Bowlby argued that the infant develops 'internal working models' of its relationship with the mother which become the basis of later relationships. He argued that the mother should be at home with the child for these behaviours to develop, and that day care was harmful.

Parag 3   Bowlby's ideas were popular with governments at the time, as there was a shortage of jobs for men returning from the Second World War: day care during the war had enabled many women to work outside the home. There was also other evidence which appeared to support Bowlby. Goldfarb (1947) compared children who had experienced continuous foster care from nine months onwards with those reared in institutions. He found that the foster children were less likely to suffer intellectual, social and emotional difficulties. Similarly, children who stayed in hospital showed distress and little affection to parents when reunited with them (Robertson 1967–73). Bowlby's own research into adolescent delinquency indicated childhood maternal deprivation as a recurring factor.

Parag 4   Much of this research evidence has since been revised. Bowlby's adolescent research was based on evacuees in the post-war years, a time of unusual trauma and disruption. With respect to Goldfarb's research, the Tizards (1970s) found that although children's homes could have a negative effect on development, this could be because of unstimulating environments and the high turnover of carers. Some four-year-olds in children's homes had more than fifty carers. Similarly, the hospital conditions of Robertson's research were stark environments where parents were discouraged from visiting and the children were very ill. This is a different situation to pleasant nurseries with healthy children who go home to their parents each evening.

Parag 5   Although Bowlby's theory of maternal deprivation has been larely discredited, Mary Ainsworth (1978) built on Bowlby's ideas about exploratory bases and separation anxiety in her now widely used 'Strange Situation' experiment. Findings based on the Strange Situation would appear to support Bowlby and the idea that child care is undesirable. However, criticisms were made of the conclusions drawn from the Strange Situation, such as that it did not take into consideration how accustomed the child was to being separated from the mother (Clarke-Stewart). Others argued that the conclusions were too culturally specific, and that cultures such as Japan's and the USA's vary in how much they valued childhood independence and so would interpret the results differently (Super-Harkness 1981). The theory traditionally focused on interactions between children and a primary care-giver. It has been further modified by those who argue that multiple attachment figures determine children's attachment patterns. Grossman et al. emphasised the role played by fathers whilst Van Ijzendoorn (2005), amongst others, proposes a 'social network' model of attachments in which infants have multiple simultaneous attachments to both family and non-family caregivers. In this model, the quality of the multiple attachments determines the infant's overall pattern of attachment. This suggests that day care would play a role in determining attachment patterns but this could be positive rather than negative.

Parag 6   One of the difficulties in evaluating research based upon Bowlby's theories has been in finding valid comparisons. Most research tends to be based on USA mothers and families under economic and social stress, who are not representative of all mothers (Burman 1994). One useful comparison group for day-care children would be children whose temperaments prevented their mothers from going to work, and mothers who then became depressed. It has been found that mothers at home with two children under five are more likely to become depressed. Depression in mothers has also been linked with delinquency in children. Research has found that three-year-old children of depressed mothers were more likely to have behaviour problems than children of mothers without depression. This suggests that day care might benefit both mother and child.

Parag 7   Bowlby's original Attachment Theory has been modified; there is now less emphasis on the 'critical period', on the irreversibility of early weak bonding, and on the necessity of exclusive, continuous maternal care. Separation and reunion behaviours are still regarded as useful indicators of later difficulties, although it is now recognised that many other factors such as marital discord have to be taken into consideration. In general, there has been greater recognition that it is the quality of care, rather than the quantity, that is important. Subsequent modifications in the theory have accompanied changes in child-care, hospital and nursery environments. Although there is still popular belief in maternal deprivation, many professionals now agree that day care can be of some benefit, if both home and day-care environments are of good quality.

References

Burman, E. (1994). *Deconstructing Developmental Psychology.* London: Routledge.
Van Ijzendoorn M. H. (2005). *Attachment in social networks: Toward an evolutionary social network model.* Human Development, 48, 85–88
Oates, J. (1995). *The Foundations of Child Development.* Milton Keynes: Open University.
Prior, V. and Glaser, D. (2006). *Understanding Attachment and Attachment Disorders: Theory, Evidence and Practice (Child & Adolescent Mental Health).* London: Jessica Kingsley Publishing.
Smith, P. K., and Cowie, H. (1988). *Understanding Children's Development.* Oxford: Blackwell.

Chapter 12

Comments

Overall this is a reasonable essay. Good points include:

- the style is very clear and precise, few words are wasted and it meets the word requirements
- there is evidence of broad reading and consideration of research into different perspectives
- the clear line of reasoning – on the whole, the essay follows the introduction, and evidence is used well to support the arguments made
- it is well structured: ideas are well ordered and generally well paragraphed

- the research evidence has been evaluated in terms of its strengths and weaknesses
- the writer's point of view (the general disagreement with Bowlby) is clear, and evidence is used to support this.

The essay could be improved, however, to get a higher mark. For example:

- *Fulfilling undertakings made in the introduction* In the introduction, the writer says she will bring together ideas on day care at the end of the essay, but she has not done so.
- *Balance* The area of day care has been rather neglected in comparison with her discussion of the theories.

- *The author's position*   An indication of the author's position and/or conclusions could come across more clearly in the introduction. This would have helped the writer to identify that the day-care issue was weaker, and would have been a stronger opening than stating that all would be 'brought together at the end'. It is best to avoid an 'all will be revealed' approach.
- *Answering the question*   Because the writer has neglected the day-care side, she has not really answered the second part of the question in full and therefore could not gain marks for this.
- *References in the text*   Although the essay is well referenced overall, paragraph 6 makes several statements without saying where the evidence comes from.
- *References at the end*   The references given in the text are written out well, but only a few of them have been given fully at the end. All references must be written out in full.

Essay 2

Now compare Essay 1 with a second essay on the same subject.

> How has Bowlby's Attachment Theory been modified by the findings of later research? How have theories about attachment affected ideas about child care?
>
> 1   The world of psychology contains many theories about children, some more useful than others, although all add something to our overall knowledge about children, so none should be dismissed as unhelpful. One such theory is that of 'attachment', which was the idea of a psychologist called Bowlby. What are the main elements of Bowlby's theory? Well, first there
>
> 5   is his early work about attachment. Second, there are his adaptations of his theory into his later ideas about maternal deprivation. There was a lot of research to support Bowlby at the time, and his ideas were very useful to society so it is not surprising that he had a big following in his day. Later, some of his ideas were discredited but some of his ideas were picked up by Mary Ainsworth. She developed something called the 'Strange Situation' which
>
> 10   has been used by many people interested in the welfare of children.
>   Bowlby actually believed that it was a tragedy for the child if the mother was not with him throughout his early childhood. He was very opposed to the idea of mothers going out to work. During the war, a lot of mothers had left their children in special nurseries set up by the Government. These nurseries enabled women to work in factories making armaments
>
> 15   or to go out to grow food and any other jobs formerly filled by men. Many women enjoyed this new-found freedom and learning new skills like building bridges, driving buses and being radar operators. Bowlby argued that the women's gains were at the expense of the child. He used examples of children that had been abandoned in the war to show that a lack of good mothering had led these children into delinquency and other serious life-long
>
> 20   problems. Later Bowlby argued that it might be acceptable for the mother to be absent if there was a suitable kind of carer who was always present so that the child got continuity. He felt that it was from this carer or the mother that the baby was able to learn how to form any relationships. So basically, if the baby did not have its mother, it did not have a sense of how

to form a relationship, so then it was not able to have the building blocks of any
25 relationship which made relationships in general always difficult. He was actually influenced
by the ideas of Lorenz who found that ducklings who lacked their mother at a critical age
adopted other objects such as toys to be their mother instead. Bowlby said that human
babies also had a critical period for bonding with their mothers – actually up to nine months
old. Harlow found that monkeys were also disturbed and when they grew up were not able
30 to look after their babies.

Mary Ainsworth found that if babies were put in a situation with a stranger, they behaved
differently depending on whether they had a good relationship with their mother. She said
that how babies behaved with a stranger and then afterwards with their mother for leaving
them alone with the stranger let you predict whether the baby would be a delinquent later.
35 She said her experiments using the Strange Situation showed that babies who were in day
care were more likely to grow up delinquent. But is this really the case? Not every
psychologist thinks so and it is important to consider other views. What about the role that
fathers play? Many would think it entirely unreasonable to dismiss the contribution that they
make to a child's upbringing and it is sexist to blame mothers only when things go wrong.
40 Bretherton says that fathers play a major role in their children's attachment. Research suggests
that children, in fact, have multiple attachments to family members and even those outside of
the immediate family.

Some people think day care may actually be good for children. Studies have shown that
day care can, in fact, make children more intelligent and better able to get on with other
45 children. Not all mothers feel fulfilled staying at home with their children and some might
end up developing mental illnesses like depression, where they feel very low and may even
be suicidal. Drug treatments and counselling can help women recover and depression is a
very treatable condition. It is surely better for a child to be in good day care, rather than
staying at home with a mother who is depressed?
50 So, there are some strong arguments for and against attachment theory. Bowlby makes
some very interesting points about the importance of mothers and the need children have
for good care. His research does seem to indicate that poor care leads to children becoming
delinquents. On the other hand, there are times when mothers would do better for their
children by being out of the home so you cannot assume that it is always best for the child
55 to be with its mother. Looking at society today, we are seeing more and more children with
problems. The rise of delinquency in children today requires greater consideration by
researchers to work out what the causes are.

References

Psychology by Richard Gross, published in paperback by Hodder Arnold in 2005
John Bowlby – *Attachment Theory*

Marking Essay 2

Using the checklists on either page 303 or 323:

1 Underline sections which you think could be improved.
2 Write comments in the margin as if you were a tutor giving the student advice.
3 Are you able to identify why Essay 1 would receive a higher mark than Essay 2?

When you have finished, compare your comments with those below.

Feedback on the exercise

Introduction   This lacks focus. The first sentence, in particular, is too general and adds nothing to the essay.

Length and conciseness   This essay is 862 words long, which is rather short. It should be 950–1050 words for a 1000-word essay (Essay 1 is 954 words long). Overall, too many words are used to say too little. This means that the writer will not cover as much relevant information in the essay as someone who writes in a more concise style, and will therefore lose marks. (See especially lines 3–4, 22–5 and 45–8.)

Line of argument   It is not clear from the introduction what the writer's line of reasoning or main argument will be. This is also the case in the conclusion, which does not identify a clear point of view.

Addressing the question   The first half of the essay does not address how Bowlby's theories were modified by research findings. The second half does not consider the impact of attachment theory on day care.

Structure   The early comments about the usefulness of Bowlby's ideas could be omitted as the essay looks at this later (lines 6–8).

Detail   The writer goes into too much unnecessary detail at various points of the essay, for example about women's work during the war and about treatment for depression. Neither is strictly relevant to this essay, and such details waste valuable words.

Paragraphing   Paragraph 2 is far too long, and its central point is not clear.

Referencing   No dates are given for the references cited, for example for the work of Lorenz (line 26), Harlow (line 29) or Bretherton (line 34). Few of the references cited within the text are listed at the end of the essay. The two texts listed at the end are not referenced correctly.

Precision   Some of the research evidence cited is rather vague. Essay 1 makes it clear that there were two stages to Bowlby's research, but this is not clear in Essay 2.

Vocabulary   Words such as 'actually' and 'basically' are not generally used in this colloquial way in academic writing (lines11, 23, 25, 28 and 42).

Clarity   Some sections (such as lines 29–30 and 32–4) could be written more clearly.

Critical comparison of two essays

Two further essays are provided below: the first essay is a final draft, and the second could be considered an earlier draft of this. These enable you to see how you can work up early drafts to develop a stronger answer – and to develop your awareness of the difference between stronger and weaker essays. Although these are on stem cell research, you do not need a science background to be able to compare and analyse them using the broad criteria provided on page 323 *What gets good marks*. The word limit is 1500 words.

Analyse essay 3 below, drawing out what you consider to be the strengths and positive features. Compare these with the comments provided on page 334.

Essay 3

The ethical implications of stem cell research outweigh the benefits – discuss.

Parag 1 Corrigan et al. (2006) describe stem cell research as 'something of a political, ethical, social and legal minefield'. In this essay I shall explore this 'minefield', examining key arguments for and against stem cell research from the perspective of both the perceived benefits and the ethics of such research. I shall argue that whilst the *potential* benefits, as opposed to the *actual* benefits, of stem cell research are great enough to justify its continuance, great care must be taken to address more subtle social ethical implications such as access to stem cell therapies and unrealistic expectations of what stem cell research can achieve.

Parag 2 Stem cells are cells from mammalian organisms which have the potential to replace themselves and to develop into specialised cell types. Stem cells are found in mammalian embryos around 5–7 days after the egg has been fertilised. These cells are 'pluripotent' – they have the ability to become any type of cell in the organism. This allows them to repair or replace absent or damaged tissues, potentially opening up new avenues for medical treatment. Less versatile stem cells can also be found in the blood of the umbilical cord and in the adult organism, where they support the development and renewal only of specific tissues such as in the nervous system.

Parag 3 Contrasting 'ethical considerations' to 'benefits' seems to suggest that there are not ethical imperatives for undertaking stem cell research. Stem cells are the only cells that we know of to date with adaptive capacity of this magnitude. This gives them enormous potential for improving health and well-being, for humans and also for animals. Research on stem cells enables scientists to study how organisms develop or respond to conditions such as illness or different medications. In turn, this can lead to stem cell therapy, where stem cells are used to repair the damage caused by injuries such as spinal cord injury or illnesses such as Parkinson's Disease. Stem cell therapy can also be used for therapeutic cloning, where genetic material is used to stop transplanted tissues being rejected by the recipient.

Parag 4 Leventhal et al. (2012) argue strongly for the benefits of stem cell research. There have, indeed, been a number of studies which have demonstrated successful use of stem cell therapies. Bang et al. (2005) found that stroke patients given stem cell transplants made better recovery and progress over a twelve month period than those in the control group, who received conventional treatments. Vidaltamayo et al. (2010) reviewed studies of the use of stem cells in the treatment of Parkinson's Disease and concluded that there was encouraging evidence to suggest that some patients could recover motor abilities after stem cell transplants. In addition, results sometimes occurred even two to three years after surgery. Tutter et al. (2006), reviewing the wide range of potential uses of stem cells, referred to them as 'a great hope for a new era of medicine'.

Parag 5 Given these potential benefits, the question arises of why anybody would object to stem cell research. One key ethical concern is whether any benefit, actual or potential, could outweigh damage to human life. One argument is that stem cell research relies on cells taken from human embryos and that is always wrong. Ethical concerns from this perspective range from the 'right to life' of cells considered to be embryos, to the risk of wastage of human cells when such cell groups, or embryos, are created but not used. Some authors, such as Doerflinger (1999), for example, believe that at the moment of fertilisation a new human life is created with the same moral rights as an adult human. Consequently, it would be wrong to destroy or make use of a human embryo of any age. McLaren (2007) refers to these as 'personal and research ethics'.

Parag 6 Conversely, evidence presented to the UK House of Lords Science and Technology Select Committee in 2002 suggested that many people believe that human life and personhood are not created at the point of conception when, in effect, there is just a mass of undifferentiated cells. In 1985 the term 'pre-embryo' was introduced to refer to groups of cells less than 14 days old. Fourteen days is the threshold where the first cell specialisation can be seen such that it becomes reasonable to refer to an 'embryo' forming; this could be regarded as the start of 'human life' and personhood. Research on pre-embryos, that is, cell groups of less than 14 days old, has generally attracted less controversy. Using pre-embryos would largely overcome this particular ethical consideration.

Parag 7 Whilst there is encouraging research which indicates the potential for the use of stem cells, the amount of evidence about the efficacy of stem cell therapy, gathered through high quality clinical trials, is limited to date. The hope that stem cells could be used to 'cure' conditions which were previously thought of as incurable has attracted a great amount of attention from scientists, the media and the general population. However, small scale findings have been heralded by the media as 'breakthroughs' in treatment, resulting in what Dresser (2001) refers to as 'therapeutic misconceptions'. This can result in a general belief that the benefits of stem cell therapy are greater than has actually been demonstrated. In practice, this has already led to what Cohen and Cohen (2010) refer to as 'International Stem Cell Tourism' where individuals with specific conditions travel to countries where stem cell therapies are readily available in the belief that therapies branded as 'innovative treatments' can cure them. Cohen and Cohen suggest that international regulation is needed to distinguish between clinically proven treatments and innovative treatments and therapies to offer protection to people who might be tempted to seek stem cell therapies.

Parag 8 Therapeutic misconceptions can also lead to the creation of 'false hope' for those taking part in clinical trials. Corrigan et al. (2006) discuss the difficulties in designing high quality clinical trials where a 'double blind' study of the impact of stem cells on neurological conditions could result in those in the control group undergoing procedures such as having holes drilled into their heads to mimic real treatment. They suggest that where there are no other recognised treatments for conditions, experimental stem cell therapies might be considered. However, it would be feasible to focus experimental treatments on terminal conditions such as end-stage Parkinson's Disease or Alzheimer's, mostly experienced by those in later life, who might be considered to have 'less to lose'.

Parag 9 If and when stem cell therapies are demonstrated to be clinically effective there will be further ethical considerations regarding access to treatments. Stem cell therapies are currently expensive and likely to remain so for many years. However, demand for them is already high and likely to rise if their efficacy is more effectively demonstrated. For state-funded health care systems like the UK National Health Service, giving access to stem cell therapies for all those in need will have major financial implications. However, failure to fund treatments would result in them only being available to those wealthy enough to afford them.

Parag 10   Although there is a wide range of ethical implications to take on board when considering stem cell research and therapies there is evidence to suggest that actions can be taken to mitigate against some of these. Overall, a balance needs to be found between managing expectations of treatment and encouraging more high quality research to enable treatments to be developed more quickly and deterring people from seeking treatments that have not yet been proven to be effective. This could be achieved, in part, through legislation, such as in the UK, where the world's first 'stem cell bank' was established in 2004 to regulate and provide stem cells for use in clinical research. Only cells which have been 'deposited' in the bank can be used in clinical research. Wilson (2009) indicated that the International Society for Stem Cell Research, formed in 2002, can play a significant role in managing the hype around stem cell therapy through issuing guidelines for research and development. Even controversial areas such as stem cell tourism may have ethical benefits. Lindvall and Hyun (2009) suggest that terminally ill patients might benefit from being able to travel to undertake 'innovative' treatments which have not yet been approved in their own country.

Parag 11   This essay has examined some of the key ethical issues relevant to the use of human stem cells in research. In considering the benefits of stem cell therapy, it indicates that the evidence for clinical efficacy is still rather limited. Moreover, the hope that stem cells will lead to cures for serious illness and injury has led to unrealistic reporting of achievements, which in turn has led some people to seek experimental treatments with little evidence that they will be successful. There is agreement between many key figures that stem cell therapy holds great potential to benefit human well-being. When this potential is aligned with good regulation that supports high quality clinical research and helps to manage expectations, then the benefits of stem cell research could be said to outweigh the negative ethical implications.

References

Bang, O. Y., Lee, J. S., Lee, P. H., Lee, G. (2005) 'Autologous mesenchymal stem cell transplantation in stroke patients', *Annals of Neurology* 57(6), pp. 874–882.

Cohen, C. B. and Cohen, P. J. (2010) 'International Stem Cell Tourism and the Need for Effective Regulation: Part I: Stem Cell Tourism in Russia and India: Clinical Research, Innovative Treatment, or Unproven Hype?', *Kennedy Institute of Ethics Journal* 20(1), pp. 27–49.

Corrigan, O., Liddell, K., McMillan, J., Stewart, A., Wallace, S. (2006) *'Ethical, legal and social issues in stem cell research and therapy'*, A briefing paper from Cambridge Genetics Knowledge Park. Available at: http://www.eescn.org.uk/pdfs/elsi_ed2.pdf (accessed 12th September 2010).

Doerflinger, R. M. (1999) 'The Ethics of Funding Embryonic Stem Cell Research: A Catholic Viewpoint', *Kennedy Institute of Ethics Journal* 9(2), pp. 137–150.

Dresser, R. (2001) *When Science Offers Salvation: Patient Advocacy and Research Ethics.* Oxford/NewYork: Oxford University Press.

Great Britain. Parliament. House of Lords (2002) *Stem Cell Research*: report of the Science and Technology Select Committee. London: The Stationery Office (HL 2001–02 (83)).

Leventhal, A., Chen, G., Negro, A. and Boehm, M. (2012) 'The Benefits and Risks of Stem Cell Technology', *Oral Diseases* 18(3) pp. 217–222.

Lindvall, O. and Hyun, I. (2009) 'Medical Innovation Versus Stem Cell Tourism', *Science* 324(5935), pp. 1664–1665.

McLaren, A. (2007) 'A Scientist's View of the Ethics of Human Embryonic Stem Cell Research', *Cell Stem Cell* July (Online). Available at: http://www.cell.com/cell-stem-cell/archive?year=2007 (accessed 8th September 2010).

Tutter, A. V., Baltus, G. A. and Kadam, S. (2006) 'Embryonic stem cells: a great hope for a new era of medicine', *Current Opinion in Drug Discovery and Development* 9(2), pp. 169–175.

Vidaltamayo, R., Bargas, J., Covarrubias, L., Hernandez, A., Galarraga, E., Gutierrez-Ospina, G., Drucker-Colin, R. (2010) 'Stem Cell Therapy for Parkinson's Disease: A Road Map for a Successful Future', *Stem Cells and Development* 19(3) pp. 311–320.

Chapter 12

Comments for essay 3

Strengths

Overall   This is a good essay. It is succinct, using the word limit to full advantage. It flows well, uses language clearly and accurately, and has been closely proof-read to remove errors.

Introduction   It has a strong introduction. Though brief, it signals a great deal to the reader, including that the essay is likely to be well-written and closely argued. The reader knows in broad terms what the content and argument of the essay will be without this being laboured. The author's own position comes across clearly, and the reader knows from the outset that the writer's position is more subtle than simply taking one side or the other. The opening sentence draws the reader in by reference to a potential 'minefield', creating a strong image and suggesting that interesting issues will be examined, albeit in the context of the set title.

The second and third paragraphs provide explanations of technical terms, and background to the issues. This is useful as a 'general reader' might not be clear what stem cells are and why they are so significant for research. This is done briefly, without excessive background description.

Use of sources and evidence   The essay demonstrates a good grasp of the issues, and engages well with debates. This is based on evidence drawn from authoritative sources. The writer uses sources well, referring to them briefly as evidence to support the points being made, but without becoming weighed down in lengthy descriptions of what they are about.

References and citations   Sources are cited correctly throughout the essay and referenced comprehensively and correctly at the end.

Critical analysis, argument and synthesis   There is excellent use of critical analysis. The writer evaluates different perspectives in an objective way, indicating how experts with different views arrived logically at their own conclusions, but

without being drawn into agreement with all of them. In particular, the writer argues that the title, itself, is contentious, and drawing a potential false dichotomy between ethics and benefits. This makes it easier for the writer to synthesise material from different sides of the debate to create his or her own position on the issue. It also indicates that they are not likely to take any statement on face value – even if in an essay title. The essay develops the argument that it is unrealistic expectations of stem cell therapy that are problematic, rather than the research itself.

Structure   The essay is well organised and structured. Paragraphs follow each other logically, each focusing on a particular perspective. This helps to develop the argument towards its conclusions. For example:

- Paragraph 4 clarifies the arguments in support of stem cell research.
- Paragraph 5 introduces an opposing argument.
- Paragraph 6 refutes the arguments given in paragraph 5.
- Parag 10, having considered counterarguments, provides a strong focus for the author's argument that negative ethical implications of stem cell research can be mitigated.

Conclusion   In the conclusion, the author summarises the arguments. The author's own position is reaffirmed in the closing sentence, which ensures that it cannot be missed by the reader.

Introducing Essay 4

Essay 3 did not arrive at this point through a single draft. 'Essay 4', below, is an earlier draft for comparison. Using the *What gets good marks sheet* (page 323), draw out what you consider to be errors and weaknesses of the essay at this stage. Assume that the writer has undertaken the same background research and reading as for essay 3. Compare your points with those made on page 337 – or by referring back to the previous essay: *The ethical implications of stem cell research outweigh the benefits – discuss.*

Essay 4

Parag 1   Stem cell research is an emotional issue, which leaves audiences divided. Is it something that might save countless human beings or an immoral activity, responsible for the deaths of thousands of babies? There are strong arguments on both sides, as this essay will show.

Parag 2   Stem cells are pluripotent cells. They have the potential to replace themselves and to develop into specialised cell types. Stem cells can be found in mammalian embryos around 5-7 days after the egg has been fertilised. Stem cells can also be found in the blood of the umbilical cord and in the adult organism, where they support the development and renewal of specific tissues such as in the nervous system. Tutter et al. refer to stem cells as 'a great hope for a new era of medicine'.

Parag 3   Much of the contention surrounding stem cells comes from the fact that the cells have to be taken from human embryos, which causes great distress to many religious people. They believe that human life begins at the minute when sperm meets egg. Therefore, even if stem cell research uses embryos young enough not to look like babies, they believe that a life is being taken. Doerflinger (1999) believe that at the moment of fertilization a new human life is created with the same moral rights as an adult human. There is also the issue that some of the stem cells cultivated for use in research might not be used and could go to waste. Consequently, it is wrong to destroy or make use of a human embryo of any age. Evidence presented to the UK House of Lords Science and Technology Select Committee in 2002 suggested that many people viewed life and personhood as developing over the course of gestation from conception to birth. In 1985 the term 'pre-embryo' was introduced to refer to embryos less than 14 days old – a threshold where the first cell specialization can be seen. Research on pre-embryos has generally attracted less controversy but is not accepted by everyone.

Parag 4   Up until now, there have been some studies which have suggested that using stem cells might have a therapeutic benefit. . Bang et al. (2005) found that when stroke patients were given stem cell transplants they tended to make more progress over a twelve month period.. Vidaltymayo et al. (2010) reviewed studies of the use of stem cells in the treatment of Parkison's Disease. They state that there is some encouraging evidence to suggest that some patients are better able to move after stem cell transplants. However, results did not always become clear quickly and in some cases took up to l two to three years after surgery to appear. This raises the question of whether the effects were actually to do with the stem cell treatment at all or might be down to other factors.

Parag 5   Stem cells have a range of potential uses. Research on stem cells allows for the study of how organisms develop or respond to conditions such as illness or different medications. Stem cell therapy involves the use of stem cells to repair the damage caused by injuries such as spinal cord injury or illnesses such as Parkinson's disease. It can also involve altering a cell's genetic material to stop transplanted tissues being rejected by the recipient. This is known as 'therapeutic cloning'.

Parag 6   Although there is some quite encouraging research about the benefits of stem cells, there have not yet been enough clinical trials to prove that stem cell therapy is beneficial. This has proved to be quite problematic. Every time that a trial is conducted and hints at a benefit for using stem cells it is blown out of all proportion by the media. A study might only show that a person getting stem cell treatment makes slightly better progress than a person getting other treatments but often this is reported in the media as if a cure has been found for the disease. This is clearly unhelpful as it makes people with incurable diseases believe that they could get better if they only had access to stem cell treatments. Cohen and Cohen (2010) warn us that there are already a number of stem cell tourists who travel to different countries in the hope of getting access to stem cell treatments. The Cohen's say that there should be laws in place to stop this from happening. The media should also be banned from reporting on stem cell research unless a cure for a fatal disease has actually been found.

Parag 7   Therapeutic misconceptions lead to the creation of 'false hope, for those taking part in clinical trials. As Corrigan et al. (2006) point out, it can be very difficult to design clinical trials where the effect of stem cell treatment is compared to patients who have required no treatment at all. For example, if the trial was looking at treatments for a neurological condition and required holes being drilled into the skull a person in the control group would have to go through this procedure without getting any treatment and would not know if they were in the treatment group or not. This would not generally be acceptable. However, it is possible that patients with incurable, terminal conditions such as end-stage Alzheimer's disease might be willing to volunteer for such trials as they might feel that they have nothing less to lose. Although this might offer a solution, it should be born in mind that patients with late-stage neurological conditions might not be considered in the best possible position to offer informed consent to take part in these trials.

Parag 8 If and when stem cell therapies are shown to have clinical benefits to patients there will be a further range of ethical issues which must be considered. As noted previously, demand for these treatments will be high and it will be vital to ensure that access is carefully controlled. For countries with publically-funded health care, the cost of stem cell therapies will be particular issue and it will be important to ensure that therapies are truly effective before public funds are committed to them. However, at the same time, if funding is not allocated to these treatments it is likely that they would only be available to those who have the money to buy them privately. This will result in a situation where the rich can afford treatment and the poor are left to die. As can be seen, there is a wide range of ethical implications to take on board when considering stem cell research and therapies. If therapies are to be used effectively, expectations of their success need to be carefully managed. This will involve a mixture of more high quality trials and better control over media reporting of trials.

Parag 9 Even with this, care will need to be taken to ensure that people cannot access treatments with limited or unproven benefits and that money is not the main factor in deciding who does or does not get treatment. This could be achieved through legislation, such as in the UK, where the world's first 'stem cell bank' was established in 2004 to regulate and provide stem cells for use in clinical research. Only cells which have been 'deposited' in the bank can be used in clinical research and treatments. This ensures quality control.. If this was repeated around the world then it is possible that stem cell tourism might start to be seen as something desirable rather than as a problem. Lindvall and Hyun (2009) suggest that terminally ill patients might benefit from being able to travel to undertake 'innovative' treatments, which have not yet been approved in their own country. After all, matters of life and death should not be decided by a postcode lottery.

Parag 10 In this essay, I have shown that the subject of stem cell research and treatment is an 'ethical minefield'. There are ways of making this less dangerous but it would appear that the field cannot entirely be cleared of mines. Furthermore, the role of faith in the lives of human beings cannot be underestimated. Even though, according to Tearfund (2007) in the UK, only x% of people go to church on a regular basis, over y% of the population identifies as being a Christian. This suggests that there will be a high percentage of the population for whom stem cell research is never going to be acceptable, whatever checks and balances are put in place. However, stem cell therapies still show great potential to improve the lives of humans and this should not be ignored. If actions can be taken to address some of the ethical concerns raised in this essay then stem cell therapies could yet prove to be the great hope for a new era of medicine" (Tutter 2006 p.1).

References

Bang, O.Y., Lee, J.S., Lee, P.H., Lee, G. (2005) 'Autologous mesenchymal stem cell transplantation in stroke patients', *Annals of Neurology* 57(6), pp. 874-882.

Cohen, C.B. and Cohen, P.J. (2010) 'International Stem Cell Tourism and the Need for Effective Regulation: Part I: Stem Cell Tourism in Russia and India: Clinical Research, Innovative Treatment, or Unproven Hype?, *Kennedy Institute of Ethics Journal* 20(1), pp. 27-49.

Corrigan, O., Liddell, K., McMillan, J., Stewart, A., Wallace, S. (2006) *'Ethical, legal and social in stem cell research and therapy'*, A briefing paper from Cambridge Genetics Knowledge Park. Available at: http://www.eescn.org.uk/pdfs/elsi_ed2.pdf (Accessed 12th September 2010).

Doerflinger, R.M. (1999) 'The Ethics of Funding Embryonic Stem Cell Research: A Catholic Viewpoint', *Kennedy Institute of Ethics Journal* 9(2), pp. 137-150.

Great Britain. Parliament. House of Lords (2002) *Stem Cell Research*: report of the Science and Technology Select Committee. London: The Stationery Office (HL 2001-02 (83)).

Lindvall, O. and Hyun, I. (2009) 'Medical Innovation Versus Stem Cell Tourism', *Science* 324(5935), pp. 1664-1665

Tutter, A.V., Baltus, G.A. and Kadam, S. (2006) 'Embryonic stem cells: a great hope for a new era of medicine', *Current Opinion in Drug Discovery and Development* 9(2), pp. 169-75.

Comments for essay 4

Overall   This draft is less economical in its use of language, and sometimes repeats points or goes into too much explanatory detail. For example, the author cites Doerflinger but this material is poorly used as it simply repeats the preceding statement about life beginning at the moment of fertilisation. Such wordiness means the author then has fewer words to allocate to providing breadth and depth or addressing more subtle issues. The essay could be better organised in parts, and many minor errors remain so it requires further proof-reading.

Introduction   This is overly brief, makes no direct reference to the title, and does not give the reader a sense of the author's position nor what the content or line of reasoning will be. The questioning style used is best avoided, not least as this creates confusion about what the 'two sides' are that the writer says the essay address: this might be either 'benefits versus ethics' or 'saving countless lives versus an immoral act'.

The essay lacks clear definitions and background explanations. In paragraph 2, the term 'pluripotent' is used – this is a technical term that the general reader might not know. Without a definition, the usefulness of stem cells, and therefore their benefits, is less clear.

Critical analysis   Rather than maintaining an objective position, the author uses emotive comments such as 'deaths of thousands of babies'. In paragraph 6, the author does not come across as dispassionate about the role of the media. The essay is further weakened by this leading to an unhelpful diversion from the topic with the writer advocating press censorship. In paragraph 7, the argument is conveyed through wordy and emotive detail on drilling through skulls rather than use of evidence.

Argument   The author presents a weak line of argument. By presenting the negative ethical considerations first (parag 3), it is less clear why anyone would want to use stem cells. From the use made of emotive examples, the author's position appears to be against the use of stem cell research on ethical grounds. However, the final sentences of the essay suggest that stem cell research could be useful. This is confusing. It is also unclear what evidence is being used to support such a position.

Although paragraph 9 had considered ways of reducing negative ethical implications, it was not made clear how that material influenced the writer's argument.

Use of sources and evidence   Given that we know the writer has undertaken the same background research, this is not fully utilised. Not all items are referred to either in the text or in the list of references. Some, such as Tutter's study (parag 2), are not correctly referenced. Evidence and language are used with less precision in essay 4 than essay 3. In paragraph 2, little evidence is given for why stem cell use is contentious and the author uses a number of vague terms such as 'many people' and 'they'. In paragraph 4, the citation of the Bang study does not indicate the comparison group against which progress was measured in the experimental group. In paragraph 6, a number of claims are made about the role of the media in increasing demand for stem cell therapies but no evidence is given for this. In paragraph 8, it is stated that demand for treatment will be high. As this is not yet known, it would be better to use a phrase such as 'it is likely that …' or 'it may be that …' demand would be high.

Structure   The essay is not well-organised. The material in paragraph 5 would be better placed towards the beginning as background information. Here, it interrupts the logical order of the argument. Paragraph 6 fits most logically after paragraph 4 as it continues to outline doubts about the potential benefits of stem cell research.

Conclusion   The conclusion is weak. The argument, mid-paragraph, that 'stem cells show great potential', is rather lost where placed. Insufficient evidence had been presented earlier in the essay to support this conclusion. New material is introduced about religious perspectives. Religion appears to be equated with being Christian. The author supposes that a high proportion of Christians would oppose stem cell research: that is an assumption that might be true but is not a conclusion that can be drawn from the data presented. Also, the conclusion states that the essay has shown that the subject is an ethical minefield: that may be the case but that is not the task set by the essay title. Similarly, the final sentence does not focus the reader back to the subject of the essay, as specified in the title.

Editing   The essay hasn't been proof-read so there are many minor errors that need tidying up:

- details of percentages still to be added or else removed
- consistency in the formatting of the referencing
- completing the references as several of the sources cited in the text are not included in the list of references

- removal of some double full stops (typing errors) and incorrect use of apostrophe: 'the Cohen's' rather than 'the Cohens' (parag 6)
- misspellings, such as 'Parkison's' (parag 4).

Review

Academic writing is not the same as writing used for other purposes. It has its own traditions and conventions. These have developed over time, partly as ways of bringing the greatest levels of accuracy and clarity to written communication, especially when read by experts in the field. This chapter looked at some of these conventions, and how they are applied within a particular kind of academic assignment, the essay. However, these also apply within other assignments such as project reports and dissertations, covered in the next chapter.

Most academic writing is influenced by the scientific model, which values objectivity and quantitative data. You will need to know which styles to use in your subject and for which purposes. For example, each academic subject varies in how much it values such aspects as use of qualitative data and/or personal experience, and awareness of subjectivity when evaluating evidence.

There are four main styles of writing used within academic writing. Some pieces of work will require you to use all of these within a single assignment. Almost all writing involves some elements of argument, evaluation, and synthesis. Generally, in academic writing at higher levels, descriptive writing needs to be used selectively and in very particular ways.

Your assignments will be designed to develop, amongst other skills, your own competence in writing in formal, clear, precise ways, using good evidence and attributing sources in appropriate ways.

Students are generally keen to know how to gain better marks for assignments. Good marks are allocated for specific reasons – not simply because you have tried hard, know a lot or are regarded as clever. It is difficult to gain the highest marks simply for being well-informed in your subject: you also have to be able to communicate your knowledge to others, using the expected conventions. The chapter provided 4 essays, with commentaries, to enable you to develop an awareness of the kinds of essays that are handed in and how these would be evaluated. Evaluating, or 'marking', essays for yourself is useful for understanding what it is that your tutors are looking for.

The strength of an essay is partly related to the formal characteristics covered in this chapter, and depends partly on how far it meets the marking criteria, including accuracy in the use of subject material. It is important to know how marks are allocated in your subject. Use your tutor's feedback constructively, and don't be put off by what seems to be criticism. Tutors want as many students to succeed as possible – and their comments are intended to help you improve your marks.

When you complete an essay, go through it yourself, checking it against the brief, the level descriptors, marking criteria provided by your tutors (as well as the checklists provided here). This will help you to develop your own independent judgement about the quality of your work – which may prove invaluable in your working life.

Chapter 13

Research projects, case studies and dissertations

Learning outcomes

This chapter offers you opportunities to:

- understand what is required for completing research-based assignments
- understand the process for undertaking larger-scale assignments such as final year projects, case studies and dissertations
- recognise the factors to consider when choosing an appropriate topic and title and developing your research proposal
- consider different research strategies to use for your assignment
- produce the content for each section of your assignment and write this up in the appropriate style.

Almost all courses set tasks which require you to undertake some kind of research yourself. This might consist of many smaller projects for which you write short reports, or larger-scale assignments such as a final year project, in-depth case study, long essay or dissertation.

Students often find such assignments daunting, especially if it is the first time they select a topic for themselves or their first large-scale assignment. However, students generally enjoy such tasks because:

- they find the assignments interesting
- typically, such assignments are set at a point in the course where you have already had practice in the underlying academic skills
- the course provides in-depth training in the more specialist skills needed.

Arguably, the most challenging and important aspects of such assignments are in:

- understanding what is required in terms of the brief and the process
- choosing a manageable topic
- planning and managing your research or dissertation as a project.

This chapter looks at:

- what is required of you
- how to approach the task and manage the process
- and how to write up your assignment.

Understanding and defining the task

Chapter 6 looked at the underlying research skills that you would call upon for such assignments. It highlighted the importance of starting out by defining the task as closely as you can.

Defining the task: starter questions
- What is the purpose? – why are such assignments set at all?
- What is the assignment brief?
- What is the end-point or 'outputs'?
- What do I know already?

What is the purpose?

An 'apprenticeship' in your field

Research is core to academic life. These kinds of assignments acquaint you with the techniques for managing research within your field.

Understanding your discipline

Undertaking a research project helps you to understand your subject better. It gives you hands-on experience of working with the raw materials typical of the discipline. You gain insights into how knowledge is constructed and advanced within your field, the difficulties that are encountered, and the issues that need to be addressed.

To give you choice and independence

Research tasks provide opportunities for you to investigate topics that are meaningful, relevant or interesting to you or your workplace.

Varied skills and employability

To accomplish such assignments successfully, you generally use and develop skills and qualities relevant to employment:
- project management – the tasks call for more advanced organisational skills
- time management, so that different aspects are completed to deadlines
- self-management – in keeping yourself motivated and focused over longer periods.

What is the assignment brief?

Your course will provide an assignment brief. This is your starting place. It details essential information such as:
- the topic – or the choices open to you
- the title, or a selection of titles from which to choose
- the word limit
- the criteria used to grade your work
- useful source materials as start places
- details of any methods, approaches, techniques, equipment or software that you are expected to use
- guidelines on presenting your work
- deadlines for hand-in.

Use the brief

- Read it many times; underline key words.
- Highlight requirements you must meet.
- Highlight, in different colours, the aspects over which you have some choice.
- Summarise the brief in your own words.
- Keep returning to it: check that your report or dissertation is meeting the brief.
- Use the marking criteria – display them where you can see them, and use them to guide your work.

What is the end-point?

- Clarify what you have to produce. Is it an essay, or a report, or a dissertation, or some other kind of output? Do you have any choice?
- What does a report or dissertation look like in your subject? What are they like to read? What kind of titles have been used in previous years? What kind of data do students use? Are any available to see, either through your library or through the department?

Defining the task: what is a project?

Characteristics of projects

Projects share the following characteristics.

- *Unique*   Each has a specific purpose, brief or angle.
- *Informed*   A project is based on research.
- *Focused*   A project focuses on one topic in depth.
- *Set apart, yet relevant*   A project is usually outside of the usual patterns of study or work.
- *Time-bound*   A project must be completed within a given time.
- *Managed*   They require organisation and planning.

Unique

In each project, there will be some aspect – the subject matter, the client group, the data or the finished product – that will make this project different from everybody else's. Your tutors will be looking to see that your work is *original*. This does not mean making major discoveries, but that you bring some new angle. This might be that you:

- test out other people's findings for yourself
- conduct a questionnaire or survey so that you could work from your own data
- apply existing research to a new area.

Informed

Although your project will be 'unique' in the ways described above, your tutors will want to see that you have used previous research to inform your own project. Your project report should make clear how you drew upon previously published materials and well-tried methods in shaping your own project. It should make clear how your own project has built on previous research or projects.

Focused

Make sure that your project brief is manageable. Choose a subject that can reasonably be researched and completed within the set time and word limits. If necessary, narrow down the topic to make the workload more realistic. Avoid large subjects that can only be covered in a superficial way within the time limit.

Identify your key questions, so that you have a clear goal. Your tutors will want to see that you can design a manageable, focused project, using an appropriate methodology. Avoid collecting and including material that, though interesting, is not directly related to the project goal.

Set apart, yet relevant

Projects are usually one-off pieces of work, related to the overall programme but covering ground chosen by the student. Make clear to your tutor how the subject you have chosen is relevant to your programme: to work covered in class, and to course texts.

Time-bound

Projects are often larger pieces of work than essays, with higher word limits and taking more time to complete. The time allocations for projects tend therefore to be greater than for essays. However, there is usually more work to do than with an essay, so the work must be carefully planned and managed.

Managed

Projects usually require that you think and plan ahead. You will need to pay attention to small details. For example, you may need to book rooms or resources well in advance, ensure that participants are available, design materials, and so forth. These tasks are not necessarily difficult, but they require time and good planning.

Typically, research projects require you to:

- break the project down into manageable tasks or steps
- make a good choice of subject
- identify appropriate methods, including ways of collating, recording and analysing source materials and data
- produce a report
- complete the project on time.

Dissertations and final year research projects

These larger-scale assignments enable you to:

- undertake a substantial piece of independent work with a great degree of choice in the topic
- pursue in depth a topic that interests you
- put your personal stamp on a piece of work.

Differences from earlier assignments

Scale   Dissertations and final year projects are larger-scale assignments based on broader reading and research, resulting in an extended piece of writing with a higher word limit.

Timing   These are usually set towards the *end* of your programme as the culmination of your study, and when you will have developed the right skills through undertaking earlier assignments.

Independence and personal involvement   You have more control over the nature and scope of your assignment. They require strong commitment. Students tend to become highly engaged in investigating their specialist topic and take pride in the end product. It is important to choose a topic that really interests you.

Time   As this is a major piece of writing, all of your time may become dedicated to managing, researching and writing it up.

Self-management and motivation   Independent study on this scale can leave students feeling isolated or adrift. You need good strategies to remain motivated and on schedule when working alone for extended periods on a topic that only you are researching in that depth.

Background research   You will read specialist material and use original documents or data. You will also find that you read far more than for other assignments. This makes it all the more important to maintain accurate, well organised records to help you to find information when needed.

Skills   Such large-scale assignments provide opportunities for you to refine and extend a wide range of skills, from collecting, analysing, summarising and presenting information, to decision-making, project management and problem-solving.

Similarities between dissertations/final year projects and earlier assignments

Essays	Project work	Reports
Like an essay, a dissertation or final year project: - follows the basic procedure for writing assignments (Chapters 11 and 12) - adheres to academic conventions (see pages 307–8) - involves research skills (Chapter 6) - includes continuous prose within most sections - requires analytical and critical reading and writing skills.	Like earlier project work, a dissertation or final year project: - requires strategy and management - requires a systematic methodology - uses data you have collected yourself - is unique – nobody else will have covered exactly the same ground or be using the same data - is a one-off, time-bound task - uses new material or approaches that you have devised, to test out theories, hypotheses or methodologies from your subject discipline.	As with other project reports, a dissertation or final year project report: - includes an abstract (see page 361) - has many of the features of a report (see page 357) - is structured in sections (page 358).

Projects and dissertations: understanding the process

Completing project reports and dissertations requires careful management. The first step is to understand that process, from start to finish.

1 Organisation and planning

Using your project brief and this process list as guidelines:

- List everything you need to do up to the end of the process
- Draw up an action plan (pages 134–5)
- Schedule each step in your diary
- Agree how you will work with your supervisor
- Plan in support from peers
- Book facilities for binding your dissertation, if required.

Preparation

2 Prepare the groundwork

- Literature search: survey the field for ideas and suitable background reading
- Brainstorm potential topics
- Focus your reading on likely topics
- Check potential topics for feasibility
- Consider ethical implications of each
- Narrow your list of topics.

3 Decide on topic, title and research strategy

- Decide on a topic
- Clarify exactly what you are setting out to investigate and demonstrate
- Specify your research question or title precisely
- Write a project hypothesis/thesis statement as required
- Decide your research strategy and methodology.

4 Draw up and agree your proposal

- Draw up a specific proposal or outline, as required
- Check with your tutor/supervisor that the project is suitable
- Gain Ethics Committee permission, if needed
- Revise the proposal if/as advised.

5 Undertake a literature review

- Read and take notes on key literature on your chosen topic
- Keep details of all works that you cite to include in your references
- Select the most relevant items for your project
- Write the review, demonstrating the relevance to your work of each item you mention.

Research

Research projects, case studies and dissertations **343**

6 Implement your research design

- Fine-tune your methodology, scaling the project to the brief
- Identify participants and/or equipment
- Design materials (if needed)
- Develop forms or databases to gather and record data
- Collect data or analyse your source materials, keeping accurate records of what you find
- Write up your methodology section.

7 Present and discuss results (for experimental research)

- Collate data, drawing up tables and graphs if relevant
- Summarise your results and their significance
- Identify whether your findings support the research hypothesis.

8 Discuss your findings and draw conclusions

- Write the discussion section, bringing critical analysis to your methods and findings
- Identify the significance of your research and ways that the topic could be further researched
- Draw conclusions and/or make recommendations based on your findings and analysis.

Analysis

9 Rework your drafts

- Go back over each section, checking that the argument and the details are consistent and that you meet the brief
- Check whether earlier sections need rewriting in the light of what you have written in later sections.

Writing up

10 Write the abstract and references

- Write your abstract or summary (if required)
- List all references and citations carefully.

11 Prepare for handing in

- Check that you meet presentation requirements in the brief
- Check heading levels and page numbering
- Add appendices, numbering these as you did in the report
- Fine-tune the phrasing
- Edit and proof-read several times.

Fine-tuning

Projects and dissertations: managing the process

Manage the scale

Manage the scale of each aspect of the project in terms of the word limit, deadline and assignment brief. This means:

- choose a topic and title which have challenge but which are feasible
- scale your reading to fit the task – don't read lots more material than you can use
- choose methods, sample sizes or source materials that give you significant results with a reasonable workload
- scale your writing of each section of the report/dissertation to match its word limit.

Manage the focus

Decide on a topic and title/research question:

- that meets the assignment brief and marking criteria
- that enables you to be specific about what you are looking for
- that enables you to envisage what your results or conclusions would look like.

Manage your time

- Start early – don't wait to get started.
- Consider your options, but aim to narrow your focus early, so that you can start to conduct your more detailed research in good time.
- Once you have chosen a topic, stay with it. Organise and plan your work, scheduling your time in detail. You need a clear sense of:
- the range of tasks to be undertaken
- the order in which you will do them
- how much time to put aside for each.

(See Chapter 5.)

Manage your supervision

Project tutors and dissertation supervisors are there to provide guidance. They will have limited time available for each student, so plan how to make best use of that time.

- Don't wait for your tutor or supervisor to contact you: make contact at agreed, regular intervals.
- Do as much as you can before contacting your supervisor.
- Prepare a list of questions in advance. Put these in order of priority.
- If you get into difficulties, ask for help. Experiment with ways of solving the problem before contacting your supervisor. Be prepared to talk through your attempted solutions and their limitations.

Draw on skills already acquired

- Research and information management skills (Chapter 6)
- Maintaining high motivation (Chapter 4)
- Applying number skills (Chapter 9)
- Analysing material critically (Chapter 7)
- Writing skills, including citing and referencing sources (Chapter 11).

Maintain contact; use support

Avoid becoming isolated:

- Maintain contact with other students to share experiences and gain different perspectives.
- Organise a support group (page 257).
- If feasible, attend lectures in related subjects to gain background information or to fire your interest and imagination.

Developing your research proposal

What kind of proposal?

Find out what kind of proposal you need to submit: the timing and contents of this vary. You may have to submit:

- just the title
- and/or a rationale and outline plan
- and/or a full or partial literature review
- or a pilot of your methods and results.

Scoping the field

Your proposal needs to show that you have a good background knowledge of the subject. You scope the field in several stages.

- Browse widely to see what is written.
- Dip into materials to look for ideas.
- Select items to read in greater depth to build your knowledge.
- Read more about areas that might provide fertile ground for a project.
- Investigate a few selected topics in depth, to find a specific project area.
- Continue to narrow your focus towards a title and hypothesis (pages 348–9).
- Check that there is sufficient literature on your chosen topic to draw upon for your literature review (page 350).
- Browse previous student dissertations to develop a feel for suitable projects.

Clarify your purpose or rationale

Once you have chosen a title, clarify your rationale for choosing it, so that you can put it into your proposal or talk it through with your supervisor/tutor. What lends it importance? For example, you might be:

- looking at documents in the light of a newly developed approach in the field
- testing out a theory or previous findings
- addressing a known gap in the data
- conducting a project for an employer
- adding data on a new population, such as fellow students or local people.

Decide on a method

Aim to draw on methods that have been covered as part of your course. Think through the practicalities. Avoid complex methods that are difficult to complete or that allow errors to creep in. Think through how your methods will provide the information or data you need.

See pages 351–64.

Consider the ethical implications

In deciding on a project, consider how your methods would be viewed by your Department's ethical committee. Address all potential issues to avoid your proposal being rejected or sent back for amendment. Ensure you can demonstrate the following.

- No one will be harmed.
- Legal requirements are met in areas such as data protection, child protection, health and safety.
- Participants understand what they will be required to do, are well informed about the project's aims and the use that will be made of the results, and how confidentiality will be maintained.
- You have gained the signed consent of participants to use their data.

Use your supervisor effectively

Supervisors and project tutors know the field and are there to guide you. Check with them that you are on the right track. Follow up on their guidance on such matters as:

- the project topic and title
- the theoretical background
- reading and source materials
- methods to use and ethical considerations
- software for analysing data
- scale and challenge: is your project over ambitious? Too basic?

Choosing a topic

Choosing the *subject* is the most important aspect of project and dissertation management.

Advancing knowledge and understanding

Reports and dissertations are expected to advance, in some small way, knowledge and understanding of an issue, methodology or application. As you look for a topic and title, consider how you would answer the question: 'In what way will this research add to what is known about this subject?' It takes time, thought, and research to identify a new angle.

Build on what has gone before

Select a topic:

- that is already well researched
- in which your lecturers have expertise
- in which there are well-established research methodologies and techniques
- to which you can bring something new (for example, where you might replicate a piece of research using a new client group, in a related area, or with a small modification)
- with few ethical and financial considerations.

Look for your own angle, much as you would when developing a new thread on a discussion board.

Develop a long list of potential topics

- Jot down many possible options: be imaginative initially so that you have a good set of angles to pursue.
- Browse journals, book reviews, other dissertations, and podcasts for ideas on what is topical in the subject.

Small is beautiful

Typical difficulties arise from topics that:

- are too broad and would take too long to complete well
- lack a research basis, so that it is hard to find a theoretical base, established methods to draw on, or material to write about in the literature review
- are too ambitious in attempting new ground – you need to be realistic: a topic is still 'original' even if it is a replication of previous research or varies in just one aspect.

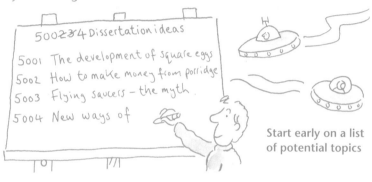

Start early on a list of potential topics

Narrow your list

Eliminate items that are likely to:

- be too complicated for this level of study
- raise ethical questions that would be too difficult to address
- take too long to research
- take too many words to write up
- fail to sustain your interest
- be covered by other students.

Identify your niche

Aim to select a topic:

- that will engage your interest, and …
- for which there are some gaps in the research (indicated by lecturers or your own reading)
- that relates to your town, your background, your year group or some other area you know well or can access easily
- that is relevant to your workplace or your employer, or that will be advantageous to your own academic or career prospects.

Specifying your title and thesis statement

Specify your research questions

As soon as you can, narrow your focus until you settle on a title. Be clear which question(s) you are setting out to address. Jot these down.

Wording the title

Although the aim of the title is to address one or more well-defined questions, for reports and dissertations this may be worded more like a statement than a question. For example:

- 'The effects of local flooding on small businesses in Smalltown'
- 'The application of ABC techniques to stimulate nitrogen fixation in leguminous plants'
- 'Using XYZ software to improve athletic performance'.

Check for feasibility

At every stage, check whether what you are setting out to do is feasible in terms of scale, time, methods, ethics, participants and resources needed. The exact wording of your title has a bearing on these considerations. Check that it is sufficiently specific.

You may find it helpful to add a subtitle that provides greater specificity. For example:

- 'The effects of local flooding on small businesses: A comparative case study of two engineering SMEs in Smalltown one year after the 2012–13 floods'.

Thesis/position statements

A thesis statement or position statement sums up your central message. It should:

- form part of your introduction
- be succinctly written: usually only one or two sentences long
- demonstrate clearly and unambiguously your position or perspective on the issue
- be the point to which you return continually, to focus your readers
- give shape to the flow of your argument
- be reinforced within your conclusion.

The value of thesis statements

Clarity   Summing up your position in this way helps you to distil and clarify your thinking.

Focus   It helps to focus your thinking before you start to gather the information and write your report. It prevents you from wasting time accumulating lots of material that you won't use, and from going off on interesting tangents.

Structure, relevance and organisation   It provides a clear reference point to which you should return, continually, as you consider whether material is relevant to include and where it fits in your overall argument. It can help you to avoid going off on a tangent.

Formulating your statement

Be well informed   Read, think, write exploratory thoughts, map these out, discuss them, until you are clear about your position on the issue.

Be specific   Be precise and clear about what you are looking for and what your position is.

Check your evidence base   Make sure there will be sufficient evidence to provide a strong basis for the position you take.

Interest and conviction   Choose a position that allows you to debate the issue in a forceful, interesting way, where you can sound convincing and draw on different angles and perspectives.

Example: Thesis statement

Although it may appear to be common sense that infants suffer if mothers go out to work, this essay argues that the stay-at-home mother is an abstract ideal, and does not represent the lived circumstances of mothers over the last 60 years. It demonstrates that it is not beneficial to either the infant or the family unit as a whole if mothers are pressurised into a particular position on whether to stay at home or go to work

---

Formulating your hypothesis

Most reports, especially in science subjects, include a **hypothesis**.

What is a hypothesis?

The hypothesis is formulated *before* you start the research, and states what you *expect* will happen – or what you are likely to find to be the case. For example:

- that there is a link between two factors
- how people will behave in certain circumstances
- what the outcome would be if two substances combined
- that x causes y

This is a theoretical assumption and should be a logical assumption based on your knowledge of the subject. Your research tests your hypothesis to see whether it can be supported by the evidence. You design your research to ensure that you test your hypothesis in an objective way.

The nature of a hypothesis

You can't 'prove' a hypothesis. You can:

Disprove it – if your evidence doesn't support it. That can be a useful thing to do and adds to knowledge of the topic, so don't be discouraged if your results do not support your hypothesis.

Provide evidence to support it – the information or data you collect can provide evidence that supports the hypothesis under the particular conditions of your own research and on that occasion. You or others might look to replicate your research and gain different results that do not support the hypothesis on that occasion.

Using your hypothesis

Your hypothesis provides a clear focus on what exactly to read, research, measure and discuss. You refer back to it in sections of your report.

- Results section: you state clearly whether the data support or do not support the research hypotheses.

- Discussion section: you analyse why the results do or do not support the hypothesis. Might the hypothesis have been supported under different conditions?
- Abstract: this focuses on your hypothesis and whether the results support it to any significant extent.

Writing the research hypothesis

The hypothesis must be worded very clearly and precisely. It usually states that something will or will not happen.

> **Example: Research hypothesis**
>
> The research hypothesis was that adults would show a preference for savoury food coloured blue over savoury food coloured with food dyes simulating natural colourings. The second hypothesis was that there would be no significant difference in the preferences of men and women.

Activity **Formulating hypotheses**

Decide whether the following are well-worded hypotheses.

Hypothesis 01   The research hypothesis was that physical activity reduces depression.

Hypothesis 02   The research hypothesis was to find out whether physical activity reduces depression.

Hypothesis 03   The research hypothesis was that 20 minutes of brisk walking a day for 8 weeks would reduce sleep disturbance as a symptom of clinical depression in women aged 30–40.

Answers are given on page 413.

Reading and reviewing the literature

Once you have chosen your title, you can conduct a more in-depth search of the literature, focused on what you now know will be relevant to your own project.

Be selective in what you read

You will be faced with a large amount of relevant material. You won't be able to read and use it all, so you will need to make choices about what you will and will not use. You need to do this in ways that will enable you to demonstrate in your literature review that you have:

- a breadth of understanding of the field
- a depth of understanding of your specialist topic
- a good grasp of what is the most significant material, and what is less so.

Know your field

- Undertake a preliminary broad survey of the material, tracing research in your topic back to its origins.
- Read the abstracts of a range of journal articles. Identify those most relevant, to read in full.
- Note recurrent key themes and issues.
- Note how the issues relevant to your project are treated by the key schools of thought in your discipline.
- Identify the leading figures relevant to your selected topic – those whose primary research, theories or writings are regarded by academics as essential to know about, even if you do not read their work in detail. What did each contribute? What did others find to be the limitations of that research? What did they do to improve upon it?
- Investigate and chart clearly the variety of

perspectives on the core issues held by experts in the field: in what ways, and why, do they agree or disagree?

- Read some specialist material, such as articles in more specialist journals, or monograms, or expert texts.

Read critically; note selectively

- Make very brief notes of materials that look relevant.
- Evaluate what you read for its relevance and significance to your own selected title, thesis statement or hypothesis.
- Look for 'chains': consider how each piece of research or set of ideas influenced others. Trace briefly how the understanding of this topic has developed through successive theories and research findings.
- Make a list of 5–10 key pieces of research or developments in theory that have had most influence on the subject. Chart briefly how each influenced others in the chain.
- Identify how your project or dissertation will follow on from what has gone before.

Write your literature review

Write up your review of the literature when:

- your research proposal is agreed (unless you need to submit the review as part of the proposal)
- you are clear on your research design
- and you know, therefore, which material will be the most relevant.

See page 359.

Chapter **13**

Research design and methods

The 'research design' refers to the way in which you will conduct your research. This includes matters such as:

- the source materials or data you need
- the exact methods for collecting these
- if relevant, the number and type of people you want to interview or to take part
- what, exactly, you want participants to do
- how you will design questions to achieve only the exact data you need
- designing forms to record and collate data.

Deciding on your raw material

Most projects and dissertations use data that you have generated or collected yourself. This may be through observation, experiment, questionnaires or similar. Alternatively, in your subject, you may select texts, artefacts, parliamentary papers, philosophical tracts, historical documents or published data and consider these from a new perspective.

Each subject has its own conventions about acceptable research methods. Your supervisor or tutors will give you details of these. Journal articles provide a good feel for how material and data are generated and analysed in your subject. However, basic principles – of being accurate, being as objective as possible, and avoiding distortion – are common to most subjects (page 287 and Chapter 12).

Precise thinking and methods

When designing your research strategy, you need to think in very precise ways. Look for conditions, or variables, that may affect your results in ways that you had not intended or that leave it open to doubt what might have given rise to your results. If there are flaws in your research design, your results will not be valid. Keep returning to the question:

- Will this method, or this wording, yield exactly what I need?

Research useful methods

When conducting your literature search:

- Look for ideas on methods to adapt.
- Look for research that employed similar methods to those you are planning to use. What insights do these provide into how you might fine-tune your own methods?

Collecting, collating and analysing data

Plan to collect enough data to achieve convincing and reliable results. Collecting and analysing data is time-consuming, however, so take advice on what is the acceptable minimum for your subject. Having too much information is not helpful for student projects: it simply means that time is wasted in collecting, sorting and selecting material that you cannot use.

Design forms to collect information in a way that helps you collate it quickly (pages 352–3). Once you have collected your information, organise it into charts or tables so that you can interpret it. Look for patterns and trends. Make relevant comparisons. Your tutors will be looking to see how well you make sense of your findings.

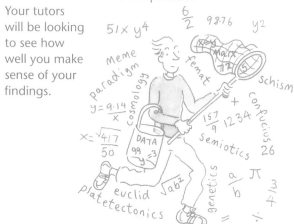

Pilot your methods

It is good practice to test out your methods in a trial run. Examine the process and the results in detail to see where you could make improvements. If you use a pilot, mention this in the methods section of your report, and include the materials in your appendices.

Designing questionnaires

Questionnaires are useful for collecting data for a range of projects. You can use them to ask participants to express preferences and opinions or to give information about their experiences and background. When compiling these, decide whether you will ask participants to:

- complete a paper version themselves
- complete electronically or online
- respond to questions verbally whilst you fill out the questionnaire yourself.

Questions for quantitative research

A small number (2–5 simple questions), if asked of a large number of people (at least 30), can deliver manageable but significant results.

To gain useful answers:

- Set short, clear, unambiguous questions. Pilot them first to ensure they cannot be misinterpreted.
- Set a small number of questions, carefully chosen to gain the information you need.
- Avoid personal questions or questions that might embarrass or distress the interviewee.
- Check that each item is a single question. (Avoid 'two questions in one'.)
- Use closed questions that give 'yes/no' answers or a response that you can count. This will make it easier for you to record and analyse the answers.
- Select a representative sample of people, appropriate to the project brief.
- Use controlled conditions, so you know exactly how the questions were delivered and who answered them.

Examples of well-structured questions

- Which font style do you prefer? *Answer 'sample 1', 'sample 2', or 'no preference'.*

- Are you a member of staff? *Yes/No*

- How often do use this train?
  (a) Every day
  (b) About once a week
  (c) About once a month
  (d) Hardly ever

Activity   Poor questionnaire technique

What is wrong with the following questions?

1   How old are you? Please circle one of the following: *0–20   20–40   40–60*

2   Do you know who is the current Secretary of State?

3   Do you believe in capital punishment? *Yes/No*

4   Do you like coming onto campus and eating in the café?

(For feedback, see page 414.)

Using scales

One way of collecting data is by giving participants a list of statements and asking them to ring the responses they prefer. Alternatively, you can ask participants to rate responses on a scale, such as the Likert-type scale in the example below.

Example of a scaled question

Please indicate your opinion of this holiday resort on a scale of 1–5, where 1 is very poor and 5 is very good.

	Very poor				Very good
Quality of hotels	1	2	3	4	5
Local transport	1	2	3	4	5
Cleanliness	1	2	3	4	5
Things for children to do	1	2	3	4	5
Shopping	1	2	3	4	5

Alternatively, each of your questions could be followed by a scale that people tick. For example:

Strongly agree	Agree	Neither agree nor disagree	Disagree	Disagree Strongly
☐	☐	☐	☐	☐

Preparation

If you wish participants to complete the questionnaire themselves, make it easy to use.

- Include a maximum of 5–6 questions.
- Bear in mind that most people will respond only to 'yes/no' or 'tick the box' questions. (Very few people write comments.)
- Bear in mind that online and postal surveys attract a very low response rate – and you do not know for sure who completed the returned surveys.
- If you include open questions or ask for comment, leave plenty of space for responses.

Recording responses

- Keep accurate records.
- Order your findings into tables.
- Devise a simple tool to collect your responses.

The following table allows the researcher to record responses quickly and clearly – in this case, about which font style is preferred, according to status and gender, for each participant.

Preferences for samples of font style		
	Female	Male
Sample 1		
Sample 2		
No preference		✓
Staff / (student)		

(This answer is from a male student with no preference.)

If you are designing a questionnaire that participants will complete electronically:

- Use the guidance provided on page 352.
- Keep the structure of your questions simple.
- Include clear instructions on how to make and submit answers.
- Ask participants to choose a response from a limited number of options, rather than asking them to type their answers.
- If asking participants to choose from a range of responses (such as between 1 and 5), use the ranges consistently.
- Ensure questions flow in a logical order.

Use the guidance provided on page 352.

Survey monkey (www.surveymonkey.com)

- An online survey generator that makes it easy to set up basic surveys.
- Free for surveys of 10 questions or fewer.
- Easy for participants to access and complete online.
- Records responses automatically and gives you an overview of these.

Questions for qualitative research

In qualitative research, typically only one or two people or items can be included in a student project. However, a good questioning technique will usually encourage interviewees to express themselves in detail.

Prepare prompts that politely encourage the interviewee to return to the subject, such as:

- I'd like to ask you more about a point you mentioned earlier …
- That's very helpful. Thank you. I'd also like to ask you about …

A few open-ended questions usually generate a great deal of material that takes considerable time to analyse. For qualitative research:

- *Good questions are open-ended.* Most encourage a response other than a simple 'yes' or 'no'.
- *Good questions are focused.* They encourage the interviewee to respond on the issue you are researching.
- *Good questions invite respondents to consider an issue from different angles.* For example, 'What were the advantages of taking part in the pilot study?' and 'What were the disadvantages?'
- *Good questions are free of bias.* They do not lead the interviewee to a particular answer (as do 'I suppose you think taking part was a bad idea?' or 'I hear you are glad you took part?')

Checklist for evaluating your questionnaire

Use the following checklist to see whether your questionnaire does what you want it to do, and will be manageable for you to use as a researcher.

Does it take a reasonable time to complete?

- ☐ 1 How long will it take to complete?
- ☐ 2 Is that time reasonable?
- ☐ 3 Is every question necessary?
- ☐ 4 Is the time required for completing the questionnaire spelt out clearly to the participant?

Will the questions yield the information I need?

- ☐ 5 Have I used closed questions to elicit precise answers when needed?
- ☐ 6 Are there sufficient options to enable people to make accurate responses?
- ☐ 7 Are any back-up questions needed in order to clarify responses?
- ☐ 8 Will the questions yield the precise data that I need?
- ☐ 9 Are there any leading questions (which would invalidate my results)?

Is it clear to participants what they have to do?

- ☐ 10 Are the instructions clear?
- ☐ 11 Are examples provided?
- ☐ 12 If participants are asked to select from a range of responses (such as between 1 and 5), is the range used in a consistent way from one question to the next?
- ☐ 13 Will it be obvious to participants how to use the rating system?
- ☐ 14 Is it clear how to submit the survey if online?

Are questions easy to answer?

- ☐ 15 Is every question a single question?
- ☐ 16 Will people understand the questions?
- ☐ 17 Could any question be interpreted in a way other than the one I intended?

Does the questionnaire encourage participants to complete it?

- ☐ 18 Does it look as if it will be quick and easy to complete?
- ☐ 19 Do questions flow in a logical order?
- ☐ 20 Are any questions too personal for people to feel comfortable answering?
- ☐ 21 Do any questions assume that participants would have specialist information or background knowledge that they might not have?

Is the questionnaire manageable for me to use as a researcher?

- ☐ 22 Will responses be easy to record?
- ☐ 23 Will responses be easy to collate?
- ☐ 24 Will responses be easy to analyse?

How do I know it will work the way I want it to?

- ☐ 25 What issues were raised by the pilot?
- ☐ 26 Have I addressed these fully?

Interview techniques

Prepare for the interview

Good preparation helps to ensure that you remain in control of the interview, keeping it focused and limited to a reasonable length.

- Prepare your questions in advance.
- Consider how you will introduce yourself at the start of the interview. This must be clear but brief: you must state that this is a student project, or name any company involved.
- You need to let participants know what happens to the data. How will you ensure confidentiality?
- If responses are to be held on an electronic database, participants must know this and agree to it.
- Decide how you will close the interview.

Consistency

If you are interviewing more than one person, it is important that you carry out all of your interviews in near-identical conditions, to ensure consistency.

- Prior to the interview, make a list of questions, with possible prompts for each.
- If there is more than one interviewer, agree questions, prompts and any other words in advance. Practise so that you phrase questions and record responses in the same way.
- Conduct the interview just as you practised it. Interview each person in the same way.

Conducting the interview

- Know your questions well so that you do not have to read them. This will engage participants better.
- Sit at right angles to the interviewee.
- Use eye contact, and smile occasionally.
- Be confident but polite.
- Keep it short: don't impose on people's time.
- Thank people for participating.

Blah
blah
blah
blah
blah
blah
blah …

Pilot the process

- Practise the whole interview. Check that it will work the way you want.
- Check that you can record the answers easily. If not, is this because the questions are too complex, or do you need a better chart to record answers?
- Analyse the answers from the pilot. Are they yielding the kind of data you want? If not, design new questions.
- Following the pilot, adapt your interview so that it is easy to conduct.

Ground rules and boundaries

Where there are a number of interviews with a single person, such as for a case study, the interviewer may become too involved. Take steps to ensure that you remain interested but detached.

- Be clear with participants what you expect.
- Explain what will happen during and after the interview, and how long it will take.
- Specify your requirements for interview space or privacy. Negotiate acceptable alternatives. If there are any risks to you, do not proceed.
- Do not make promises.
- Do not get drawn into sharing personal experiences, as this can lead to unforeseen consequences. It can also distort the kind of information you receive in answer to your questions.

After long interviews

- Write up your notes as soon as possible.
- If you are required to transcribe the interview, write down exactly what was said, indicating pauses, coughs, 'ums' and 'ahs', and so on.
- Go through your notes with coloured pens or pencils, marking all sections that refer to similar themes.
- Write a list of the themes, and where you can find these in your notes.

Presenting and analysing the data

Presenting your results

Decide which method of presentation will show your results most clearly. You may wish to use a table, chart, or graph (see Chapter 9).

Tables

Add up responses for each question. If you divide the responses – by age, gender, location, job or similar – state this clearly in the title of the table.

Table 1: Preferences for samples of font style, by gender

	Women	Men	Totals
Sample 1	8	15	23
Sample 2	13	5	18
No preference	9	10	19
Totals	30	30	60

Tables are useful for setting out information in clear categories. For example, Table 2 indicates preferences (three options) by gender (two options) and occupation (two options).

Table 2: Preferences for samples of font style, by gender and occupation

	Sample 1	Sample 2	No pref.	Totals
Male staff	13	2	0	15
Female staff	4	6	5	15
Male students	2	3	10	15
Female students	4	7	4	15
Totals	23	18	19	60

Bar charts

When presenting information in bar charts, select two things that can be compared against each other. Label the horizontal line (axis) with the details of what is being compared. In the example below, the horizontal axis refers to sample preferences. Label the vertical axis with the difference that is being measured. In the example here, this is the number of people who indicated a given preference.

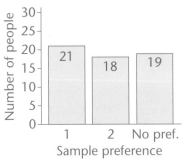

Figure 1: Preferences for samples of font style, by sample

Pie charts

Pie charts are useful for presenting information in a way that the eye can take in at once.

Figure 2: Preferences for samples of font style, by occupation

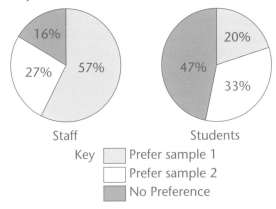

Staff   Students

Key ☐ Prefer sample 1
     ☐ Prefer sample 2
     ▓ No Preference

Analyse the data

It is easier to look for patterns and to draw conclusions when you have organised your data according to categories, as in the charts and tables above. It is important to organise results in different ways and to compare the results.

- Analyse your data. What do they tell you? Is this what you expected? Do the data support your research hypothesis?
- How do your findings compare with those in the research literature?
- What questions are you not able to answer because of the way you designed your research? Could the design be improved?
- What questions are raised by your research?

Characteristics of reports

What is a report?

A report is the formal method of communicating the results of a project or research assignment. It may cover a laboratory experiment, survey, questionnaire, case study. Dissertations based on those research methods require similar, though more extended, reports. Reports are structured in broadly similar ways so that readers can find information quickly – and are different to essays.

Reports …	Essays …
1 originate from outside an educational context: they are typical of writing required for the world of work	**1** originate in academic settings: they are rarely used anywhere else
2 present research data and findings that you have collected yourself	**2** focus on analysing or evaluating theory, past research by other people, and ideas; they seldom present the findings of new research
3 are structured as on page 358	**3** are structured as on page 290
4 are divided into separate sections	**4** do not have distinct sections, apart from unheaded paragraphs; they flow as a continuous piece of text
5 contain tables, charts, and appendices	**5** do not include tables or appendices
6 are divided into sections, each with a heading (see page 358). Each point is numbered (see the diagram on page 362).	**6** do not include section headings or numbering (if these are used during drafting, remove them before handing in the essay)
7 utilise several writing styles, depending on the section (see pages 359–61). They are written concisely, and give precise details.	**7** use a consistent writing style throughout
8 include descriptions of the methods used	**8** do not refer to the method used in arriving at conclusions
9 include a discussion section that identifies how the research could have been improved, and areas for further research	**9** are not usually reflective about the process of researching and writing the essay itself
10 may include recommendations for action	**10** do not include recommendations

Different goals

The style and content of your report should be appropriate to the readers for whom you write.

- If you make recommendations for action, evaluate different options.
- For business reports, include details of costs, losses and potential profits for each option.
- For a report based on an experiment, describe the experiment and the conditions under which it took place.
- If you are writing for a client (such as a work placement employer), tailor your report to the client's own requirements.

Reports and dissertations: structure and content

Check your course requirements. Typically, you would include some or all of the following sections.

Title   Write this in the centre of the first page, with the course title, and the date.

Acknowledgements   List people you wish to thank for help given.

Abstract   Give a succinct summary of your project report or dissertation, clarifying why the subject is significant or worthy of study, and your conclusions. For experimental reports, state your research proposal or hypotheses, the methods used to test these, the results, whether these were significant, and whether they supported the hypotheses.

Abstracts may be reproduced and read separately from the rest of the report, so repeat information included in other sections.

Contents   List the main sections and the page on which each begins (including appendices).

Tables and illustrations   List any illustrations, charts, maps and so on, giving the page number for each.

Introduction   Briefly discuss what the research is about – why is it important or significant? State your proposals or hypotheses briefly: what are you going to show or test through your research?

Review of the literature   Discuss the most important writings on the subject, highlighting the key contribution of their findings or perspectives to the development of this line of enquiry within your field. Focus on how previous research leads up to your research. Introduce your experimental hypothesis, if you have one.

Method   How did you conduct your research? What methods did you use? Did you replicate methods used by other researchers?

Exactly what were the conditions of the experiment? How many people or items were included? How did you select them? What instructions did you give to participants?

Measurement criteria   Discuss the kinds of data you gathered. How did you analyse them? How reliable or accurate were your data?

Results   Present your main findings briefly, using headings for clarity. Give results in the order in which you conducted any experiments, or start with the most important. Be honest about your results: do not assume these are 'poor' if they don't prove your hypothesis. The integrity of your results and reporting are more important.

Discussion   This is a longer section. Analyse and explain your findings. Were they what you had expected? Were they consistent with your hypothesis? How are they significant? Did they support or challenge existing theories?

Demonstrate that you understand your results and findings: what had an impact on them? How could your research design, methods or sources be improved, refined or extended – such as by using new variables, sources or data?

Conclusions   If a conclusion is required, summarise your key points and show why your hypothesis was supported or should be rejected.

Recommendations   In subjects such as social policy, business or health, you may be asked to give a numbered list of suggestions for action.

References   List, in alphabetical order, the sources you cited in your report or dissertation. Use the format required on your course.

Bibliography   If required, list relevant further reading, again in alphabetical order.

Appendices   Include essential items only, such as instructions given to participants, materials developed for your research, tables and graphs. Include only items mentioned (and numbered) in your report.

Writing the report: the opening sections

Writing it all up

If you write up sections of the assignment as you complete each set of related tasks, you will find it easier once you come to draw your report or dissertation together. Different sections of reports require different writing styles – further details are given on pages 359–62.

Introduction

Your introduction provides a succinct summary of your research. It includes your rationale for the research (page 346) and the thesis statement For science reports, state the research hypothesis (page 349). Summarise what you did, the results, whether the hypothesis was supported or not, and whether the results were significant. For shorter reports, the introduction may also incorporate a review of the literature. Write succinctly, fitting in as much key information as you can in as few words as possible.

Other types of introduction

If your report was commissioned by a business or agency, the introduction would usually give more background about:

- who commissioned the report
- why the report was commissioned
- the scope of the report: what it will cover
- definitions of any terms
- the methodology
- a summary of findings and recommendations.

The Literature Review

For larger projects and dissertations, this forms a separate section. Avoid describing the content of previous literature. Focus on what each item you mention contributes to the line of enquiry, such as its use of new sources, data, populations, how it led to a refining of theory, changes in method, or opened up new avenues for enquiry.

Reports or dissertations with longer word limits require reference to a greater number of items, but would not usually include more information about each unless some were highly significant. In the example below, note how few words would be devoted to any one piece of previous research. The final paragraph shows how the student's project will build on previous research.

Example: The literature review

It has been argued (Ayer 2000; Bea 2002) that diet can be affected by the colour of food. For example, Bea found that 15% of participants in a series of six experiments showed strong aversions to certain food colour combinations. People were less likely to eat food if they disliked the colour combination. Dee (2004) found that food colour preferences are affected by age, with green being the least popular food colouring amongst children. However, Evans challenged Dee's results. Evans (2006, 2007) found that children's preferences for colour only applied to certain types of food. For sweet foods, for example, children showed a strong preference for red products, but chose green as frequently as other colour options.

Jay extended this area of research to non-natural food colours. Early indications (Jay 2008a) suggest children are likely to select blue coloured food even though blue foods do not often occur naturally. This research was replicated by Kai (2007). Similar results were also found for adults (Jay 2008b). However, Jay's research included only sugar-based products. As Evans has shown that there are different colour preferences for sweet and savoury produce, Jay and Kai's findings may not hold true across all food products, especially for savoury foods.

Jay's research (2008b) indicated strong adult preferences for sweet food coloured blue; Jay argued this was probably due to its 'novelty value'. The aim of the current research was to see whether adults showed the same preferences for blue food colouring when presented with savoury food options. The research hypotheses were that … [see page 349]. It was assumed that the 'novelty effect' would hold true for savoury products.

Writing the report: the body of the report

The main body of a project report details your research design, your methods, your results, and an analysis of these.

Methodology or 'research design'

This section details how you gained your data and analysed it, so that readers can decide whether your results or conclusions are reliable. It also enables others to replicate your research to test your findings. The writing is descriptive, and lists actions in the order undertaken: 'First this was done, then that was done …'.

Example: Methodology

Participants
The research participants were 32 adult students, all aged over 25. There were equal numbers of men and women.

Materials
Four types of food were prepared (potato salad, chapati, rice, couscous) and each was divided into 4. Four different food dyes were used; three were dyes used in the food trade designed to look like a 'natural' food colour; the fourth dye was pale blue. A quarter of each of the four food types was dyed a different colour so that all foods were available in each colour, to give 16 possible options.

Method
Firstly, participants were told that all of the food was coloured using artificial dyes. Each person was then allowed to choose three items to eat. This meant they could not select one of each colour. A record was kept of the colours selected by each person. The results were then calculated according to food colour preference overall, and preferences by gender.

Results

The results section simply presents the data: it does not discuss them. Keep this section short; include only relevant and representative data. State whether your results support the research hypotheses. Often they do not: this is neither 'good' nor 'bad'.

Normally you would present results both in a brief paragraph, and in tables or charts which summarise the data. You may be asked to present your data as appendices only.

Example: Results

24 of the 32 participants (75%) did not select a blue food item. The findings do not support the first research hypothesis. However, 7 of the 8 participants who did select a blue option were women. 44% of women selected a blue option compared with 6.25% of men. This does not support the second research hypothesis.

Discussion

This section makes a critical analysis of the data. It draws out interesting findings such as:

- the significance of your results and whether these support or differ from previous research
- your conclusions, and the evidence for these
- if relevant, your reasons for why the research hypothesis was not supported
- suggestions of how improvements or variants to the research could yield different outcomes or further useful research
- how your results could be applied elsewhere.

For the research above, the discussion might analyse:

- *The sample*   Was it representative? Could the ethnic mix or age range, or asking students only, have made a difference?
- *The method*   Could this have been improved? Did the blue food look unpleasant rather than simply 'unnatural'? Would there have been a different response to an unnatural-looking green?
- *Future research*   What research is needed to clarify these results further? For example, do colour preferences apply to all foods or only to some? How long does the 'novelty factor' last?

Example: Part of the Discussion section

The research indicated that even when participants were told that all food options were artificially coloured, they still chose savoury food that looked 'natural' rather than food dyed blue. This suggests that adults have a preference for natural colours in savoury food. However, the blue dye was streaky; this might have distorted the results.

Chapter **13**

Writing the report: conclusions, recommendations and abstracts

Conclusions

Conclusions sum up your research, setting out its significance and your findings. No new information or references are included. The conclusions are also included in the abstract, the introduction, and the discussion.

For the research above, the conclusions might include:

- a note that your research findings are not consistent with previous research findings
- a brief summary of *why* your results may be different (for instance, adult participants rather than children, and savoury food rather than sweet)
- notes of any shortcomings of the research (the streakiness of the blue colouring might have distorted results).

Example: Conclusions

The research suggests that adults do not select savoury foods dyed blue, if given the choice of other options of dyed food. The 'novelty effect' of blue products, suggested by previous research, did not hold true for savoury foods. The research suggests that people choose savoury food on a different basis from sweet food. However, this hypothesis would need to be tested further by researching the choices made for sweet and savoury products by a single group of participants (etc.).

Recommendations

The purpose of recommendations is to suggest ways forward. They might propose how to improve current ways of working, or action that needs to be taken. They are numbered. For example, if you were undertaking research for an agency, your recommendations might be:

1 Undertake further research using a larger sample.
2 Avoid use of blue food dyes in the manufacture of savoury food products for adults.

Research undertaken from an academic or scientific perspective rather than, for example, a marketing one, does not usually include recommendations.

Abstracts

Although the abstract is presented at the start of the report, before the contents page, it is more efficient to write this last. Leave plenty of time for this: it can take a number of drafts to rephrase it in order to fit everything in. The abstract sums up your aims, your research hypothesis, your methodology, your findings and your conclusions. You may be set a tight word limit, such as 50–100 words. An abstract needs to be both brief and concise.

Example 1: Abstract (50-word limit)

This report suggests that research into truancy has neglected the critical role of school play-time. In-depth interviews with 6 former truants, now students, highlight the pivotal role of group dynamics within the playground. The interviews suggest that 'feeling like an outsider' at play-time encourages initial acts of truancy.

Example 2: Abstract (100-word limit)

This report presents an analysis of adults' responses to dyed savoury foodstuffs. The initial hypotheses, based on Jay's research (2008b), were that adults would show a preference for food dyed blue over natural-looking foods, and there would be no gender differences. This project replicated Jay's methods, substituting savoury for sweet foods. 32 adults aged over 25 were asked to select three items from a selection of 16 choices. Neither hypothesis was supported, as 75% did not select a blue option, and 44% of women selected a blue item compared with 6.25% of men. However, only the first result was statistically significant.

Summaries

Some subjects require a summary rather than an abstract. This is usually longer than an abstract, but still no more than a page. The summary contains the aims and objectives, a brief outline of the research problem, the methodology, the key findings, the conclusions and the main recommendations.

Writing the report: layout, presentation and style

Style and presentation vary depending on your discipline and assignment: a case study requires a more qualitative, text-based report whilst a scientific report will focus on the presentation and analysis of quantitative data. In scientific reports, sections will generally be numbered, whereas sub-headings are generally used for reports in arts, humanities and social sciences.

Headings for sections

Give each main section of your report a heading to indicate what it covers (see page 358). Use brief section headings to break up your report and to introduce different kinds of subject matter within each section. For reports on experimental research, number each section in a logical way, as below.

9	**Results**
9.1	***Results of experiment A***
9.1.1	In experiment A, none of the participants completed …
9.1.2	On the second attempt, 4% of participants completed …
9.1.3	On the third attempt, 17% of participants completed the …
9.2	***Results of experiment B***
9.2.1	In experiment B, 33% of the participants completed …
9.2.2	On the second attempt, 64% of participants completed …
9.2.3	On the third attempt, 97% of participants completed the …

Levels of heading

Headings are organised into levels: 'A', 'B', 'C', 'D'. To avoid confusion, be consistent in your usage throughout your report and avoid using more than four levels. An example would be:

A   Main heading: the title, in large print.
B   Section headings: in a slightly larger font than the text, and in bold type.
C   Sub-headings: may be in italics or bold.
D   Other lesser headings: should stand out clearly.

Presenting the text

- Number the pages in order. On the contents page, give the page number for each section.
- Use fonts that are easy to read.
- Leave clear margins at each side.
- Avoid fancy graphics, unless specified.
- Use a clear layout. Include only essential tables and diagrams in the body of the report. Place others as appendices at the end.

Writing style

All writing in a report or dissertation is:

- *formal* – avoid slang and abbreviations
- *focused* – address only the project brief
- *concise* – avoid tangents and unnecessary examples
- *subject-specific* – follow the style appropriate to your subject.

Writing for a purpose

The content will depend on the purpose of the report. For example, the report on pages 359–61 is written about research undertaken on campus. However, if you undertook similar research for a company wanting to launch a range of picnic food, the research and the report would reflect those different purposes. For example:

- The introduction would state briefly what the company wanted the research to achieve.
- The sample would be bigger, focusing on members of the public rather than students.
- If the sample were bigger, the method should be simpler. For example, you could offer a choice of only two food items, one dyed and one not, followed by fewer questions.
- The discussion would focus on the implications of the results for the proposed range of new foods.
- You would probably make a recommendation – in this case, not to use blue colouring.

Project or dissertation report: checklist

Use the checklist before completing your final draft. Mark items with a tick ✓ once you are satisfied these are completed correctly.

Done ✓	Item
	1 The whole report meets the assignment brief and marking criteria
	2 The assignment is true to the agreed proposal (if relevant)
	3 The title is precisely worded and makes clear what the report is about
	4 The abstract or summary is succinct and meets any word limits
	5 All required sections are included
	6 All material is in the right sections
	7 The Contents page is complete, accurate and includes page numbers
	8 The thesis (or position) statement, or hypothesis, is precisely worded
	9 The rationale or purpose comes across clearly
	10 The Introduction is succinct and covers all sections in brief
	11 The literature review is succinct and demonstrates breadth, depth and the relevance of previous research
	12 The research method is accurately written, with full details written precisely and succinctly
	13 The results or findings are presented clearly and accurately
	14 It is clearly stated whether the results support the hypothesis and are significant or not
	15 The report analyses, critically, the results or findings in the light of previous research, and critiques the research design
	16 Conclusions or recommendations are included, if required
	17 All the information is relevant
	18 The writing style is correct in each section
	19 It is clear and easy to read
	20 All sections are clearly headed and numbered
	21 It meets the word limit
	22 Citations and references are complete and accurate
	23 All necessary appendices are there, and include only relevant material
	24 Appendices are numbered in the same way as numbered in the report
	25 Pages are numbered
	26 It has been carefully proof-read
	27 It is neat, presented as required, and bound if necessary
	28 Any necessary cover sheets are competed, such as integrity statements

Chapter 13

Case studies

A case study is an in-depth study of a single example. It offers a chance to analyse one case – such as a single person, group, company, event, or geographical area – as an example of a general type. It allows you to look at something in much more detail than is typical of other research methods.

Characteristics of a case study

A case study allows you to test out techniques or theory in a real-life or simulated situation.

- It involves detailed analysis of a single example of an issue, a technique, a member of a client group, or the like.
- It is factual and is usually based on a real-life subject.
- It brings an issue vividly to life.
- You must relate the case study to a theoretical framework, and show how it either illustrates or contradicts the theory.
- You must show how your case study either illustrates or contradicts previous related research.
- You may be required to use the case study to analyse a problem and to make recommendations.

Advantages of case studies

- Case studies are useful in illustrating a point.
- They allow more investigation into small details; these details can throw new light upon how something really works in practice.
- As they are drawn from 'real life', case studies may show up complexities that do not emerge under controlled conditions such as experiments.
- They can be used to test out a theory.
- The level of detail considered can be helpful in advancing the theoretical framework.

- Case studies may open up new lines of enquiry for research.
- They are useful in identifying how rules, theory or work practice should be adapted to meet the needs of special cases.
- They can draw out examples of good or bad practice in the workplace.

Limitations of case studies

- Case studies may not be representative of what happens in general.
- Care must be taken in drawing up general rules from only one case study or from only a small number of case studies.
- Case studies are time-consuming, so only a few can be undertaken.

Case studies as qualitative research

Case studies are examples of *qualitative* research. (Differences between qualitative and quantitative research are discussed on page 313.) A research strategy for a case study would include some or all of the following:

- *Identifying the purpose.* Is the study undertaken in order to understand an issue? To test out a theory? To trial a product? To recommend change?
- *Reading background information.* Read the history of the case until you know it thoroughly.
- *Identifying relevant theory and research methods.*
- *Observing or questioning.* This is usually open-ended in the early stages, so that you do not prejudge the outcomes.
- *Analysing early data* for emerging themes.
- *Focusing further observation or questions* on specific themes, or on gaps in the information. Check that what you have been told is accurate.
- *Identifying probable causes of problems.*
- *Evaluating or testing potential solutions.*
- *Making recommendations* for action.

Writing a case study

Structuring a case study

Introduction

The introduction outlines why the case study was undertaken, and gives a brief overview.

Background

As a student, you may be expected to include in your case study a summary of related research on the issues raised by your study.

Sections of the case study

The body of the report organises issues raised by the case study into sections under appropriate headings. Likely sections include:

- background information
- research methods used (if relevant)
- a statement of the problem, issue or focus
- early action or intervention, if any
- current action or intervention
- client responses to any action or intervention
- other people's responses
- an overall evaluation of the intervention or action
- any outstanding issues or problems
- probable causes of any outstanding problems
- possible solutions to outstanding problems
- an evaluation of these possible solutions.

Conclusions

Draw together your main findings. How far does this case study illustrate or contradict previous research and existing theory? How typical is it of other cases?

Recommendations

List any recommendations suggested by the case study. Good recommendations are:

- *based on real needs*
- *reasoned* – they make a good case, based on the evidence, for what action is needed, and state what outcomes can be expected if that action is taken
- *clear about alternatives*
- *suitable* – they fit the culture of the organisation or the situation of the individual

- *realistic* – they can reasonably be afforded and carried out, within relevant timescales and with the expertise available
- *specific* – it is clear exactly what must be done, by whom and when.

Writing style

Example: Case study writing

Rabina was then referred to an educational psychologist, who told her she was dyslexic. The psychologist's report describes her as 'very bright', with the 'cognitive ability to succeed at university'.

Rabina had also been referred to several ear specialists as she appeared to have difficulties with listening and processing spoken information. The results suggested her hearing was within normal range. This surprised Rabina and her parents. However, research has shown that dyslexic people often show hearing differences when given a wider range of hearing tests. For example, the Baltic Dyslexia Research Laboratory has found associations between dyslexia and left ear dominance and other auditory processing anomalies (Johansen 1991, 1994). The tests undertaken at the Baltic Centre were not available for Rabina so she may have hearing difficulties that have not yet been identified.

Rabina reported that as a child, she had thought she was 'going mad' when words 'fell off the edge of the page'. It is not unusual for people to attribute aspects of dyslexia to a range of reasons that 'make sense' to them as children. Usually, these are associated with events that caused them extreme embarrassment and shame. Edwards (1994) has shown that the scars can last well into adulthood. In Rabina's case, this was manifested in being withdrawn and reluctant to join in classroom activities. She …

Note in this example how the writing:
- focuses on a particular individual
- gives more detail than is typical of essays
- links Rabina's experience to wider research
- brings out what is particular about Rabina's experience.

Review

As a student, you may be asked to undertake a variety of research-based assignments, from smaller projects through to larger-scale projects, dissertations or in-depth case studies.

Once you have learnt how to do projects and write essays and reports, then larger-scale assignments such as dissertations and other final year projects should be much more manageable tasks. They are challenging because you are more in control. You have to make the decisions and manage the process for yourself. They require more reading, the collection of a larger set of data or the use of primary sources, and take more time to analyse and present. They require excellent forward planning and attention to detail.

Projects and dissertations provide opportunities to cover a subject that really interests you so they can be extremely rewarding and enjoyable. Through the decisions that you make, you will bring an element of originality to the assignment although it is not usually expected that you will make major discoveries.

The best student projects, whether small scale or a major piece of work, are clear and well-defined. They are carefully thought through so as to be manageable within the time limits, word

constraints and project brief. Working within such constraints is part of the brief. The objectives may seem minor compared with published research, but this is not a problem as long as the project is well managed, has clearly written outcomes, and is linked to previous research.

It can be a good idea to apply previous research methods to a small sample that has not been researched before. For example, you could use examples from your own age group, from a minority ethnic group, from a local area, or your workplace. This could make the project more interesting and relevant for you, and it would add to the overall body of knowledge about the subject.

If there are opportunities for independent or group projects, consider them seriously. Although they can be demanding, they give you practice in applying a range of skills, not least in project management and organisation. They generally require you to work with a high degree of independence and are a good test of your problem-solving skills, resourcefulness and self-reliance. Because of this, it is likely that you will find that a successful outcome is all the more satisfying.

Chapter 14
Revision and exams

Learning outcomes

This chapter offers you opportunities to:

- take charge of the exam experience
- consider some advantages of examinations
- become aware of some common pitfalls – and learn how to avoid them
- develop ideas for approaching revision in the long term and in the build-up to exams
- consider other preparation needed apart from revision
- develop strategies and techniques to help during the exam itself
- learn ways of managing stress in order to facilitate your learning
- feel you have some control over the exam experience.

The prospect of examinations can be daunting. However, you can take charge of many aspects of the exam process so that, when you enter the exam room, you feel in the best possible position to perform well.

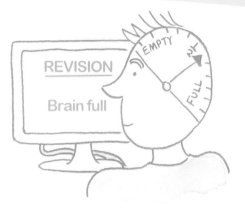

Knowing the purpose of exams, understanding some ways that exams can be an advantage to you, and having techniques and strategies that you can use, can all help to create the positive mindset needed for a successful exam experience.

The purpose of exams

The main purpose of exams is for lecturers to check that you understand the work covered on the course and to ensure that the work which demonstrates this is entirely your own. Preparing for exams involves a high release of energy and an unusual degree of focus. These produce a very intense kind of learning that is not easy to reproduce under any other conditions.

Some advantages of examinations

There are some positive benefits from exams!

- You cannot be expected to give very long or detailed answers in exams: you need to use less information than in a comparable piece of coursework. As a result, less in-depth research and reading may be needed than if you were set additional coursework.

- You don't have to write out references or bibliographies in full at the end.

- Examiners are generally more sympathetic about weak presentation, minor grammatical errors, spellings, and forgotten details than lecturers are for coursework.

- Compared with continual assessment, there is less pressure on you throughout the year.

What does revision involve?

Revision is the process of reviewing the work to be examined, going over it to:

- check you have covered the syllabus in sufficient breadth and depth
- remind yourself of what you have learnt
- check your understanding
- employ strategies to help recall in the exam room.

The pressure of the exam stimulates you to draw together the strands of your study, and to acknowledge areas that need more work. You can view this pressure either:

- negatively – as stress and the likelihood of failure
- or positively – as a challenge encouraging you to heighten your own expertise.

Before an exam approaches, it is useful to make adequate preparations.

- *Organise your notes* – the process of sorting out what is 'essential' helps to reminds you of material covered during the year.
- *Reduce your notes* – to key headings, points and citations (name and date only).
- *Make master cards* – using memory triggers. You could also use pattern notes or concept pyramids.
- *Check your learning.* Work interactively with materials. Write out or record what you have to recall. Test your recall. Write and test recall of difficult material several times to build your memory.

Use past exam papers

Past exam papers are your best resource. The phrasing of these might feel off-putting: questions may seem vague as they cannot 'give away the answer'. It is good to become familiar with such wording before the exam.

- Remember that each question links to an area of the course. You need to find that link and consider which issues the question is directing you towards.
- Look for patterns of recurring questions.
- Check the minimum number of topics you could have revised to complete that paper.

Select what to revise

The revision process is especially one of selection.

- Select which topics you are going to revise. If you will need to answer three exam questions, revise at least five topics.
- Work out answers to a range of possible exam questions for each topic, so that you feel able to deal with almost any question that might be set on the topics you have chosen.
- Select the most important theories, references and evidence for each topic. It is much easier to do this before the exam than during it.
- Organise the selected information so that it is easier to remember (see Chapter 8).

Draw up a timetable

Work out exactly how much time you have to revise, given potential 'emergencies', and time to relax.

- If they carry equal marks, divide the time equally between the subjects you are studying, and then between the selected topics.
- Set aside time for practising past papers.
- Read about time management (Chapter 5).

Build up writing speed

Quality and relevance are more important than quantity. Concise answers can get high marks. However, if you are used to word-processing most of your work, your handwriting speed may have diminished. Practising timed essays – or writing anything at speed every day – will help build the muscles needed for handwriting at speed.

New reading just before the exam

Opinion varies on whether you should read new material just before exams. It can keep your thinking fresh and bring your work into perspective. If reading new material confuses you, however, just focus on the notes you have already.

Effective revision

Ten common pitfalls in revision ...	... and how to avoid them
1 Leaving revision until the last minute.	Revision is a way of pulling your understanding together in preparation for the exam. You can include and plan for revision from the *beginning* of the course. Here are some examples. ● When planning and reading for a part of the course, write alternative essay titles on separate pages. Jot brief notes, or page references to material, under each title. ● Make your notes readable, attractive and visually compelling as you go through the course – this builds the memory. ● Start to over-learn names, dates and key points early in the year, using notes or 'flash cards' in spare moments (see page 214). Even if you forget them, they will be easier to learn a second time round. ● Begin intense revision about four weeks before the exam. ● Read the sections on 'Exams' (pages 374–8) well before the exam.
2 Reading through notes over and over again.	● Use creative and interactive strategies (see Chapters 4 and 8). This keeps your mind alert, and helps to integrate information. ● Instead of just reading, read in order to *find out*. The best way to do this is to look for material related to possible exam answers. Ask in the library for past exam papers for your course, and invent your own questions. ● Discussing past exam questions with friends makes this process more interesting. ● Time yourself writing some essays without looking at your notes. This not only shows you which areas need more work but helps to increase your handwriting speed and your ability to think and write under pressure.
3 Writing notes out over and over again.	● This can be a good strategy if you learn through 'motor memory'. Working to *different* essay plans keeps the information fresh and develops your thinking about the subject. ● Some people find that rewriting notes interferes with visual recall of their original set of notes. For them, it is preferable to develop one good complete set of notes, plus a series of flash cards. ● Reduce information to a series of memory triggers. Reduce a set of triggers to one key word or image.
4 Writing out essays and learning them off by heart.	This is time-consuming and counter-productive – it is unlikely that the identical question will come up in your exam. It is better to spend time reflecting on, and practising, a range of answers, so that you over-learn the material (see page 214). You will then be able to work with it flexibly during the exam, selecting exactly what you need for the exact title given.

Ten common pitfalls in revision ...	... and how to avoid them
5 Finding ways of putting off revision (such as 'urgent' things that need to be done, watching TV, or chatting with friends or family).	• Make a revision timetable which leaves empty spaces to cater for real emergencies. Do a spell of revision before each 'urgent task'. • Use watching television or other distractions as a reward – put them in your timetable. • See *Tricks for getting started* (page 279). • You may be missing company. Have a go at revising with other students, or involve others in your revision. Explain a subject to them: can they understand your explanation? Ask them to test you on your memory triggers, or to ask you questions from your notes.
6 'I can't force myself back to study.'	• Go back over Chapter 4. Check your motivation. • Rather than 'forcing' yourself, *encourage* and *entice* yourself to study through short-term goals, challenges, creativity, and studying with others. • Check that your timetable has sufficient breaks for rest.
7 'I start to panic. I feel I'm never going to get through it all or remember it.'	• Work with positive-minded people. • Read about *Dealing with stress* (pages 379–81) and *Memory* (Chapter 8). • Work steadily to small goals (page 117). • Speak to a professional counsellor at the university.
8 'I can't cope with the boredom of it. I start to daydream or wonder why I'm bothering.'	• Work in many shorter spells rather than long revision sessions. • Boredom suggests that you are not using a variety of interactive learning techniques, nor using your creativity (Chapters 4 and 8). • Look for ways of introducing variety into your study sessions. • Look for unusual angles on the material you have, or images that sum up the material. Think of ways in which seemingly unrelated material could be linked. Invent an essay or a test for yourself. • To stretch your mind and increase your interest, set yourself greater challenges. For example, read a more advanced article on the subject and consider how you could weave any relevant material into your exam answers.
9 'I have too many responsibilities to make revision practicable.'	• Make use of short spells of time, on buses, during tea breaks, and the like. • Divide your material into short sections. Always carry some with you. • Carry an exam question in your head and jot down ideas as they occur.
10 Stopping revision before the process of over-learning is complete.	• Check back repeatedly over what you have learnt, reducing your material to shorter, key memory triggers as your recall improves. • Keep asking yourself: 'How can I use this material to answer other questions that might come up?' • Over-learning takes time – use spare moments well.

Revision strategies

A good revision mentality requires creativity, interactive study techniques, a high degree of motivation, time management, working well with others, writing skills and being able to use your powers of selectivity, critical thinking and memory.

As you can see, if you have used the strategies suggested in earlier chapters, you have already advanced towards doing well in your exams. Tick the boxes beside specific revision activities listed below if you consider that they would help you. Work these into an *Action plan* (page 373).

Have a revision mentality for the whole term or year

☐ Make your notes clear, visual, colourful, dynamic, and memorable. Leave lots of space to add new information later.
☐ Make flash cards of key information as you go along.
☐ Go over material at regular intervals so that you have less to do at the last minute.
☐ See 'Revision pitfalls' (1) on pages 369–70.

Use time carefully

☐ Start as early in the year as possible.
☐ Draw up a revision timetable.
☐ Draw up a *Priority organiser* (pages 134–5).
☐ Make a *Time circle* for revision (pages 131–3).
☐ Use stray moments for revision.

Keep a positive mindset

☐ Work on your motivation (Chapter 4) and your attitude towards exams. Regard difficulties as challenges for which you can devise new strategies.

Work with others

☐ Arrange revision sessions with friends.

Ask for help

☐ Find out from tutors how exam answers differ from course essays.

Use memory triggers

☐ Devise memory triggers (Chapter 8).
☐ Distil your notes to key points, key words, and memory triggers.
☐ Learn by heart essential information only, such as dates, names and formulae.

Revise by ear

☐ Record yourself answering questions – listening to your own voice can help memory.

Stay healthy

☐ Sleep, relax and take plenty of breaks.

Use exam papers from former years

☐ Check which questions come up regularly.
☐ Brainstorm answers to past questions.
☐ Make outline plans for as many questions as you can.
☐ Time yourself writing *some* of these, to build writing speed and for general practice.
☐ Discuss questions with others. Work out plans together.
☐ Consider in advance what detail needs to be *left out* of exam answers.

Revision and exam preparation

SELF-EVALUATION

Preparing for exams: checklist

☐ 1   I can find something positive for me in taking these exams

☐ 2   I can develop the right frame of mind for these exams

☐ 3   I know exactly when the exams are

☐ 4   I am aware how many questions are required for each exam

☐ 5   I have read the course or module details carefully to check what I am expected to know about the subject

☐ 6   I have organised my notes so that the material is easy to learn

☐ 7   I can work out how many topics I need to revise for each exam

☐ 8   I am aware of the range of questions that can come up for each topic

☐ 9   I have made a realistic revision timetable, with clear priorities

☐ 10 I know how to work on exam answers using past papers

☐ 11 I have started to practise writing out answers at speed

☐ 12 I am aware of the memory strategies I need to revise for the exam

☐ 13 I know how the marks are weighted for each question

☐ 14 I am aware of how to use time most effectively in the exam

☐ 15 I am aware of how to avoid common pitfalls in exams

☐ 16 I am aware of the differences between exam answers and coursework

☐ 17 I know how to manage stress and use it effectively

Reflection: Improving revision strategies

In what ways have your past revision strategies and your approach to exams helped or hindered your exam success? What can you change or improve for your next set of exams?

Revision: seven-point action plan

1 **Positive state of mind,** e.g. checking my motivation; giving myself positive messages; working on stress; accepting the challenge. *Things I will do to stay positive:*

2 **Time,** e.g. going over my work from early in the year in different ways; organising a timetable, *Priority organiser* (page 135) or *Time circle* for revision (pages 132–3); dealing with my excuses for not revising; using spare moments. *I will:*

3 **Variety,** e.g. working in many short spells; using varied and interesting ways of going over my material. *I will:*

4 **Over-learning,** e.g. rewriting notes, flash cards, new essay plans, memory triggers. *I will:*

5 **Practice,** e.g. doing past questions; working under exam conditions; having a trial run. *I will:*

6 **People,** e.g. revising with other people where possible. *I will:*

7 **Selection**   What topics will I revise? What level of detail can I really use under exam conditions? *I will:*

Advance preparation for the exam

Find out basic information

- How many exams will you have?
- When are the exams?
- What are these exams?
- How will you be assessed?
- Are any mock exams provided?
- Where can you get past papers?

Keep a record of this information – see the *Exams* checklist on page 375.

Find out the exam 'instructions'

Familiarise yourself with the instructions, or 'rubric', on exam papers: these can be difficult to understand if you read them for the first time under the stress of the exam itself. They usually indicate where to write your name or exam number, and how many questions you have to answer. (The invigilator may read the instructions aloud at the start of the exam.)

Plan out your exam time in advance

For each paper, work out the times that you will start and finish each question – this is one less thing to do in the exam room. Remember these and, when you enter the exam room, jot them down and keep sight of them.

Practise

Like most things, exam performance improves with practice. Attend any mock exams provided, even if you feel you are not at all ready – the experience is important. If no mocks are provided, arrange your own with friends or by yourself.

- Pick out an old exam paper or make up your own questions.
- Arrange the seating so that you cannot see each other's papers.
- Write the answers within a set time limit – work alone, in silence.
- Afterwards, discuss your answers with each other.

The week before

- Drink plenty of water in the week before the exam so that you are not dehydrated.
- Build in movement and exercise so that you work off excess adrenalin.
- Work daily on relaxation, so that your thinking remains clear and focused. You will still feel some nervous energy, which is useful for exams.
- Learn the information on your 'flash' cards. Check your understanding and memory. Find ways of keeping up interest and motivation.
- Organise cover for any domestic or employment responsibilities. Plan for emergencies. If possible, arrange for child care or other support from the day *before* the exam, so that you are free for final revision.
- Avoid people who may make you feel unsure of yourself – those who are super-confident, and those who panic!
- Visit the exam room and get the feel of it.

The night before

- Check over any exam details you have.
  - Prepare what you will need – pens, ruler, water, a snack, the exam room number, your identity card, a jumper, and so on.
  - Avoid people who panic.
  - Have a snack and a hot, relaxing bath before bed. Leave plenty of time to sleep.

The day of the exam

- Eat well before the exam, to keep up your stamina. Slow-releasing carbohydrates, such as bread and cereals, are best.
- Leave plenty of time for the journey in case of delays.
- Plan to arrive at the exam room as it opens: it may take time to find your seat.

Exams

Subject area:	**Exam title:**
Date:	**Day:** **Time:**
Campus:	**Building:**
Length of exam:	**Room:**

Number of questions I have to answer (in each section, where applicable):

Preparation: time needed for reading through questions; choosing questions; planning answers.
Final check: time needed to check for sense, for errors, that questions are correctly numbered, neatening the script, and so on.

Total preparation and final check time needed:

Time left for writing answers (total time *minus* preparation and final check time):

Total marks available for each question	Length of time to spend on each question	Time to start each new answer
1		
2		
3		
4		
5		

Any unusual features of the paper or exam conditions?

Which aids – dictionaries, calculators, etc. – are permissible for this paper?

What must I take to the exam room? Identity card? Pens? Coloured pencils? Any special equipment? A jumper? Water? Snacks, to be eaten quietly? Glucose tablets?

Chapter 14

In the exam

First things

- Orientate yourself.
- Find a positive, calm, focused state of mind.
- Check that you have been given the right exam paper. (Mistakes *have* happened!)
- Read the instructions slowly, at least twice.
- Fill out personal details exactly as required.
- Read the whole paper. Always check both sides, even if you think one side is blank.
- Divide your time equally among questions that carry the same marks. Jot down the times you will begin each question.

Selecting exam questions

- Read each question through at least twice.
- Work out what is expected, in general, for each question. Which part of the course does it refer to? Towards which issues is the question directing you?
- If a question sounds like one you have done before, check the wording very carefully before you select it. A slight difference in wording might require a very different answer.
- Tick all questions you could attempt. Tick twice the ones you could answer best. Don't rush this – it's vital that you choose the questions that will do you justice.
- For the questions you select, highlight key words in the title. Notice how many parts there are to the question. Read questions through phrase by phrase to make sure you have not misread or misinterpreted them. At this stage you may realise that a question is not what you thought, and may need to select a different one.
- At any time, jot down ideas you have about any of your selected questions on a separate sheet. Note the relevant question number beside each idea.

Writing exam essays

Follow a similar procedure to that used when writing any other essay. Use structure, organisation, evidence and a clear line of reasoning – without these, you will get very few marks for content.

Exam essays can be *easier* to write because:

- you need less evidence and fewer examples than for coursework
- you can write less about each point
- you can miss out some background detail
- you don't need to give a bibliography or supply detailed references
- minor grammatical and spelling errors, and rushed handwriting (provided it's readable), are generally less important.

'What if I go blank?'

- Don't try too hard to remember. Leave a space – it may come back later.
- You may be too tense – use a relaxation exercise you have used before (pages 379–81).
- Use a 'getting started' trick: see page 279.
- Keep writing. On spare paper, jot down any words that have anything to do with the question. These should eventually start to prompt your memory into action.
- Ask yourself questions, starting with the most basic – who? when? what? how? – until you become more focused.

Use pyramid questions to guide you

Learn the pyramid questions (page 296) as a song, a list or a chant. Use them to guide your essay plan in the exam room. This is especially useful if you experience great difficulty in organising and structuring information at speed, or if you go blank in exams.

Doing well in exams

Common pitfalls in examinations ...	... and how to avoid them
1 Doing silly things Silly things can fail exam candidates or lose marks or the examiner's goodwill.	Well before the exam, find out what is required. Make sure you turn up at the right exam centre on the right day. Check that you have been given the right exam paper. Be sure to write your name or exam number on the answer paper and on additional sheets. Read the questions. Check the back of the exam paper. Answer the right number of questions. Put time aside to check such details carefully.
2 Mystifying the exam The examiner won't pore over your script for hours, nor see through your answer to what you don't know. There is no 'magical ingredient' you have to deliver.	Examiners have a large pile of scripts. They want to get through these as quickly as they can, with just a few minutes for each. They may check your introduction and conclusion for the gist of your argument, skim the answer to evaluate your line of reasoning, check that you are using material from the course to support your answers, and evaluate roughly what grade the work is worth. They are unlikely to mark it as closely as tutors mark coursework. Often a second marker goes through the same process: if she or he disagrees, the external examiner's opinion will be asked. Only excessively bad grammar, spelling errors or handwriting are likely to stand out.
3 Using exam time poorly and answering too few questions	Give equal time to questions that carry equal marks – and more time to any that carry extra marks. The law of diminishing returns applies to the amount of time spent on any one question: if you spend twice as long on one question, you are very unlikely to get twice as many marks. You are more likely to pass if you give reasonable answers to the set number of questions than if you spend all your time writing some brilliant essays but miss out one question completely. If you run out of the time you have allocated to one answer, leave a space – there may be time to come back to it at the end.
4 Writing everything you know about a topic There is no value in simply writing down all you know to prove you've learnt it.	The examiner is not interested in how much you know – indeed, you may get no marks at all for simply listing a lot of information. Just as for coursework, marks are given for showing you can make sense of the question, relate it to course issues, develop a line of reasoning, evaluate opposing viewpoints, and offer supporting evidence.
5 Abandoning structure and the usual essay writing techniques	Because of the speed at which exam markers work, they appreciate answers with clear, well-organised structures, good introductions and conclusions, correctly numbered questions, and clearly labelled scripts which are easy to read. You lose goodwill if your script is messy, illegible or confusing to read.

Exam strategy

Do I ...	Yes	No	Things to do, or to watch out for
read the whole exam paper carefully?	☐	☐	
follow all instructions?	☐	☐	
answer the correct number of questions in full?	☐	☐	
plan time well, so that I can check through my answers?	☐	☐	
know exactly how long I have for each question?	☐	☐	
share out time according to the marks available?	☐	☐	
use all of the available time?	☐	☐	
read each question at least twice?	☐	☐	
spend time working out what all the questions mean?	☐	☐	
ask myself what the examiner is looking for?	☐	☐	
spend enough time considering the best questions for me?	☐	☐	
feel confident about what I am expected to do?	☐	☐	
find questions that are similar to ones I have practised?	☐	☐	
find I have revised enough topics?	☐	☐	
know what a 'good' answer looks like?	☐	☐	
know which writing style is appropriate?	☐	☐	
know the correct format or layout?	☐	☐	
plan my answers (on paper or in my head)?	☐	☐	
develop a clear argument (where appropriate)?	☐	☐	
use examples from the course materials?	☐	☐	
keep strictly to answering the question set?	☐	☐	
avoid irrelevant detail and going off at tangents?	☐	☐	
get to the point quickly?	☐	☐	
avoid flowery language and vague introductions?	☐	☐	
include an introduction and a conclusion?	☐	☐	
keep focused on the exam during the exam?	☐	☐	
check my answers for mistakes?	☐	☐	
check my answers to see if they make sense?	☐	☐	

If you answered 'yes' to most of these questions, then your chance of exam success is high.

If not, look again through the relevant sections of this *Handbook* and work out what you need to practise. If you are still uncertain about any aspects, consult with your tutor.

Dealing with stress

A *mild* degree of stress can be helpful, providing a challenge with stimulation, excitement, and focus. Some people deliberately search out stress to make life more exciting.

Studying towards deadlines and exams involves different amounts of stress for each student. Added life pressures, such as shortage of money, difficult relationships, bereavement, or changes in your work, family or housing situation, can all add to your stress level. Excess stress can severely affect physical and emotional health, concentration and memory.

If you suffer from excess stress, you need to take steps to reduce it. The signs can be extremely varied.

Know your own triggers

When do you start getting worked up?

- [ ] When things are not going your way?
- [ ] When work mounts up?
- [ ] When you are trying to please too many people apart from yourself?
- [ ] When other people seem to be doing things badly, or better than you?
- [ ] When you set yourself unrealistic goals?
- [ ] In traffic jams, or using public transport?
- [ ] Other triggers?

Spot the signs

Do you ...

- [ ] lie awake worrying?
- [ ] feel guilty when you aren't working?
- [ ] get frustrated easily?
- [ ] get a dry mouth, heavy pounding or a 'butterfly' feeling in the heart, sweaty hands, nausea, or twitching muscles?
- [ ] grit or grind your teeth?
- [ ] flare up easily at other people?
- [ ] regularly eat in a hurry, or go on binges?
- [ ] smoke or drink 'to unwind'?
- [ ] drop or break things frequently?
- [ ] notice signs of increased irritability, tearfulness or moodiness?

Reflection: Stressful situations

In your journal, list the times when you get most stressed – or what makes you feel tense. Describe what happens. What do you do to handle the situation? What else *could* you do?

Reflection: Managing stress

Look at the suggestions on the following page. Tick things you could try out. Which *one* will you try first, or next?

Managing stress

Stay relaxed

Sleep properly

☐ Aim to sleep for 7 hours each day. More or less than this can tire you.

Take breaks

Give yourself regular breaks in whatever you are doing.

Use the STOP! exercise

☐ Let yourself stop everything for a moment. Breathe slowly or count to 100.

- Let yourself smile – even if this is difficult.
- Spread out your hands and relax your fingers. Let your hands and feet be still.
- Repeat 'Stop' to yourself until you feel calm.

Monitor your state of mind

One aspect of stress is the attitude we take towards challenges. The situation and feelings that panic one person may excite and interest another.

Listen to the voice in your head

☐ If you tend to think, 'I can't …', 'Other people can …' or 'I'm useless at …', you need to change the record!

- Turn the message round: 'I can …', 'I have already …', 'I am able to …', 'I am going to …'

Question your way of thinking

Ask yourself questions such as:

☐ Is there another way of thinking about this?
☐ Am I being a perfectionist?
☐ Am I expecting too much of myself (or others) in the current circumstances?
☐ Am I getting things out of proportion?
☐ What is the effect on me of having this attitude?
☐ Am I blaming myself for things that can't be helped?
☐ What can I do to improve matters?

Manage your time

Be organised

☐ Organise yourself to avoid stress. Make timetables and action plans to avoid predictable crises and panics. Take control of your time.

Set priorities

☐ Work out your priorities and when you will do each of the tasks. Work out which things can wait – and let them (see pages 134–5).

Take care of your body

Get exercise

☐ Do something energetic – walk, swim, run, play a game, clean the room, do some gardening. Get rid of pent-up energy and excess adrenalin (see pages 208–9).

Have a healthy diet

☐ Check what you are putting into your body. Could you fill it with less coffee, less smoke, less alcohol and fewer chemicals? Does your body need bigger helpings of substances that help it renew itself – such as food and water?

Relax

Treat yourself

☐ Take a relaxing bath. Don't rush it. Light a candle, or treat yourself to aromatherapy oils.

☐ Put some time aside every day just to enjoy yourself or to do nothing. Try to get at least 20 minutes on your own in quiet.

Celebrate success

☐ Reflect on your achievements over the day or week – and reward yourself.

Daydream

☐ Imagine that the floor is a cloud or a big ball of cotton wool, and that you are lying down on this, sinking down into it and floating away.

☐ Imagine that you are on a magic carpet. Look down at the landscape moving beneath you. Where would you like to visit?

☐ Imagine that you are on a mountain top, enjoying the view.

Use a relaxation exercise

☐ Take time to relax, consciously.

1 Lie on the floor or sit in a comfortable chair.

2 Close your eyes and breathe out slowly several times. Don't force the breathing.

3 If your mind is racing, do the 'Stop!' exercise (page 380).

4 Notice where your body feels tense. Then do each of the following several times.

5 Clench your toes tightly, count to three, then 'let go'. Repeat this several times.

6 Repeat this with all the muscles you can, working from your toes up to your neck.

7 Pull your shoulders right up to your ears – and let them drop. Repeat several times.

8 Screw up all the face muscles. Then relax. Open your mouth into a big yawn.

9 Imagine yourself in a peaceful, beautiful, safe place. Listen for sounds and look at the colours there. It can be any place, real or imaginary. This can be a safe 'retreat' in the mind for you to go when stressed.

Breathe calmly

☐ After relaxation, sit or lie comfortably. Close your eyes. Put on relaxing music if you wish.

1 Imagine that you are breathing in calm and tranquillity with each in-breath, and letting go of stress with each out-breath.

2 Think of one word you find soothing, and repeat this in your mind.

3 Do this for about ten minutes – or longer if you like.

☐ If you find that difficult, just stay still and be quiet. Listen to the sounds around you.

☐ Meditation classes may also be helpful.

Further reading

- NHS Website http://www.nhs.uk/ livewell/stressmanagement/Pages/ Stressmanagementhome.aspx
- Wilkinson, G. (1997). *Understanding Stress*. London: British Medical Association ('Family Doctor' series).
- Wilson, P. (1997). *Calm at Work*. London: Penguin.

Review

Examinations are a culmination of your term's or your year's learning – not just of the course content but also of strategies you have developed over the year. Many of the strategies that help you to do well at exams are similar to those needed for any assignment: organisation, selection, developing your point of view and line of reasoning, and structured writing skills.

This means that revision and exam preparation are not separate events, completely divorced from the other learning activities you undertake in the year. If you have worked steadily all year, the exam period will be more manageable.

Don't build the exam out of proportion. If you don't pass, you are usually offered a second chance. If you *still* don't pass it, it's not the end of the world – there's life beyond exams, and success without a degree. Your health, family and friends are not worth sacrificing for the sake of a degree. However, if you revise well and stay calm, it is highly probable that you will pass your exams.

Regard heightened nervous energy and some stress as a useful friend. However, take care to relax and keep stress to a manageable level. Remember that the examiners – often your tutors – generally *want* you to do well. They will be looking for ways to give you marks and help you pass.

If you wish to hone your revision and exam skills, you may find it helpful to read further: Stella Cottrell, *The Exam Skills Handbook: Achieving Peak Performance, second edition* (Palgrave Macmillan, 2012). Exams can be an exciting time. By the time the exam is over you will probably feel that you really know your subject!

Immediately after the exam, you may feel a little deflated – be prepared for that possibility. Arrange something enjoyable and relaxing as a reward.

Celebrate your achievements.

Part E
Drawing it together

15 Planning your next move

Once you have been a student for a while, worked on a number of assignments and had occasion to develop your study skills, it is likely that your academic performance will have developed substantially. Students often do not appreciate just how far they have improved until they look back at their earlier work and reconsider the issues that had been more problematic earlier. Many small, incremental changes can add up to large gains in confidence and achievement. It can be a real boost to your confidence to see how far you have travelled.

It is also true that progress can be uneven, with great advances in some areas and less in others. The increasing demands made of you throughout your course can mean that you find that some skills need continual development or fine-tuning.

It is useful, at this point, to consider where to fine-tune some skills beyond the generic level of this book. You may find it helpful to go into more detail about particular skills, such as critical analysis, preparation for exams, or writing up a larger-scale assignment such as a dissertation, depending on what is most live for you at the moment.

For most students, the relationship between the skills that they are developing as a student and those that they can apply in the workplace becomes increasingly important as they move through their course. It is usually best to consider your broader skills set within the context of career planning from as early as possible in your course.

For all of these reasons, it is useful to stand back and to take stock of where you are now, what you will do with the skills that you have gained, and what further advances you would like to make.

Chapter 15
Planning your next move

Learning outcomes

This chapter offers you opportunities to:

- identify your study achievements so far
- evaluate your achievements
- understand what is meant by 'personal development planning'
- identify your personal planning to date
- identify the next set of targets for your own progress.

This chapter is an opportunity to take stock of what you have achieved so far. If you have worked through one or more chapters of the book already, then the *Evaluating achievement* chart on page 386 is one place where you can record your evaluation of what you have learnt.

To make an accurate judgement about what you have achieved – neither understating it nor overstating it – you will need to consider a number of points:

- What do you *believe* you have achieved? What can you do now that you could not do before?
- What is the *evidence* of your achievement – how do you *know* that you succeeded?
- What is the *significance* of your achievement – what does it mean, and how does it help?
- What is still *left* to do? There is always room to fine-tune skills so that you can work more creatively, more effectively, with less stress, and so forth. In addition, you may lose skills if you do not make use of them. Plan opportunities to *practise* your skills.
- What new challenges do you wish to set yourself? How can you broaden your range of skills or your perspectives on life, and open up new opportunities?

Study skills are part of a developmental process. This book has suggested study strategies and concepts that can be applied to *most* aspects of study. They have been used effectively by students at all levels, including postgraduates.

However, successful study also benefits from a range of ancillary skills more commonly associated with the concepts of 'personal development' or 'continuous professional development' than traditionally linked with the term 'study skills'. Developing your skills and experience on a broad front can have a positive impact on academic work, on career outcomes, and on personal well-being.

This chapter introduces the concept of personal planning. It maps out personal development already addressed through this book, and begins the process of setting targets towards a wider set of personal goals.

Evaluating achievement

Identify one study skill achievement that particularly pleases you, or of which you are proud. You can use the following table to analyse your achievement in more detail and evaluate your progress. When you have completed this sheet, you might like to repeat the process with another of your achievements.

Prompt	Evaluation
What I have achieved What has changed? (For example, what can I do now that I couldn't do before?)	
How I know I have achieved this What is the evidence for my achievement? (For example, how I feel, comments from other people, or changes in my marks.)	
What I did to achieve this What steps did I take? (Did I change my attitudes, habits or behaviour? Did I have a good strategy? Did I ask for support? Did I practise skills? Did I reflect on my performance?)	
The significance or relevance of the achievement What is significant or meaningful about this achievement? (Why is it relevant or important? Why am I pleased or proud about it?)	
Taking it further What can I do to build upon this success? (How can I fine-tune my skills further? Could I apply these skills to a new situation? What is my next step?)	

Chapter 15

Planning your future

Personal planning

Study skills activities are part of a wider process of personal development or personal planning. This is not a task you undertake once and for all: rather, it is an attitude towards your future. It has no limits; it does not come to an end.

Personal planning is a process that helps you to:

- deepen your understanding of yourself
- become more aware of what really motivates you
- identify what you want for your life and career
- become aware of what the opportunities are that are open to you, and what you would need to do to access these
- plan over the longer term towards goals that are important to you
- identify strengths and consider how to make best use of these
- identify personal limitations and address these realistically, such as through training, further qualifications or adapting your goals
- consider how you come across to others, such as employers
- make more effective use of work-based processes such as annual review or appraisal.

What does personal planning involve?

- *Reflection*   The focus of your reflection will change over time, but involves thinking deeply about issues such as what kind of person you are now, who or what you want to be in future, why this is what you want, your alternatives and opportunities in life, and what kind of life journey you want.
- *Increasing self-awareness*   Personal planning requires you to be aware of your individual strengths, interests, inspirations, preferences, qualities, and ambitions – and of your own weaknesses and shortcomings.
- *Being informed*   You are active in finding out about opportunities and choices that are open to you, and in broadening your perspective.
- *Taking personal responsibility*   You take charge of your education, training, choices and forward planning.
- *Developing a strategy to get where you want to be*   Personal planning helps you review your position, set yourself goals and targets, take action, develop skills, and identify further training needed.

Seven benefits of personal planning

Universities and colleges generally offer careers guidance and opportunities for personal planning so that students are better prepared for life and work. There are many benefits to this: here are just seven of them.

1 It gives you a clearer sense of your direction and purpose. Many students are unclear about what they want to do after university, and may make the wrong choices early on.
2 Direction and purpose make study more meaningful. This builds motivation, which you can direct to achieve your academic goals.
3 The reflective, strategic, analytical and creative thinking skills associated with personal planning are relevant to academic study, and are useful in most life contexts.
4 It gives you a better sense of who you are in the world and what you want: this in turn will give you more control over your future.
5 Typically, it spurs you on to develop skills and to take on activities that give you a broader portfolio of experience when you leave university or college. This enables you to compete for better jobs and to cope in the wider world.
6 It can increase your self-confidence, based on better knowledge of yourself and your opportunities, and advance planning.
7 You will receive more than just a degree from your education.

Activity ⟳ Personal planning

- What other benefit, if any, would you add to the list above?
- Which three benefits are the most important to you?
- Which aspects are *not* very important to you?

Personal development already undertaken

Personal development as a student

Earlier sections of this book have already introduced strategies that support personal development. Below are some examples.

- Understanding skills development in relation to different contexts:
  - identifying skills and personal qualities (Chapter 2)
  - understanding personal learning styles and preferences (Chapter 3).
- Planning:
  - setting goals and targets so that you can measure your progress (pages 117 and 397)
  - clarifying what you want from your studies in order to increase your focus (Chapters 1, 2 and 4).
- Developing a strategy:
  - using your own goals, experience, learning styles and preferences to develop personalised strategies (Chapter 4).
- Monitoring and evaluating performance:
  - self-evaluations (pages 51, 97–8 and 386).

Your personal development history

Even before you entered Higher Education, you were engaged in processes of personal planning. For example, you may have selected qualifications at school or college, chosen part-time work for experience, picked the most suitable university or college, or even moved home.

Reflection: Personal planning

- In what ways are you using personal planning now, to make choices that affect your future – for example, how you choose to spend your time, how you make subject choices, how you choose work experience, any volunteering you do, and any other extracurricular activities?
- What do you hope to achieve through these choices?
- How could you improve your personal planning so as to prepare better for your future and to broaden your horizons?

Activity Personal development history

Identify ☑ which types of personal planning you have already undertaken.

- ☐ Researching and planning in order to complete a qualification or programme at school or college.
- ☐ Researching and planning a major life event (such as the birth of a child, or moving home).
- ☐ Researching and planning an event (such as a party, festival or degree show).
- ☐ Researching and planning to inform your choice of college or university.
- ☐ Research and planning to inform your choice of course.
- ☐ Research and planning to find a part-time or full-time job.

- ☐ Planning a study project or work project.
- ☐ Thinking through how to give someone bad news.
- ☐ Balancing a busy schedule.
- ☐ Planning how you will develop a skill over time (such as driving, technical skills, or in sports or arts).
- ☐ Thinking long-term when making choices.
- ☐ Taking specific courses to develop personal awareness (such as in management, coaching or counselling).
- ☐ Taking courses to develop your personal interests.
- ☐ Travelling in order to challenge your ideas and broaden your perspective.
- ☐ Building my CV through activities outside my course.

Planning towards a career

Plan ahead

If you wish to gain a good job as a graduate, the process of preparation cannot begin too soon. By themselves, your degree subject and grade will not usually be enough to impress employers. They will also be looking to see how well you can demonstrate skills and attributes they value. They will be looking, for example, for people who can:

- take responsibility for themselves, for other people, and for the work they will be given
- plan ahead to address future needs
- spot and create opportunities
- make the best use of opportunities that arise
- demonstrate an understanding of the employer's needs
- take responsibility for personal development and for improving performance.

Ideally, planning should start in your first year of study, so that by the time you apply for jobs as a graduate you are in a strong position.

Plan the steps ahead

Develop a 'rounded portfolio'

When you apply for a job, the subjects and extracurricular activities you have been engaged in will count. When you make job applications, you will be asking:

- 'How have I used my time …?'
- 'What have I done that will make my application stand out?'
- 'What will make this company consider me rather than somebody else?'
- 'What evidence have I got that I can deliver the skills they are asking for?'
- 'What experience can I offer …?'

Your time at college or university is an investment. Obviously, it is important to spend time gaining your degree. However, you do not have to invest *all* your time in study. There are 'smart' ways of using your time and putting a degree together, so that you leave with a rounded portfolio.

Typically a rounded student portfolio will contain 'investment' in at least three of the following:

1. the degree subject(s)
2. complementary subjects
3. skills development
4. unusual technical expertise
5. work experience
6. volunteer activity
7. contributing to the community
8. a position of responsibility
9. a broad set of skills that could be transferred to the workplace.

Chapter 15

Activity 〇 Personal portfolio

- In which of the nine areas listed above have you invested already?
- Realistically, what else could you undertake in the next six months to develop your personal portfolio?

Career readiness

Below are suggestions of steps you can take now to develop your readiness for later when you apply for graduate jobs.

Career plan
18 Shop assistant
25 Manager
30 Director
35 Prime Minister
45 Take over the World
50 ?

Visit your Careers Service

It is never too early to use the Careers Service. Choices made in the first year and early in the second year can have long-term effects. Most Careers Advisers would prefer that students visit the Careers Service in their first year. An early chat about your aspirations and goals can point you in the right direction, help you make good decisions, and save you time and money later.

Your Careers Service will have a library of up-to-date information about employers and different professions. Find out the full range of career and academic choices that are open to you as a result of the subject options you are taking – almost half of graduates enter careers that have little obvious connection with their degree subject.

What the Careers Service can offer

The Careers Service can advise you on how to make the best use of your time while you are a student, so that you:

- develop your ideas about the kinds of jobs you really want
- choose the right subject options for careers that interest you or suit you best
- are aware of the skills and qualities employers want in the fields of work that interest you
- make the best use of opportunities open to you as a student
- prepare well in advance for the kinds of jobs that interest you
- are aware of the range of opportunities available to you, through university and beyond.

University Careers Services often have a jobshop or similar facility to help you gain student jobs or work placements while you are studying.

Prepare questions for the Careers Adviser

It may help to ask the Careers Adviser:

- What kinds of jobs are open to me because of my degree subject?
- What kinds of jobs do most students with my degree enter?
- What further training would I need for the career I have in mind?
- What competition is there for that career?
- What additional things will employers be looking for, apart from my degree?
- What can I do while at university to improve my chances of getting a good job in the area that interests me?

Labour market trends

Ask Careers Advisers about current trends in the labour market, and how these may affect you. What opportunities are there?

Find out what kinds of jobs graduates enter when they leave your discipline. Decide whether these interest you. If so, how can you put yourself in a good position to compete for them?

If those jobs do not interest you, there is no cause for alarm. A very wide range of jobs are open to graduates from any discipline.

Decide what is important to you

Many students find it useful to talk with a Careers Adviser about what is involved in pursuing a certain career. Before you commit yourself to a particular route, make sure that you know what the job would entail.

Beware of the apparent glamour of some jobs: search below the surface for details of what day-to-day work would be like, and think whether this would suit you. For example:

- Are long hours expected of employees in these kinds of jobs? If so, would you be prepared to work those hours?
- Would you be willing to work for many years on a training wage until you were fully qualified?
- Would you be prepared to take more qualifications in order to pursue your chosen career?
- Can you afford the further training?
- Would you like the kind of people who are usually attracted to this kind of work?
- Would a lot of travel be required? If so, would this be acceptable to you?
- Would you be likely to be moved to different parts of the country, or to other countries? Would you mind?
- How stressful is the job? How much stress would you be prepared to put up with?
- Are there any health and safety risks associated with this kind of work?
- What would be the effects of this kind of job on family life? Would you be prepared to accept these?
- Would you be expected to socialise regularly with colleagues? Is that something that would appeal to you?

Your answers to these questions are not simply about the type of *work* you think you would like but about the kind of *life* you want to lead, the sort of *person* you want to be, and the *people* with whom you wish to mix.

Choices of study options

It pays to consider the full range of subject options open to you. Consider whether you could:

- take a complementary subject that would give you an unusual but marketable range of expertise
- develop new skills or languages
- develop an international perspective
- develop business skills
- develop relevant professional skills
- create an opportunity for work experience.

However, bear in mind that there will be many learning opportunities throughout your life when you could catch up in areas that you have missed.

Stand out from the crowd

Consider what opportunities you can make use of now so that later, when competing with others for jobs or academic places, you stand out as 'distinctive'.

Stand out from the crowd

Develop your CV

When you apply for a job, you will probably be asked to send in a curriculum vitae (CV). On this, you list your educational and work history, your interests, and other activities you have undertaken. Your academic qualifications form only one part of a CV. If you do nothing but study whilst at university, you may have very little to write on your CV or to discuss at interview.

You can expect employers to ask for examples of:

- where you have demonstrated certain skills
- how you dealt with certain kinds of situation typically encountered in the workplace (such as dealing with the public)
- voluntary work or public service.

It is worth planning ahead to ensure that you build up at least some experience upon which you can draw for application forms and interviews. This may be through work experience, performing, putting on an exhibition, or some other activity.

Write a CV

Write a CV and keep it up to date. Maintain good records and keep track of experience, jobs, dates and addresses of employers. You may need to send out a CV at short notice, so update it regularly.

Update your personal records

Keep a good portfolio of your personal records.

Every six months, write a thumbnail sketch about yourself. Include the following.

- What inspires you most at present?
- How have you used existing skills in new contexts?
- What personal qualities have you developed out of recent experience?
- What are your long-term goals now?
- What are your immediate goals and targets?

Gain work experience

There is no substitute for work experience – it builds a range of skills and attitudes that are hard to learn through study. Work experience need not necessarily be in a relevant area. If you want to enter a career quickly after graduating, it can pay to have *any* kind of work experience during your time as a student – especially if you have not been in paid employment before.

There is a wide range of choices:

- paid employment
- voluntary work schemes
- sandwich programmes, work-based learning modules or work placements
- work placements abroad
- internships
- mentoring-in-schools projects
- artists in residency (for arts students)
- Student Union work.

Broaden your life experience

Identify ways of broadening your outlook, your range of skills, and your ability to deal with a wider range of people. Build your confidence in coping with a wider set of circumstances and situations.

Give serious attention to undertaking a range of activities *apart* from study. Take on positions of responsibility so that you can develop and demonstrate your ability to cope with difficulties and show leadership skills.

If you work, see whether you can take a work-related study option to make the most of the experience – many universities and colleges now offer these. Consider undertaking community work, Student Union work, drama, music, or political activity – there is usually a wide range of activities on offer.

Lifelong learning?

What is lifelong learning?

The rapid rate of change in knowledge, technology and society means that it is now essential to keep updating skills and expertise. In addition, there are far more opportunities, today, to change career or to develop specialisms long after leaving college and university. Increasingly, employers expect graduates to demonstrate personal commitment to continued personal development (CPD) and an appreciation of lifelong learning.

Universities and colleges contribute to lifelong learning, providing opportunities for graduates to develop expertise in new areas. This can be very useful if you did not make ideal academic choices first time around.

Developing skills as a student

As you reach the end of this study skills book, you may feel you know all you want to know about skills development. It may indeed be time for a break. However, the challenge of continued personal development will remain.

- No one person is likely to have a perfect set of skills and strategies which will meet every eventuality. There is always something that can be improved or updated.
- At each level of study at school, college and university, the skills needed will be more sophisticated than at the previous level. At each new level, more will be expected. You will need new strategies and ways of thinking.

New opportunities for personal advancement

Many universities and colleges now offer opportunities for a wide range of additional learning, including the following:

- *Postgraduate or higher-level programmes.*
- *Continuous professional development courses.*
- *Short courses* at various levels, including courses to update skills.

- *Additional modules* – the chance to take a few units of study to suit your needs, rather than an entirely new degree.
- *Credit accumulation* – this enables students to build up academic credits over a long period of time, to suit their work and life circumstances.
- *Extra-mural studies* – these 'continuing education' programmes enable people to follow up on interests either before or after their degree.
- *Work-based learning* – programmes offered in the workplace, or with workplace assignments.
- *Work-related learning* – at college or university, but centred on work.

Even while you are taking your degree, it is worth finding out about the range of future study options on offer. This may help you now, when making choices about optional aspects of your course. For example, you may prefer to leave some specialist areas relevant to your career interests to a future post-graduate course.

Activity 6 **Identifying opportunities**

- What opportunities are open to you for adapting your degree programme or for taking options that develop unusual skills?
- If there are aspects of your programme that do not interest you now, can they be studied in the future instead?
- What opportunities are there for gaining credit for work-based learning?

Where next?

This book has taken a broad approach to academic development. It provided opportunities to:

- develop your understanding of a range of concepts that can assist the learning process
- undertake reflective activities that can increase your awareness of your own learning development
- learn how to study successfully while working with other people
- develop skills of prioritising, action planning and self-evaluation.

Most of these developmental skills will remain important in advancing your academic, personal and professional success. The next step is to identify which of these skills would be usefully developed further. The following table will help you explore your experience and skills at a more advanced level than that covered by this book so that you can identify your next set of personal targets. Resources that you might find helpful with these areas are listed on pages 402–3.

Knowledge, skills, qualities and experience	Already good	Want to know more	Want to develop further	Order of importance
1 Understanding success and self-management • Understanding more about my personal motivation, inspiration, goals and values • Understanding factors that contribute to success and improving personal performance • Managing 'goal inertia' • Working at my 'personal edge' • Developing emotional intelligence • Keeping myself organised				
2 People skills • Developing rapport and mutual trust • Building on teamwork skills • Using 'Action sets' for mutual support • Developing assertiveness and skills in persuasion and negotiation • Dealing with difficult people and situations • Exercising leadership				
3 Creative thinking and problem-solving • Using the brain more effectively to generate ideas and improve performance • Developing confidence in creative problem-solving and 'thinking outside of the box' • Taking and managing creative risks • Employing strategies for addressing basic and complex problems • Managing tasks and projects successfully • Using performance indicators (PI)				

Chapter **15**

Knowledge, skills, qualities and experience	Already good	Want to know more	Want to develop further	Order of importance
4 The art of reflection • Understanding 'reflective practitioner' models and approaches • Understanding different stages in the reflective process • Applying reflection in useful ways • Presenting reflection within assignment				
5 Successful job applications • Choosing a graduate job • Understanding more about what employers are looking for • Making good job applications • Being more effective at job interviews • Starting a new job				
6 Critical and analytical thinking • Developing skills in clear thinking • Improving the use of critical analysis in written assignments • Understanding how to build well-structured, consistent arguments • Evaluating evidence • Identifying flaws in other people's arguments				
7 Improving performance at exams and assignments • Understanding more about what examiners are looking for • Improving revision and exam techniques • Developing strategies for various kinds of exam, such as multiple choice, essay-based and viva exams • Using technology to support my studies • Undertaking larger-scale assignments such as dissertations and research projects				
8 Improving underlying academic skills • Improving my use of grammar • Improving punctuation • Improving my writing style • Knowing more about referencing				

Clarifying personal targets

- Look at the previous activity (pages 394–5), and note the skills you wished to pursue further.
- Of those you identified, which *three* are your top priorities?
- To focus your thinking on these, complete the boxes below for your three chosen targets.

	Target 1	Target 2	Target 3
1 What is the point of developing this skill? (What are the benefits to you?)			
2 What is your goal or target?			
3 How will you make time to do this?			
4 What support or guidance will you need? Where will you go for this, and when?			
5 What would demonstrate that you had achieved your aim?			

Action plan for personal development planning goals

Main things to do	Steps to take (milestones)		What indicates successful completion?	Start date	Target completion date	Done
1	a					
	b					
	c					
2	a					
	b					
	c					
3	a					
	b					
	c					

What now?

Although this is the end of the book, it is not the end of your development as a student.

Using *The Study Skills Handbook* after a first reading

The Study Skills Handbook is not designed to be worked through a single time. As you develop as a student, you will find things of benefit that you missed the first time around. Browse through the text from time to time – you may be surprised at what catches your eye.

Monitoring your progress

As the *Handbook* has emphasised, as an adult student you are ultimately responsible for monitoring your own progress. If you keep a study journal, read back over it and note changes in your ideas. Return to the self-evaluation questionnaires and complete these again. Compare your current answers with your earlier responses. What changes do you note? How have you changed as a person? What did you identify for improvement, which you then forgot all about? Does this still need attention?

Need help?

If you feel you are not making the progress you would like, make an appointment to see a study adviser or counsellor, your personal tutor, or your year tutor. When you meet, take evidence of your difficulties as well as your attempts to resolve them. Tutors can help you best if they see how far you can manage on your own, what you have already tried, and where they need to focus the support. If you turn up empty-handed, there may be very little they can do to help.

Looking backwards, looking forwards …

In this chapter you have returned, in some ways, to the starting point of the book. The book began by inviting you to review your skills and to identify your own priorities. In this chapter you have reviewed your achievements and evaluated some that are most important to you. You have also begun to identify next steps forward in your own personal development.

Having been through different levels of study at school and now at university or college, you will have become aware that where one stage of learning ends, another begins. Increasingly this process of personal development is a feature of professional life. Many jobs you may enter as a graduate will expect you to take responsibility for this process of:

- evaluating your own performance
- identifying areas to improve
- identifying your training needs
- developing a strategy and an action plan to address these
- monitoring your own progress
- evaluating successful achievement.

Whereas the book has focused mainly on study skills, this chapter has encouraged you to consider your skills development in the wider context of your life and career ambitions. The final activities, on pages 393–7, encouraged you to think about different, often more advanced, aspects of skills you have already developed. It is up to you whether you take this further.

Good luck!
Enjoy your learning and experience success with your studies.

Appendix 1
Quick multiplier

Use the grid below to see what number results when you multiply a number from the top row with a number from the left-hand column. The diagonal shaded row shows each number multiplied by itself.

Spend time seeing whether you can detect any patterns in the numbers. For example, look at the final digits in the *4* column, the *5* column, the *9* column and the *11* column.

0	1	2	3	4	5	6	7	8	9	10	11	12	13	14	15	16	17	18
1	1	2	3	4	5	6	7	8	9	10	11	12	13	14	15	16	17	18
2	2	4	6	8	10	12	14	16	18	20	22	24	26	28	30	32	34	36
3	3	6	9	12	15	18	21	24	27	30	33	36	39	42	45	48	51	54
4	4	8	12	16	20	24	28	32	36	40	44	48	52	56	60	64	68	72
5	5	10	15	20	25	30	35	40	45	50	55	60	65	70	75	80	85	90
6	6	12	18	24	30	36	42	48	54	60	66	72	78	84	90	96	102	108
7	7	14	21	28	35	42	49	56	63	70	77	84	91	98	105	112	119	126
8	8	16	24	32	40	48	56	64	72	80	88	96	104	112	120	128	136	144
9	9	18	27	36	45	54	63	72	81	90	99	108	117	126	135	144	153	162
10	10	20	30	40	50	60	70	80	90	100	110	120	130	140	150	160	170	180
11	11	22	33	44	55	66	77	88	99	110	121	132	143	154	165	176	187	198
12	12	24	36	48	60	72	84	96	108	120	132	144	156	168	180	192	204	216
13	13	26	39	52	65	78	91	104	117	130	143	156	169	182	195	208	221	234
14	14	28	42	56	70	84	98	112	126	140	154	168	182	196	210	224	238	252
15	15	30	45	60	75	90	105	120	135	150	165	180	195	210	225	240	255	270
16	16	32	48	64	80	96	112	128	144	160	176	192	208	224	240	256	272	288
17	17	34	51	68	85	102	119	136	153	170	187	204	221	238	255	272	289	306
18	18	36	54	72	90	108	126	144	162	180	198	216	234	252	270	288	306	324
19	19	38	57	76	95	114	133	152	171	190	209	228	247	266	285	304	323	342
20	20	40	60	80	100	120	140	160	180	200	220	240	260	280	300	320	340	360

Appendix 2
Online research tools

General help sites and academic search engines

Google Scholar

A specialist branch of the main Google search engine that focuses searches on 'scholarly' material such as peer-reviewed articles:

- http://scholar.google.com/

Web of knowledge

Very wide content on a range of subjects:

- http://wokinfo.com

The Open Course Ware Consortium (OCW)

Provides students with access to free course materials from Higher Education institutions.

- www.ocwconsortium.org (UK and USA)

BASE

The Bielefeld Academic Search Engine is an open source database which allows you to search for academic articles and materials on any topic:

- www.base-search.net

COPAC

The Catalogue for the Consortium of University Research Libraries:

- http://copac.ac.uk

IngentaConnect

Access to online journal abstracts and articles, many free of charge:

- http://www.ingentaconnect.com

OneLook

Will quickly check through over 150 online dictionaries for you:

- www.onelook.com

EBSCO EJS

Provides access to electronic journals from various publishers:

- http://ejournals.ebsco.com

Athens AMS

Access to journals and online content to students in participating HEIs:

- http://auth.athensams.net/my

Find Articles

Access to articles from magazines, journals, trade publications and newspapers:

- http://findarticles.com

Questia

A large online library with a broad selection of complete books and journal articles in the humanities and social sciences. There is no charge for searching the library, but a subscription is required to access publications:

- http://www.questia.com

Internet tutorials

Several sites provide tutorials on using the internet, and some teach basic research strategies. You can choose tutorials on general internet skills or skills specific to your subject:

- http://www.vtstutorials.co.uk
- http://www.netskills.ac.uk

Digital Repositories

JSTOR

Has over 1000 academic journals, and a wide range of primary source materials such as documents, data and images relevant to those undertaking academic study and research:

- www.jstor.org

The Universal Digital Library

Has digitised versions of many printed sources, and is aiming to offer at least 10 million books online:

- www.ulib.org

Wikipedia

See page 163 for more information.

- http://en.wikipedia.org/

Subject sites

Arts and humanities

- http://www.jurn.org/

Biology

- http://www.biologybrowser.com

Chemistry

- http://www.chemistryguide.org/

Computing

- http://arxiv.org/corr/home

Education

ERIC and the British Education Index:

- http://www.eric.ed.gov/

Engineering

- http://www.techxtra.ac.uk/

Geography

- http://www.geointeractive.co.uk

History

- http://www.connectedhistories.org/

Law

- http://www.infolaw.co.uk/

Mathematics

- http://mathworld.wolfram.com/

Medical, biomedical and pharmaceutical

Pubmed: medicine and biomedicine:

- www.ncbi.nlm.nih.gov/pubmed
- http://www.embase.com/

Nursing and health

- http://www.nursing-portal.com/

Psychology

- http://www.apa.org/psycinfo/

Science:

- http://www.scirus.com

Social science resource databases:

- http://infomine.ucr.edu
- http://www.ssrn.com/
- http://www.eldis.org/

Subject directories

Websites for finding lists of subject directories:

- http://www.ipl.org
- http://www.sweetsearch.com
- http://searchenginewatch.com

Appendix 3

Further resources on managing and studying as a student

1 Resilience, self-management and managing as a student

Cottrell, S. M. (2013 and annually). *The Palgrave Student Planner*. Basingstoke: Palgrave Macmillan. Resources to help you plan and organise life as a student. It includes diary pages, a term/semester planner, revision timetables, financial planners, checklists, travel planners, sheets to record birthdays and events, tutor tips, library books you have on reserve, and lots of websites and information relevant to managing day-to-day life as a student.

Goleman, D. (2011). *The Brain and Emotional Intelligence: New Insights*. Northampton, MA: More than Sound.

Lucien, L. (2013). *Student Brain Food: Eat Well, Study Better*. Basingstoke: Palgrave Macmillan.

http://www.mhhe.heacademy.ac.uk   Enhancing learning and teaching about mental health in Higher Education: free resources and information to support the mental health and resilience of students, including subject-specific materials.

http://mind.org.uk/help/diagnoses_and_conditions/stress_of_student_life   How to cope with the stress of student life: website from mental health charity Mind with downloadable resources.

http://www.nhs.uk/livewell/stressmanagement/Pages/Stressmanagementhome.aspx: Free National Health Service website with lots of information about managing stress.

2 Employment and personal development

Cottrell, S. M. (2010). *Skills for Success: Personal Development and Employability,* 2nd edn. Basingstoke: Palgrave Macmillan.

Chartered Institute of Personnel and Development (CIPD) (March 2010). *Focus on graduate jobs.*

www.cipd.co.uk/hr-resources/survey-reports/graduate-jobs-focus.aspx

Connor, H. and Brown, R. (2009) *Value of graduates: employers' perspectives* (2009) Council for Industry and Higher Education (CIHE)

www.cihe.co.uk/wp-content/themes/cihe/document.php?file=0911VoGsummary.pdf 2009

Office for National Statistics (2011). www.ons.gov.uk/ons/dcp171776_233872.pdf
Provides information about graduate earnings over the last decade.

www.prospects.ac.uk   Information about graduate employment.

www.jobs.ac.uk   Guidance and jobs for school leavers and graduates.

www.insidecareers.co.uk   Career guidance and jobs for students.

www.milkround.com   Career guidance for students.

www.companieshouse.gov.uk   Lists all UK public companies.

http://vault.com   What it is like to work for named companies.

3 Thinking skills: critical thinking, problem solving, reflection

Cottrell, S. M. (2010). *Skills for Success: Personal Development and Employability*, 2nd edn. Basingstoke: Palgrave Macmillan.

Cottrell, S. M. (2011). *Critical Thinking Skills: Developing Effective Analysis and Argument,* 2nd edn. Basingstoke: Palgrave Macmillan.

de Bono, E. (2007). *How to Have Creative Ideas: 62 Exercises to Develop the Mind*. London: Vermilion; Random House.

Michalko, M. (2011). *Creative Thinkering: Putting Your Imagination to Work*. Novato, CA: New World Library.

Moon, J. A. (2004). *A Handbook of Reflective and Experiential Learning: Theory and Practice*. London: Routledge.

Schon, D. A. (1987). *Educating the Reflective Practitioner: Toward a New Design for Teaching and Learning in the Professions.* San Francisco: Jossey Bass.

Thompson, S. and Thompson, N (2008). *The Critically Reflective Practitioner*. Basingstoke: Palgrave Macmillan.

Thomson, A. (2009). *Critical Reasoning: A Practical Introduction*, 3rd edn. Abingdon, Oxon: Routledge.

4 Other academic skills

Cottrell, S. M. (2012). *The Exam Skills Handbook: Achieving Peak Performance.* 2nd edn. Basingstoke: Palgrave Macmillan.

Cottrell, S. M. and Morris, N. (2012). *Study Skills Connected: Using Technology to Support Your Studies*. Basingstoke: Palgrave Macmillan.

Cottrell, S. M. (2013). *Dissertations and Research Projects: A Step by Step Guide*. Basingstoke: Palgrave Macmillan.

Strong, S. I. (2010). *How to Write Law Essays & Exams*. Oxford: Oxford University Press.

Strunk Jr, W. and White, E. B. (2008). *The Elements of Style*, 50th Anniversary edition. Needham Heights, MA: Pearson Education.

Thomas, J. and Monaghan, T. (eds) (2007). *Oxford Handbook of Clinical Examination and Practical Skills* (Oxford Medical Handbooks). Oxford: Oxford University Press.

Truss, L. (2003). *Eats, Shoots and Leaves*. London: Profile Books.

Pears, R. and Shields, G. (2013). *Cite them Right: The Essential Referencing Guide*, 9th edition. Basingstoke: Palgrave Macmillan.

5 People skills for study, and learning with others

Beaty, L. and McGill, I. (2001). *Action Learning: A Practitioner's Guide*. Abingdon, Oxon: RoutledgeFalmer.

Bolton, R. (1986). *People Skills: How to Assert Yourself, Listen to Others and Resolve Conflicts*. New York: Simon & Schuster.

Cottrell, S. M. (2010). *Skills for Success: Personal Development and Employability*, 2nd edn. Basingstoke: Palgrave Macmillan.

Goleman, D. (1996). *Emotional Intelligence: Why it Can Matter More Than IQ*. London: Bloomsbury.

Learn Higher (2009). Making Groupwork Work, http://learnhigher.ac.uk/resources/files/Group%20work/groupwork_booklet_200109.pdf (accessed 26 August 2012).

Glossary
Terms useful to know in Higher Education

Asynchronous conferencing Online communication whereby individuals leave messages and make contributions at times that suit them, rather than in live discussion.

Blended learning A combination of e-learning and conventional learning approaches. Increasingly, technology is used to 'blend' or personalise most learning.

Blog (weblog) A web-based log or diary that can be seen by other people. Some students use blogs to keep friends up to date with their news.

Bibliographic database A database of details about published books, journal articles, research papers, and conference proceedings and books, with links to the text.

Boolean operators Search terms (such as AND, OR, NOT) to help limit or extend online searches.

Bursary Financial support offered by HEIs is often called a bursary. Each HEI decides how much financial support to give as bursaries, and to whom. At some universities these are referred to as 'scholarships'.

Campus The site on which the majority of a university's or college's buildings are located. Some HEIs have several campuses, sometimes spread across a single city, sometimes in different towns and cities.

Citation Referring to source material in a text, such as student assignments, giving the surname of the author and date of publication (e.g. Smith, 2013). Full details of the source would be given in the list of references at the end of the document.

Classification Typically, degrees in the UK are classified as first class, 2.1, 2.2, 3rds and fails.

Conferencing Linking up with others via the Internet for classes, discussions or project work.

Course Short-hand for your 'programme of study'.

Credit In Britain, each full year of study is the equivalent of a number of credits. A three-year undergraduate degree is the equivalent of 360 credits. Each credit is assumed to be roughly the equivalent of 10 hours of study.

For some degrees, you can take larger or smaller modules or units of study, each equivalent to different amounts of credit. You would need to check that the total amount of credits achieved at each level was appropriate.

Curriculum vitae (CV) A CV is a document used to summarise up-to-date key details about your education, qualifications, employment to date, skills and experience; you submit this to employers when applying for jobs.

Discussion board An online tool that you can use to communicate with others and share information. It is also referred to as a 'notice board', 'chat room' or 'message board'.

E-learning Learning that makes use of electronic tools and information. Most courses now include this. See also 'Blended learning'.

E-portfolio An electronic portfolio or folder in which you gather records of your learning and experience, including your academic and non-academic activities. It may be linked to a portal or VLE. (See page 56 for a list of typical portfolio contents.)

Degree A qualification gained through higher level study. These may be at undergraduate or post-graduate level. There are other qualifications that you can gain in Higher Education that are less than a degree, such as a Certificate of Higher Education or HNC (equivalent to one year of full-time study) or a Foundation Degree, HND or Diploma (equivalent to two years of full-time study).

Dissertation A longer piece of work, usually based on your own research, typically undertaken in your final year of study.

Elective Some HEIs allow you to make up part of your year's study through a free choice of units or modules. These may be unconnected to the rest of your programme.

Enrolment Once you have registered for a programme, you may also have to enrol on particular modules or units.

Essay A typical assignment in Higher Education. These have a particular structure and are used to check students' ability to present reasoned, written argument and demonstrate their understanding of the subject.

Formative assessment An assignment, mock exam, test, quiz or trial run that is used to develop your skills and understanding and does not count towards your marks or grades.

Foundation Degrees A two-year qualification in its own right and an alternative route to gaining a degree. These are the equivalent of the first two years of full-time study for an honours degree, usually with a strong workplace element. Students can then opt to take a 'top up' year to complete an honours degree.

Foundation level These programmes prepare students for higher study and are pitched at the same level as 'A' level study. Foundation level programmes are common for some subjects such as Art. They are also helpful if you decide late on at school that you want to study a science or medical programme.

Freshers' Week A week used to welcome new students, typically the week before formal teaching begins.

Gap year A year taken out either between school and Uni, or between Uni and employment or further study.

Graduate Once students have been awarded their qualification, they are referred to as 'graduates'.

Graduation The ceremony at which students who have successfully completed a qualification are awarded their degree.

Hall; Halls; Halls of Residence Many HEIs refer to student accommodation as 'Halls' or 'Hall'. Some also refer to their formal dining space as 'Hall'.

Honours degree Most full-time three-year undergraduate degrees (or part-time equivalents) lead to Honours, provided you earn 360 credits at the appropriate levels. There may also be Ordinary degrees awarded if you gain fewer than 360 credits.

Internships HEIs often have arrangements with employers for their students or recent graduates to undertake a workplace project or placement so that the student gains experience of that kind of work. Sometimes employers pay for the work undertaken but this is not always the case. There is usually a lot of competition to gain each internship, even if not paid, as students want work experience that can help them to find a job later.

Labs. Short for 'laboratory'. Laboratory work is a typical feature of science programmes.

Lecture A method of teaching typical in Higher Education. These usually consist primarily of a lecturer talking to the class about the subject, often providing an overview of a topic, and students listening and making notes. Often, these are followed up by smaller group teaching such as seminars or workshops, where the issues raised can be discussed.

Lecturer The name given to teaching staff at Uni. Teaching staff may also be referred to as 'lecturers' and, at some Unis, as 'dons'.

Masters A post-graduate qualification, normally taken only once you have received a degree in Higher Education already.

Matriculation Formal admittance to the HEI. There are usually minimum requirements for previous qualifications in order to matriculate. The grades that you are required to achieve to gain a place on your programme would usually be higher than that minimum. For example, the HEI may require a minimum of a grade C maths at GCSE whereas the entry requirement for your programme might be an A or B.

Module At some HEIs, the year's study is divided up into sections; these may have different names depending on the HEI; typically they are referred to as 'modules' or 'units'.

Netiquette Netiquette is an abbreviation of 'internet etiquette'. This refers to a set of developing conventions and courtesies to guide online behaviour, especially for commenting on blogs and taking part in chat rooms, and for safeguarding others' information.

Option As part of your degree programme, as well as compulsory units, you may be able to choose some optional units/modules.

Peer In the context of Higher Education, this refers to other students, especially those at the same level of study. The term is used in phrases such as 'peer support' or 'peer feedback'.

Personal tutor Many HEIs provide each student with a named personal tutor who is their main point of contact for the programme. Generally, these offer academic advice and may also be required to offer pastoral support.

Ph.D (or D.Phil) Doctor of Philosophy. A post-graduate qualification, typically involving original research, normally taken only once you have a degree in Higher Education and after starting on a Masters-level programme.

Placement year A year structured into your programme of study during which you spend all or most of your time in a placement at work or overseas.

Programme Your programme of study may be referred to as either your 'programme' or your 'course' for short.

Podcast One or more audio files which are published on the Internet in a file format, and sometimes used by lecturers to record lectures. You can subscribe to these using podcasting software or tools. You can also produce your own.

Reference At the end of your assignments, you are usually expected to provide the full details of the source materials you cited in your assignment (see 'citation' above). These are known as 'references'. (See page 179 for examples.)

Registration If you have been accepted as a student at the HEI, you usually have to register for the programme in order to be recognised as a student for that year. You would normally register each year. You may need to enrol separately onto individual modules or units of study.

Scholarships 'Scholarships' are usually awarded to recognise academic achievement or excellence; depending on the HEI, scholars may be awarded money, accommodation rights or other privileges. At some HEIs, the term is also used to refer to bursaries offered to support those on low incomes.

Sandwich course A course that includes a set period of time out of study where you undertake a period of employment. This might be for a whole year on placement, or for shorter work placements.

Semester Many universities and colleges organise study over two longer semesters rather than three terms.

Seminar A taught session typical at many HEIs. These can vary in size from small groups through to 60 students or more. They tend to involve more discussion and student input than traditional lectures.

STEM subjects Subjects in Science, Technology, Engineering and Maths.

Term Some universities and many colleges organise study in three terms, similar to the school system. At Oxford and Cambridge, the terms are named Michaelmas, Hilary and Trinity.

Top up year The final level of an honours degree, taken by students who have previously successfully completed a Foundation Degree.

Tutorial Teaching or support offered in a relatively small group. In some HEIs, these are short sessions on an individual basis, with your personal tutor or year tutor.

Undergraduate Students are known as 'undergraduates' or 'post-graduates'. When you first go to Uni or college, you are usually an undergraduate. Post-graduate study is at a higher level, such as masters degrees.

Unit At some HEIs, the year's study is divided up into sections; these may have different names depending on the HEI; typically they are referred to as 'modules' or 'units'.

Vice Chancellor Usually, the chief executive officer, or equivalent, of a university. Names vary, so at some HEIs, these may be referred to as the Provost, Rector, Principal, etc.

VLE Virtual Learning Environment. Online learning space provided for organising learning resources for the university or college, typically with dedicated space for each programme of study.

Wiki An online document that can be edited by many users, following given conventions for the site. Wikipedia is one example.

Year tutor At some HEIs, there is a designated tutor to provide oversight of the programmes and support for all students in a given year of each programme.

Answers to activities

Chapter 4   Effective and efficient study (page 101)

1   Linking new information to what you already know or have studied. *Effective. This helps you to understand and remember your subject.*

2   Learning difficult information 'off by heart'. *Virtuous. Whether or not it is effective depends on what you are learning and why. You may need to learn formulas, equations, names and dates by heart. For written text, however, this is an ineffective method. (See Chapter 8.)*

3   Copying chunks from textbooks – because the writer says it better than you could. *Neither. You are expected to show that you understand your material and can write it in your own words. Even your notes should be in your own words: this also helps you to avoid plagiarism (see page 177).*

4   Questioning whether what you have heard is really true or representative. *Effective. You need to develop your knowledge and understanding by asking questions. (See Chapter 7.)*

5   Writing fast so that you can take down almost everything the lecturer says. *Neither. This is an ineffective strategy. You need to note the main points in your own words. You will also end up with more notes than you need and have to spend time editing them. (See Chapter 6.)*

6   Reading your essays and other writing slowly and out loud before you hand it in. *Effective. Reading out loud helps you spot mistakes which you need to correct.*

7   Studying when you are too tired to concentrate. *Virtuous, as you are keeping going. This may not be as effective as taking a break and returning to study when you feel refreshed and better able to focus your attention.*

8   Changing to a new topic or type of study activity if you find that your mind is wandering to other matters. *Effective. This adds interest to the study session. If you are bored reading, for example, you can bring more focus to this by* setting yourself a challenge such as those listed under 'Active learning', page 108–10.

9   Asking for help as soon as you find something difficult. *Neither. This is not, normally, either virtuous or effective. It is good to tackle a difficult study challenge from several different angles, and to gain the satisfaction of finding your own solution. Ask for help when you really need it, leaving time to take on board the advice you may receive.*

10 Relating your studies to real life. *Effective. This can help to make your studies more relevant, interesting and meaningful, making it easier to understand the material and to remain motivated.*

Chapter 6   Detecting plagiarism and copying (page 178)

Text 1   This is plagiarism (page 66). Although a few words have been changed, this is copied out almost entirely word for word, and there are no references. It is not acceptable.

Text 2   This is not an example of plagiarism because it summarises the original text (pages 60–86) in the writer's own words. The quality of the text could be strengthened by including some references. However, the summary is sufficiently general to mean that references are not essential in order to avoid plagiarism. It is acceptable.

Text 3   This plagiarises the original text (pages 61–4). It copies, almost word for word, a sentence or bullet point from each of these pages. Tutors refer to this as 'cut and paste' or 'scissors and paste' writing. It is not acceptable.

Text 4   Text 4 is almost identical to text 3, but is properly referenced. However, tutors would not be pleased to see so little in the student's own words. If this continued throughout the essay, it would receive a very low mark. It would simply be well-referenced copying – which is not acceptable.

Text 5   This text is in the student's own words. The student has made his or her own connections between different parts of the original text in a meaningful way, rather than simply 'cutting and pasting'. The student has read other material on the subject and included this. There is proper referencing both of the source of ideas and of individual pieces of research. This is acceptable work.

Text 6   This student simply paraphrases the source text (page 61). This might be acceptable for writing a summary or a journalistic type of article. However, there are no references and little evidence of any independent thinking or 'working' with the material. This may not be deemed to be plagiarism or copying, but for an essay or report it would receive a low mark.

Chapter 6   Advanced online searches (page 161)

1   False. AND it excludes references that do not contain both words, so there are likely to be fewer references. (Page 160.)

2   True. (Page 160.)

3   *A*. (Page 160.)

4   *C* – the search will find only matches of the exact phrase. (Page 160.)

5   **design*** would find **design, designers** and **designs**, but would also find irrelevant entries such as **designate**.

6   *A* A suitable search string would be: **nurs* AND method***. This would find additional references such as pages that mention **nursing, nurses, method, methodology** or **methodologies**.
    B A suitable search string would be: **monopoly? as a trend? in world? trade?** You might then retrieve an item such as *Monopolies as a developing pattern in the global market*.

7   *B* – this focuses on relevant items but looks for relevant alternatives such as **world, designers** and **designs**. *A* might narrow your search too far, and *C* might include many irrelevant items such as **global warming, globalisation**, or **local design**, yet omit reference to **designers**.

Chapter 7   Critical thinking when reading (pages 189–95)

Passage 1: Rochborough Health

Activity 1: Line of reasoning

'Outdoor play is good for children's health, so Rochborough needs better facilities for it.'

Activity 2: Vested interests

The article was published by the Playcouncil, who are likely to have a vested interest in arguing for more supervised play spaces.

Activity 3: Types of evidence used

The main evidence is of two kinds: surveys and anecdotes. The detail about the Arkash family is anecdotal (it is just one person's experience). There is also a statistic about garden ownership.

Activity 4: Evaluating the evidence

The evidence about health and parental attitudes comes from official sources which could be considered relatively good 'authorities' and thus reliable. This evidence is relevant and contributes to the argument.

On the other hand, the writer generalises from only one set of health factors (those related to the lungs). It is possible that children who play outdoors have *different* health problems – such as skin complaints or broken ankles. Alternatively, it is possible that the children who played indoors did so because they were more prone to sickness already (such as asthma and pollen allergies). Sickness may have been the *cause* of their playing indoors, rather than the *effect*.

We don't know how representative the children in the survey were of all Rochborough children.

The anecdotal details about the Arkash child and the fox are emotive, and not really relevant to the main argument. The anecdote provides human interest for journalistic writing, but would be unacceptable in most academic writing.

No source is given for the figure of 18% garden ownership: we can't judge whether it is reliable.

The writer twice mentions the effects of outdoor play on social interaction, but gives no evidence or details. She or he could link this in more to the main argument.

Activity 5: Conclusions

The conclusion is that Rochborough should provide more supervised outdoor play areas.

Activity 6: Implicit conclusions

1   There is no explicit conclusion. The implicit conclusion is that you should buy this plant.

2   The explicit conclusion is that the election was unfair. The implicit conclusions are that the election results shouldn't count and that the election should be held again.

3   The explicit conclusion is that the tree is dangerous. The implicit conclusion is that it should be made safe or removed.

Activity 7: Use of evidence

The writer makes a reasonable case and gives supporting evidence. However, there is insufficient evidence to support the conclusion that 'in order to improve the health of its children, Rochborough needs to provide more supervised outdoor play areas'. We don't know what it is about playing outdoors that led to the health improvements. For example, it may be that children ran about more when they were outdoors, and that an indoor running area would have the same effect.

Underlying assumptions

The passage assumes:

1   That playing outdoors is better for all children's health. This may not be the case.

2   That the health of children who play indoors at present would necessarily improve by playing outdoors. This may not be true.

3   That playing outside decreases the incidence of asthma and bronchial conditions.

4   That beneficial effects are available only from outdoor play areas. In fact it may have been other factors about the outdoor play, such as space to run or things to climb, that led to improved health indicators.

5   That there are not enough supervised play areas already for Rochborough children. No figures are quoted for existing supervised play areas so we do not know whether more spaces are needed. The sources the writer quoted don't mention a need for more play spaces. We do not know what percentage of children already play outdoors. All these gaps mean that the writer has not given sufficient evidence to support the conclusion.

Activity 8: Critical analytical thinking

On the right is Passage 3 again, with reference numbers added.

> **Passage 3: Children at Play**
> Children need to play outdoors (1) and yet it is amazing how few children (2) get that opportunity today. Although Smith (2004) argues that 48% of children prefer to play inside, Jones (1964) found that 98% of children in Britain prefer to play outdoors (2b). I spoke to some parents in Rochborough (2) who said their children missed out by not being able to play down by the river or roam the countryside in safety (3). Most children are now television addicts or, worse, are addicted to computer games (4). Everybody knows that this is damaging children educationally (5), and yet nothing is done about it. This is certainly true of Rochborough's children (4), and the main reason is that they do not have anywhere to play (6). Hardly anybody in Rochborough has a garden (2). It would be better for their health if they played outdoors (7), but parents say they won't let them unless supervised play areas are provided (2). The parents are worried that they cannot see their children when they are playing. What chance is there for the health of citizens in Rochborough if its children do not get to play outdoors, and end up as TV addicts? (8)

Logical progression: the line of reasoning

This kind of writing is likely to receive a comment such as 'What is your point?' It is difficult to identify the thread running through the passage: the line of reasoning is weak. The writer hops backwards and forwards between different types of information, as at (8), having already mentioned these points earlier. The final sentence does not add to what has been stated earlier, at (4).

The conclusion

The conclusion is not clear. The nearest approximation to a conclusion is at (1), 'Children need to play outdoors', as this largely sums up the passage. The writing does not draw its information towards a final conclusion, and the final lines of the passage don't lead anywhere. Compare this with the 'Rochborough Health' passage, which leads to a clear conclusion.

The evidence

The evidence is weak, with insufficient detail. The places marked (2) all require further evaluation of the evidence: 'How many children? How many parents? How representative are they of Rochborough parents as a whole? What other views were expressed? How many exactly have gardens? How do we know this?'

A tutor might also comment that the writer has not analysed the sources. At (2b), although the writer uses statistics, these are not recent. She or he offers no possible explanations for why Smith's and Jones' research had different findings – such as that they were looking at two different generations of children. The evidence cited confuses the argument rather than supporting it.

Offering evidence to support reasoning

At (7) and (5), issues about health or education could be developed into interesting points, but no evidence or details are given so the reasoning is weak. Compare (7) with the same point in the 'Rochborough Health' passage, which is more convincing.

The evidence: emotive language

At (3) the writer appeals to a 'golden age' when childhood was safer or better. Referring to children as 'addicts' is also very emotive.

The evidence: sources of information

The assertions at (4) may or may not be true. No reliable sources are quoted, so these may be just speculation.

Underlying assumptions

That 'Everybody knows' (5) is an assumption on the part of the writer. How does he or she know what 'Everybody knows'? Our own experience might suggest to us that most children are not 'addicts'.

Does the reasoning support the conclusion?

The main conclusion, that children need to play outdoors, is poorly supported by the reasoning. Although some reasons are given, these are in a jumbled order, without supporting evidence, and are mixed in with irrelevancies such as computer addiction. It is not clear whether an argument is being made on grounds of children's health.

Activity 9: Descriptive or critical? (page 199)

Passage 1

This is mainly descriptive writing. The writer describes the way that the living world was divided between animals and plants, and gives information about recent research. The passage consists mostly of statements. The statements are not linked and ordered in such a way that they build up clearly towards the conclusion. There is little weighing of the evidence in the build-up to the conclusion. The significance of the conclusion itself is not very clear.

Passage 2

This writing is more critical than the previous writing as it gives a reasoned account for the difficulties in classifying bacteria. It draws on research to show why the difficulties existed, and evaluates the significance of the research for the wider question of classifying life forms.

Passage 3

This is critical, analytical writing. The writing evaluates the evidence for the theory that the right brain is associated with creativity. The writer draws out aspects about current findings that may prove to be significant in the long term. The writer questions 'reasonable assumptions', making clear what has and has not been proved at the time of writing.

Passage 4

This is descriptive writing. It describes one aspect of how the brain works.

Passage 5

This is descriptive writing. It describes Bowlby's theories but does not critically evaluate them. Compare this with the critical analytical writing on pages 325–7.

Chapter 9   Confidence with numbers

Using fractions (page 227)

1 a $\frac{1}{5}$

  b $\frac{2}{3}$ ($\frac{22}{33}$) is bigger than $\frac{7}{11}$ ($\frac{21}{33}$)

  c $\frac{4}{7}$ ($\frac{36}{63}$) is bigger than $\frac{5}{9}$ ($\frac{35}{63}$)

  d $\frac{4}{5}$ ($\frac{24}{30}$) is smaller than $\frac{5}{6}$ ($\frac{25}{30}$)

2 a $\frac{1}{3}$ and $\frac{1}{2} = \frac{2}{6} + \frac{3}{6} = \frac{5}{6}$

  b $\frac{1}{6}$ and $\frac{1}{8} = \frac{4}{24} + \frac{3}{24}$
    $= \frac{7}{24}$

  c $\frac{1}{2}$ and $\frac{5}{6} = \frac{3}{6} + \frac{5}{6} = \frac{8}{6} = 1\frac{2}{6} = 1\frac{1}{3}$

  d $\frac{1}{4}$ and $\frac{2}{3} = \frac{3}{12} + \frac{8}{12}$
    $= \frac{11}{12}$

  e $\frac{2}{7}$ and $\frac{3}{5}$
    $= \frac{10}{35} + \frac{21}{35} = \frac{31}{35}$

  f $\frac{1}{9}$ and $\frac{3}{4} = \frac{4}{36} + \frac{27}{36}$
    $= \frac{31}{36}$

3 a $\frac{2}{3}$ of £750:
    $750 / 3 = 250$
    $250 \times 2 = 500$

  b $\frac{3}{4}$ of 160:
    $160 / 4 = 40$
    $40 \times 3 = 120$

  c $\frac{5}{6}$ of 72:
    $72 / 6 = 12$
    $12 \times 5 = 60$

  d $\frac{2}{9}$ of 81:
    $81 / 9 = 9$
    $9 \times 2 = 18$

  e $\frac{3}{5}$ of 620:
    $620 / 5 = 124$
    $124 \times 3 = 372$

  f $\frac{2}{7}$ of 91:
    $91 / 7 = 13$
    $13 \times 2 = 26$

4 a $\frac{1}{2} = 100$:
    $100 \times 2 = 200$

  b $\frac{1}{4} = 100$:
    $100 \times 4 = 400$

  c $\frac{1}{3} = 50$:
    $50 \times 3 = 150$

  d $\frac{2}{3} = 50$:
    $\frac{1}{3} = 50 / 2 = 25$
    $25 \times 3 = 75$

  e $\frac{3}{4} = 120$:
    $\frac{1}{4} = 120 / 3 = 40$
    $40 \times 4 = 160$

  f $\frac{1}{7} = 10$:
    $7 \times 10 = 70$

  g $\frac{2}{7} = 10$:
    $\frac{1}{7} = 10 / 2 = 5$
    $5 \times 7 = 35$

  h $\frac{4}{5} = 20$:
    $\frac{1}{5} = 20 / 4 = 5$
    $5 \times 5 = 25$

5 a $\frac{1}{2} \times \frac{1}{2} = \frac{1}{4}$

  b $\frac{1}{2} \times \frac{1}{4} = \frac{1}{8}$

  c $\frac{1}{4} \times \frac{1}{4} = \frac{1}{16}$

  d $\frac{1}{3} \times \frac{1}{3} = \frac{1}{9}$

  e $\frac{1}{3} \times \frac{1}{2} = \frac{1}{6}$

  f $\frac{2}{3} \times \frac{1}{2} = \frac{2}{6} = \frac{1}{3}$

Calculating percentages from fractions: 1 (page 229)

  a $\frac{4}{8} = 50\%$

  b $\frac{44}{88} = 50\%$

  c $\frac{19}{56} = 33\%$

  d $\frac{76}{145} = 52\%$

  e $\frac{9}{11} = 81\%$

  f $\frac{196}{567} = 34\%$

  g $\frac{11}{91} = 12\%$

  h $\frac{128}{256} = 50\%$

  i $\frac{117}{327} = 35\%$

  j $\frac{67}{84} = 79\%$

  k $\frac{87}{181} = 48\%$

  l $\frac{12}{96} = 12\%$

  m $\frac{667}{713} = 93\%$

  n $\frac{19}{38} = 50\%$

  o $\frac{765}{999} = 76\%$

  p $\frac{65}{230} = 28\%$

Calculating percentages from fractions: 2 (page 229)

  a 6 of the 11 plants are deciduous: 54.5% are deciduous; 45.5% are not. (54.5 + 45.5 = 100%.)

  b 41 out of 230 children in the school have reading difficulties: 17.8% have reading difficulties; 82.1% do not have reading difficulties. (17.8% + 82.1% = 99.9%: the numbers are rounded down slightly.)

c 23,456 of the town population went to see the film out of a population of 234,560: 10% of the town saw the film; 90% did not. (10% + 90% = 100%.)

d 873 of 9,786 participants took part in the competition online, 2,314 by texting, the rest by phone-in: 8.9% took part online; 23.6% by texting. 8.9% + 23.6% = 32.5%. The percentage who took part by phone-in is 100% − 32.5% = 67.5%.

Rounding up and down (page 230)

a $41.34675 \rightarrow 41.3$

b $912.172 \rightarrow 912.2$

c $22.222 \rightarrow 22.2$

d $99.88 \rightarrow 99.9$

e $1.714 \rightarrow 1.7$

f $10.08 \rightarrow 10.1$

g $66.55 \rightarrow 66.6$

h $6.10987 \rightarrow 6.1$

Calculating averages: the mean (page 232)

a $1 + 2 + 3 + 5 + 6 + 7 + 8 + 9 + 11 + 15 + 17 = 84$
Mean = 84/11 = 7.6

b $234 + 19 + 1 + 66 + 2002 + 7 = 2329$
Mean = 2329/6 = 388.2

c $7 + 7 + 6 + 8 + 9 + 8 + 11 + 7 + 6 + 11 + 2 + 14 + 5 = 101$
Mean = 101/13 = 7.8

d $11 + 22 + 33 + 44 + 55 + 66 + 77 + 88 + 99 + 111 = 606$
Mean = 606/10 = 60.6

e $7 + 14 + 19 + 8 + 6 + 11 + 21 + 32 + 8 + 19 + 21 + 5 = 171$
Mean = 171/12 = 14.3

f $23 + 36 + 42 + 56 + 57 + 58 + 59 + 59 + 59 + 69 + 69 = 587$
Mean = 587/11 = 53.4

Calculating averages: the median (page 233)

a 1, 2, 3, 5, 6, 7, 8, 9, 11, 15, 17
Median = 7

b 234, 19, 1, 66, 2002, 7
19 + 66 = 85
Median = 85/2 = 42.5

c 7, 7, 6, 8, 9, 8, 11, 7, 6, 11, 2, 14, 5
Median = 7

d 11, 22, 33, 44, 55, 66, 77, 88, 99, 111
55 + 66 = 121
Median = 121/2 = 60.5

e 7, 14, 19, 8, 6, 11, 21, 32, 8, 19, 21, 5
11 + 14 = 25
Median = 25/2 = 12.5

f 23, 36, 42, 56, 57, 58, 59, 59, 59, 69, 69
Median = 58

Comparing means, medians and modes (page 234)

a 1, 1, 1, 3, 3, 4, 7, 7, 10
Mean = 37/9 = 4.1
Median = 3 (mid-point)
Mode =1
Note the impact of a small minority of scores of 1 on the mode and on the mean.

b 28, 14, 21, 28, 26, 62
Mean = 179/6 = 29.8
Median = 27
Mode = 28
The extreme value (62) makes little noticeable difference.

c 19, 170, 17, 19, 19, 16, 20
Mean = 280/7 = 40
Median = 19
Mode =19
The extreme value (170) makes no difference to the mode or median, but distorts the mean.

Using five-number summaries (page 236)

a Set of class scores: 10, 31, 39, 45, 46, 47, 48, 55, 56, 57, 58, 59, 61, 63, 64, 65, 66, 67, 68, 69, 71
Five-number summary:
10; 46.5; 58; 64.5; 71.

b Number of pets per household: 0, 0, 0, 0, 0, 0, 0, 0, 1, 1, 1, 1, 1, 1, 1, 2, 2, 2, 2, 2, 2, 2, 3, 3, 4, 4, 5,17
Five-number summary:
0; 0; 1; 2; 17.

c Life expectancy for males in sample families (in years): 32, 39, 41, 56, 58, 64, 65, 67, 69, 70, 71, 71, 73, 73, 73, 73, 74, 77, 77, 78, 81, 84, 89, 92
Five-number summary:
32; 64; 71; 77; 92.

Interpreting graphs (page 238)

a What was the average salary for Aremian men in October?
Answer: $40,000.

b In which quarter did Aremian women's earnings rise
above $20,000?
Answer: July–October.

Interpreting charts: 1 (page 240)

Group A's scores are closer to those of the university as a whole, so are more representative than those for group B. The pattern of scores is also more similar for group A and the university overall. In group B, men's scores are relatively higher than the women's. This is not typical of the university overall.

Interpreting charts: 2 (page 240)

The 24 students in the two groups are not representative of the whole university in that the pattern of subject choices is very different. For example, none of the students in these groups study nursing and medicine, whereas these are the main subjects studied overall. On the other hand, geology is the main subject studied in the two groups (25%), but a small proportion in the university overall. Of students in Groups A and B, 12.5% studied Film compared to only 5% for the university overall.

Chapter 10 Being fair to everyone in the group (page 256)

- Does everybody get a chance to contribute, or do some people (or groups) dominate?
- If people have accents, or dialects, or stutters, are they treated with the same respect when they speak?
- Is everybody's experience and background included in the way subjects are discussed? Are there assumptions that everybody is married, in a relationship, or wants to be? Or shares the same cultural background and assumptions? Or is able to get about easily?
- When people make comments or ask questions, are they sensitive to the feelings of others – or aware of issues that might cause distress?
- Where does the group meet? Can everybody get there, even in a wheelchair or using a stick?
- Do you know when somebody is trying to lip-read? What could group members do to make this easier? Examples include keeping their hands and writing materials away from their faces, and not sitting in silhouette against the source of light.
- What might cause interference or pain for someone using a hearing-aid?
- What words or behaviour might other people find offensive?
- Are there people who look left out, or uncomfortable, or angry? Why is this happening?

Chapter 11 Devising your own essay title (page 286)

1 The title is far too general. Compare this with a stronger title such as: 'To what extent have reptiles been more successful than amphibians in adapting to environmental challenges?'
2 The title is too general. You could give more focus by adding: 'Discuss with reference to …' and add a specific region, timescale and field of enquiry. For example: 'Discuss with reference to the control of nuclear waste in Europe and the Pacific rim' or 'Discuss with reference to the impact of mobile phones on personal safety'.
3 This title is too long and contains too many questions. An alternative question for this topic could be: 'Domestic technology since 1970: labour-saving or labour-creating?'
4 The title is biased towards one (negative) point of view, and contains no obvious question.
5 Descriptive essays are unlikely to give opportunities for the critical, analytical reasoning that gains good marks. Contrast this with: 'How effective have placebos been in testing medical interventions for children?'

Chapter 13   Designing questionnaires (page 352)

1   It is not clear which box should be completed by a person who is 20 or 40. The text should read '0–19   20–39   40–60' or '0–20   21–40   41–60'. Also, no provision has been made for people older than 60.

2   The question does not capture accurate information. Secretary of State? If they say 'yes', how do you know whether they really do? It should read: 'Who is the current Secretary of State for … [named Department, such as Education]?'

3   This question does not capture the variety of positions people might hold on the issue. It could read: 'Which of the following positions is nearest to your own?' and then list several numbered options.

4   This contains two questions. The person might like coming onto campus but not eating in the café, or vice versa. These two issues should be separated out. If the question is about whether people like eating at the café on campus, it could be worded: 'Do you like eating at the café on campus?'

Chapter 13   Formulating your hypothesis (page 349)

Hypothesis 01: This hypothesis is worded clearly but is not precise. It states that physical activity would reduce depression but it does not give any details about what kind of activity and how much of it would have what kind of impact upon whom.

Hypothesis 02: This is not worded as a hypothesis because it does not state what the research is expected to reveal.

Hypothesis 03: This is clear, precise and states exactly what amount and kind of exercise over what timescales would have what sort of impact for which population.

References

Ainsworth, M. D. S., Blehar, M. C., Waters, E. and Wall, S. (1978). *Patterns of Attachment: A Psychological Study of the Strange Situation.* Hillsdale, NJ: Erlbaum.

Association of Graduate Recruiters (2012). 'The AGR Graduate Recruitment Survey 2012 Summer Review'. Available at www.agr.org.uk/write/docs/Summer%202012%20Review%20Final.pdf (accessed 27 August 2012).

Bachelor, L. (2012) 'Graduate careers: the importance of employability skills. Available at www.guardian.co.uk/money/2012/jun/08/graduate-careers-employability-skills (accessed 26 August 2012).

Bang, O. Y., Lee, J. S., Lee, P. H., Lee, G. (2005). 'Autologous mesenchymal stem cell transplantation in stroke patients', *Annals of Neurology* **57**(6), 874–82.

Beaty, L. and McGill, I. (2001). *Action Learning: A Practitioner's Guide.* Abingdon, Oxon: RoutledgeFalmer.

Bower, G. H., Clark, M., Lesgold, A. and Winzenz, D. (1969). 'Hierarchical retrieval schemes in recall of categorised word lists', *Journal of Verbal Learning and Verbal Behaviour* **8**, 323–43.

Bowlby, J. (1951). *Maternal Care and Mental Health.* Report to the World Health Organisation. New York: Shocken Books.

Bowlby, J. (1969). *Attachment and Loss: Attachment.* New York: Basic Books.

Bretherton, I. (2010). 'Fathers in attachment theory and research: a review', *Early Child Development and Care* **180**(1–2), 9–23.

Burman, E. (1994). *Deconstructing Developmental Psychology.* London: Routledge.

Butterworth, G. (1992). 'Context and cognition in models of cognitive growth'. In Light, P. and Butterworth, G. (eds), *Context and Cognition.* London: Harvester.

Buzan, T. (1993). *The Mind Map Book.* London: BBC.

Buzan, T. and Keene, R. (1996). *The Age Heresy: You Can Achieve More, Not Less, As You Get Older.* London: Ebury Press.

Clarke, A. M. and Clarke, A. D. B. (1976). *Early Experience: Myth and Evidence.* London: Open Books.

Clarke-Stewart, A. (1988). 'The "effects" of infant day care reconsidered: risks for parents, children and researchers', *Early Childhood Research Quarterly* **3**, 292–318.

Cohen, C. B. and Cohen, P. J. (2010). 'International Stem Cell Tourism and the Need for Effective Regulation, Part I: Stem Cell Tourism in Russia and India: Clinical Research, Innovative Treatment, or Unproven Hype?', *Kennedy Institute of Ethics Journal* **20**(1), 27–49.

Colon, J. (1982). *A Puerto Rican in New York and Other Sketches,* 2nd edn. New York: International Publishers.

Corrigan, O., Liddell, K., McMillan, J., Stewart, A., Wallace, S. (2006). *Ethical, legal and social in stem cell research and therapy.* A briefing paper from Cambridge Genetics Knowledge Park. Available at: http://www.eescn.org.uk/pdfs/elsi_ed2.pdf (accessed 12 September 2010).

Cottrell, S. M. (2010). *Skills for Success: Personal Development and Employability,* 2nd edn. Basingstoke: Palgrave Macmillan.

Cottrell, S. M. (2011). *Critical Thinking Skills: Developing Effective Analysis and Argument,* 2nd edn. Basingstoke: Palgrave Macmillan.

Cottrell, S. M. (2012). *The Exam Skills Handbook: Achieving Peak Performance,* 2nd edn. Basingstoke: Palgrave Macmillan.

Cottrell, S. M. (2013 and annually). *The Palgrave Student Planner.* Basingstoke: Palgrave Macmillan.

Cottrell, S. M. and Morris, N. (2012). *Study Skills Connected: Using Technology to Support Your Studies*. Basingstoke: Palgrave Macmillan.

Cottrell, S. M. (2013). *Dissertations and Project Reports: A Step by Step Guide*. Basingstoke: Palgrave Macmillan.

Doerflinger, R. M. (1999). 'The Ethics of Funding Embryonic Stem Cell Research: A Catholic Viewpoint', *Kennedy Institute of Ethics Journal* **9**(2), 137–50.

Donaldson, M. (1978). *Children's Minds*. Glasgow: Fontana.

Dresser, R. (2001). *When Science Offers Salvation: Patient Advocacy and Research Ethics*. Oxford and NewYork: Oxford University Press.

Flanagan, K. (1997). *Maximum Points, Minimum Panic: The Essential Guide to Surviving Exams*, 2nd edn. Dublin: Marino.

Freeman, R. and Mead, J. (1991). *How to Study Effectively*. Cambridge: National Extension College.

Fuhrman, J. A., McCallum, K. and Davis, A. A. (1992). 'Novel major archaebacterial group from marine plankton', *Nature* **356**,148–49.

Gardner, H. (1993). *Frames of Mind: The Theory of Multiple Intelligences*, 2nd edn. London: Fontana.

Glaser, E. (1941). *An Experiment in the Development of Critical Thinking.* New York: Teachers' College, Columbia University.

Goldfarb, W. (1947). 'Variations in Adolescent Adjustment of Institutionally-Reared Children', *American Journal of Orthopsychiatry* **17**(3), 449–57.

Great Britain. Parliament. House of Lords (2002). *Stem Cell Research*, Report of the Science and Technology Select Committee. London: The Stationery Office (HL 2001-02 (83)).

Harlow, H. (1958). 'The Nature of Love', *American Psychologist* **13**, 673–85.

Harris, J. E. and Sunderland, A. (1981). 'Effects of age and instructions on an everyday memory questionnaire'. Paper presented at the British Psychological Society Cognitive Psychology Section Conference on Memory, Plymouth, 1981.

Karmiloff-Smith, A. (1992). *Beyond Modularity: A Developmental Perspective on Cognitive Science.* Cambridge, MA: MIT Press.

Keane, M., Kahney, H. and Brayshaw, M. (1989). 'Simulating analogical mapping difficulties in recursion problems'. In Cohn, A. G. (ed.), *Proceedings of the Seventh Conference of the Society for the Study of Artificial Intelligence and Simulation of Behaviour.*

Lauffman, M. Cited in Kahney, H. (1993). *Problem Solving: Current Issues*, 2nd edn. Buckingham: Open University Press.

Leventhal, A., Chen, G., Negro, A. and Boehm, M. (2012). 'The Benefits and Risks of Stem Cell Technology', *Oral Diseases* **18**(3), 217–22.

Lindvall, O. and Hyun, I. (2009). 'Medical Innovation Versus Stem Cell Tourism', *Science* **324**(5935), 1664–5.

Lorenz, K. (1979). *The Year of the Greylag Goose.* London: Eyre Methuen.

Lucien, L. (2013). *Student Brain Food: Eat Well, Study Better.* Basingstoke: Palgrave Macmillan.

Mackintosh, N. J. and Mascie-Taylor, C. G. N. (1985). 'The IQ question'. In *Report of the Committee of Inquiry into Education of Children from Ethnic Minority Groups.* London: HMSO, pp. 126–63.

McLaren, A. (2007). 'A Scientist's View of the Ethics of Human Embryonic Stem Cell Research', *Cell Stem Cell* July (Online). Available at: http://www.cell.com/cell-stem-cell/archive?year=2007 (accessed 8 September 2010).

Oates, J. (1995). *The Foundations of Child Development.* Milton Keynes: Open University.

O'Connor, J. and McDermott, I. (1996). *Principles of NLP.* London: Thorsons.

O'Dochartaigh, N. (2012). *Internet Research Skills*, 3rd edn. London: Sage.

Oke, A., Keller, R., Mefford, I. and Adams, R. N. (1978). 'Lateralization of norepinephrine in human thalamus'. *Science* **200**, 1411–13.

Prior, V. and Glaser, D. (2006). *Understanding Attachment and Attachment Disorders: Theory, Evidence and Practice (Child & Adolescent Mental Health).* London: Jessica Kingsley.

Prospects 'What do graduates do? What do employers want?'.Available at: www.prospects.ac.uk/what_do_graduates_do_employers.htm (accessed 27 August 2012).

Reed, S. K., Dempster, A. and Ettinger, M. (1985). 'Usefulness of analogous solutions for solving algebra word problems', *Journal of Experimental Psychology; Learning, Memory and Cognition* **11**(1), 106–25.

Resnick, L., Levine, J. and Teasley, S. D. (eds) (1991). *Perspectives on Socially Shared Cognition.* Washington, DC: American Psychological Association.

Rose, C. (1985). *Accelerated Learning.* Aylesbury: Accelerated Learning Systems.

Simon, H. (1974). 'How big is a chunk?' *Science* **183**, 482–8.

Smith, P. K., and Cowie, H. (1988). *Understanding Children's Development.* Oxford: Blackwell.

Spearman, C. (1927). *The Abilities of Man.* London: Macmillan.

Springer, S. P. and Deutsch, G. (1981). *Left Brain, Right Brain.* San Francisco: W. H. Freeman.

Sternberg, R. J. (1984). 'Facets of intelligence'. In Anderson, J. R. and Kosslyn, S. M. (eds). *Tutorials in Learning and Memory: Essays in Honor of Gordon Bower.* San Francisco: W. H. Freeman.

Sternberg, R. J. (1985). *Beyond IQ: A Triarchic Theory of Human Intelligence.* Cambridge: Cambridge University Press.

Tearfund (2007). *Churchgoing in the UK.* Available at: http://news.bbc.co.uk/1/shared/bsp/hi/pdfs/03_04_07_tearfundchurch.pdf (accessed 29 August 2012).

Terman, L. M. (1975, first published 1916). *The Measurement of Intelligence.* New York: L. L. Arno Press.

Thompson, A. (1996). *Critical Reasoning: A Practical Introduction.* London: Routledge.

Thurstone, L. L. (1960). *The Nature of Intelligence.* Totowa, NJ: Littlefield Adams.

Tizard, B. (1991). 'Working mothers and the care of young children'. In Woodhead, M., Light, P. and Carr, R. (eds), *Growing Up in a Changing Society.* London: Routledge.

Tutter, A. V., Baltus, G. A. and Kadam, S. (2006). 'Embryonic stem cells: a great hope for a new era of medicine', *Current Opinion in Drug Discovery and Development* **9**(2), 169–75.

Van Ijzendoorn M. H. (2005). 'Attachment in social networks: toward an evolutionary social network model', *Human Development* **48**, 85–8.

Vidaltamayo, R., Bargas, J., Covarrubias, L., Hernandez, A., Galarraga, E., Gutierrez-Ospina, G., Drucker-Colin, R. (2010). 'Stem Cell Therapy for Parkinson's Disease: A Road Map for a Successful Future', *Stem Cells and Development* **19**(3), 311–20.

Vygotsky, L. (1978). *Mind in Society.* Cambridge, MA: Harvard University Press.

Wilkinson, G. (1997). *Understanding Stress* ('Family Doctor' Series). London: British Medical Association.

Wilson, P. (1997). *Calm at Work.* London: Penguin.

Woese, C. R. (1994). 'There must be a prokaryote somewhere: Microbiology's search for itself', *Microbiological Reviews* **58**: 1–9.

Index

Notes

Notes

Notes